Environmental Law in Malaysia

Environmental Law in Malaysia

Fifth Edition

Maizatun Mustafa

This book was originally published as a monograph in the International Encyclopaedia of Laws/Environmental Law.

Founding Editor: Roger Blanpain
General Editor: Frank Hendrickx
Volume Editor: Kurt Deketelaere

Wolters Kluwer

Published by:
Kluwer Law International B.V.
PO Box 316
2400 AH Alphen aan den Rijn
The Netherlands
E-mail: lrs-sales@wolterskluwer.com
Website: www.wolterskluwer.com/en/solutions/kluwerlawinternational

Sold and distributed by:
Wolters Kluwer Legal & Regulatory U.S.
7201 McKinney Circle
Frederick, MD 21704
United States of America
E-mail: customer.service@wolterskluwer.com

ISBN 978-94-035-4741-1

e-Book: ISBN 978-94-035-4502-8
web-PDF: ISBN 978-94-035-4932-3

The Author

Dr Maizatun Mustafa holds an LLB from the International Islamic University Malaysia (IIUM) in 1992, an MCL from the same university in 1993 and a PhD from the School of Oriental and African Studies, the University of London in 2001 and has been a lecturer at the IIUM since then. She is currently an Associate Professor in the Department of Legal Practice. Her major areas of interest are environmental law, pollution law and climate change. She has been appointed as a consultant by several Ministries in Malaysia for environmental-related projects and involves in capacity building and training of Malaysia's environmental court judges on environmental law. She has authored many articles that have been published in numerous publications and presented at many conferences, local and international. Currently she is the coordinator for the Climate Change Policy and Law Centre, Ahmad Ibrahim Kulliyyah of Laws, IIUM, and a consultant with the Property Law Research Unit Ahmad Ibrahim Kulliyyah of Laws, IIUM. At the International level, she is an active member of the International Union for Conservation of Nature (IUCN) Academy of Environmental Law and the IUCN World Commission on Environmental Law.

The Author

Table of Contents

Table of Contents

List of Abbreviations

ASEAN	Association of Southeast Asian Nations
ASTM	American Society of Testing and Material
BAT	Best Available Techniques
CBU	Completely Built-Up
CITES	1973 Washington Convention on International Trade in Endangered Species of Wild Fauna and Flora
CKD	Completely Knocked Down
CLJ	Current Law Journal
dB(A)	Decibels
DG	Director General
ECE	Economic Commission for Europe
EIA	Environmental Impact Assessment
EQA	Environmental Quality Act
GVW	Gross Vehicle Weight
IIUM	International Islamic University Malaysia
ILMA	International Law & Maritime Unit
ITTO	International Tropical Timber Organization
LMO	Living Modified Organisms
MLJ	Malayan Law Journal
MLJU	Malayan Law Journal Unpublished
MNRE	Ministry of Natural Resources and Environment
MW	Megawatts
MYR	Malaysian Ringgit
NGO	Non-governmental Organizations
SIRIM	Standards and Industrial Research Institute of Malaysia
TEFs	Toxicity Equivalency Factors
WQI	Water Quality Index

General Introduction

§1. General Information

I. Geography and Population

1. Malaysia is geographically divided into two parts, covering a total of 329,750 sq.km: the Peninsular Malaysia and the North Bornean territories of Sabah and Sarawak, also referred to as East Malaysia. The former accounts for 40% of the total land area, whereas the latter represents 60% of the land area of the country.

2. There are about 31 million people in the country, 50% of whom constitute Malay, 33% Chinese, 9% Indian, plus indigenous tribes of Peninsular Malaysia, and the natives of Sabah and Sarawak. The capital city of Malaysia is Kuala Lumpur, which houses a total population of 1.7 million.

II. Legal and Political Structure

3. In 1957, Malaysia, then known as the Federation of Malaya, gained her independence from the British. In 1963, the Federation of Malaysia was formed, comprising the states of Malaya, Sabah, Sarawak and Singapore. In 1965, Singapore left the federation to establish an independent republic.[1] At present, Malaysia has a federal system of government and practises democracy and constitutional monarchy.

4. Malaysia comprises thirteen states, namely Perlis, Kedah, Pulau Pinang (or Penang), Perak, Selangor, Negeri Sembilan, Melaka (or Malacca), Johor, Pahang, Terengganu, Kelantan, Sabah and Sarawak. There are also three federal territories in Malaysia, namely Kuala Lumpur, Putrajaya and Labuan. The supreme legislative power resides in the Parliament. However, each of the thirteen states has a state legislature and a state government. Within the three levels of government, the first two are those at the federal and state levels. Below these is the local level, which include city, municipal and district administrations. These local government bodies operate under the exclusive jurisdiction of their respective state governments.

1. *See* Cheah Boon Kheng (ed.), *The Encyclopedia of Malaysia: Volume 7: Early Modern History* (Archipelago Press 2001).

5. The federal and state governments are elected by means of a general election once every five years. The appointment of the monarch is by means of a five-year rotation among the nine ruling Sultans of the Malay states.

III. Economic Characteristics

6. Malaysia is well endowed with natural resources in areas such as agriculture, forestry and minerals.[2] In terms of agriculture, Malaysia is one of the leading exporters of palm oil, which, together with rubber, sawn logs and sawn timber, cocoa, pepper, pineapple and tobacco, dominate the growth of the sector. Palm oil is also a major generator of foreign exchange.

7. Tin and petroleum are two other main mineral resources available in Malaysia. Tin played a predominant role in the Malaysian economy in the nineteenth and twentieth centuries.

8. It was only in 1972 that petroleum and natural gas took over from tin as the mainstay of the mineral extraction sector, and they have contributed greatly to the Malaysian economy. However, since the 1980s, the industrial sector has been the primary source of economic growth, particularly the manufacturing of electronics for export.

IV. Social and Cultural Characteristics

9. The population of Malaysia is made up of different races and religious groupings, but can be categorized into main two groups. First are those who have cultural affinities indigenous to the region, such as the Malays, aboriginal tribes (*Orang Asli*), and natives of Sabah and Sarawak. The second group consists of those who are linked culturally elsewhere, such as the Chinese, Indians and much smaller communities of Arabs, Europeans and Eurasians. Since independence, a common national identity has solidified among these groups, but ethnic divisions remain apparent in many aspects of daily life.

10. The official language of Malaysia is *Bahasa Malaysia*, or the Malay Language. Other commonly spoken languages include English, Mandarin, Cantonese and Tamil. Islam is the official religion, but freedom of religion is constitutionally guaranteed. Apart from Islam, other religions such as Christianity, Buddhism, Taoism and Sikhism are also practised.

2. *See* Rani Osman (ed.), *The Encyclopedia of Malaysia: Volume 13: The Economy* (Archipelago Press 2001).

V. Main Environmental Problems

11. While Malaysia's economic development for the past thirty years has been impressive, it also has had detrimental effects on the environment and on the depletion of natural resources.[3] Various aspects of the environment have been affected by development activities. The main problems are the following:[4]

- inland water and marine pollution from various sources;
- air pollution from industry, traffic and agricultural activities;
- deforestation due to logging and land clearance activities;
- mismanagement of waste and sewage discharges; and
- dangerous discharge of hazardous and toxic wastes.

12. Another environmental problem faced by Malaysia is the recurring incidence of the haze phenomenon, which is mainly due to transboundary air pollution. Land and forest fires in several provinces in Sumatra and Kalimantan, Indonesia, coupled with the direct influence of south-westerly winds, have contributed to the deterioration of air quality during these periods and have caused the emergence of haze.[5] Malaysia is also facing direct or indirect consequences of climate change. These include rising in temperature and sea level and extreme rainfall and winds. Currently, climate change and its potential impacts are given priority within the national environmental policy, both in relation to mitigation and adaptation.[6]

13. At present, climate change is the most urgent and profoundly complex environment-related problem for Malaysia. Surface mean temperatures continue to rise, and the country is expected to experience increasingly unpredictable weather systems. This, in addition to challenges associated with changes in land use and land cover, urbanization, environment and air quality degradation, is expected to increasingly impact agriculture and food security, safe water supplies, public health and the delivery of essential social services. Climate change can also impact environmental quality such as that of the atmosphere. Factors affecting the formation of ozone include heat and concentrations of precursor chemicals. Particulate matter concentrations are affected, among other factors, by wildfire emissions and haze episodes. Health problems related to climate change facing Malaysia can be a result of direct exposure patterns such as heat waves and air pollution.

---

3. *See* Sir R. Aiken et al., *Development and Environment in Peninsular Malaysia* (McGraw-Hill Intl 1982).
4. Dept. Envt. Malay., *Environmental Quality Report 2012* 4 (Dept. Envt. Malay. 2012).
5. *The Encyclopedia of Malaysia: Volume I: The Environment* 110–111 (Sham Sani ed., Archipelago Press 1998).
6. For further details on climate change initiatives for Malaysia, *see* the Ministry of Natural Resources and Environment's official website at http://www.nre.gov.my/sites/climatechange/Pages/default.aspx, July 2018.

§2. BASIC PRINCIPLES OF ENVIRONMENTAL LAW

I. The Constitution

14. In Malaysia, there is no specific provision in the Federal Constitution which speaks about the recognition or protection of the public's right to a healthful environment. Consequently, Malaysia's approach to environmental management through policy and legal measures has not evolved from a Constitutional mandate to afford the public a right to clean air, water and environment. Rather, these measures are more a response to intolerable environmental conditions.[7]

15. However, Article 5 of Part II of the Constitution does contain a provision on fundamental liberties, which states that 'no person shall be deprived of his life or personal liberty save in accordance with the law'. While this article does not specifically deal with environmental rights, it is possible for this article to be construed liberally to allow for the right to a healthful environment.[8] It is fair to say that efforts have indeed been made by some Malaysian judges to try to deal with issues pertaining to the right to a clean environment in a more liberal manner. One example is the observation of Judge Mahadev Shankar in *Sinuri bin Tubar v. Syarikat East Johor Sawmills Sdn. Bhd*,[9] when he said that 'Human calls for nature do not wait for governments to function. Clean water is a birthright of every human being as much as clean air.'[10]

II. The Institutional and Legal Framework on Sustainable Development

A. *Agencies*

16. Malaysia's commitment towards sustainable development within its legislative framework is well defined in the long-term Outline Perspective Plans and the five-year development plans which have encompassed national development policy for the country.

17. The Outline Perspective Plans and the five-year development plans are produced by the Economic Planning Unit, under the Prime Minister's Department.[11] This Department is the central government agency that has ultimate responsibility for national development planning and coordination in Malaysia.

---

7. *See*, Maizatun Mustafa, *Clean Water: Right and Remedies Under Environmental Law in Malaysia*, in *Integrated Water Resources Management in Malaysia: Experiences and Practices* 209–217 (Ann Anton et al. eds., Malaysian Water Partnership 2004).
8. Abdul Haseeb Ansari, *Right to Healthful Environment As a Means to Ensure Environmental Justice: An Overview with Special Reference to India, Philippines and Malaysia*, 4 MLJ xxv (1990); and Abdul Aziz Bari, *Right to Life under the Federal Constitution and Environmental Issues*, 1 MLJ lx (1999).
9. (1987) 1 MLJ 315.
10. (1987) 1 MLJ 315, at 319.
11. Refer to the Prime Minister's Department's official website at http://www.epu.gov.my/en, July 2018.

18. Since then, environmental sustainability has been included in the Outline Perspective Plans and consistently addressed in Malaysia's development plans, starting from the Third Malaysia Plan (1976–1980), up to the Eleventh Malaysia Plan (2016–2020)[12] and the present Twelfth Malaysia Plan (2021–2025)[13] themed 'A Prosperous, Inclusive, Sustainable Malaysia' aims to steer Malaysia out of the COVID-19 pandemic and put the economy back on track. Malaysia also incorporated Agenda 21, which was adopted at the United Nations Conference on Environment and Development in June 1992 and integrated into the national planning process.[14]

19. There are various ways to apply the principles of sustainable development introduced by the Economic Planning Unit. Following the Brundtland Report in 1987 and the United Nations General Assembly Resolutions 44/228 on the recognition that economic development issues are intricately linked with the environment, a National Conservation Strategy was drawn up by the Economic Planning Unit.[15] This is to ensure that future development and the environment in Malaysia are properly coordinated in line with the sustainable-development concept.

20. The Economic Planning Unit also introduced the Malaysian Quality of Life Index in 1999, which coincides with Chapter 35 of Agenda 21. The Index provides a means of tracking progress towards development that is economically sound and sustainable in a broad sense. It relies on data routinely collected and published by the Department of Statistics, Malaysia, the Department of Environment, Malaysia, and by other government departments.[16]

21. The Department of Statistics under the Prime Minister's Department enhanced environmental sustainability through the establishment of the Environmental Statistics Section in 1998 and the publication of the Compendium of Environment Statistics, Malaysia. The objectives of the section are to enhance the national ability to assess progress towards sustainable development, and to allow the Department to become the central repository for all environmental statistics in Malaysia. The main objective of the publication of the Compendium is to provide the latest environment statistics in Malaysia.[17]

---

12. *See* the report of the *First Malaysia Plan* to the *Eleventh Malaysia Plans* (1966–2016) at Jabatan Perdana Menteri, Unit Pemodenan Tadbiran dan Perancangan Pengurusan, Malaysia, Kuala Lumpur, Jabatan Percetakan Negara.
13. *See* the *Twelfth Malaysia Plan* (12021–2025) at Jabatan Perdana Menteri, Unit Perancang Ekonomi, Kuala Lumpur, Jabatan Percetakan Negara.
14. *See* Persidangan Pertubuhan Bangsa-Bangsa Bersatu Mengenai Alam Sekitar dan Pembagunan, *Agenda 21, Program Tindakan Untuk Pembangunan Mapan: Deklarasi Rio: Kenyataan Mengenai Prinsip Hutan* (Jabatan Alam Sekitar 1997).
15. *See* Economic Planning Unit, *Malaysian National Conservation Strategy* (Kuala Lumpur, Economic Planning Unit 1993).
16. *See* the latest 2011 Malaysia Quality of Life Data at http://www.epu.gov.my/en/archive/qualityoflife, July 2018.
17. For details, *see* the Department of Statistics official website at https://www.dosm.gov.my/v1/, July 2018.

B. Legislations

22. Serious efforts to ensure environmental sustainability in Malaysia started with the enactment of the Environment Quality Act in 1974, which provides the legal basis for the protection and control of environmental pollution and the enhancement of environmental quality.[18] This Act is continuously being amended to include new regulations to incorporate the objective of sustainable development. This includes the amendment in 1996 to include legal measures that can reconcile economic and environmental objectives which are central to the achievement of sustainable development.[19]

23. Agenda 21 was incorporated by the Federal Town and Country Planning Department, under the Ministry of Housing and Local Government, Malaysia, through the Town and Country Planning Act 1976. In 1995, this Act was amended in order to incorporate sustainable indicators within land-use planning.[20] For example, under section 21B, the proponent of any development proposal must submit a development-proposal report along with their application for planning permission, which must contain, among other things:

- a description of the land, including its physical environment, topography, landscape, geology, contours, drainage water bodies and catchments and natural features;
- a survey of trees and all kinds of vegetation;
- a land-use analysis and its effects on adjoining lands;
- lay out plans; and
- prepared according to the requirements of the Act.

§3. Historical Background

24. As in most countries, laws concerning the environment in Malaysia did not develop as 'environmental law'. An early form of management response to impending environmental problems was the introduction of the Water Enactments in 1920.[21] Other earlier legislations include the F.M.S. Forest Enactment, 1934;[22] the Merchant Shipping Ordinance, 1952;[23] the Land Conservation Act, 1960;[24] the Fisheries Act, 1963;[25] and the Factories and Machinery Act, 1967.[26]

18. *See* Maizatun Mustafa, *The Environmental Quality Act 1974 as a Significant Legal Instrument towards Environmental Protection and Sustainable Development in Malaysia: Prospects and Challenges*, a paper presented at the *6th Asian Law Institute Conference* (H.K.U. 2009).
19. The Environmental Quality (Amendment) Act 1996, Act 953.
20. The Town and Country Planning (Amendment) Act 1995, Act 933.
21. Cap. 148.
22. Cap. 153.
23. No. 70 of 1952.
24. Act 385.
25. Act 210.
26. Act 139.

25. However, many of these legislations were not originally designed to address environmental problems, but rather to promote sound housekeeping practices in specific sectors, in line with the government policies at the time. They were also largely sectoral in nature, focusing on specific activity areas. Thus, during that time, not much thought was given to the idea of an integrated approach to environmental concerns.

26. Strong environmental awareness among developing countries like Malaysia started to emerge during the 1970s, particularly after the commencement of the United Nations Conference on the Human Environment that took place in Stockholm in 1972. Pursuant to this Conference, Malaysia subsequently introduced its first ever environmental policy directive, which was embodied in the Third Malaysia Plan,[27] and significantly, enacted the Environmental Quality Act (EQA) in 1974. This Act relates to 'the prevention, abatement, control of pollution and enhancement, and for the purposes connected therewith'.[28] It also forms the basic legislation for achieving national environmental objectives and policies.

27. Apart from the EQA 1974, there are over forty different environment-related statutes for environmental management and conservation. This distribution of legislative powers renders both federal and state governments' competency to deal with environmental matters, both legislatively and administratively. Coincidently, such competency also results in the existence of various agencies, at all levels of government, dealing with various aspects of environmental management. This is the main reason for the rather piecemeal approach to environmental legislation in Malaysia.

§4. The Role of Government Institutions in the Shaping and Administration of Environmental Law and Policy

I. Governmental Institutions and Their Competencies

A. Constitutional Set Up

28. In Malaysia, the environmental administration is rather complex as it stems from the Constitution's distribution of powers between the federal and state governments. The Constitution, known as the Federal Constitution, is the supreme law of the land, and any law that is inconsistent with it is void. The Federal Constitution is extensive, as it covers basically all that is required for the governance of a nation.

29. The constitutional provision with the most profound effect on the environment is the division of law-making powers between the state and federal governments. This division of power can be found in Part VI of the Constitution. Article

27. Jabatan Perdana Menteri, Unit Pemodenan Tadbiran dan Perancangan Pengurusan, Malaysia, *Third Malaysia Plan 1976–1980* (Jabatan Percetakan Negara 1976).
28. Preamble of the Environmental Quality Act 1974.

73 provides, as a general principle, that 'Parliament may make laws for the whole or any part of the federation and laws having effect outside as well as within the federation', while 'the legislature of a state may make laws for the whole or any part of the state'.

B. Legislative Lists

30. Within the Ninth Schedule of the Constitution, there is a division of legislative powers between federal and state governments under what is known as the 'Federal List', the 'State List' and the 'Concurrent List'. The Constitution provides that the federal government can make law on matters under List I, the Federal List, whereas the State List (List II) has the areas where the state government can make laws. The Concurrent List (List III) has the areas where either the state or the federal government can make laws. The main objective of having this legislative division between the two tiers of government is to provide for a suitable division of responsibility between federal and state, without introducing the kind of rigidity which would make the system unworkable.[29]

31. The Federal List enumerates matters to which only the federation, that is, Parliament, can make laws. They are external affairs; defence and security; citizenship; finance; trade and industry; shipping; education; health; labour and many other matters. Areas relevant to the environment that can be found in the Federal List include treaties, agreements and conventions with other countries; trade, commerce and industry; development of mineral resources, mines, mining, minerals, factories, fisheries, maritime; communication and transport; federal works and power; water supplies, rivers and canals, except those within one state; electricity; gas and gas works; welfare of the aborigines; and control of agricultural pests.

32. However, matters under the State List for which the states can legislate laws include Muslim law and Malay customs; land, agriculture, forestry; state works and water; and local government. There are several environmental-related items that come under this List, including land tenure; permits and licences for prospecting for mines; agriculture and forestry; local government outside the federal territories of Kuala Lumpur, Putrajaya and Labuan, including obnoxious trades and public nuisances in local authority areas; water (excluding water supplies), rivers and canals; control of silt, riparian rights; turtles; and riverine fishing.

33. The Concurrent List, where both the federal and state legislatures have the power to enact laws, includes matters pertaining to animal husbandry; town and country planning except in the federal capital; public health, sanitation (excluding

29. For details on the Malaysian Constitution, *see* Andrew Harding, *Law, Government and the Constitution in Malaysia* (Kluwer L. Intl. 1996).

sanitation in the federal capital) and the prevention of diseases; drainage and irrigation; protection of wild animals and wild birds; national parks; prevention of cruelty to animals; veterinary services; animal quarantine; rehabilitation of mining land which has suffered soil erosion; and subject to the Federal List, water supplies and services.

34. In order to avoid any conflict of law, the Constitution provides that the state cannot legislate on any matter which is contrary to the federal law.[30] However, the case of land is different. Even though land is a state matter, Parliament is allowed to make laws with respect to land, including matters such as land tenure, and landlord and tenant.[31] This is because, in matters pertaining to law and policy relating to land and local government, the Constitution recognized the special need for uniformity among the states and cooperation between the federation and the states. For this purpose, the law on land does not have to be approved by state legislature before it takes effect to become federal law.

35. The Constitutional distribution of powers thus renders both federal and state governments' competency to deal with environmental matters, both legislatively and administratively. Coincidently, such competency also results in the existence of various agencies, and at all levels of government, dealing with various aspects of environmental management.

II. Administrative Set Up

A. Federal Level

36. Executive power is vested in the Cabinet, which is the highest coordinating executive body of all government activities and is led by a Prime Minister. The Malaysian Constitution stipulates that the Prime Minister must be a member of the lower house of Parliament which, in the opinion of the *Yang di-Pertuan Agong* or the king, commands a majority in Parliament.

37. The Prime Minister's main functions are to preside over the Cabinet and to coordinate policies and efforts of the various portfolios in the government. He also has certain constitutional and statutory functions, such as to advise the *Yang di-Pertuan Agong* on the appointment of judges and to fill certain senior posts in the civil service.

38. Ministers are appointed on the advice of the Prime Minister. The Cabinet meets regularly under the chairmanship of the Prime Minister to formulate the policy of the government. The Ministers hold different portfolios and are collectively responsible for all decisions made by the Cabinet, which is the highest policy-making body in the country.

30. Preamble of the Environmental Quality Act 1974.
31. Article 76(4) of the Federal Constitution.

39. Administratively, Malaysia is organized in a three-tier system of government: federal, state and local governments. In carrying out its duties as enumerated in the Federal and Concurrent Lists of the Constitution, the federal government has established a number of ministries, departments and agencies, apart from public enterprises, statutory bodies and corporations.

40. At the federal level, the main components of the federal government's administrative machinery are ministries and departments. A ministry is the highest federal administrative body and is headed by a minister, who holds a portfolio. Government departments, established within ministries, are the second highest federal body, and they are responsible for implementing the federal government's policies. A department is headed by a director general (DG), who is also the chief administrative officer.

B. State Level

41. At the state level, states have their own governments and constitutions. State governments are composed of a legislative assembly, a speaker of the House and a head of state. Legislative assembly members are elected by single-member constituencies, and assembly members in turn elect the speaker. Legislative assemblies may make or enact laws not reserved for the federal legislature and on subjects under the concurrent purview of federal and state governments.

42. Heads of state are hereditary rulers, namely the *Sultan* or Ruler. He acts on the advice of the State Executive Council that is chaired by the *Menteri Besar* or chief minister.[32] Exceptions are the states of Melaka, Pulau Pinang, Sabah and Sarawak, which have governors appointed by the king upon the chief minister's advice.

43. The head of state appoints a chief minister from among legislative members, may dissolve assemblies on the chief minister's advice and must approve all legislation. In practice, chief ministers handle state administrative matters, assisted by a cabinet of ministers.

44. At the state level, the state's Executive Council is the federal cabinet equivalent and is the highest coordinating body on all matters of interest to the state. The state legislature has the autonomy to pass any law within its competency as provided by the Federal Constitution. State-level agencies enforce and administer state laws, just as federal agencies do for federal laws.

45. At the state level as well, state departments are the highest administrative machinery and they can be divided into two: those within the state government, and

32. In the states where there is no hereditary ruler, a governor is appointed by the *Yang di-pertuan Agong* or King to be the state's ceremonial head, as in the case of Penang, Melaka, Sarawak and Sabah.

those that come under the federal government, namely, branches of federal departments. State departments of the first type include the State Secretary's Office. Federal department branches, which are the responsibility of the federal government, include the Education Department and Department of Environment.

C. Local Level

46. At the local level, the local government or local authority forms another part of the government. Under Item 4 in List II of the Ninth Schedule, the Federal Constitution stipulates that local government is to be a subject under the State List. Hence, all local authorities fall under the exclusive jurisdiction of the state governments.

47. Local governments in Malaysia include city councils, municipal councils or district councils, and the Commissioner of the City of Kuala Lumpur. Except for Kuala Lumpur, Putrajaya and Labuan, all other local governments are placed under the state authorities, which have the power to declare any area in that state a local authority area and to determine the status of that local authority. Local governments are headed by the mayor, for city councils, or the president, for municipalities or district councils.[33] Prior to 1965, local council heads and their members were elected; however, at present they are appointed by the respective state governments.[34]

D. Statutory Bodies/Corporatization

48. One of the government's ways of transferring public services is through corporatization. In Malaysia, statutory bodies are established under specific laws with the objective of implementing certain duties and responsibilities in line with national objectives.

49. Usually, corporations are set up to take over the duties and responsibilities of certain government departments. As such, corporate statutes typically give corporations the ability to own property, sign binding contracts and pay taxes in a capacity that is separate from that of its shareholders. The advantages of setting up corporations are to enable benefits derived from the government to be integrated with the benefits from the private sector.

50. Every public corporation has officers of its own to manage it. The chief administrator of a public corporation is called the General Manager, who is responsible for management and administration in accordance with the corporations' objectives. To ensure smooth administration, a corporation has certain divisions

---

33. *See* Siew Nooi Phang, *Sistem Kerajaan Tempatan di Malaysia* (Dewan Bahasa dan Pustaka 1989).
34. In 1974, the Local Government (Temporary Provisions) Act 1973 (Act 124) abolished all elected local authorities, and the power to appoint local authorities was given to the state governments.

assigned with special tasks. Every corporation has a board of directors. In the case of statutory bodies, their board of directors are appointed by the minister responsible for its establishment.

51. A number of corporate bodies have been created through legislation. One of these corporations, relevant to environment matters, is the *Suruhanjaya Perkhidmatan Air Negara* or National Water Services Commission. This body was set up by virtue of the National Water Services Commission Act 2006 in order to regulate the Water Services Industry Act 2006. The objective of this Corporation is to centralize water services for the whole country.

52. Another relevant body corporate is the Solid Waste Management Corporation, established under the Solid Waste and Public Cleansing Management Act 2007. Its objective is to provide comprehensive regulation and control of solid waste and public cleansing management throughout Malaysia.

E. Privatization

53. Malaysia's privatization programme began in 1983 as a mean to transfer certain government functions to the private sector. In Malaysia, privatization is undertaken in order to take advantage of the private sector management skills to provide better service to the public. It also helps to promote economic growth, reduce the government's administrative and financial burden, and increase government revenue.

54. Malaysia's privatization policies were set out in the Privatization Master Plan published in 1991. The privatization process is managed by the Economic Planning Unit in the Prime Minister's Department.[35]

55. Together with the Privatization Master Plan, the federal government introduced the Privatization Action Plan, which is a two-year rolling plan to assist the annual implementation of the programme. At the end of 1995, there were twelve different methods of privatization in use, including sale of equity, sale of assets, lease of assets, management contract, build-operate-transfer, build-operate-own, build-operate, build-transfer, land development, management buy-out, joint ventures and asset swap.

56. Several environmental-related sectors have been privatized under the privatizing policy. They include the privatization of water management to reduce the financial burden on state governments. Until now, water authorities in several states, such as Johor, Penang and Kelantan, have already been privatized. Sewage treatment is another area which has been privatized in Malaysia. A company known as

---

35. *See* the Economic Planning Unit's official website for detail at http://www.epu.gov.my/en/dasar-penswastaan, January 2014.

the Indah Water Konsortium, formed in 1993, was given a contract and assigned the responsibility of operating public-sewage-treatment facilities.

F. State and Federal Coordination

57. In Malaysia, the Federal Constitution dictates that environmental management is not strictly a prerogative of either state or federal government, due to the fact that environmental matters fall under different legislative lists.

58. The Federal Constitution provides for avenues of federal influence over the state governments for coordination. Such influence is exercisable over matters that are even listed under the State List of the Constitution. This is done through the establishment of specific councils, such as the National Council for Local Government,[36] the National Land Council[37] and the National Finance Council.[38] These Councils are chaired by the prime minister or his appointee. Representatives from both the federal and state governments sit on these committees.

59. For example, in order to ensure uniformity of law and policy, the Federal Constitution provides for the establishment of a national development plan under Article 92(3). The plan is for the development, improvement or conservation of the natural resources of a development area, the exploitation of such resources, or the increase of means of employment in the area.

60. Clause (1) of Article 92 states that:

> if, after a recommendation from an expert committee and after consultation with the National Finance Council, the National Land Council and the Government of any State concerned, the Yang di-Pertuan Agong or the King is satisfied that it is conducive to the national interest that a development plan be put into operation in any area or areas in one or more of the States, the Yang di-Pertuan Agong may proclaim the area or areas as a development area; and thereupon Parliament shall have power to give effect to the development plan or any part thereof.

Therefore, within the decentralization of Malaysia's legal and institutional frameworks, there are provisions in the Constitution that provide for an exception to that notion.

61. In the national administrative system, government agencies at all levels play an important role in implementing government policies. Although each government agency has its own corporate objectives, generally government agencies carry out

36. Article 95A of the Federal Constitution.
37. Article 91 of the Federal Constitution.
38. Article 108 of the Federal Constitution.

their duties and responsibilities, as well as their activities, in line with national aspirations and objectives. The close cooperation among the various agencies is imperative to stabilize administration and services to society.

62. There is also a specialized agency that was set up by the federal government to monitor and coordinate the implementation of development programmes.
The Implementation and Coordination Unit was established directly under the Prime Minister's Department,[39] and its task is to determine the coordination of implementing policies, programmes and development strategies in the federal and state governments.

63. Another mechanism that has a significant influence on federal and state environmental policies is the Meeting of Ministers and State Executive Councillors Responsible for Environmental Matters. This is a venue at which federal and state authorities meet to discuss environmental issues, to formulate uniform and coordinated policies, and to monitor the development of the implementation of those policies across states.

III. The Actual Role of the Governmental Institutions

A. Federal Level

64. Malaysia is a country of decentralized administrative jurisdiction of federal, state and local governments, where each of the governments has its own administrative body to exert control over their respective spheres of jurisdiction as specified in the Federal Constitution, including those relating to the environment.

65. The existence of agency relating to the environment at ministerial level in Malaysia started in 1976 when the Ministry of Technology, Research and Local Government which was set in 1973 was re-established as the Ministry of Science, Technology and Environment (MOSTE) to include new functions and responsibilities related to environment. During that time, until 2004, functions and responsibilities related to environmental issues came directly under MOSTE through the Department of Environment (DOE) which was created in 1976 with the main purpose of enforcing the Environmental Quality Act 1974.

66. While MOSTE was a key agency in terms of environmental management and protection, it was also mandated to develop and expand science and technology activities for national development, while preserving the quality of life and the country's natural resources. Thus, apart from the DOE, the implementation of this mandate was also tasked to several departments within MOSTE, including the Department of Wildlife and National Parks. In 2004, there was a restructuring of MOSTE, and the Ministry's name was changed to Ministry of Science, Technology and Innovation (MOSTI) in order to spearhead the development of national ICT,

39. *See* its official website at http://www.icu.gov.my/pg/1icu.php, January 2014.

multimedia and innovation. At the same time, a new Ministry was created to exclusively deal with the environment, namely the Ministry of Natural Resources and Environment (MNRE). Under the MNRE, the DOE continues to become the main body dealing with environmental protection and management and to advise and assist the relevant minister in performing his duty. However, after Malaysia's general election in May 2018, which saw the change of government, a number of reorganizations took place within several Ministries. In relation to environmental matters, two new Ministries were established. One of which was the Ministry of Energy, Green Technology, Science and Climate Change (MESTECC). This new Ministry was the reorganization of three former Ministries, namely (i) the Ministry of Science, Technology and Innovation; (ii) the Ministry of Energy, Green Technology and Water; and (iii) the MNRE. At the same time, the MNRE was replaced by the Ministry of Water, Land and Natural Resources which was responsible for overseeing the management of water, natural resources, wildlife, minerals, irrigation, drainage, land, mapping and forest in Malaysia. It is also responsible for the administration of the marine parks of Malaysia.

67. However, the established MESTECC and Ministry of Water, Land and Natural Resources were short-lived. After another political crisis in March 2020, restructuring exercise occurred the second time. The two key ministries, MESTECC and Ministry of Water, Land and Natural Resources were then reconfigured into three different ministries, namely (i) Ministry of Science, Technology and Innovation;[40] (ii) Ministry of Environment and Water;[41] and (iii) Ministry of Energy and Natural Resources.[42] In August 2021, there was yet another change in the government for Malaysia which has therefore seen three federal governments over a period of two years. However, for the 2021's political crisis, existing environmental-related ministries have been retained, whereas the national focal point for environmental issues as well as climate change and the UNFCCC continues to reside under the Ministry of Environment and Water from 2020 until now.

68. The Department of Environment was established in 1975 and originally belonged to the Ministry of Science, Technology and Environment. The Department of Environment has comprehensive jurisdiction over environmental administration and is charged with formulating environmental rules and regulations, enforcing legislation, carrying out monitoring of environmental pollution, and conducting Environmental Impact Assessments (EIAs).

69. For administrative purposes, the EQA 1974[43] provides for the office of Director General of Environmental Quality. The DG's duties, as contained in section 3(1), are to administer the Act and its Orders and Regulations, to coordinate all activities relating to the discharge of wastes into the environment and to control such activities through the issue of licences of wastes or substances which are of

40. See the official website at https://www.mosti.gov.my/en/
41. See the official website at https://www.kasa.gov.my/ms/
42. See the official website at https://www.ketsa.gov.my/en-my/Pages/default.aspx
43. Act 127.

danger to the quality of the environment. He also gives recommendations to the Minister with regard to environmental policy, as well as standards and criteria of the quality of the environment.

70. Besides the DG, the Act also provides for the establishment of the Environmental Quality Council under section 4. The main duty of the Council is to advise the Minister in charge of the environment on matters pertaining to the EQA 1974.

71. The Environmental Quality Council comprises nineteen members who are representatives of relevant bodies concerned with the environment and pollution. They include[44] a Chairman, who is the representative of Ministers who are charged with the following responsibilities: for natural resources and environment; for science, technology and innovation; for international trade and industry; domestic trade and consumer affairs; for agriculture and agro-based industry; for human resources; for transport; for housing and local government; for energy, green technology and water; and for health. Besides these, seven of the following persons are also appointed as members of the Council: One representative each from Sabah and Sarawak; one representative each from the petroleum industry, the palm oil industry, the Federation of Malaysian Manufacturers, the rubber industry; a member who shall be appointed by the Minister from among the academic staff of a higher learning institution; and two members who shall be appointed by the Minister from among the registered non-governmental organizations (NGO) who are active in promoting and enhancing environmental quality.[45]

B. State Level

72. Environmental management at the state level is more complex. Government departments at the state level are divided into two, namely, state departments and branches of federal departments. An example of a branch of federal government is the federal department of environment state branches. State departments responsible to the state government include the State Secretary Office, State Financial Office, State Legal Advisor's Office and State Economic Planning Unit.

73. Federal department branches, such as those of the Department of Environment, are the responsibility of the federal government, although they are subject to coordination efforts of the state administration. To meet state needs, heads of branches are invited to committee meetings of the State Government Council and the State Action Council. They also become members of the State Development Committee and other state committees.

44. Section 4(1) of the Environmental Quality Act 1974.
45. Subsection Act A1441 of the year 2012. In addition, s. 7 has been amended to include subs. (6) which allows the Minister to invite a person who is not a member of the Council to attend the Council meeting for the purpose of giving advice on the matter under discussion. However, this person has no voting rights.

74. The states of Sabah and Sarawak have more state departments, as a result of the 1963 Malaysia Agreement,[46] which gave both these states more power than that given to states in Peninsular Malaysia. However, due to an integration process, most of the departments have slowly been taken over by the federal government.

75. The main state departments in Sabah[47] and Sarawak,[48] which are under the jurisdiction of the state governments, are similar to those in Peninsular Malaysia.

C. *Local Level*

76. At the lowest level of government, the local government is also involved, either directly or indirectly, with the administration of the environment and the control of pollution within its own area. They also have the power to enforce various legislative provisions on the matter as provided by the Local Government Act 1976, the Town and Country Planning Act 1976, and the Street Drainage and Building Act 1974.

77. Generally, the environmental functions of the local government are maintenance and improvement of the environment within its locality. This includes such matters as those pertaining to parks and gardens; planning activities; conservation of physical features such as rivers, streams and trees; and prevention of air, water and land pollution. Other related functions include obligatory services, such as cleansing, collection and disposal of solid wastes, proper drainage and sewage, operating a sewerage system, sanitation and solid waste management system, and the cleaning of drains and roads.

§5. Sources of Environmental Law

I. Written Laws

78. In Malaysia, environmental competences are attributed to a number of authorities, largely due to historical development of the country's legal system. Sources of Malaysian environmental law can generally be classified into written and unwritten law. Apart from that, Malaysia's international environmental obligation is another source of environmental law.

46. Malaysia Agreement is Malaysia Treaty of 9 Jul. 1963, concluded between the Federation of Malaya, the United Kingdom of Great Britain and Northern Ireland, North Borneo, Sarawak and Singapore.
47. For details regarding Sabah, refer to Sabah state's government official website at http://www.sabah.gov.my/main/, January 2014.
48. For Sarawak, refer to the state government's official website at http://www.sarawak.gov.my/, January 2014.

79. Written law is the most important source of law in Malaysia, with the Federal Constitution being the principal source of law for the whole country. The Constitution may declare the law on a given matter, including environmental law. It may also designate the bodies that can make the law. When these bodies make law, the laws they make owe their legitimacy to the Constitution.[49]

80. Apart from the Federal Constitution, which is applicable to the whole of Malaysia, each state also possesses its own constitution regulating the government of that state. State constitutions generally make provisions concerning the ruler of that state, the state executive council and state legislative assemblies.

81. Written laws include legislation enacted by Parliament and state legislative assemblies, as well as subsidiary legislation made by persons or bodies under power conferred on them by Parliament's Acts or state legislative assemblies. Thus, within the three levels of government in Malaysia, there may exist federal and state legislations relating to the environment.

82. In Malaysia, many of the sources of environmental law come in the form of written laws, that is, statutes or legislation, with the EQA 1974, a federal law, being the most comprehensive law on the matter.

83. Following its enactment, the EQA 1974 was amended nine times, in 1985, 1996, 1998, 2001, 2007, 2009, 2012, 2014 and 2015. These amendments were made following changes in Malaysia's environmental status and developments within legal and administrative processes affecting the Act such as that pertaining to investigation, prosecution and prevention of environmental crime.[50]

84. The 1985 amendment[51] was made in response to growing public concern about destruction of the natural environment by development activities. It introduced the EIA system, under section 34A, for large-scale development projects as a means of preventing environmental destruction.

85. The 1996 amendment[52] was the most extensive one. First, the amendment increased fines and penalties for non-compliance with environmental regulations. The stiffer penalties prescribed in this amendment include increasing the term of imprisonment for offences involving scheduled wastes from two years to five years, and raising the maximum fine from Malaysian Ringgit (MYR) 10,000–MYR 500,000. Second, the prohibition against emission discharge was widened from that

49. Refer to Andrew Harding, *Law, Government and the Constitution in Malaysia* (Kluwer L. Intl. 1996).
50. *See* Maizatun Mustafa, *Environmental Quality Act 1974: Development and Reform*, 2 MLJ (March/April 2009); Maizatun Mustafa, *Environmental Quality Act 1974: A Tool towards the Implementation and Achievement of Malaysia's Environmental Policy*, 19 IIUM L.J. (2011); and Maizatun Mustafa & Nurah Sabahiah Mohammed, *The Development of Environmental Crime and Sanction in Malaysia*, 11 Eur. Scientific J. (2015).
51. The Environmental Quality (Amendment) Act 1985, Act 636.
52. The Environmental Quality (Amendment) Act 1996, Act 953.

of 'waste' only to other discharges such as 'environmentally hazardous substances' and 'pollutants'.[53] Powers of the DG were also widened to require pollution-prevention equipment and actions by operators and to issue a prohibition order.[54]

86. The 1996 amendment also introduced new provisions such as the requirement of environmental auditing on any vehicles, ships or prescribed premises;[55] and the requirements of labelling and recycling on any substance prescribed as an environmentally hazardous substance or on any prescribed product.[56] Other new provisions include deposit and rebate of products,[57] establishment of an environmental fund,[58] and compensation for damage to property belonging to a third party as a result of the violation of the Act.[59]

87. The 1998 amendment[60] incorporated a complete ban on 'open burning' because of the major haze incidents occurring in Malaysia. However, the 2001 amendment[61] provided for situations where a person may be exempted from the prohibition of open burning.

88. The amendment in 2007[62] involved two separate provisions. The first, in section 34B, involved a stiffer punishment imposed on any person convicted of offences involving scheduled wastes, which is a fine not exceeding MYR 500,000 and a jail term not exceeding five years. Another amendment, in section 43, extended liability to include that of the chief executive officer of a company in addition to the existing liability of company directors. Under this amendment, the chief executive officer would be equally liable if his company, firm or society committed such offences.

89. In 2009, the Act was amended in order to revoke one of its Regulations, the Environmental Quality (Sewage and Industrial Effluents) Regulations 1979, and to replace it with two new Regulations, namely the Environmental Quality (Sewage) Regulations 2009, and the Environmental Quality (Industrial Effluent) Regulations 2009. The former apply to any premises which discharge sewage onto or into any soil, or into any inland waters or Malaysian waters, other than any housing or commercial development or both having a population equivalent of less than 150

53. Section 2 of the Environmental Quality Act 1974.
54. Section 31A of the Environmental Quality Act 1974.
55. Section 33A of the Environmental Quality Act 1974.
56. Section 30A of the Environmental Quality Act 1974.
57. Section 30B of the Environmental Quality Act 1974.
58. Section 36A, 36B, 36C and 36D of the Environmental Quality Act 1974.
59. Section 46E of the Environmental Quality Act 1974.
60. The Environmental Quality (Amendment) Act 1998, Act 1030.
61. The Environmental Quality (Amendment) Act 2001, Act 1102.
62. The Environmental Quality (Amendment) Act 2007, Act 1315.

people.[63] Whereas the latter apply to any premises which discharge or release industrial effluent or mixed effluent, onto or into any soil, or into inland waters or Malaysian waters.[64] With the introduction of these two Regulations, matters relating to sewage and industrial effluents are now being treated separately by the Act, including those involving their acceptable conditions and enforcement.

90. During the same year, other Regulations were introduced, namely the Environmental Quality (Control of Pollution from Solid Waste Treatment Station and Landfill) Regulations 2009. These Regulations apply to solid waste transfer stations and landfills which discharge or release leachate[65] in relation to noise and air pollution, as well as the pollution of soil, surface water and groundwater.[66]

91. In 2012,[67] amendment was made to improve existing sections such as that of environmental audit in section 33A, and that of EIA in subsections (2A), (2B) and (2C) of section 34A. In addition, a new section was introduced, section 34AA[68] which complements section 34A in providing for the power to the DG to issue any prohibition order or stop work order to the person carrying out the prescribed activities. The 2012 amendment also inserted a number of new sections, mainly to deal with processes pertaining to investigation of environmental offences such as that of section 37A, 37B and 37C, and matters relating to evidence in new sections 38AA, 38AB and 48AC. Procedures relating to forfeiture of seized items such as vehicle, ship and book for purposes of investigation and related matters have been improved by the Act through the amendment of section 46B and 46D, and the introduction of new sections 46BA, 46BB, 46BC and 48AA. Other new sections introduced by the 2012 amendment include that of section 48AB on the presumption of scheduled wastes; section 48AC on the execution of power given to the DG for the execution of the Act; section 48AD on offences relating to obstruction of search; section 48AE on joinder of offences; section 49B on payment of reward to informers; and section 50A on protection of informers.

92. Two most recent amendments to date were in 2014[69] and 2015.[70] The former was done in order to revoke one of its oldest Regulations, the Environmental Quality (Clean Air) Regulations 1978, and to replace it with the Environmental Quality (Clean Air) Regulations 2014. The 2014 Regulations are meant to provide for new methods towards controlling air pollution from stationary sources through management and operational changes, and more stringent standards and advanced strategies. Whereas the EQA's 2015 amendment was meant to revoke the Environmental

63. Regulation 3 of the Environmental Quality (Sewage) Regulations 2009.
64. Regulation 3 Environmental Quality (Industrial Effluent) Regulations 2009.
65. Regulation 3 of the Environmental Quality (Control of Pollution from Solid Waste Treatment Station and Landfill) Regulations 2009.
66. Regulation 5 of the Environmental Quality (Control of Pollution from Solid Waste Treatment Station and Landfill) Regulations 2009.
67. Environmental Quality (Amendment) Act 2012, Act A1441.
68. Act A1441.
69. P.U. (A) 151/2014.
70. P.U. (A) 195/2015.

Quality (Prescribed Activities) (EIA) Order 1987 and to introduce a new Order, known as Environmental Quality (Prescribed Activities) (EIA) Order 2015. The new Order contains important changes such as the incorporation of the term 'environmentally sensitive area'[71] within its scope of application, the requirement of public participation on certain activities and the revision of activities that are considered to be 'prescribed activities'.

93. The EQA 1974 is a framework law, which means that for its provisions to take effect there is a need for the making of rules and regulations. Similarly, environmental terms defined in section 2 of the Act do not stand on their own, but must be read together with any relevant provision, and for this provision to take effect there is a need for rules and regulations to be gazetted on the matter.

94. Regulations, rules and orders have continuously been passed under the aegis of the Act, through the delegation of legislative power to the Minister of Environmental Quality.[72] They are as follows:[73]

(1) the Environmental Quality (Prescribed Premises) (Crude Palm Oil) Regulations 1977;[74]
(2) the Environmental Quality (Licensing) Regulations 1977;[75]
(3) the Environmental Quality (Clean Air) Regulations 1978;[76]
(4) the Environmental Quality (Prescribed Premises) (Raw Natural Rubber) Regulations 1978;[77]
(5) the Environmental Quality (Sewage and Industrial Effluents) Regulations 1979;[78]
(6) the Environmental Quality (Control of Lead Concentration in Motor Gasoline) Regulations 1985;
(7) the Environmental Quality (Motor Vehicle Noise) Regulations 1987;[79]
(8) the Environmental Quality (Prescribed Activities) (EIA) Order 1987;[80]

71. 'Environmentally sensitive area' is defined by the Order to mean 'any area specified as such in the development plan or national physical plan under the Town and Country Planning Act 1976, or any area specified as environmental protection area or environmental conservation area under any Enactment in the State of Sabah or any Ordinance in the State of Sarawak'.
72. In normal situations, Parliament or a state legislative assembly would exercise its legislative power by making law. However, it is also possible for the legislature to delegate its law-making power into some other person or body to form a delegated or subsidiary legislation within the purview of any Act of Parliament.
73. These Regulations, Orders and Rules were enacted by the Minister under the powers conferred to him by s. 51 of the Environmental Quality Act 1974.
74. P.U. (A) 342/77.
75. P.U. (A) 198/77.
76. P.U. (A) 280/78.
77. P.U. (A) 338/78.
78. P.U. (A) 12/79.
79. P.U. (A) 244/87.
80. P.U. (A) 362/1987.

(9) the Environmental Quality (Prescribed Premises) (Scheduled Wastes Treatment and Disposal Facilities) Regulations 1989;[81]
(10) the Environmental Quality (Control of Emission from Petrol Engines) Regulations 1996;[82]
(11) the Environmental Quality (Control of Emission from Diesel Engines) Regulations 1996;[83]
(12) the Environmental Quality (Refrigerant Management) Regulations 1999;[84]
(13) the Environmental Quality (Halon Management) Regulations 1999;[85]
(14) the Environmental Quality (Appeal Board) Regulations 2003;[86]
(15) Environmental Quality (Control of Emission from Motorcycles) Regulations 2003;[87]
(16) the Environmental Quality (Dioxin and Furan) Regulations 2004;[88]
(17) the Environmental Quality (Scheduled Wastes) Regulations 2005;[89]
(18) the Environmental Quality (Control of Petrol and Diesel Properties) Regulations 2007;[90]
(19) the Environmental Quality (Sewage) Regulations 2009;[91]
(20) the Environmental Quality (Control of Pollution from Solid Waste Treatment Station and Landfill) Regulations 2009;[92]
(21) the Environmental Quality (Industrial Effluent) Regulations 2009;[93]
(22) the Environmental Quality (Compounding of Offences) Rules 1978;[94]
(23) the Environmental Quality (Compounding of Offences) (Open Burning) Rules 2000;[95]
(24) the Environmental Quality (Prescribed Premises) (Crude Palm Oil) Order 1977;[96]
(25) the Environmental Quality (Prescribed Premises) (Raw Natural Rubber) Order 1978;[97]
(26) the Environmental Quality (Prescribed Activities) (EIA) Order 1987;[98]

---

81. P.U. (A) 241/87.
82. P.U. (A) 429/96.
83. P.U. (A) 141/89.
84. P.U. (A) 451/99.
85. P.U. (A) 452/99.
86. P.U. (A) 115/2003.
87. P.U. (A) 464/2003.
88. P.U. (A) 104/2004.
89. P.U. (A) 294/2005.
90. P.U. (A) 145/2007.
91. P.U. (A) 432/2009. The Environmental Quality (Sewage and Industrial Effluents) Regulations 1979 [P.U. (A) 12/79] is revoked.
92. P.U. (A) 433/2009. The Environmental Quality (Sewage and Industrial Effluents) Regulations 1979 [P.U. (A) 12/79] is revoked.
93. P.U. (A) 434/2009. The Environmental Quality (Sewage and Industrial Effluents) Regulations 1979 [P.U. (A) 12/79] is revoked.
94. P.U. (A) 281/78.
95. P.U. (A) 310/2000.
96. P.U. (A) 199/77.
97. P.U. (A) 250/78.
98. P.U. (A) 362/87.

(27) the Environmental Quality (Prescribed Premises) (Scheduled Wastes Treatment and Disposal Facilities) Order 1989;[99]
(28) the Environmental Quality (Delegation of Powers on Marine Pollution Control) Order 1993;[100]
(29) the Environmental Quality (Prohibition on the Use of Chlorofluorocarbon and other Gases as Propellants and Blowing Agents) Order 1993;[101]
(30) Environmental Quality (Delegation of Powers on Marine Pollution Control) Order 1994;[102]
(31) the Environmental Quality (Prohibition on the Use of Controlled Substance in Soap, Synthetic Detergent and Other Cleaning Agents) Order 1995;[103]
(32) the Environmental Quality (Delegation of Powers) Order 1999;[104]
(33) the Environmental Quality (Prescribed Activities) (Open Burning) Order 2000;[105]
(34) the Environmental Quality (Delegation of Powers) (Investigation of Open Burning) Order 2000;[106]
(35) the Environmental Quality (Delegation of Powers) (Halon Management) Order 2000;[107]
(36) Environmental Quality (Delegation of Powers) (Perbadanan Putrajaya) Order 2002;[108]
(37) Environmental Quality (Declared Activities) (Open Burning) Order 2003;[109]
(38) the Environmental Quality (Prescribed Conveyance) (Scheduled Wastes) Order 2005;[110]
(39) Environmental Quality (Delegation of Powers) Order 2005;[111]
(40) Environmental Quality (Delegation of Powers) (Investigation on Erosion and Sediment Control) Order 2012;[112]
(41) Environmental Quality (Clean Air) Regulations 2014;[113] and
(42) the Environmental Quality (Prescribed Activities) (EIA) Order 2015.[114]

95. Apart from the EQA 1974, there are various others legislations in Malaysia that are directly or indirectly related to environmental protection, conservation and pollution control. They are as follows:

---

99. P.U. (A) 140/89.
100. P.U. (A) 276/93.
101. P.U. (A) 434/93.
102. P.U. (A) 537/94.
103. P.U. (A) 115/95.
104. P.U. (A) 501/99.
105. P.U. (A) 308/2000.
106. P.U. (A) 311/2000.
107. P.U. (A) 490/2000.
108. P.U. (A) 233/2002.
109. P.U. (A) 460/2003.
110. P.U. (A) 293/2005.
111. P.U. (A) 365/2005.
112. P.U. (A) 436/2012.
113. P.U. (A) 151/2014.
114. P.U. (A) 195/2015.

(1) Aboriginal Peoples Act 1954, revised 1974;[115]
(2) Access to Biological Resources and Benefit Sharing Act 2017;[116]
(3) Animals Act 1953, revised 2006;[117]
(4) Animal Welfare Act 2015;[118]
(5) Atomic Energy Licensing Act 1984;[119]
(6) Baselines of Maritime Zones Act 2006;[120]
(7) Civil Law Act 1956, revised 1972;[121]
(8) Continental Shelf Act 1966;[122]
(9) Criminal Procedure Code, revised 1999;[123]
(10) Drainage Works Act 1954, revised 1988;[124]
(11) Exclusive Economic Zone Act 1984;[125]
(12) Factories and Machineries Act 1967, revised 1974;[126]
(13) Fisheries Act 1985;[127]
(14) Food Act 1983;[128]
(15) International Trade in Endangered Species Act 2008;[129]
(16) Irrigation Areas Act 1953,[130] revised 1989;
(17) Land Acquisition Act 1960, revised 1992;[131]
(18) Land Conservation Act 1960, revised 1989;[132]
(19) Local Government Act 1976;[133]
(20) Malaysian Maritime Enforcement Agency Act 2004;[134]
(21) Malaysian Quarantine and Inspection Services Act 2011;[135]
(22) Merchant Shipping Ordinance 1952;[136]
(23) Mineral Development Act 1994;[137]
(24) National Forestry Act 1984;[138]
(25) National Heritage Act 2005;[139]

115. Act 134.
116. Act 795.
117. Act 647.
118. Act 772.
119. Act 304.
120. Act 660.
121. Act 67.
122. Act 83.
123. Act 593.
124. Act 354.
125. Act 311.
126. Act 134.
127. Act 317.
128. Act 281.
129. Act 686.
130. Act 386.
131. Act 486.
132. Act 385.
133. Act 171.
134. Act 633.
135. Act 728.
136. No. 70 of 1952.
137. Act 524.
138. Act 313.
139. Act 645.

(26) National Land Code;[140]
(27) National Parks Act 1980;[141]
(28) Occupational Safety and Hazardous Act 1994;[142]
(29) Penal Code, revised 1997;[143]
(30) Pesticides Act 1974;[144]
(31) Petroleum Mining Act 1966, revised 1972;[145]
(32) Protection of Wildlife Act 1972;[146]
(33) Renewable Energy Act 2011;[147]
(34) Road Transport Act 1987;[148]
(35) Solid Waste and Public Cleansing Management Act 2007;[149]
(36) Solid Waste and Public Cleansing Management Corporation Act 2007;[150]
(37) Street, Drainage and Building Act 1974;[151]
(38) Suruhanjaya Perkhidmatan Air Negara Act 2006;[152]
(39) Sustainable Energy Development Authority Act 2011;[153]
(40) Territorial Sea Act 2012;[154]
(41) Town and Country Planning Act 1976;[155]
(42) Water Services Industry Act 2006;[156]
(43) Water Act 1920, revised 1989;[157] and
(44) Wildlife Conservation Act 2010.[158]

II. Unwritten Law

96. Unwritten law is the part of Malaysian law which is not enacted by parliament or state legislative assemblies. It is found in cases decided by the courts or case law.

97. Case law decided by the superior courts is one of the sources of environmental law. In Malaysia, superior courts are the High Court, Court of Appeal and

140. Act 56.
141. Act 226.
142. Act 514.
143. Act 574.
144. Act 149.
145. Act 1995.
146. Act 76. Revoked by Act 716.
147. Act 725.
148. Act 333.
149. Act 672.
150. Act 673.
151. Act 133.
152. Act 654.
153. Act 726.
154. Act 750.
155. Act 172.
156. Act 655.
157. Act 418.
158. Act 716.

the Federal Court.[159] This is based on the hierarchical system known as *stare decisis* or the doctrine of binding judicial precedent. This doctrine is based on the principle that decisions of higher courts bind lower courts, and some courts are bound by their own decisions. Cases from the United Kingdom and commonwealth countries have persuasive authority on the decisions of the Malaysian courts.[160]

98. Reported cases on the environment in Malaysia, which are very few, are based on either statute law or common law and may provide an authority for future cases. They are to be found mainly in the following reports:

- Malayan Law Journal;
- current Law Journal; and
- all Malayan Reports.

99. The principles of English common law and equity, recognized by virtue of the Civil Law Act 1956,[161] are unwritten sources of Malaysia's environmental law.

100. English common law and rules of equity continue to be applied in Malaysia. However, England's common law and rules of equity that form part of Malaysian law are limited to section 3 of the Act. This section provides for cut-off dates for the application of English law to specific parts of Malaysia. For Peninsular Malaysia, the courts must apply the common law of England and the rules of equity as administered in England on the seventh day of April 1956. In Sabah and Sarawak, the courts must apply the common law of England and the rules of equity, together with statutes of general application, as administered or in force in England on the first day of December 1951 and the twelfth day of December 1949 respectively. However, where there is a conflict between English law and written law in Malaysia, Malaysian written law prevails.[162]

101. In Malaysia, common law remedies in the form of tort principles are available to any person who has suffered injury as a result of environmental pollution. Civil litigation in respect of environmentally related matters can be made based on these principles. For example, the tort principle of public nuisance was applied in the case of *Majlis Perbandaran Pulau Pinang v. Boey Siew Than & Others*,[163] where an action was taken by the local authority of Pulau Pinang against the defendants for carrying out structural alteration and using the premises as an eating house without licence. Private nuisance is another tort principle applied in Malaysia for

159. Sources of Malaysian law can also be found in the then Supreme Court, Federal Court and the Judicial Committee of the Privy Council. The two later courts were part of the Malaysian judicial system until 31 Dec. 1986 and decisions made by them are still binding on the present courts, whereas the Supreme Court was part of the judicial system from 1 Jan. 1987 to 23 Jun. 1994.
160. For detail, *see* Ahmad Ibrahim & Ahilemah Joned, *The Malaysian Legal System* 116–141 (Dewan Bahasa dan Pustaka 1995).
161. Act 67, revised 1972.
162. *See* Ahmad Ibrahim & Ahilemah Joned, *The Malaysian Legal System* 81–91 (Dewan Bahasa dan Pustaka 1995).
163. (1978) 2 MLJ 145.

environment-related cases such as the case of *Renal Link (KL) Sdn. Bhd. v. Dato' Dr Harman Singh.*[164] The appellant in this case was alleged to have emitted noxious and toxic fumes and gases from his premises to the detriment of respondent's beneficial use of his premises. It was held that the appellant was liable for the loss suffered by the respondent under the tort of private nuisance. The tort principle of negligence was recognized and applied by the Malaysian court in the case of *McGowan & Another v. Wong Shee Fun & Another,*[165] when the defendants caused damage to the plaintiff's stream by failing to take all reasonable steps to prevent siltation of that stream. The rule in *Rylands v. Fletcher* on strict liability is yet another tort principle relevant in environmental cases, applied in the case of *Woon Tan Kan & Others v. Asian Rare Earth Sdn. Bhd.*[166]

102. Another form of unwritten law in Malaysia is custom of the local inhabitants.[167] The Malaysian definition of law under Article 160 of the Federal Constitution includes 'customs and usages having the force of law'. However, the application of customary law as a source of law is very limited. It is mainly applied by natives of Sabah and Sarawak on specific matters only.[168]

103. Generally, native customary laws in Sabah and Sarawak are found in administrative codes, legislations, judicial decisions and unrecorded oral traditions. All customary law gazetted or enacted become legal documents and are subjected to a system of binding precedents applied similarly to that of common law principles. Disputes involving customary laws are decided by the Sabah Native Courts[169] and Sarawak Native Courts[170] for the states of Sabah and Sarawak respectively. Native customary laws of Sabah and Sarawak deal mainly with matters pertaining to native land tenure, inheritance, family law and minor criminal law.

104. Some of these customary laws relate indirectly to environmental matters. For example, the Land Code 1958[171] has provisions recognizing native customary rights to land.[172] Such rights can be created through several methods, such as through the felling of virgin jungle and the occupation of the cleared land; the planting of land with fruit trees; the occupation or cultivation of land; the use of land for

164. (1997) 2 MLJ 373.
165. (1966) 1 MLJ 1.
166. (2001) 1 CLJ 8.
167. For details on customary laws in Malaysia, *see* Wan Arfah Hamzah & Ramy Bulan, *An Introduction to the Malaysian legal System* 151–180 (Fajar Bakti 2003).
168. Legislative definition of a native for the purpose of Sabah and Sarawak can be found in Art. 161 A(6) and (7) of the Federal Constitution; s. 3 of the Sabah Interpretation (Definition of Native) Ordinance 1952; and Schedule to the Sarawak Interpretation Ordinance (Cap. 10) (Revised Laws of Sarawak 1958).
169. The Natives Courts in Sabah were established under the Native Courts Enactment 1992 (En. 3 of 1992).
170. The Native Courts in Sarawak were established under the Native Courts Ordinance 1992, No. 9 of 1992.
171. Cap. 81, Revised Laws of Sarawak 1958.
172. Section 5(1) of the Land Code 1958.

burial ground or shrine; and the use of land for any class for rights of way.[173] In the case of *Nor anak Nyawai & Ors. v. Borneo Pulp Plantations Sdn. Bhd. & Superintendent of Land & Survey & Anor*,[174] the civil court recognized the existence of Iban native customary right to land based on a ground survey and a map produced by the community with reference to various mountains, hills, ridges and trees, according to the traditional way of demarcating boundaries.

105. It is also relevant to mention that Islamic law is another important source of Malaysian law.[175] The application of this law is very limited and applies to Muslims only, and is administered by a separate system of courts known as the *Syariah* court.[176] However, the jurisdiction of this court is confined to family matters such as divorce, marriage and inheritance of Muslims, and minor criminal offences. Matters pertaining to business law such as Islamic banking and insurance are dealt with by the civil court.

106. Matters pertaining to the environment do not come within the jurisdiction of the *Syariah* court. However, recently Islamic principles have been recognized and adopted as a part of environmental principles within Malaysia's development policy. In the Ninth Malaysia Development Plan (2005–2010),[177] the National Development Policy has embraced an Islamic concept known as *Islam Hadhari* within its environmental policy statement.[178] This concept, which means 'civilizational Islam' is a theory of government based on the principles of Islam derived from the *Quran*. This concept aims to achieve ten main principles which Muslim nations must demonstrate, namely:

(1) faith and piety in Allah;
(2) a just and trustworthy government;
(3) a free and independent people;
(4) mastery of knowledge;
(5) balanced and comprehensive economic development;
(6) a good quality of life;
(7) protection of the rights of minority groups and women;
(8) cultural and moral integrity;
(9) protection of the environment; and
(10) strong defences.

---

173. Section 5(2) of the Land Code 1958.
174. (2001) 2 CLJ 769.
175. The position of 'Islam' in Malaysia is provided in Art. 3 of the Constitution.
176. Islamic law is a state matter under the State List of the Constitution, except in the federal territories, where it is a federal matter. Thus, each state has its own *Syariah* courts and can enact its own *Syariah* enactments.
177. *See* Jabatan Perdana Menteri, Unit Pemodenan Tadbiran dan Perancangan Pengurusan, Malaysia, *Eighth Malaysia Plan 2006–2010* 453–463 (Jabatan Percetakan Negara 2006).
178. *See* Mohd Zuhdi Marsuki, *Etika Alam Sekitar Dari Perspektif Islam, Timur dan Barat* (PTS Publications 2002).

III. Environmental Policy

A. Historical Development

107. Malaysia's environmental policy can be traced back to the early 1970s when the country participated in the United Nations Conference on the Human Environment in Stockholm in 1972. Pursuant to this Conference, Malaysia subsequently introduced its first ever environmental policy directives, embarked on by the Third Malaysia Five-Year Plan, enacted the EQA in 1974, and established the Department of Environment in 1975.[179]

108. Malaysia's development policy, together with environmental policy, is set out in the First Outline Perspective Plan (1991–2000), the Second Outline Perspective Plan (2001–2010)[180] and the five-year development plans. Since then, environmental policy has been consistently addressed in Malaysia's development plans starting from the Third Malaysia Five-Year Plan (1976–1980)[181] up to the present Twelfth Malaysia Five-Year Plan (2021–2025).[182]

109. During the era of the First Outline Perspective Plan, Malaysia had no specific environmental policy, but there were environmental policy objectives introduced within the Third Malaysia Five-Year Plan and subsequent Plans. It was only during the era of the Second Outline Perspective Plan that Malaysia introduced an environmental policy known as the National Policy on the Environment. This Policy was approved by the cabinet ministers on October 2002 and provided guidance for environment and natural resource management under the Seventh Malaysia Plan onwards.[183] The policy aims at promoting economic, social and cultural progress through environmentally sound and sustainable development.

B. Content of the Policy

110. The National Policy on the Environment provides a framework for a comprehensive approach to natural resource development and provides guidance to all federal and state agencies and to every industrial sector and local community on environmental stewardship. The objectives of the Policy are to achieve a clean, safe, healthy and productive environment for present and future generations; conservation of the country's unique and diverse cultural and natural heritage with effective

179. Then referred to as the Division of Environment Malaysia.

180. Refer to the Economic Planning Unit's official website at http://www.epu.jpm.my/, May 2008.

181. Jabatan Perdana Menteri, Unit Pemodenan Tadbiran dan Perancangan Pengurusan, Malaysia, *Third Malaysia Plan 1976–1980* (Jabatan Percetakan Negara 1976).

182. Jabatan Perdana Menteri, Unit Perancang Ekonomi, *Twelfth Malaysia Plan 2021–2025* (Jabatan Percetakan Negara 2021).

183. The full policy statement is available at the Department of Environment's official website. *See* http://www.doe.gov.my/portalv1/wp-content/uploads/2013/01/dasar_alam_sekitar_negara.pdf, January 2014.

participation by all sectors of society; and sustainable lifestyles and patterns of consumption and production. This policy is based on eight principles that harmonize economic development and environmental imperatives. They are:

- stewardship of the environment;
- conservation of nature's vitality and diversity;
- continuous improvement in the quality of the environment;
- sustainable use of natural resources;
- integrated decision-making;
- role of the private sector;
- commitment and accountability; and
- active participation in the international community.

The National Policy on the Environment also adopts Malaysia's Green Strategies for promoting environmental soundness. These strategies are directed towards the following key areas, namely: education and awareness; effective management of natural resources and the environment; integrated development planning and implementation; prevention and control of pollution and environmental degradation; strengthening administrative and institutional mechanisms; proactive approach to regional and global environmental issues; and formulation and implementation of Action Plans.

111. Malaysia uses the five-year plans to implement environmental strategies and programmes within the legal and institutional framework. The results of Agenda 21 and sustainable development were incorporated and integrated into the national planning process. The environmental policy statement embodied in the Third Malaysia Five-Year Plan highlights important factors to be taken into account by the overall environmental policy, namely:

- the impact of population growth and man's activities in resources development, industrialization and urbanization on the environment;
- the critical importance of maintaining the quality of the environment relative to the needs of the population, particularly in regard to the productive capacity of the country's land resources in agriculture, forestry, fisheries and water;
- the need to maintain a healthy environment for human habitation;
- the need to preserve the country's unique and diverse natural heritage, all of which contribute to the quality of life; and
- the interdependence of social, cultural, economic, biological and physical factors in determining the ecology of man.[184]

112. During the Ninth Malaysia Plan (2006–2010),[185] the general environmental objective was for a more integrated and holistic management of the environment

184. *See* Jabatan Perdana Menteri, Unit Pemodenan Tadbiran dan Perancangan Pengurusan, Malaysia, *Third Malaysia Plan 1976–1980* 219 (Jabatan Percetakan Negara 1976).

185. *See* Jabatan Perdana Menteri, Unit Pemodenan Tadbiran dan Perancangan Pengurusan, Malaysia, *Eighth Malaysia Plan 2006–2010* (Jabatan Percetakan Negara 2006).

and natural resources through the incorporation of environmental considerations into planning and development. Environmental stewardship under this Plan was based on the principles of sustainable development and the Islamic principle of *Islam Hadhari*.[186] It was also during the era of the Ninth Malaysia Plan that Malaysia began to directly address the issue on climate change, and to put an emphasis on preventive measures to mitigate and minimize pollution, and to address other adverse environmental impacts arising from development activities.[187] Among programmes initiated by the Plan to address climate change issues include to increase the supply and utilization of alternative fuel such as renewable energy; to encourage energy efficiency in industrial, building and transport sectors; and to protect forest areas via sustainable forest management to ensure the forest areas are maintained as sinks.[188]

113. The previous environmental policy directives for Malaysia were provided for in the 10th Malaysia Plan (2011–2015).[189] They were aimed at protecting the environmental quality of life, caring for the planet, while harnessing economic value from the process. Among agenda of this Plan were the creation of a stronger incentive for investments in renewable energy in order to achieve a renewable energy target of 985 MW by 2015; promotion of energy efficiency to encourage productive use of energy; improvement of solid wastes management; conservation of forests; reduction of emissions to improve air quality; enhancement of forest and wildlife conservation efforts; and assurance of equitable and sustainable utilization of resources.[190]

114. Unlike the previous Malaysia Plans, the Tenth Malaysia Plan specifically and directly addressed the issues of climate change. For this purpose, the Plan adopted a dual strategy in addressing climate change impacts. First is the adaptation of strategies to protect economic growth and development factors from the impact of climate change. Second is the mitigation of strategies to reduce emission of greenhouse gases. Major efforts introduced under the 10th Malaysia Plan to reduce greenhouse gases emission intensity were focusing on five areas, namely, creating stronger incentives for investments in renewable energy; promoting energy efficiency to encourage productive use of energy; improving solid waste management; conserving forests; and reducing emissions to improve air quality.[191]

---

186. Jabatan Perdana Menteri, Unit Pemodenan Tadbiran dan Perancangan Pengurusan, Malaysia, *Eighth Malaysia Plan 2006–2010* 453–463 (Jabatan Percetakan Negara 2006).
187. *See* Jabatan Perdana Menteri, Unit Pemodenan Tadbiran dan Perancangan Pengurusan, Malaysia, *Ninth Malaysia Plan 2006–2010* 453 (Jabatan Percetakan Negara 2006).
188. *See* Jabatan Perdana Menteri, Unit Pemodenan Tadbiran dan Perancangan Pengurusan, Malaysia, *Ninth Malaysia Plan 2006–2010* 458–463 (Jabatan Percetakan Negara 2006).
189. Jabatan Perdana Menteri, Unit Pemodenan Tadbiran dan Perancangan Pengurusan, Malaysia, *Tenth Malaysia Plan 2011–2015* (Jabatan Percetakan Negara 2011).
190. Jabatan Perdana Menteri, Unit Pemodenan Tadbiran dan Perancangan Pengurusan, Malaysia, *Tenth Malaysia Plan 2011–2015* 302–308 (Jabatan Percetakan Negara 2011).
191. Jabatan Perdana Menteri, Unit Pemodenan Tadbiran dan Perancangan Pengurusan, Malaysia, *Tenth Malaysia Plan 2011–2015* 303–304 (Jabatan Percetakan Negara 2011).

115. Under the Tenth Malaysia Plan, the government were guided by sustainable production practices to decouple economic growth from environmental degradation, and developed business models to compete sustainably in the global economy in ways that help address some of the world's most profound social, economic and environmental challenges.[192] To achieve these objectives, Malaysia has introduced several progression policies to set the national agenda on environmental protection and conservation such as the National Renewable Energy Policy 2009, National Green Technology Policy 2009, and the National Climate Change Policy 2009.[193]

116. Specifically, the National Renewable Energy Policy 2009[194] is a policy for change that gives emphasis to the importance and necessity of sustainable development. Malaysia's ratification of the Kyoto Protocol in 2002 is a move to show the government's seriousness and commitment to reduce carbon footprints through escalating green technology applications in all sectors of the economy. The National Renewable Energy Policy 2009 is intended to transform Malaysia to become a leader in renewable energy and also in green technology applications, and develop into a nation that is able to satisfy its own energy needs from indigenous renewable energy resources, while able to conserve its natural environment. At the moment, several new initiatives anchored upon the Policy have been undertaken to achieve a renewable energy target of 985 MW by 2015, contributing 5.5% to Malaysia's total electricity generation mix.[195]

117. Another Policy, the National Green Technology Policy[196] was launched in 2009 to spearhead green technology sector development in Malaysia. This Policy has a strategic role which spans beyond achieving energy autonomy and mitigating climate change, which is one of the emerging drivers of economic growth for Malaysia. The four pillars of this Policy: energy; environment; economy; and social, seek to achieve the following: Attainment of energy independence and promotion of efficient utilization; Conservation and enhancement of the natural environment and promotion of mitigation measures; Enhancement of the national economic development through the use of technology; and Improvement of the quality of life for all.[197]

---

192. Jabatan Perdana Menteri, Unit Pemodenan Tadbiran dan Perancangan Pengurusan, Malaysia, *Tenth Malaysia Plan 2011–2015* 303–304 (Jabatan Percetakan Negara 2011).
193. Jabatan Perdana Menteri, Unit Pemodenan Tadbiran dan Perancangan Pengurusan, Malaysia, *Tenth Malaysia Plan 2011–2015* 298 (Jabatan Percetakan Negara 2011).
194. Ministry Energy, Green Tech. & Water Malay, *National Green Technology Policy* (Putrajaya, Ministry Energy, Green Tech. & Water Malay. 2009).
195. Jabatan Perdana Menteri, Unit Pemodenan Tadbiran dan Perancangan Pengurusan, Malaysia, *Tenth Malaysia Plan 2011–2015* 302 (Jabatan Percetakan Negara 2011).
196. Ministry Energy, Green Tech. & Water Malay, *National Green Technology Policy* (Putrajaya, Ministry Energy, Green Tech. & Water Malay. 2009).
197. Jabatan Perdana Menteri, Unit Pemodenan Tadbiran dan Perancangan Pengurusan, Malaysia, *Tenth Malaysia Plan 2011–2015* 303 (Jabatan Percetakan Negara 2011).

118. The National Climate Change Policy[198] which was launched in 2009 is another national policy created to provide the framework to mobilize and guide government agencies, industry, community, other stakeholders and major groups in addressing the challenges of climate change in a holistic manner. The objectives of the policy are: mainstreaming of measures to address climate change challenges through strengthened economic competitiveness, wise management of resources, environmental conservation and enhanced quality of life for sustainable development; integration of responses into national policies, plans and programmes to strengthen the resilience of development from arising impacts and challenges of climate change; and strengthening of institutional and implementation capacity to better harness opportunities in reducing and addressing negative impacts of climate change.

119. The Climate Change Policy is based on the following principles: Development on a Sustainable Path; Sustainability of Environment and Natural Resources; Integrated Planning and Implementation; Effective Participation; and Common but Differentiated Responsibilities. Each principle is supported by a few strategic thrusts. For example, the first principle, which is Development on a Sustainable Path, is supported by three strategic thrusts: facilitate the harmonization of existing policies, institute measures to make development climate-resilient and support climate-resilient development and investment. Each thrust has specific key actions.

120. The Tenth Malaysia Plan (2011–2015) was followed by the Eleventh Malaysia Plan (2016–2020).[199] Environmental policy directives of this Plan are based on Malaysia's target to become an advanced economy by 2020. In order to achieve this target, the policy is to shift from the conventional and costly 'grow first, clean-up later' path to a more greener trajectory, 'Green Growth' which will ensure that socio-economic development is pursued more sustainably, beginning at the planning stage, and continuing throughout the implementation and evaluation stages.[200] In order to pursue green growth, the Plan focuses on four Focus areas, namely:

(a) strengthening the enabling environment for green growth through fundamental transformations in regulations, including to provide relevant policy and institutional framework for green growth, enhancing awareness of all stakeholders to create shared responsibility, and establishing sustainable financing mechanisms;[201]
(b) adopting the sustainable consumption and production concept in prominent sectors such as industry, power generation, infrastructure and transportation

198. Ministry of Natural Resources and Environment Malaysia, *National Climate Change Policy 2009* (Putrajaya, Ministry of Natural Resources and Environment Malaysia. 2010).
199. Jabatan Perdana Menteri, Unit Pemodenan Tadbiran dan Perancangan Pengurusan, Malaysia, *Eleventh Malaysia Plan 2016–2020* (Jabatan Percetakan Negara 2016).
200. *Ibid.*, 6–9.
201. *Ibid.*, 6–13.

based on strategies on creating green markets, increasing the share of renewable energy mix, enhancing demand side management, encouraging low-carbon mobility and managing waste holistically;[202]

(c) conserving natural resources for present and future generations by laying the regulatory framework on access to biological resources and benefits sharing in order to ensure natural resources security, and to enhance alternative livelihood for indigenous and local communities through their involvement in biodiversity conservation and alternative economic opportunities;[203] and

(d) strengthening resilience against climate change and natural disasters through resilience of growth and preparing a comprehensive disaster risk management framework. These will be achieved through strategies to strengthen disaster risk management, improving flood mitigation, and enhancing climate change adaptation by developing a national adaptation plan and strengthening resilience of infrastructure.[204]

Through these four Focus areas, the Eleventh Malaysia Plan seeks to strengthen the enabling environment in terms of policy and regulatory framework, human capital, green technology investment and financial instruments. This enabling environment will facilitate a shift in the economy towards more sustainable patterns of consumption and production. According to the Plan, such transformation is meant to ensure sustainability of natural resources, minimize pollution and strengthen energy, food and water security. By conserving biodiversity, the continuity of their function as a natural buffer against climate change and natural disaster can be strengthened. This buffer, complemented by structural approaches such as innovative flood mitigation and green infrastructure, as well as non-structural approaches like hazard risk maps and warning system, will strengthen disaster risk management and ultimately improve the well-being and quality of life.

The Twelfth Malaysia Plan (2021–2025)

121. The Twelfth Malaysia Plan (2021–2025)[205] is a medium-term plan with the objective of 'A Prosperous, Inclusive, Sustainable Malaysia'. This Plan was initially planned for tabling in the Parliament in August 2020 but was delayed twice to January 2021 and then to October 2021 due to the COVID-19 pandemic as well as change in Malaysia's leadership landscape. This Plan was designed to pave the way forward for comprehensive policy responses in facing the challenging situation brought about by the COVID-19 pandemic, whereas policy directives under this Plan are structured to achieve sustainable economic growth, with a focus on equitable wealth distribution, public well-being and environmental sustainability. Thus,

202. *Ibid.*, 6–15.
203. *Ibid.*, 6–21.
204. *Ibid.*, 6–25.
205. Jabatan Perdana Menteri, Unit Perancang Ekonomi, *Twelfth Malaysia Plan 2021–2025* (Jabatan Percetakan Negara 2021).

national development priorities of the Twelfth Plan will continue to be aligned to the Sustainable Development Goals (SDGs) of the 2030 Agenda based on the principle of 'leaving no one behind'.[206]

122. The three themes of the Plan are resetting the economy; strengthening security, well-being and inclusivity; and advancing sustainability.[207] Of these, Theme 3[208] provides matters related to the environment on advancing green growth and enhancing energy sustainability as well as a shift to more sustainable economic practices and lifestyles that value natural endowments and environmental health. This shift would address the issues of climate change, unsustainable consumption and production practices, loss of biodiversity, lack of coherence in the implementation of policies and inefficient water resources management.

123. In the Twelfth Malaysia Plan, green growth will be augmented to achieve sustainability and resilience based on shared responsibility in moving towards a low-carbon nation and the promotion of equal benefit-sharing from the utilization of natural resources. Theme 3 seeks to embrace circular economy[209] and adopt the Integrated Water Resources Management[210] in order to contribute to sustainable and resilient growth as well as the achievement of the 2030 Agenda.

124. Specifically, Chapter 8: 'Advancing Green Growth for Sustainability and Resilience'[211] as part of Theme 3 is the centrepiece of the green economy agenda under the Twelfth Malaysia Plan.

125. Chapter 8 promotes efforts towards striking a balance between socio-economic development and environmental sustainability.[212] This will be done through the introduction of economic model on the green economy to determine the linkages between economic growth and the use of natural resources as well as environmental impact, which will be a key reference for policy-making.

126. The Twelfth Malaysia Plan is built upon the green growth initiatives of the Eleventh Plan by implementing the clean, green and resilient development agenda and enhancing sustainability and resilience by addressing issues such as: climate change and pollution, reducing disaster risks, managing natural resources efficiently and strengthening the enabling environment for effective governance. There are three priority areas of A, B and C relating to environmental protection under the Plan together with related strategies for each priority area.[213] Specifically for Priority Area A 'Implementing a Low-Carbon, Clean and Resilient Development'[214],

206. *Ibid.,* p.23-24.
207. *Ibid.,* 1-12.
208. *Ibid.,* T3-2.
209. *Ibid.,* T3-5.
210. *Ibid.,* T3-6.
211.
212. *Ibid.,* 8-2.
213. *Ibid.,* 8-8.
214.

there are four strategies provided, namely Strategy A1 'Moving Towards a Low-Carbon Nation', Strategy A2 'Accelerating Transition to the Circular Economy', Strategy A3 'Sharing Responsibility in Pollution Prevention', and Strategy A4 'Increasing Resilience against Climate Change and Disasters'[215]. For Priority Area B 'Managing Natural Resources Efficiently to Safeguard Natural Capital'[216], the four identified strategies are: Strategy B1 'Conserving Natural Ecosystems', Strategy B2, 'Protecting and Conserving Species and Genetic Resources', Strategy B3 'Ensuring Sustainable Utilisation and Benefit Sharing', and Strategy B4 'Enhancing Conservation of Water Resources'[217]. Lastly, for Priority Area C 'Strengthening the Enabling Environment for Effective Governance'[218], there are three strategies identified which are: Strategy C1 'Strengthening Environmental Governance', Strategy C2 'Scaling-up Green Financing and Investments', and Strategy C3 'Instilling Sense of Ownership and Shared Responsibility'.[219]

127. Among the highlights of the Plan's environmental strategies are on strategies relating to climate change and energy, namely: to conduct a feasibility study on carbon pricing, carbon tax and emission trading scheme; to encourage adoption of fuel economy standards to increase fuel efficiency for new vehicles; and to regulate the use of energy by high-intensity consumers in the industrial and commercial sectors through the introduction law relating to energy conservation.[220] Whereas strategies relating to pollution control and waste management include: to review the Environmental Quality Act of 1974 and other existing laws to regulate emerging pollutants and increase penalties based on the polluter-pays principle; to review and develop relevant policies, legislation and economic instruments to facilitate the transition to the circular economy and to incorporate eco-design requirements, including the use of recycled materials; to review existing law to control waste imports and exports; to introduce regulations on household e-waste and extended producer responsibility particularly packaging materials and single-use plastics; and to construct integrated waste management facilities, and integrated scheduled waste treatment and disposal facilities.[221]

Shared Prosperity Vision 2030

128. The Shared Prosperity Vision 2030[222] which is officially launched on 5 October 2019 is Malaysia's new policy statement which seeks to affirm the nation's commitment towards achieving sustainable growth along with fair and equitable distribution, across income groups, ethnicities, regions and supply chains, as well as strengthening political stability, enhancing the nation's prosperity and unity. This

215.
216.
217. *Ibid.*
218. *Ibid.*, 8-25.
219. *Ibid.*
220. *Ibid.*, 8-8.
221. *Ibid.*, 8-8.
222. Ministry of Economic Affairs, *Shared Prosperity Vision 2030* (Ministry of Economic Affairs 2019).

Policy is a continuation from Vision 2020 three decades ago to propel the country's economic and provide a decent standard of living to all Malaysians by 2030.[223]

129. This Vision lays out three overarching objectives, namely: Development for All; Addressing Wealth and Income Disparities; and United, Prosperous and Dignified Nation[224], and supported by fifteen guiding principles and eight enablers.[225] In addition, there are seven strategic thrusts which are developed as a key to accomplish the Vision's initiatives and three objectives. [226]All thrusts are developed based on guiding principles that emphasize policy formulation and implementation of Government programmes aiming at addressing socio-economic and administrative system issues. In relation to economic and environmental sustainability, Strategic Thrust 2 on Key Economic Growth Activities (KEGA) is most relevant.[227] KEGA is defined by the Vision as a future economic activity that demonstrates the potential for rapid growth in line with the country's aspiration to achieve high-value economic development. [228] Under Strategic Thrust 2, 15 KEGA have been selected to be a new priority with emphasis on generating significant and sustainable growth.[229] Specifically, KEGA 9 'Coastal and Maritime Economies (International Waters)' promotes the development of coastal and maritime economy as new economic centres as well as a means to rehabilitate the natural resources of the area.[230] Another one is KEGA 11 'Renewable Energy' proposes that by 2025, the target contribution of renewable energy to electricity generation is 20% through the progression in activities relating to mini-hydro, solar, algae, biomass, biogas and municipal solid waste. [231] Finally, KEGA 12 'Green Economy' proposes low-carbon activities as well as effective and inclusive sources.[232] Green Economy encompasses diverse activities such as green buildings, sustainable transportation and mobility, food sovereignty and security, energy and maritime, plastic substitute products, smart and sustainable cities, sustainable coastal development, environmental preservation and rehabilitation, climate-adapted technology and organic farming. Green Economy also refers to the creation of a circular economy that is capable of operating without emitting waste. These are considered to be new approach towards Malaysia's economic and social management whereby economic development is aligned with endeavours to preserve the environment and the well-being of the society.[233]

---

223. *Ibid.,* 1-01.
224. *Ibid.,* 0-04.
225. *Ibid.,* 0-01.
226. *Ibid.,* 0-02.
227. *Ibid.,* 6-08.
228. *Ibid.*
229. *Ibid.,* 6-10.
230. *Ibid.,* 6-12.
231. *Ibid.,* 6-13.
232. *Ibid.*
233. *Ibid.,* 6-14.

130. Within the guiding principles, the one that is most relevant to the environment is Guiding Principle 15 'Sovereignty & Sustainability'.[234] This Vision recognizes the impact of Malaysia's rapid development process puts pressure on the environment and natural resources which arises from land clearing for infrastructure, agriculture, plantation, industrial and housing development.[235] The Vision also acknowledged that development that neglects environmental sustainability will result in fragmentation of flora and fauna habitat and the degeneration of the forest ecosystem, whereas the rising population has resulted in higher demand on resources and increased waste production.[236] Therefore, to ensure proper management of natural resources and the environment, Guiding Principle 15 emphasizes the following outcomes: including compliance to the Environmental Impact Assessment and Social Impact Assessment; and strengthening environmental conservation and natural resources in development planning.[237] To further enhance these outcomes, Guiding Principle 15 is supported by Enabler 7 'Sustainability' which highlights the importance of sustainability in harmonizing socio-economic development with the preservation of the environment and natural resources to meet the needs of the present generations without neglecting the future generations.[238] In line with the Twelfth Malaysia Plan, Enabler 7 is an effort to drive national development through green growth, which emphasizes low-carbon development, resource efficiency, resilience and inclusivity. The proposed strategies for sustainability enabler are as follows: 'reviewing environmental laws and legislation by taking into account current issues and future challenges; strengthening and coordinating the enforcement of environmental laws and legislation at various levels of Government; improving the methodology of EIA implementation by taking into account the impact on the ecosystem as a whole; and maximising resource utilisation efficiency and minimising waste production through the concept of circular economy at various stages of production and consumption'.[239]

The National Policy on Biological Diversity 2016–2025

131. National Policy on Biological Diversity 2016–2025[240] is a multi-sectoral policy which serves as a guide for Malaysia's biodiversity management which emphasizes the need for continued conservation, sustainable utilisation and the sharing of benefits from biodiversity in a fair and equitable manner. This Policy also complements Malaysia's obligation under the United Nations Convention on Biological Diversity's Strategic Plan for Biodiversity 2011–2020[241], and Agenda 2030's Sustainable Development Goals (SDG).[242] This Policy consists of five principles as

234. *Ibid.,* 5-01.
235. *Ibid.,* 5-20.
236. *Ibid.*
237. *Ibid.*
238. *Ibid.,* 7-16.
239.
240. Ministry of Natural Resources and Environment, *National Policy on Biological Diversity 2016 – 2025* (Ministry of Natural Resources and Environment 2016).
241. *Ibid.,* 10.
242. *Ibid.,* 36.

follows[243]: Principle 1: Heritage (Biological diversity is a national heritage. It must be sustainably managed, wisely utilized and conserved for future generations), Principle 2: Precautionary (The lack of full scientific certainty should not be used as a reason to postpone measures to minimize biodiversity loss), Principle 3: Shared responsibility (The conservation and sustainable utilization of biodiversity are the shared responsibility of all sectors of society), Principle 4: Participatory (Planning and management of biodiversity must be carried out in a participatory manner), and Principle 5: Good governance (Good governance, including accountability and transparency, is crucial to biodiversity conservation).

132. Additionally, the Policy has five overarching goals encompassing stakeholder empowerment, reducing pressures on biodiversity, safeguarding ecosystems, species and genetic diversity, ensuring fair and equitable sharing of benefits from the utilization of biodiversity and building the capacity of all stakeholders.[244] These five goals are supported by 17 national biodiversity targets which address all key facets of biodiversity conservation including:[245]

- awareness raising;
- mainstreaming biodiversity;
- implementing good management practices in various economic sectors;
- strengthening of protected areas;
- preventing extinction of species;
  addressing invasive alien species;
- ensuring biosafety;
- addressing capacity building;
- increasing our knowledge; and
- improving financing.

133. Each of the said targets is accompanied by a set of 57 actions that spell out the steps that we have to take to achieve the targets and, ultimately the goals. These actions have measurable key indicators for the purpose of monitor of progress. As a whole the Policy provides an enabling framework for action by stakeholders at all levels and sets out goals and targets to be achieved. The main lead agency for the purpose of this policy is the MNRE (presently the Ministry of Environment and Water).

National Transport Policy 2019-2030

134. The National Transport Policy 2019-2030[246] was launched to provide an overarching policy to various regulatory agencies as well as to implement policy

243. *Ibid.*
244. *Ibid.*, 37.
245. *Ibid.*
246. Ministry of Transport Malaysia, *National Transport Policy 2019-2030* (Ministry of Transport Malaysia 2019).

thrusts which include, among others developing and streamlining transport initiatives towards a common goal, resulting in effective and efficient use of resources, and reduce the negative impact of the transport system on the environment. This Policy consists of 8 key trends, namely[247]: Growing and increasingly ageing population; Increasing urbanization; Advances in real time information and digitalization; Expansion of e-commerce market; Shift towards Environmentally sustainable transport; Move towards bigger vessels, consolidation and containerization; Increasing passenger travel and impact of Low Cost Carriers; and Proliferation of new technology. At the same time, the Policy seeks to secure five policy thrusts[248] and 23 strategies taking into consideration future trends of the transport sector.[249] The five policy thrusts aim to[250]:

i. Strengthen the governance to create a conducive environment for the transport sector,
ii. Optimize, build & maintain transport Infrastructure, services and networks for efficiency,
iii. Enhance safety, integration, connectivity & accessibility for seamless journey,
iv. Advance towards green transport ecosystem, and
v. Expand global footprint and promote internationalization of transport services.

135. Specifically, the Policy's vision is anchored on three inter-related principles economic competitiveness, social impact, and environmental impact[251], and based on Agenda 2030's SDG particularly Goals 9 and 11, which emphasized on sustainable transport system for all and resilient infrastructure to ensure, among others, clean and resilient with minimal impact to the environment and natural resources.[252] Among environmental objectives of the Policy include to reduce the carbon footprint of the transport sector by embarking on low-carbon mobility; to encourage use of cleaner fuels for transport; to adopt international environmental standards and emulate best practices that support the objective of sustainable transport; and to achieve green growth via low-carbon mobility.[253] In its vision, the Policy stresses on the need to reduce fuel consumption and GHG emission/ pollution control, promotes environmental protection and conservation, and encourages sustainable consumption and production.[254]

136. In line with the present focus towards the environment, specific thrusts have been formulated which ensures that environmental aspects are addressed

247. *Ibid.*, 14-22.
248. *Ibid.*, 23.
249. *Ibid.*
250. *Ibid.*
251. *Ibid.*, 7.
252. *Ibid.*, 58.
253. *Ibid.*, 25.
254. *Ibid.*, 24.

through efficient and sustainable use of resources and minimize environmental pollution. For example, Policy Thrust 4 on 'Advance towards a green transport ecosystem'[255] includes strategies targeting at complying to the law and to shift towards international environmental standards; prioritizing public transport network as fundamental structure in charting out sustainable spatial and transportation growth in urbanized areas; accelerating implementation of low-carbon mobility initiatives; instituting measures to control pollution, noise and waste from the transport sector; and developing effective communication, education and public awareness to create behavioural change towards practices of sustainable transport. Within Strategy 4.4 of Thrust 4, the Policy seeks to institute measures to control pollution, noise and waste from the transport sector particularly from vessel traffic along Malaysia's coastline which have been causing water-borne pollution and impacting.[256] Whereas Trend 5 'Shift towards environmentally sustainable transport' acknowledges the possible increase of price for the world's petroleum and other liquid fuels, and the needs for the sector to move towards sustainable transport and to capture the demand for a green supply chain which is becoming prominent. [257] As a whole, the National Transport Policy 2019-2030 gives emphasis on ensuring that development of infrastructure is carried out in a sustainable manner, conserving natural resources and cutting down pollution, based on the 2030 Agenda of the SDG.

National Marine Litter Policy and Action Plan 2021–2030

137. Another recent environmental-related policy for Malaysia launched in November 2021 is the National Marine Litter Policy and Action Plan 2021–2030[258] which was developed by the Ministry of Environment and Water to guide nationwide actions to address marine litter pollution. This Policy is guided by existing international and regional frameworks on marine litter such as the 2030 Agenda for Sustainable Development, International Maritime Organisation's Action Plan 2018, and the Regional Action Plan for Combating Marine Debris in the ASEAN Member States (2021–2025).[259]

138. Under this Policy, some of the relevant terms are defined as follows:[260]

i. Marine litter: 'Any persistent solid material, manufactured or processed, that is disposed of directly or indirectly into the marine environment. Marine debris, marine litter are often used interchangeably.'
ii. Marine environment: 'Environment in the aquatic area where marine litter is found to occur, including along the shoreline, sea surface or water column, and seafloor.'

---

255. *Ibid.,* 56.
256. *Ibid.,* 62.
257. *Ibid.,* 19.
258. Ministry of Environment and Water, *National Marine Litter Policy and Action Plan 2021 – 2030* (Ministry of Environment and Water 2021).
259. *Ibid.,* 12.
260. *Ibid.,* 06.

iii. Marine plastic: 'Term commonly used to designate plastic fragments or pieces found in the marine environment. They are used interchangeably with marine plastic debris, marine plastic litter or marine plastic particles and include macro- and micro-plastic debris.'
iv. Microplastic: 'Small plastic particles which can be formed from the degradation of larger pieces. Their size definition falls within < 5 mm or < 1 mm.'
v. Nanoplastic: 'Plastic particles that result from the degradation of larger plastic particles and are of the sub-micrometre scale.'
vi. Plastic waste: 'Plastic that is deemed to be at the end of its life cycle, unable to be recycled or repurposed.'

139. The main aims of the National Marine Litter Policy and Action Plan 2021–2030 are to reduce marine plastic pollution through strategic actions along the value chain of plastic life cycle, based on the following purposes:[261]

i. to address marine litter pollution through robust policy development;
ii. to document concrete steps ahead on tackling marine litter pollution based on scientific evidence and lessons;
iii. to learn from international, regional and local efforts;
iv. to coordinate efforts at every level of the Federal Government, State Government, local government, as well as public, private and social sectors;
v. to foster further research and innovation to prevent, monitor and tackle marine litter pollution;
vi. to deploy and implement cutting-edge technologies and innovation backed with strong national standards and guidelines, as well as strengthened institutional and legal framework to ensure Malaysia is at the forefront of global efforts in tackling marine plastic pollution;
vii. to promote the sharing of best practices and lessons learned, while enhancing regional and international cooperation, and creating awareness and instigating behavioural change; and
viii. to increase access to finance and facilitating private sector engagement to promote investment, trade and market creation, and market-based incentives in industries and activities that enable marine litter management and prevention.

140. The National Marine Litter Policy and Action Plan 2021–2030 is guided by five pillars and substantiated with 17 action plans and 103 proposed activities to be implemented in tandem objectives of the Twelfth Malaysia Plan in Chapter 8 relating to the implementation of circular economy as a catalyst for resource sustainability. Specifically, these five Pillars are as follows:[262]

i. Policy Adoption and Implementation: Advance and improve engagement on addressing marine litter pollution from land- and sea-based sources through mainstreamed policy measures and priorities, sharing of information and

261. *Ibid.,* 14.
262. *Ibid.,* 14-15.

knowledge, and enhancing coordination with stakeholders and policymakers to reduce and mitigate marine litter pollution,

ii. Deployment of Technologies, Innovation and Capacity Building: Drive innovative technology deployment, backed up by robust standards to ensure evidence-based outcomes. Meanwhile, work towards building local capacity for advanced testing of new solutions between public-private-academic partnerships,

iii. Improve Monitoring and Data Collection on Marine Litter: Establish a national marine litter monitoring programme, hotspots evaluation and publish assessments on marine litter.

iv. Communication, Education and Public Awareness, Outreach and Engagement: Raise awareness at all levels of society in addressing marine plastic pollution through behavioural change, new practices, advocating product/packaging labelling towards zero single-use plastic and extended producer responsibility schemes, and

v. Adopting Whole-of-Nation and Multi-Stakeholders Approach in Harmonising Cross-Cutting Objectives: Improve engagement and cooperation through multi-stakeholders and whole-of-nation approach including with the informal sectors, and establishing Public-Private Partnerships by implementing pilot projects (island and inland) as well as through potential avenues including access to research, data and information and funding opportunities to tackle marine litter problems collectively, and through better understanding the source to sea interactions. Aspects towards advancing the inclusiveness, human rights and gender equality are also to be assured, as well as rights of indigenous people and disadvantaged groups.

141. In addition to the five Pillars, this Policy is further supported by seven Principles to guide in its implementation, namely:[263] (i) enhancement of implementation of relevant international and regional conventions on marine debris pollution; (ii) reduction of marine plastic pollution loadings from land and sea-based sources; (iii) demonstrating good practices and experiences in integrated river basin and estuaries, and coastal area management; (iv) behavioural change through transformation and modification of lifestyle into sustainable living and environmentally friendly approaches; (v) impacts assessment guideline review to strengthen the pillars and goals on national marine litter actions; (vi) robust solutions that are environmentally sound and socially just used to increase effectiveness in reducing marine plastic pollution through; and (vii) innovative approaches using advanced technology along the whole plastic value chain.

142. Framework for the implementation of national actions on marine litter prevention and mitigation is based on top-down and bottom-up approaches. All stakeholders including civil society, private sector and local communities, academia as well as the society at large would be engaged in their respective roles and functions to participate in the implementation and monitoring of the Action Plan. The Policy

263. *Ibid.*, 15.

provides three roadmaps[264]: short term, medium term, and long term, with the final target, among others, to develop and standardize national standards in line with regional and international and to establish National legal framework.

The Malaysia Forest Policy 2021

143. Malaysia as a nation consists of three regions, namely, Peninsula Malaysia and the Borneo states of Sabah and Sarawak. Since independence, the forest policies of Peninsular Malaysia,

144. Sarawak and Sabah have developed independently of each other. In 1978 the National Forestry Policy Peninsular Malaysia was introduced to provide guidance on the development of the forestry sector with the main objectives of forest conservation and management based on the principles of sustainable management.[265] In 1992, the Policy which was fully adopted by all states in the Peninsula Malaysia was revised to incorporate matters relating to biological diversity conservation and sustainable utilization of genetic resources, as well as relating to the role of local communities in forest development.[266] For the state of Sabah, the Sabah Forest Policy was launched in 2018 to provide an overarching framework which focuses on sustainable forest management in line with Agenda 2030's SDG.[267] For the state of Sarawak, the Sarawak Forest Policy[268] was introduced in 2019 to provide guiding principles to ensure that its strategic direction is in line with the national and international agenda including the SDG.

145. In 2021, Malaysia launched the first-ever federal-level forest policy known as the Malaysia Forest Policy.[269] This new Policy would replace the National Forestry Policy 1978 (Revised 1992) of the Peninsula Malaysia. At the same time, the Policy is inclusive which takes into account key aspects of the three forestry policies Peninsula, Sabah and Sarawak towards achieving sustainable development as well as responsible and sustainable forest management. Thus, the Malaysia Forest Policy, which is in line with the commitment of Shared Prosperity Vision 2030[270], would be a reference as well guidelines for the three regions in formulating action plan and strategies in their respective regions.

146. In its policy statement, the Malaysia Forest Policy seeks to recognize forests as heritage and national treasures and commits to maintain the forest for the

264. *Ibid.*, 39.
265. Ibu Pejabat Perhutanan Semenanjung Malaysia, *National Forestry Policy Peninsular Malaysia 1978* (Ibu Pejabat Perhutanan Semenanjung Malaysia 1978).
266. Jabatan Perhutanan Perhutanan Semenanjung Malaysia, *National Forestry Policy Peninsular Malaysia 1978 (Revised 1992)* (Jabatan Perhutanan Perhutanan Semenanjung Malaysia 1992).
267. Sabah Forestry Department, *Sabah Forest Policy 2018* (Sabah Forestry Department 2018).
268. Forest Department Sarawak, *Sarawak Forest Policy 2019* (Forest Department Sarawak 2020).
269. Kementerian Tenaga dan Sumber Asli, *Dasar Perhutanan Malaysia* (Kementerian Tenaga dan Sumber Asli 2021).
270. Ministry of Economic Affairs, *Shared Prosperity Vision 2030* (Ministry of Economic Affairs 2019).

purposes of ecosystem services, biodiversity conservation, environmental protection and resource utilization towards socio-economic development and welfare of the present and future generations.[271]

147. The rationale of having this national-level policy is for the adoption by the states on the Peninsula Malaysia, Sabah and Sarawak in line with provisions of the Constitution which provides direction for the management of forests through good governance and best practice to ensure that the forest sector continues to contribute to towards sustainability.[272]

148. This Policy has five objectives, namely[273]:

i. to ensure adequate forest areas are managed through good governance and best practices for biodiversity conservation and ecosystem services;
ii. to preserve, restore and manage permanent reserve forest or forest reserve or permanent forest based on the principles of forest management;
iii. to ensure a continuous source of raw materials from native forest areas and plantation forests for the continuation of the development of the wood and non-wood based industry;
iv. to encourage the participation of indigenous communities, native and local people in forest conservation and protection; and
v. to empower capacity building; research and development, and commercialization; and innovation including providing human and financial resources sufficient to improve forest management and the use of forest resources.

149. The Malaysia Forest Policy would be implemented by the ministry responsible for forestry which has the function to coordinate and monitor policy implementation among the federal and state government ministries as well as various other stakeholders including the community, private sector and researchers.[274] Although the federal government drives the implementation of this policy, that jurisdiction is only limited to providing guidance and support to states in all three regions. The Peninsula, Sabah and Sarawak will implement the Policy in their respective states based on state forestry policies and regulations according to the needs of the state. The implementation would also be based on detailed targets, goals and regional strategies of the respective Peninsula Malaysia, Sabah and Sarawak policies which would be applicable only to the respective state.

150. It has been reiterated by the Malaysia Forest Policy that the Policy should be read together with other policies relating to forest management, namely the Forestry Policy of Peninsular Malaysia, Forest Policy Sabah, and Sarawak Forest

271. *Ibid.*, 8.
272. *Ibid.*, 9.
273. *Ibid.*, 11.
274. *Ibid.*, 12.

Policy. These policies complement each other, and nothing in this Policy is construed as limiting state's right to take action relating to forest management in line with objectives and the provisions of this Policy.[275]

Malaysia's Nationally Determined Contribution (NDC)

151. As a state party to the Paris Agreement, Malaysia is required to submit its Nationally Determined Contribution (NDC) which is a national commitment to reduce emissions and adapt to impacts of climate change. Malaysia's NDC implementation time frame is from 2021 to 2030. It is a requirement that every five years, an updated NDC has to be sent to the secretariat of the United Nations Framework Convention on Climate Change (UNFCCC) secretariat. It is also a requirement that each successive NDC must show progress from the previous version. When Malaysia submitted its first NDC in 2015, the commitment undertaken was a 35% unconditional emissions reduction target with an additional 10% conditional upon receipt of climate finance, technology transfer and capacity building from developed countries, by 2030 compared to 2005 levels.[276] For this 2015's NDC, the scope coverage for gases were carbon dioxide, methane, and nitrous oxide. However coverage for economy-wide emissions intensity of GDP was confined to the following sectors: energy, industrial processes, waste, agriculture, and land use, land use change and forestry.[277]

152. However, in July 2021, Malaysia has revised its mitigation ambition with an unconditional target to cut carbon intensity against GDP by 45% by 2030 compared to 2005 levels. This is the first modification made to its NDCs and it represents a 10% increase in ambition.[278] In addition, the coverage of 2021's NDC is expanded to seven greenhouse gases which are: carbon dioxide, methane, nitrous oxide, hydrofluorocarbons, perfluorocarbon, sulphur hexafluoride and nitrogen trifluoride.[279] As to the status of Malaysia's NDC target at present, the Twelfth Malaysia Plan provides that the country has achieved 29.4% reduction in GHG emissions intensity per unit of GDP by the end of 2016, compared to 2005 levels.[280] Details as regard to Malaysia's action plans in meeting the NDCs are provided in two types of reports, the National Communication (NC) as well as the Biennial Update Report (BUR) to the UNFCCC, which is required of Paris Agreement signatories. At present, Malaysia has produced the following NC and BUR:

275. *Ibid.*, 12.
276. UNFCCC 2015, https://www4.unfccc.int/sites/submissions/INDC/Published%20Documents/Malaysia/1/INDC%20Malaysia%20Final%2027%20November%202015%20Revised%20Final%20UNFCCC.pdf.
277. *Ibid.*
278. UNFCCC 2021, https://www4.unfccc.int/sites/ndcstaging/PublishedDocuments/Malaysia%20First/Malaysia%20NDC%20Updated%20Submission%20to%20UNFCCC%20July%202021%20final.pdf.
279. *Ibid.*
280. Jabatan Perdana Menteri, Unit Perancang Ekonomi, *Twelfth Malaysia Plan 2021–2025* (Jabatan Percetakan Negara 2021), 8-1.

(i) Malaysia Initial Communication 2000[281]
(ii) Malaysia Second National Communication to the UNFCCC 2011[282]
(iii) Malaysia Biennial Update Report to the UNFCCC 2015[283]
(iv) Malaysia Third National Communication and Second Biennial Update Report to the UNFCCC 2018[284]
(v) Third Biennial Update Report to the UNFCCC 2020.[285]

IV. International Law

A. *The Constitution*

153. At the international level, Malaysia has signed and ratified a number of international treaties related to the environment. However, such instruments do not have domestic effect until Parliament enacts legislation to implement their contents. A possible jurisdictional basis for the federal government to enact law on this matter can be derived from Article 76(1)(a) of the Constitution. It provides that Parliament may make laws with respect to any matter enumerated in the State List for implementing any treaty, agreement or convention between the Federation and any other country, or any decision of an international organization of which the Federation is a member.

B. *United Nations Conventions*

154. Malaysia's diplomatic association at regional and international levels has impacted policy and law pertaining to the environment of the country. Since independence, Malaysia has fully committed itself to the United Nations. Malaysia's environmental policy and law were highly influenced by the United Nations conventions, starting from the United Nations Conference on the Human Environment 1972, the 26 principles of the Stockholm Declaration, of which Malaysia was a signatory, and the 126 recommendations of the Action Plan. Other international conventions and treaties relating to the environment ratified or signed by Malaysia include:

281. Ministry of Science, Technology and The Environment, *Malaysia Initial Communication 2000* (Ministry of Science, Technology and The Environment 2000)
282. Ministry of Natural Resources and Environment Malaysia, *Malaysia Second National Communication to the UNFCCC 2011* (Ministry of Natural Resources and Environment Malaysia2011)
283. Ministry of Natural Resources and Environment Malaysia, *Malaysia Biennial Update Report to the UNFCCC 2015* (Ministry of Natural Resources and Environment Malaysia 2011)
284. Ministry of Energy, Science, Technology, Environment and Climate Change, *Malaysia Third National Communication and Second Biennial Update Report to the UNFCCC 2018* (Ministry 0f Energy, Science, Technology, Environment and Climate Change 2018)
285. Ministry of Environment and Water, *Third Biennial Update Report to the UNFCCC 2020* (Ministry of Environment and Water 2020)

- Convention on International Trade in Endangered Species of Wild Flora and Fauna 1973;
- United Nations Convention on the law of the Sea 1982;
- Convention on Biological Diversity 1992;
- United Nations Framework Convention on Climate Change 1992;
- International Tropical Timber Agreement 1983;
- Convention on Wetlands of International Importance Especially as Waterfowl Habitat 1971;
- Kyoto Protocol;
- United Nations Framework Convention on Climate Change;
- Montreal Protocol on Substances that Deplete the Ozone Layer 1987;
- Convention Concerning the Protection of the World's Cultural and Natural Heritage 1972;
- Basel Convention on the Control of Transboundary Movements of Hazardous Wastes and their Disposal 1989;
- The Paris Agreement 2015.

C. Commonwealth of Nations

155. Another international association joined by Malaysia is the Commonwealth of Nations. It comprises sovereign nations previously under British rule. The Commonwealth of Nations is a voluntary association of independent sovereign states, each responsible for its own policies, consulting and cooperating in the common interests of their peoples and in the promotion of international understanding and world peace.

156. The Commonwealth of Nations' framework is outlined in the Singapore Declaration of Commonwealth Principles 1971, and reinforced in the Harare Declaration 1991. Both are important documents to the Commonwealth's uncodified constitution.

157. The main decision-making forum of the organization is the biennial Commonwealth Heads of Government Meeting, where Commonwealth presidents or prime ministers assemble to discuss matters of mutual interest, including that of the environment, such as, notably, the Langkawi Declaration on the Environment 1989.

D. Association of Southeast Asian Nations

158. At the regional level, Malaysia is a party to the Association of Southeast Asian Nations (ASEAN). This association was established on 8 August 1967 in

Bangkok by the five original member countries, namely, Indonesia, Malaysia, Philippines, Singapore and Thailand. Brunei Darussalam joined in 1984, Vietnam in 1995, Laos and Myanmar in 1997 and Cambodia in 1999.[286]

159. Member Countries adopt fundamental principles in their relations with one another, based on the Treaty of Amity and Cooperation in Southeast Asia 1976, including principles on environmental protection. The ASEAN leaders also adopted the ASEAN Vision 2020 – a shared vision of ASEAN as a concert of Southeast Asian nations.

160. The highest decision-making organ of ASEAN is the Meeting of the ASEAN Heads of State and Government. All the ASEAN countries have established ministries or bureaus of the environment to deal with environmental protection and are implementing national and regional legislation. ASEAN also has several specialized bodies and arrangements promoting inter-governmental cooperation in various fields including the ASEAN Regional Centre for Biodiversity Conservation.

161. Various bilateral and multilateral commitments between Malaysia and other ASEAN countries have been entered into, which further complement and reinforce Malaysia's environmental law and policy. They are:[287]

- the Manila Declaration 1981;
- the Bangkok Declaration 1984;
- the Jakarta Resolution on Sustainable Development 1987;
- the Langkawi Declaration 1989;
- the Kuala Lumpur Accord on Environment and Development 1990;
- the Singapore Resolution on Environment and Development 1992;
- the Bandar Seri Begawan Resolution on Environment and Development 1994;
- ASEAN Cooperation Plan on Transboundary Pollution 1995;
- Jakarta Declaration on Environment and Development 1997;
- ASEAN Agreement on Transboundary Haze Pollution 2002;
- Yangon Resolution on Sustainable Development 2003;
- Agreement on the Establishment of the ASEAN Centre for Biodiversity 2005;
- ASEAN Declaration on the 13th Session of the Conference of the Parties (COP) to the United Nations Framework Convention on Climate Change (UNFCCC) 2007;
- Singapore Declaration on Climate Change, Energy and the Environment 2007;
- ASEAN Regional Action Plan to Tackle Plastic Pollution (2021–2025).

---

286. For further details on ASEAN and its environmental commitment, *see* the official website at http://environment.asean.org/, January 2014.
287. For details on ASEAN environmental agreements, *see* the official website at http://environment.asean.org/, January 2014.

Part I. Pollution Control

Chapter 1. General Law

§1. Environmental Quality Standards in Malaysia

162. In Malaysia, the primary law on pollution control is the EQA 1974.[288] This Act is a federal statute, and section 1(1) of the Act specifies that it shall apply to the whole of Malaysia.[289]

163. Part IV of the Act concerns the prohibition and control of pollution and contains sections relating to various aspects of environmental pollution, such as: air pollution (section 22); noise pollution (section 23); soil pollution (section 24); pollution of inland waters (section 25); pollution caused by oil in the Malaysian waters (section 27); pollution caused by the discharge of waste into the Malaysian waters (section 29) and open burning (section 29A).

164. Under the Act, the control of the discharge of pollutants is based on relevant effluent standards or acceptable conditions, whereby the discharge exceeding these standards is considered an offence.

165. The term 'acceptable condition' presupposes an environmental standard, which is used as a baseline criterion of the acceptability or restriction stipulated in the EQA 1974, and is central to the management of pollution control in the Act.

166. The main provision that deals with acceptable conditions is section 21, which permits the Minister, after consultation with the Environmental Quality Council, to specify the acceptable conditions for the discharge of pollutants into the environment exceeding which the discharge is prohibited or restricted.

288. Act 127.
289. *See* Maizatun Mustafa, *Environmental Quality Act 1974: Development and Reform*, MLJ (March/April 2009).

§2. LICENCES

I. General

167. Part III of the EQA 1974 deals with licences. The licence authority is assigned to the Director General of the Department of Environment as provided in section 10 of the Act. Licence application must be made in accordance with the procedures specified under the Environmental Quality (Licensing) Regulations, 1977.[290]

168. Through a concept of 'maximum allowable limit' of pollution, a person is prohibited from discharging any effluent into the environment, in contravention of acceptable conditions, unless he is licensed to do so.

169. Under the EQA 1974, licences are required for the following:

- section 18(1) to occupy or use prescribed premises;
- section 22(1) to emit or discharge wastes into the atmosphere in contravention of the acceptable conditions specified under section 21;
- section 23(1) to emit or cause or permit to be emitted any noise greater in volume, intensity or quality in contravention of the acceptable conditions specified under section 21;
- section 24(1) to pollute or cause or permit to be polluted any soil or surface of any land in contravention of the acceptable conditions specified under section 21;
- section 25(1) to emit, discharge or deposit any wastes into any inland waters in contravention of the acceptable conditions specified under section 21; and
- section 29(1) to discharge wastes into Malaysian waters.

II. Licence Conditions

170. Once a licence is granted, a licence holder is required to pay the licence fee which is prescribed by section 17(1) of the Act. The amount payable is not fixed but is imposed by the DG after taking into consideration the following factors, namely, the class of premises; the location of such premises; the quality of wastes discharged; the pollutant or class of pollutants discharged; and the existing level of pollution.[291]

171. In granting any application for a licence or for a renewal or transfer thereof, the DG, by virtue of sections 11 and 12, may do so either subject to conditions or unconditionally. During the currency of the licence, the DG has the discretionary power to revoke or vary any condition attached to the licence or attach new conditions thereto.[292]

290. P.U. (A) 198/1977.
291. Regulation 17(2) of the Environmental Quality (Licensing) Regulations, 1977.
292. Section 11(3)(b) of the Environmental Quality Act 1974.

172. Any licensee who fails to comply with any terms or conditions of the licence is guilty of an offence and may be liable to a fine not exceeding MYR 25,000 or to imprisonment for a period not exceeding two years or both, and to a further fine of MYR 1,000 for every day that the offence is continued after a notice has been served upon him.[293]

III. Contravention Licence

173. One of the two types of licence introduced under the EQA 1974 is a contravention licence. It is applicable for the discharge of pollution under sections 22–25 and 29 of the Act. Under these sections, the prohibition on the discharge of pollution into the environment is not an absolute one. The prohibition is subject to the application of a contravention licence.

174. Under this licence, the control of pollution is achieved through the imposition of 'acceptable conditions', as provided in section 21. This section empowers the Minister to specify any acceptable condition for the emission of wastes into any area of the environment. Acceptable conditions on the discharge of effluent are specified in the licence.

175. Acceptable conditions which are regulated through contravention licences are provided in the following Regulations:

- the Environmental Quality (Sewage) Regulation 2009;
- the Environmental Quality (Industrial Effluent) Regulation 2009;
- the Environmental Quality (Clean Air) Regulations 1978;
- the Environmental Quality (Motor Vehicle Noise) Regulations 1987;
- the Environmental Quality (Control of Emission from Petrol Engines) Regulations 1996;
- the Environmental Quality (Control of Emission from Diesel Engines) Regulations 1996;
- the Environmental Quality (Control of Emission from Motorcycles) Regulations 2003; and
- the Environmental Quality (Control of Petrol and Diesel Properties) Regulations 2007.

IV. Prescribed Premises Licence

176. The second type of licence is 'prescribed premises' licence provided under sections 18–20 of the EQA 1974. This licence is specifically applied to regulate the discharge of palm oil and rubber effluents.

293. Section 16 of the Environmental Quality Act 1974.

177. Under section 18 of the Act, the Minister is empowered to prescribe that all premises carrying out palm oil and rubber activities are prescribed premises and consequently provide for specific regulations to regulate their activities.

178. Two specific regulations have been introduced for these purposes, which contain effluent standards to be attached to licences for prescribed premises. They are:

- the Environmental Quality (Prescribed Premises) (Crude Palm Oil) Regulation 1977; and
- the Environmental Quality (Prescribed Premises) (Raw Natural Rubber) Regulation 1978.

179. Licences for prescribed premises are based on effluent limits that are provided in the respective Regulations. This licence needs to be applied for by the owner or occupier of any prescribed premises.

180. Failure to obtain the prescribed premises licence is considered an offence and any person found guilty may be liable to a fine up to MYR 50,000 or imprisonment for a period not exceeding two years, or both.[294]

181. However, unlike a contravention licence, the prescribed premises licence is issued based on a gradual effluent standard. For palm oil effluent, its Regulations have formulated a seven-generation set of effluent standards,[295] with the objective of allowing palm oil factories adequate time to comply with the required limits. Hence, during the early period of introduction of the Environmental Quality (Prescribed Premises) (Crude Palm Oil) Regulations 1977, no condition was imposed on the discharge of palm oil effluent. Subsequently, licences issued after the said period were required to contain conditions limiting the parameters of the effluent according to the respective periods. The parameter limits of this effluent is stated in the licence itself, and the DG is empowered either to impose a more stringent or a less stringent limit than that prescribed.[296]

182. Likewise, prescribed premises licences for rubber effluent also provide for a gradual limit of effluent that is allowed to be discharged.[297] The objective of the imposition of such limits is also the same, namely to allow rubber factories adequate time to comply with the effluent standards. Thus, during the first two years of its

---

294. *See* s. 18(3) of the Environmental Quality Act 1974. A further fine of MYR 1,000 a day for every day that the offence is continued will also be imposed after the Director General has sent the person a notice requiring that person to cease the act.
295. *See* Second Schedule of the Environmental Quality (Prescribed Premises) (Crude Palm Oil) Regulations 1977.
296. *See* Regulations 11 and 12 of the Environmental Quality (Prescribed Premises) (Crude Palm Oil) Regulations 1977.
297. *See* Regulation 11 of the Environmental Quality (Prescribed Premises) (Raw Natural Rubber) Regulations 1978.

introduction, no condition was imposed on the discharge of rubber effluent. Following that period, every licence issued should contain conditions limiting the discharge in accordance with the five-generation set of standards.[298] The DG is empowered to regulate the licence, including the power to impose a more stringent limit than that prescribed by any parameter,[299] in addition to other administrative and operational authorities.

§3. EIA IN MALAYSIA

183. Since 1986, the EQA 1974 provides for EIA to be carried out for certain types of activities. EIA is defined in the Act as 'a study to identify, predict, evaluate and communicate information about the impacts on the environment of a proposed project and to detail out the mitigating measures prior to project approval and implementation'.[300] The authority in charge of overseeing the EIA process is the Department of Environment.

184. The EIA requirement is made compulsory on activities deemed to have adverse effects on the environment. This was through the incorporation of an EIA provision under section 34A of the EQA 1974, in 1985.

185. Previously, from 1987 up until 2015, lists of activities that require EIA, or 'prescribed activities' were provided within the Environmental Quality (Prescribed Activities) (EIA) Order 1987.[301] In 2015, this Order was repealed and replaced by the Environmental Quality (Prescribed Activities) (EIA) Order 2015.[302] Prescribed activities are activities considered by the Minister as having the possibility of causing significant environmental impacts. Any person intending to carry out any of the listed activities is required to submit a report containing an assessment of the impact the activity is likely to have on the environment to the DG for his approval.[303]

186. Under the repealed Order, there were nineteen types of activity prescribed by the Act for the assessment, namely:[304]

- Item 1 on agriculture;
- Item 2 on airports;
- Item 3 on drainage and irrigation;

298. First to Fourth Schedules of the Environmental Quality (Prescribed Premises) (Raw Natural Rubber) Regulations 1978.
299. *See* Regulation 18 of the Environmental Quality (Prescribed Premises) (Raw Natural Rubber) Regulations 1978.
300. *See* Dept. Envt., *Environmental Impact Assessment (EIA) Procedure and Requirement in Malaysia* 1 (Dept. Envt. 1993). *See also* Dept. Envt., *Environmental Requirements: A Guide for Investors* (Dept. Envt. 2010).
301. P.U. (A) 362/87.
302. P.U. (A) 195/2015.
303. Section 34A(2) of the Environmental Quality Act 1974.
304. *See* Schedule of the Environmental Quality (Prescribed Activities) (EIA) Order 1987.

- Item 4 on land reclamation;
- Item 5 on fisheries;
- Item 6 on forestry;
- Item 7 on housing;
- Item 8 on industry;
- Item 9 on infrastructure;
- Item 10 on ports;
- Item 11 on mining;
- Item 12 on petroleum;
- Item 13 on power generation and transmission;
- Item 14 on quarries;
- Item 15 on railways;
- Item 16 on transportation;
- Item 17 on resort and recreational development;
- Item 18 on waste treatment and disposal; and
- Item 19 on water supply.

187. The lists of prescribed activities have been revised by the 2015 Order, whereby all activities specified in the First Schedule do not require public display and public comment unless otherwise instructed, in writing, by the DG, whereas activities specified in the Second Schedule require public display and public comment.[305] Activities included in the First Schedule of the 2015 Order are as follows:

- Item 1 on agriculture, covering land development schemes for an area of 20 ha or more but less than 500 ha to bring forest into agricultural production; and development of agricultural estates covering an area of 500 ha or more involving changes in types of agricultural use;
- Item 2 on Aerodrome, for the expansion involving a runway of 1,000 m or longer;
- Item 3 on Drainage and Irrigation, for the construction of man-made lakes and enlargement of artificial lakes with surface areas of 100 ha or more, and for irrigation schemes covering an area of 500 ha or more;
- Item 4 on Fisheries, covering land-based aquaculture projects accompanied by clearing of mangrove forest, peat swamp forest or fresh water swamp forest for an area of 20 ha or more but less than 50 ha;
- Item 5 on Forestry, for (a) the conversion of forest at 300 m or more above mean sea level to other land use covering an area of 20 ha or more but less than 100 ha; (b) logging, or cutting or taking of timber for the purpose of conversion from forest to other land use covering an area of 100 ha or more but less than 500 ha; (c) logging, or cutting or taking of timber from forest at less than 300 m above mean sea level covering an area of 100 ha or more, outside permanent reserved forest; (d) conversion of an area of mangrove forest; peat swamp forest; or fresh water swamp forest for industrial, housing or agricultural use covering an area of 20 ha or more but less than 50 ha; or (e) development of planted forest covering an area of 100 ha or more but less than 500 ha;

305. Order 4 of the Environmental Quality (Prescribed Activities) (EIA) Order 2015.

- Item 6 on Industry, covering (a) chemical production capacity of each product or combined products of 100 tonnes or more per day; (b) cement grinding plant with cement production capacity of 200 tonnes or more per day; (c) production of 100 tonnes or more per day of burnt lime using rotary kiln or 50 tonnes or more per day of burnt lime using vertical kiln; (d) production capacity of each product or combined product of less than 50 tonnes per day; and (e) shipyards with dead weight tonnage of 5,000 tonnes or more;
- Item 7 on Land Reclamation along riverbanks involving an area of less than 50 ha;
- Item 8 on Mining covering (a) ore processing outside mineral tenement area, including concentrating of aluminium, copper, gold, iron, tantalum or rare earth element; (b) sand mining on land or river or in coastal area or in territorial waters not exceeding 3 nautical miles measured from the low-water line, involving an area of 20 ha or more; and (c) sand mining in continental shelf area;
- Item 9 on Petroleum relating to (a) development of oil field, gas field, or oil and gas field; (b) construction of 30 km or more in length of offshore pipelines, onshore pipelines, or offshore pipelines and onshore pipelines; (c) construction of oil separation, processing, handling and storage facilities; gas separation, processing, handling and storage facilities; or oil and gas separation, processing, handling and storage facilities; and (d) construction of product depot for the storage of petrol, gas or diesel which has the combined storage capacity of 60,000 barrels or more (excluding service station) within 3 km from any commercial, industrial or residential area;
- Item 10 on Ports including (a) expansion of port involving an increase of 50% or more in handling capacity per annum; and (b) expansion of fishing port involving an increase of 50% or more in fish landing capacity per annum;
- Item 11 on Power Generation and Transmission relating to the (a) construction of steam generated power station using fossil fuels (other than coal) and having the capacity of 10 MW or more, with or without transmission line; (b) construction of combined cycle power station, with or without transmission line; and (c) construction of transmission line in environmentally sensitive area;
- Item 12 on Development in Coastal and Hill Area covering (a) the construction of building or facilities with eighty rooms or more in coastal area; and (b) construction of hill-station resort or hotel at 300 m or more above mean sea level covering an area of 20 ha or more;
- Item 13 on Development in Slope Area involving the development or land clearing less than 50% of an area with slope greater than or equal to 25° but less than 35°.
- Item 14 on Waste Treatment and Disposal including (a) scheduled waste relating to the construction of recovery plant (off-site), construction of wastewater treatment plant (off-site) and construction of storage facility (off-site); (b) solid waste including the construction of composting plant and construction of recovery plant or recycling plant; and (c) sewage relating to the construction of sewage treatment plant with 20,000 population equivalent or more and sludge treatment facilities;
- Item 15 on Dredging, including capital dredging and disposal of waste dredged materials;

- Item 16 on Housing development covering an area of 50 ha or more;
- Item 17 on Industrial Estate Development of industrial estate covering an area of 20 ha or more;
- Item 18 on New Township construction consisting of 2,000 housing accommodation units or more or covering an area of 100 ha or more;
- Item 19 on Quarrying of rock material;
- Item 20 on Road, covering the construction of expressways; highways; and road, tunnel or bridge traversing or adjacent or near to environmentally sensitive areas;
- Item 21 on Water Supply involving the groundwater development for industrial, agricultural or urban water supply of 4,500 m^3 or more per day.

Under the Second Schedule of the 2015 Order, prescribed activities require public display and public comment. According to the Order, public display and public comment are a display of a report, at a place and within the time determined by the DG, to obtain public comment in relation to that report. The list of prescribed activities under the Second Schedule are as follows:

- Item 1 on agriculture, involving (a) land development schemes for an area of 500 ha or more to bring forest into agricultural production; and (b) new pig farming area of 2,000 or more standing pig population;
- Item 2 on Aerodrome, for (a) the construction of a new aerodrome involving a runway of 1,000 m or longer; and (b) construction of aerodrome in or adjacent or near to any state park, national park, national marine park, island surrounding marine park or environmentally sensitive area;
- Item 3 on Drainage and Irrigation, for (a) the construction of man-made lakes and enlargement of artificial lakes with surface areas of 50 ha or more in or adjacent or near to environmentally sensitive area; and (b) Any drainage of wetland, wildlife habitat or of dry inland forest covering an area of 20 ha or more;
- Item 4 on Fisheries, covering land-based aquaculture projects accompanied by clearing of mangrove forest, peat swamp forest or fresh water swamp forest for an area of 50 ha or more;
- Item 5 on Forestry, for (a) the conversion of forest at 300 m or more above mean sea level to other land use covering an area of 100 ha or more; (b) logging or conversion of forest to other land use within: (i) a catchment area of reservoirs used for municipal water supply, irrigation or hydropower; (ii) an area adjacent or near to any state park, national park or national marine park; (iii) any state park, national park or national marine park; or (iv) an area gazetted as water catchment forest under the National Forestry Act 1984; (c) logging, or cutting or taking of timber from forest at 300 m or more above mean sea level covering an area of 100 ha or more, outside permanent reserved forest; (d) logging, or cutting or taking of timber covering an area of 500 ha or more; (e) development of planted forest covering an area of 500 ha or more; (f) conversion of an area of mangrove forest, peat swamp forest or fresh water swamp forest for industrial, housing or agricultural use covering an area of 50 ha or more; and (g) clearing of mangrove forest, peat swamp forest or fresh water swamp forest on islands adjacent to any national marine park;
- Item 6 on Industry, relating to (a) the non-ferrous covering primary smelting aluminium (all sizes), primary smelting copper (all sizes) and primary smelting other

non-ferrous (producing 50 tonnes product or more per day); (b) cement with clinker production capacity of 30 tonnes or more per hour; (c) iron and steel using iron ore as raw materials for production of 100 tonnes or more per day and using scrap iron as raw materials for production of 200 tonnes or more per day; (d) petrochemicals with production capacity of each product or combined product of 50 tonnes or more per day; EUR pulp, or pulp and paper with production capacity of 50 tonnes or more per day; and (f) recycle paper industry with production capacity of 50 tonnes or more per day;

- Item 7 on Land Reclamation involving (a) coastal reclamation or land reclamation along riverbanks involving an area of 50 ha or more; (b) coastal reclamation or land reclamation along riverbanks within or adjacent or near to environmentally sensitive areas; and (c) reclamation for man-made island;
- Item 8 on Mining of minerals in new areas involving large-scale operation; and mining of minerals within or adjacent or near to environmentally sensitive area;
- Item 9 on Petroleum relating to the construction of oil refineries, gas refineries, and oil and gas refineries;
- Item 10 on Ports including construction of a new port and new fishing port;
- Item 11 on Power Generation and Transmission relating to (a) the construction of coal fired power station and having the capacity of 10 MW or more with or without transmission line; and (b) construction of nuclear-fuel power station with or without transmission line;
- Item 12 on Development in Coastal and Hill Area, National Park and State Park involving the development of tourist facilities, recreational facilities or other facilities in any national park or state park; or on any island in surrounding waters which has been gazetted as a national marine park or marine reserve under the Fisheries Act 1985;
- Item 13 on Development in Slope Area involving (a) the development or land clearing of 50% or more of an area with slope greater than or equal to 25° but less than 35°; and (b) Construction of road, tunnel or bridge traversing an area with slope greater than or equal to 35°.
- Item 14 on Waste Treatment and Disposal covering (a) scheduled waste involving the construction of thermal treatment plant; the construction of off-site recovery plant for lead acid battery wastes; the construction of off-site recovery plant or treatment facility that generates significant amount of wastewater which is located at the upstream of public water supply intake; and the construction of secure landfill facility; and (b) solid waste involving the construction of thermal treatment plant, sanitary landfill facility and transfer station;
- Item 15 on Construction of Dam relating to (a) impounding reservoir for irrigation, flood mitigation, control of siltation, recreational, water supply or any other reason with a surface area of 100 ha or more; (b) dam and hydroelectric power scheme with dam of 15 m or more in height and ancillary structures covering a total area of 40 ha or more; or reservoir with a surface area of 100 ha or more;
- Item 16 on Transportation including the construction of new routes or branch line for a mass rapid transport project, or new railway route or railway branch lines;
- Item 17 on Radioactive materials and Radioactive Waste covering any activity specified in this Schedule and the First Schedule using radioactive materials and generating radioactive wastes.

188. In 2000, the Environmental Quality (Prescribed Activities) (EIA) Order 1987 was amended[306] to exclude its application to Sabah and Sarawak in certain prescribed activities.[307] For the state of Sabah, the law applicable on the prescribed activities[308] is the Conservation of Environment (Prescribed Activities) Order 1999.[309] For the state of Sarawak, the applicable law is the Natural Resources and Environment (Prescribed Activities) Order 1994.[310] However, notwithstanding the said exception, prescribed activities listed as Items 2, 5(a) and (b), 8, 9, 10, 12, 13(a), (b) and (c), 15, 16 and 18 in the Schedule of the Environmental Quality (Prescribed Activities) (EIA) Order 1987 continue to apply in the states of Sabah and Sarawak.[311]

189. The exclusion of certain prescribed activities' application to Sabah and Sarawak continues to be reiterated by the 2015 Order. However, items that are still applicable to Sarawak are items 2, 6, 9 and 10 and sub-items 11(a) and (b) and 14(a) of the First Schedule; and items 2, 6, 9, 10, 11, 16 and 17 and sub-item 14(a) of the Second Schedule.[312] Whereas activities that are still applicable to Sabah are items 2, 6, 9 and 14 and sub-items 11(a) and (b) of the First Schedule; and items 2, 6, 9, 11, 14 and 17 of the Second Schedule.

190. Section 34A of the EQA 1974 requires that, before a person can carry out any of the prescribed activities, and before any approval for the carrying out of such activity is granted by the relevant approving authority, the person must submit a report to the DG for his assessment.

In 2012, several amendments, insertions and substitutions were made to section 34A in relation to EIA procedures and requirements pertaining to the EIA consultants. Under section 34A (2),[313] any person intending to carry out any prescribed activity is required to appoint a qualified person to conduct an EIA and to submit the EIA report thereof to the DG. Subsection (2A) of section 34A was inserted[314] to require the DG to maintain a list of qualified persons who may carry out the EIA and submit the report. Responsibilities of such qualified person pertaining to the submission of EIA report are provided by section 34A (2B).[315] They include responsibility pertaining to EIA and its recommendations apart from ensuring that the report and the recommendation do not contain any false or misleading information, and take a professional indemnity insurance for any liability arising from the EIA and its recommendations.

306. Amendment P.U. (A) 489/2000.
307. *See* Order 3 of the Environmental Quality (Prescribed Activities) (EIA) Order 1987.
308. Except Item 7 (viii) listed in the First Schedule of the Environment (Prescribed Activities) Order 1999.
309. Published under the Second Supplementary of the Sabah Government Gazette on the 30 Aug. 1999.
310. Published under Part II of the Sarawak Government Gazette on the 18 Aug. 1994.
311. *See* Order 4 of the Environmental Quality (Prescribed Activities) (EIA) Order 1987.
312. *See* Order 4 (1) of the Environmental Quality (Prescribed Activities) (EIA) Order 2015.
313. Subs. Act A 1441, 2012.
314. Ins. Act A1441, 2012.
315. Ins. Act A 1441, 2012.

As regard the report, section 34A (2C)[316] requires that it must be done in accordance with the guidelines and must contain an assessment of the impact such activity will have or is likely to have on the environment; and the proposed measures that shall be undertaken to prevent, reduce or control the adverse impact on the environment. On the part of the DG, he would approve the report if upon examining the report he is of the opinion that the report satisfies the requirements of subsection (2C).[317] However, if the DG is of the opinion that the report is not in accordance with the development plan or physical plan approved by the relevant approving authority, or it does not satisfy the requirements under subsection (2C), then he will not approve the report.[318]

191. The EIA process is provided in guidelines known as *A Handbook of Environmental Impact Assessment Guidelines*.[319] The Guidelines require that the EIA process is done in two stages. The first stage is the preliminary assessment, where the report is reviewed by a technical committee within the Department of Environment. The second stage is the detailed assessment, which is reviewed by an ad hoc review panel whose members are appointed.

192. The approving authority is the government authority that has the task of deciding whether or not a project should proceed. The authorities include the National Development Planning Committee for federal government sponsored projects; the State Executive Council for state government sponsored projects; the various local authorities or Regional Development Authority with respect to planning approval within their respective areas; and the Ministry of Trade and Industry for industrial projects.

193. Once the EIA report has been approved, the Department of Environment may attach conditions to its approval of either a preliminary or a detailed assessment. The project proponent must provide proof that the conditions have been complied with.[320]

194. Any person intending to carry out a prescribed activity shall not carry out such activity until the EIA report is submitted to the DG and approved.[321] Contravening section 34A is an offence and may comprise any of the following actions or omissions, namely:

– non-compliance with the provisions of section 34A;

316. Ins. Act A 1441, 2012.
317. Section 34A (3) of the Environmental Quality Act 1974. (Am. Act A 1441, 2012).
318. Section 34A (4) of the Environmental Quality Act 1974. (Subs. Act A1441, 2012).
319. These are non-statutory guidelines and contain directions to assist project initiators in the preparation of their EIA reports. *See* Dept. Envt., *Handbook of Environmental Impact Assessment Guidelines* (Dept. Envt. 1995). *See also* Dept. Envt., *Environmental Requirements: A Guide for Investors* (Dept. Envt. 2010).
320. Section 34A(7) of the Environmental Quality Act 1974.
321. Section 34A (6) of the Environmental Quality Act 1974.

– non-compliance with the implementing measures for mitigating and for the abatement of an impact on the environment; and
– non-compliance with the 'terms of reference'.[322]

195. Previously, section 34A (8) prescribed that the guilty person shall be liable to a fine up to MYR 100,000 or imprisonment up to five years or both and to a further fine of MYR 1,000 for every day that the offence is continued, after a notice by the DG requiring him to comply with the Act has been served on him.[323] However, this subsection has been amended whereby the amount of fine is now increased to MYR 500,000.[324]

Another addition to the EIA provisions is the insertion of section 34AA[325] relating to prohibition order. This section gives the power to the DG to issue a prohibition order or stop work order to the person who carries out the prescribed activities without the approval under subsection 34A(3); who violates any conditions attached to the approval of the report; or which in the opinion of the DG are being carried out in a manner that is likely to cause environmental damage.[326] Such prohibition order or stop work order may be issued for preventing the prescribed activities from continuing either absolutely or conditionally; for such period as the DG may determine; or until requirements to remedy as the DG may direct have been complied with.[327] Penalty prescribed by section 34AA for its contravention is a fine not exceeding MYR 500,000 or to imprisonment for a period not exceeding five years or both and to a further fine of MYR 1,000 for every day that the offence is continued, after a notice by the DG requiring him to comply with the Act has been served on him.

196. One decided case that relies on section 34A of the Act is *Tenggara Gugusan Holidays Sdn. Bhd. v. Public Prosecutor.*[328] In this case, the appellant was convicted and fined MYR 20,000 by the sessions court judge for carrying out construction of coastal resort facilities, which is a prescribed activity under Item 17(a) of the Environmental Quality (Prescribed Activities) (EIA) Order 1987. However, he did not submit an EIA report to the DG and did not get his approval, as required under section 34A. The appellant appealed against the conviction, but the appeal court dismissed the appeal and ruled that the construction of more than eighty coastal chalets by the appellant was a prescribed activity. Section 34A(2) imposes a duty on any person intending to carry out any of the prescribed activities to submit an EIA report before any approval for the carrying out of such activities is granted. Unless and until such report is submitted and approved by the DG, no person would be allowed to carry out such activity.

322. Terms of reference are terms submitted to the project proponent by the review panel before carrying out detailed assessment.
323. Section 43A(8) of the Environmental Quality Act 1974.
324. Am. Acts A953, A 1441, 2012.
325. Ins. Act A.1441, 2012.
326. Section 34AA (1) of the Environmental Quality Act 1974.
327. Section 34AA (2) of the Environmental Quality Act 1974.
328. (2003) 1MLJ 508.

§4. PUBLIC PARTICIPATION

197. In Malaysia, principles for public participation have been accepted as criteria within certain practices involving environmental matters. The amendment of the EQA through the revocation of the Environmental Quality (Prescribed Activities) (EIA) Order 1987, and replaced by the Environmental Quality (Prescribed Activities) (EIA) Order 2014 was meant, among other things, to legally require public participation. This obligation is imposed on certain prescribed activities which require that information of the projects to be displayed to the public for comment. Such public display and comment refer to a display of the EIA report at a place and within the time determined by the DG in order to obtain public comment in relation to that report.[329]

198. Within the local government level, public participation applies within the Local Authority Act 1976[330] through the appointment of councillors in the local councils. These councillors are appointed from among persons the majority of whom must be ordinarily resident in the local government area.[331] These councillors are representatives of the areas from where they hail, or they represent various business communities or interest groups, and they provide a channel of communication between the local government and the local residents.[332]

199. The element of public participation has also been incorporated within the Town and Country Planning Act 1976.[333] Under this Act, every local government is deemed to be the local planning authority of the area[334] and is empowered to prepare the Structure Plan[335] for the area. A second tier of the development plan is the Local Plan.[336] The role of the Local Plan[337] is to ensure a detailed implementation of the policies and strategies laid down in the Structure Plan.[338]

200. The Town and Country Planning Act 1974 requires that the local planning authority must consider representations from the public through publicity[339] and

329. *See* Order 3 (5) of the Environmental Quality (Prescribed Activities) (EIA) Order 2015.
330. Act 171.
331. Section 10 of the Local Authority Act 1976.
332. Section 10(2) of the Local Authority Act 1976.
333. Act 172.
334. *See* s. 5 of the Town and Country Planning Act 1976.
335. 'Structure plan', is defined by s. 2 of the Town and Country Planning Act 1976, in relation to an area, means the structure plan for the area, and any alteration of the plan, having effect in the area by virtue of s. 10(6); and, in relation to any land or building, means the structure plan, as so defined, for the area in which the land or building is situated; and 'draft structure plan' shall be construed as the context requires.
336. *See* s. 12(8) of the Town and Country Planning Act 1976.
337. 'Local plan', is defined by s. 2 of the Town and Country Planning Act 1976, in relation to an area, means the local plan for the area, and any alteration of the plan, for the time being having effect in the area by virtue of s. 15(1); and, in relation to any land or building, means the local plan, as so defined, for the area in which the land or building is situated; and 'draft local plan' shall be construed as the context requires.
338. Section 12(3) of the Town and Country Planning Act 1976.
339. Sections 9, 12A, and 13 of the Town and Country Planning Act 1976.

access both the draft Structure and Local Plans. During the preparation of these Plans, public participation is spelt out under sections 9 and 10 of the Act in two stages. The first is when the local planning authority is deciding on the matters to be included in the draft plan.[340] The second is when the draft structure plan has been completed and the public is invited to inspect a copy of the document and send objections.[341] The local planning authority is required to consider those objections through a public hearing.[342]

201. Under the Act, the State Planning Committee would receive all objections from the public against the Structure Plan, and a public local enquiry would be formed to study these objections and suggestions.[343] Both the plans may be changed and modified after taking into consideration the views of the public.

§5. ENVIRONMENTAL MANAGEMENT SYSTEMS AND AUDITS

I. Mandatory Standards

202. There are two types of standards for environmental management systems in Malaysia, voluntary and mandatory standards. Mandatory standards were introduced by amendments to the EQA 1974 in 1996 in the form of environmental audits under 33A.[344] According to the Department of Environment, the primary objective is to assess the compliance status of industrial facilities and development projects that are subject to the EQA 1974 and to provide a systematic approach to ensuring compliance. The longer-term goal is for industry and developers to eventually self-regulate their environmental management and help achieve Malaysia's sustainable development objectives.[345]

203. Under the Act, 'environmental audit'[346] is defined as 'a periodic, systematic, documented and objective evaluation to determine the compliance status to regulatory requirements; the environmental management system; and the overall environmental risk of the premises'. The primary type of environmental audit that will be required by the Department of Environment is a regulatory compliance-type audit which is meant to identify conditions that are out of compliance and for bringing the condition back into compliance as soon as practicable.[347]

204. Section 33A on the requirement of environmental audits, empowers the Department of Environment to require an occupier of any premises, vehicle or ship

340. Section 9(1)(b) of the Town and Country Planning Act 1976.
341. Section 9(2)(3) of the Town and Country Planning Act 1976.
342. Sections 9(4) and 10(3) of the Town and Country Planning Act 1976.
343. Section 14(1) of the Town and Country Planning Act 1976.
344. Environmental Quality (Amendment) Act 1996, Act 953.
345. *See* Dept. Envt. *Environmental Audit Guidance Manual* 1 (Dept. Envt. 2011).
346. Section 2 of the Environmental Quality Act 1974.
347. *See* Dept. Envt. *Environmental Audit Guidance Manual* 1 (Dept. Envt. 2011).

to carry out an environmental audit; and to submit an audit report in the manner prescribed by the Minister in regulations made under the Act.

205. Under section 33A, environmental audit includes the requirement of evaluating the environmental management system which is defined as 'a system comprising of an organizational structure with its responsibilities, practices, procedures, processes and resources for implementation and maintaining the system relating to the management of the environment'.[348]

206. The section also requires the occupier, who is directed to carry out and submit an environmental audit report, to appoint qualified personnel who are registered to assist with the audit. The environmental audit is to be carried out by competent and independent third-party auditors. Thus, an organization's internal auditors are disallowed from conducting the compliance-type audit for their own organization. In order to fulfil the requirement of section 33A, the Department of Environment has established the online Environmental Auditor Registration Scheme. Only audit reports prepared by registered environmental auditor will be accepted. It is a requirement for the auditor to use a customized audit protocol that is relevant to the particular industry and location that is being audited. The regulatory checklist would include the Environmental Quality (Sewage Regulations) 2009; Environmental Quality (Industrial Effluent Regulations) 2009; Environmental Quality (Control of Pollution from Solid Waste Transfer Station and Landfill) Regulations 2009; and Environmental Quality (Clean Air) Regulation 1978. Apart from the general regulatory checklist, other items shall be extracted from other relevant documents such as those relating to conditions of approval for licences or EIA.[349]

207. It is a requirement that environmental audit process is to be conducted in accordance with the Department of Environment's *Environmental Audit Guidance Manual.* Failure to comply with the environmental audit requirements is a violation against the EQA 1974.[350]

208. Section 33A does not include a penalty provision. However, the existing section 41 covers penalties for offences not otherwise provided for in the EQA 1974. Here, the offender may be liable to a fine not exceeding MYR 10,000 or to imprisonment for a period not exceeding two years, or both.

II. Voluntary Standards

209. Apart from the mandatory standards, voluntary environmental management standards are available for producers and manufacturers, but punitive action is not taken in cases of non-compliance with those standards.

---

348. Section 2 of the Environmental Quality Act 1974.
349. *See* Dept. Envt. *Environmental Audit Guidance Manual* 1 (Dept. Envt. 2011).
350. *Ibid.*

210. Voluntary standardization of environmental management systems is applied in Malaysia under the ISO 14000 scheme, developed by the International Organization for Standardization, and applies uniformly to companies in any industry and of any size.

211. The Standards and Industrial Research Institute of Malaysia (SIRIM) acts as the standards setting and certifying agency for the ISO scheme. This institute was established under the Ministry of Science, Technology and the Environment[351] by virtue of the SIRIM (Incorporation) Act 1975.[352]

212. This Act was later repealed by the Standards of Malaysia Act 1996.[353] In 1996, the Institute was corporatized under the Companies Act 1965,[354] and it is now known as SIRIM Berhad.

213. SIRIM Berhad is appointed by the Department of Standards Malaysia as the sole national standards development agency. This Department is the national standardization and accreditation body established under the Ministry of Science, Technology and Innovation in accordance with the Standards of Malaysia Act 1996. The use of Malaysian Standards is voluntary unless they are made mandatory by regulatory authorities by means of legislation.

351. Now under the Ministry of Science, Technology and Innovative, Malaysia.
352. Act 157. *See* s. 23 of the Standards of Malaysia Act 1996.
353. Act 549.
354. Act 125.

Chapter 2. Air Pollution

§1. General

214. The quality of air pollution in Malaysia is very much dependant on the level and pace of development, both in urban and rural areas.[355] In urban areas, the two largest sources of air pollution are motor vehicles and industries. Most emissions occur in the form of carbon monoxide, nitrogen oxides and sulphur oxides. In rural areas, air quality deterioration occurs by dust emitted from ploughing fields, rock quarries or smoke from wood and crop fire, palm oil mills, sawmills and paddy mills.

215. Motor vehicle emission is also a contributor towards air pollution. According to the Ministry of Transport, in 2015 the total number of vehicles in Malaysia was 28,181,203 units as compared to 20,188,565 units of registered vehicles in 2010. Overall, there were 13,288,797 cars and 12,933,042 motorcycles registered in 2015, in addition to the 185,035 public service vehicles and 1,205,744 goods vehicles.[356] In September 2018, the total number of vehicles in Malaysia further increased to 29,666,187 Unit.[357] The increasing number of motor vehicles on the road has contributed towards the discharge of gases such as hydrocarbons, nitrogen oxides, carbon monoxide, lead and black smoke.

216. Another source of air pollution is uncontrolled open burning of industrial, municipal and agricultural wastes. In Malaysia, uncontrolled open burning has been identified to be a major contributor towards the haze phenomenon which has been gaining prominence in Malaysia in the 1990s. Haze is caused by the presence of a large number of particles suspended in the air. These include particulate matter including dust, dirt and smoke, and chemicals such as carbon monoxide, nitrogen dioxide, sulphur dioxide, carbon monoxide, ozone, nitric oxide and others. It is a form of air pollution which is exacerbated at certain times of the year under specific weather conditions.[358]

217. In Malaysia, the EQA 1974 is the main law that contains provisions on air pollution. The Act empowers the Minister to set air quality standards and emission standards for the whole country. Various types of air pollution are controlled through the application of ambient standards as provided in the relevant regulations. Under the Act, the Department of Environment has monitoring and enforcement duties on air pollution.

---

355. Refer to the data provided on the status of air quality and sources of air pollutants by the Department of Environment in Kementerian Sumber Asli dan Alam Sekitar Malaysia, *Malaysia Environmental Quality Report 2012* 6–13 (Jabatan Alam Sekitar 2012).
356. *See* the website of the Ministry of Transport Malaysia at http://www.mot.gov.my/en/resources/yearly-statistic/, November 2018.
357. https://www.ceicdata.com/en/malaysia/motor-vehicles-registration/number-of-motor-vehicle-total, January 2019.
358. *See The Encyclopedia of Malaysia: Volume 1: The Environment* 108–111 (Sham Sani ed., Archipelago Press 1998).

§2. AIR POLLUTION INDEX

218. The air quality status for Malaysia is determined and disseminated according to the Air Pollution Index. This index, which is comparable to the corresponding air quality standards recommended by the World Health Organization, was developed by the Department of Environment in 1993. This Index is monitored by the Department for continuous monitoring of air quality throughout Malaysia using fifty-two air quality monitoring stations.[359]

219. The Air Pollution Index system includes the major air pollutants which could cause potential harm to human health should they reach unsafe levels. The pollutants included in this Index are ozone, carbon monoxide, nitrogen dioxide, sulphur dioxide and suspended particulate matter less than 10 microns in size. The pollutant with the highest reading in any twenty-four-hour period is taken as the Air Pollution Index reading for the whole period.[360] To reflect the status of the air quality and its effects on human health, the ranges of index values could then be categorized as follows: good, moderate, unhealthy, very unhealthy and hazardous.

220. The index values may also be categorized according to episode or action criteria, such as air pollutant levels within stipulated standards, or levels signifying conditions for alert, warning, emergency and significant harm, using the scale of 0–500. The key reference point in these air pollution index systems is the index value of 100, which is the 'safe' limit, whereas air quality with Air Pollution Index values exceeding 100 are considered likely to affect the health of the general public.[361]

§3. STATIONARY AIR POLLUTION

221. Previously, from 1978 up until 2014, the main regulations pertaining to the control of stationary sources air pollution were the EQA 1974, and ambient standards for stationary air pollution are specified under the Environmental Quality (Clean Air) Regulations 1978.[362] These Regulations, which relied upon the application of acceptable conditions based on parameters limit, were applied to the following situations:[363]

---

359. *See* Kementerian Sumber Asli dan Alam Sekitar Malaysia, *Environmental Quality Report 2012* 6–13 (Jabatan Alam Sekitar 2012).
360. *See* the latest Air Pollution Index for the whole of Malaysia at the Department of Environment's official website at http://www.doe.gov.my/, January 2019.
361. *See* Sham Sani (ed.), *The Encyclopedia of Malaysia: Volume 1: The Environment* 110–111 (Archipelago Press 1998).
362. P.U. (A) 280/78.
363. Regulation 3 of the Environmental Quality (Clean Air) Regulations 1978.

- any premises used for any industrial or trade purposes, or on which matter is burnt in connection with any industrial or trade purposes including burning of waste, irrespective of whether such premises are prescribed under section 18 of the Act or not;
- any facility or process that discharges or is capable of discharging air impurities into open air;
- every chimney;
- every industrial plant; and
- any fuel burning equipment.

222. Part II of the 1978 Regulations concerned industrial facilities adjacent to residential areas,[364] whereas Part IV of the Regulations dealt with dark smoke. The emission of dark smoke of any colour from any new facility was controlled based on shade No. 1 on the Ringelmann Chart;[365] or shade No. 2 on the Ringelmann Chart for fuel burning equipment utilizing solid fuel.[366]

223. Air pollution in the form of air impurities was controlled by 1978 Regulations through emission standards. Permissible limits of emission, discharge or deposit from the particular trade, industry or process was done according to three standards: Standards A, B and C. These Standards apply to the following air impurities:

- solid particle concentration in heating of metals;[367]
- solid particle concentration in other operations;[368]
- metal and metallic compounds;[369]
- gaseous substances;[370]
- asphalt concrete plants;[371]
- Portland cement plants;[372] and
- facilities discharging asbestos and free silica.[373]

224. When these emission standards came into effect in 1978, they were enforced as phased regulations over three stages of A, B and C. Existing facilities were required to satisfy the most lenient regulations, Standard A, no later than two years after enactment, and to achieve Standard B no more than three years after enactment. New facilities have to meet the most stringent regulations, Standard C, from the outset. In the case of the control of air impurities, the 1978 Regulations

364. Regulations 4–6 of the Environmental Quality (Clean Air) Regulations 1978.
365. The definition of the Ringelmann Chart is provided in Regulation 2 of the Environmental Quality (Clean Air) Regulations 1978.
366. Regulation 14 of the Environmental Quality (Clean Air) Regulations 1978.
367. Regulation 24 of the Environmental Quality (Clean Air) Regulations 1978.
368. Regulation 25 of the Environmental Quality (Clean Air) Regulations 1978.
369. Regulation 26 of the Environmental Quality (Clean Air) Regulations 1978.
370. Regulation 27 of the Environmental Quality (Clean Air) Regulations 1978.
371. Regulation 28 of the Environmental Quality (Clean Air) Regulations 1978.
372. Regulation 29 of the Environmental Quality (Clean Air) Regulations 1978.
373. Regulation 30 of the Environmental Quality (Clean Air) Regulations 1978.

required that every new facility shall comply with Standard C, and every existing facility shall comply with Standard A within two years, and shall comply with Standard B within three years from the date these Regulations come into force.

225. The discharged standards for air pollutants were regulated by the 1978 Regulations using the acceptable condition licence which prohibits any person from emitting or discharging any waste into the atmosphere in contravention of the acceptable conditions under section 22(1) of the EQA 1974 unless licensed. Application for a licence under section 22(1) shall be made in accordance with the procedures specified in the Environmental Quality (Licensing) Regulations 1977.

226. The 1978 Regulations also adopted the best practical means requirement order to prevent the emission of noxious or offensive substances and to render them harmless and inoffensive. The Regulations required that any occupier of any industrial or trade premises use the best practicable means for the following purposes:[374]

- the size, design and inherent operation characteristics of the plant or process;
- the provision, if necessary, and appropriate use of mist eliminator, dust arrestor, gas absorber and control instrumentation;
- the use of suitable raw material or suitable fuel;
- the alternative process within the capacity and design capability of the plant;
- the alternative manner of operation or procedures within the capacity and design capability of the plant or process;
- the proper conduct and adequate supervision of operations; and
- regular and efficient maintenance of plant and control equipment.

227. The 1978 Regulations imposed penalty for offences committed based on the contravention of the Regulations without licence[375] whereby any person who emits or discharges waste in contravention without a licence issued under section 22(1) of the Act shall be guilty of an offence and shall be liable to a fine not exceeding MYR 10,000 or to a term of imprisonment not exceeding two years or both and to a further fine not exceeding one MYR 1,000 a day for every day that the offence is continued after a notice by the DG requiring him to cease the act specified therein has been served upon him.[376]

228. In 2014, the 1978 Regulations were repealed and replaced by the Environmental Quality (Clean Air) Regulations 2014.[377] The 2014 Regulations' approaches on air pollution control depart substantially from that of the previous ones in term of scope, approaches and targets. The 2014 Regulations are applicable to premises that are used for any industrial or trade purposes, or on which matter is burnt in connection with any industrial or trade purposes, including burning of waste; any other

374. Regulation 32(3) of the Environmental Quality (Clean Air) Regulations 1978.
375. Regulations 7, 14–16, 21, 24–32, 34 and 35 of the Environmental Quality (Clean Air) Regulations 1978.
376. Regulation 56(1) of the Environmental Quality (Clean Air) Regulations 1978.
377. P.U. (A) 151/2014. The passing of these Regulations also revoked the Environmental Quality (Dioxin and Furan) Regulations 2004, P.U. (A) 104/2004.

premises or process that discharges or is capable of discharging air pollutants into the open air; any industrial plant; and any fuel burning equipment, which include any furnace, boiler, fireplace, oven, retort, internal combustion engine, vessel, or any other apparatus, device, mechanism, stack, chimney or structure used in connection with the burning of any combustible material.[378] The term 'air pollutants' here means smoke, cinders, solid particles of any kind, gases, fumes, mists, odours and radioactive substances or any other substances which the Minister by notification in the *Gazette* declares to be air pollutants for the purposes of these Regulations. Whereas the term 'chimney' includes any opening, vent, flue, conduit, outlet or any structure constructed or arranged from or through which air pollutants may emit, and any reference to a chimney which serves the whole or a part of the facilities though structurally separate from such facilities or building thereon.[379]

229. The 2014 Regulations require the owner or occupier of new premises to comply with limit values and technical standards specified therein, whereas owners of existing premises must comply with such values within five years from the date of the Regulations.[380] They are also required to notify the DG before carrying out the following: any change in operation of the premises; any work on any premises that may result in a source of emission; construct on any land, any building or premises designed or used for a purpose that may result in a new source of emission; make, cause or permit to be made any change of, to, or in any plant, machine, or equipment used or installed at the premises that causes a material change in the quantity or quality of emission from an existing source; or carrying out any changes or modifications to an existing air pollution control system.[381]

Under the 2014 Regulations, every premises are required to be equipped with an air pollution control system, and to operate and maintain it in accordance with sound engineering practice.[382] These premises are also required to be equipped with facilities to conduct performance monitoring of the air pollution control system, as well as to maintain records of manufacturing processes, and of maintenance and performance monitoring of the air pollution control system.[383]

In relation to opacity, any owner or occupier is not permitted to cause emission darker than shade No. 1 on the Ringelmann Chart or greater than 20% opacity when measured with a transmissometer. However, this imposition is not applicable where the emission is not darker than shade No. 2 on the Ringelmann Chart for an aggregate of less than five minutes in any period of one hour, or in cases of start-up conditions where the emission is not darker than shade No. 2 on the Ringelmann Chart. In addition, any premises that emits 2.5 kg/h of dust or more or has a potential to emit smoke darker than shade No. 2 on the Ringelmann Chart is required to install

378. Regulation 3 of the Environmental Quality (Clean Air) Regulations 2014.
379. Regulation 2 of the Environmental Quality (Clean Air) Regulations 2014.
380. Regulation 4 of the Environmental Quality (Clean Air) Regulations 2014.
381. Regulation 5 of the Environmental Quality (Clean Air) Regulations 2014.
382. Regulation 7 of the Environmental Quality (Clean Air) Regulations 2014.
383. Regulations 9 and 10 of the Environmental Quality (Clean Air) Regulations 2014.

and operate a transmissometer.[384] The term 'Ringelmann Chart' means the Ringelmann scale for grading the density of smoke published by the latest British Standard in the BS 2742 series or an equivalent Malaysian Standard, or any chart, recorder, indicator or device for the measurement of smoke density which is approved by the DG as the equivalent of the said Ringelmann scale.[385]

Measures to reduce emission applied by the 2014 Regulations are in accordance with the concept 'Best Available Techniques Economically Achievable' (BAT) and are applicable to premises involved in any activity listed in the First Schedule of the Regulations.[386] This concept is defined by the Regulations to mean 'the effective method in preventing pollution and, where that is not practicable, generally to reduce emissions into the air from the industrial activities and their impact on the environment as a whole'.[387] Activities that are subjected to BAT include fuel burning, including heat and power generation in boilers, combustion turbines or generator; production and processing of ferrous and non-ferrous metals; oil and gas industries; non-metallic industry in cement production; all stationary asphalt mixing plants in form of liquid, solid or gas; pulp and paper industry; chemical and petrochemical industry; production of pharmaceutical products, plant health products and biocides, and mixing and packaging of chemicals, pesticides, pharmaceutical products; solvent use in industry for dressing, printing, coating, degreasing, waterproofing, painting; and waste incinerators.[388]

For all activities and industries that require BAT, they are required to comply with the limit values and technical standards as specified in the Second and Third Schedules of the Regulations. For this purpose, emission is calculated in terms of mass of pollutant per volume of the waste gases (expressed as mg/m^3), whereas any fuel burning equipment that is rated to consume pulverized fuel or any solid fuel at 30 kg or more per hour or any liquid or gaseous matter at 15 kg or more per hour is required to comply with the limit values and technical standards as specified in the Second Schedule. The limit values and technical standards for emission of dioxin and furan are expressed as 2, 3, 7, 8 tetrachlorinated dibenzo-para-dioxin toxicity equivalent which is calculated by summing the concentration of each 2, 3, 7, 8 congener in the sample multiplied by the appropriate Toxicity Equivalency Factors (TEFs) as prescribed in the Fourth Schedule.[389] The sampling and analysis of pollutants shall be carried out in accordance with the Malaysian Standards MS 1596 or MS 1723 or the Methods published by the United States Environmental Protection Agency or any other standards as determined by the DG.[390]

The Regulations allow any owner or occupier of a premise to apply for a licence under section 22 of the EQA to contravene the acceptable conditions of emission of pollutants into the atmosphere in relation to limit values and technical standards, as well as opacity.[391]

---

384. Regulation 12 of the Environmental Quality (Clean Air) Regulations 2014.
385. Regulation 2 of the Environmental Quality (Clean Air) Regulations 2014.
386. Regulation 6 of the Environmental Quality (Clean Air) Regulations 2014.
387. Regulation 2 of the Environmental Quality (Clean Air) Regulations 2014.
388. First Schedule of the Environmental Quality (Clean Air) Regulations 2014.
389. Regulation 13 of the Environmental Quality (Clean Air) Regulations 2014.
390. Regulation 23 of the Environmental Quality (Clean Air) Regulations 2014.
391. Regulation 25 of the Environmental Quality (Clean Air) Regulations 2014.

Any owner or occupier of a premise is required to use the best practicable means to prevent the emission of hazardous substances and to render harmless and inoffensive those substances necessarily discharged.[392] The Regulations also require such owner or occupier to conduct periodic monitoring if required under the relevant Schedules,[393] and carry out continuous emission monitoring as specified in the Second and Third Schedules.[394] Any owner or occupier of a premises, which carries out any of the activities or industries specified in the First Schedule, shall for every calendar year submit to the DG an emission declaration.[395]

Other requirements imposed on any owner or occupier include the requirements to measure, take samples of, analyse, monitor, record and report any environmentally hazardous substances, air pollutants or emissions containing pollutants; comply with stricter limit values, parameters or equivalent technical measures than those prescribed in the Schedules; use certain types of fuel; or take any other action which the DG considers necessary.[396] Such requirements would apply if the DG is of the opinion that the prescribed conditions or standards will not adequately protect public health, safety or welfare, or the quality of the environment, due to the following factors:

- the accumulation or concentration of air pollutants in a certain area;
- the proximity of a residential area to the premises that is carrying out activities that discharges or is capable of discharging air pollutants into the atmosphere; or
- the instances where, based on the BAT, the prescribed conditions or standards under these Regulations will not be sufficient, have been exceeded or are expected to be exceeded.[397]

For the purpose of the Regulations, the term 'residential area' means an area designated as a residential zone having clearly demarcated boundaries as defined, which appears in the Gazette local plan prepared by the appropriate local planning authorities under Part III of the Town and Country Planning Act 1976, in the case of Sabah the Town and Country Planning Ordinance, and in the case of Sarawak the Sarawak Land Code or, in the absence of such Gazette local plan, a housing estate or an area situated within 1,000 m of the nearest dwelling.

In a situation where the DG is of the opinion that a failure in the operations of any premises, or any control equipment used on any premises, can cause an accumulation of air pollutants to such level so as to threaten public health, safety or welfare, or the quality of the environment, the DG may require the premises to do the following: to submit a comprehensive emergency response plan detailing out the equipment, chemicals and personnel requirement, as well as measures and steps to be taken by parties concerned in the event of such emergency; to install of necessary public warning or alert systems; to keep in adequate stock such equipment or

392. Regulation 15 of the Environmental Quality (Clean Air) Regulations 2014.
393. Regulation 16 of the Environmental Quality (Clean Air) Regulations 2014.
394. Regulation 17 of the Environmental Quality (Clean Air) Regulations 2014.
395. Regulation 18 of the Environmental Quality (Clean Air) Regulations 2014.
396. Regulation 22 of the Environmental Quality (Clean Air) Regulations 2014.
397. Subregulation (2) of Regulation 22 of the Environmental Quality (Clean Air) Regulations 2014.

chemicals as may be required in such emergency; and to comply with any other directions which the DG considers necessary in dealing with such emergency.[398]

The Regulations imposes a prohibition order in the event of any undesirable occurrence as specified in the Sixth Schedule and the DG is of the opinion that the continued operation of any premises or process in question should not be permitted in order to safeguard public health, safety or welfare. In such situation, the DG may by notice in writing issue an order to the owner or occupier of a premises prohibiting further operation of such premises or process absolutely or conditionally, or for such period as he may direct, or until remedial requirements as directed by him have been complied with.[399]

The combination of administrative and criminal sanctions is also being applied by the Regulations for ensuring compliance. In a situation where the DG is of the opinion that the circumstances surrounding a failure to comply with the requirements so warrant, he may issue a schedule of required actions to bring the owner or occupier of a premise into compliance within a fixed period of time. The schedule of required actions shall set interim standards which may reduce the levels of operation pending the installation of adequate control equipment and may establish a series of deadlines for the installation of specific control equipment. However, failure to comply with any of the conditions or deadlines specified shall render the owner or occupier liable to the penalty prescribed for the original violation.[400]

In the event that any person provides any information under these Regulations which he knows to be false or misleading, he shall be guilty of an offence and shall be liable to a fine not exceeding MYR 100,000 or to imprisonment for a term not exceeding two years or both.[401] Whereas general penalty imposed on any person contravening any provisions of these Regulations shall be guilty of an offence and shall be liable to a similar fine not exceeding MYR 100,000 or to imprisonment for a term not exceeding two years or both.[402]

§4. Mobile Air Pollution

230. The EQA 1974 controls the emission of air pollution from mobile sources that use either a diesel or a petrol engine, for regulating gaseous emissions and black smoke as discussed below. The Act also regulates the standard of fuel used in any internal combustion engine and in industrial plants. This is provided under the Environmental Quality (Control of Petrol and Diesel Properties) Regulations 2007[403] which require that fuel which is produced, stored, distributed, transported, supplied, sold or offered for sale[404] within Malaysia shall comply with specific standard of properties, namely the European emission standards of EUR 2 for both petrol and

398. Regulation 20 of the Environmental Quality (Clean Air) Regulations 2014.
399. Regulation 24 of the Environmental Quality (Clean Air) Regulations 2014.
400. Regulation 26 of the Environmental Quality (Clean Air) Regulations 2014.
401. Regulation 28 of the Environmental Quality (Clean Air) Regulations 2014.
402. Regulation 29 of the Environmental Quality (Clean Air) Regulations 2014.
403. P.U. (A) 145/2007.
404. Regulation 4(3) of the Environmental Quality (Control of Petrol from Diesel Properties) Regulations 2007, Am. P.U. (A) 278/2013.

diesel.[405] If the fuel supplier contravene this provision, he shall on conviction be liable to a fine not exceeding MYR 100,000 or imprisonment for a term not exceeding two years or both, and to a further fine not exceeding MYR 50,000 a day for every day that the offence is continued.[406] To determine the properties of the prescribed fuel, the representative samples of the fuel shall be collected according to American Society of Testing and Material D 4057.[407]

I. Diesel Engine

231. Under the EQA 1974, emission standards for mobile air pollution from motor vehicles are provided by the control of emission from diesel engines, under the Environmental Quality (Control of Emissions from Diesel Engines) Regulations 1996.[408] The Regulations control smoke emission from every motor vehicle irrespective of whether it is in use or stationary, or in any bus terminus, taxi stand or private premises or on any private road.[409] The maximum concentration of smoke from these vehicles is tested based on the Ringelmann Smoke Chart No. 2.[410]

232. The Regulations restrict the installation or replacing of engine systems[411] and require the assembler or manufacturer to conduct tests to verify the prescribed emission of pollutants standards.[412]

233. Emission standards of pollutants for a diesel engine are provided in the First Schedule of the Regulations, whereas emission standards of pollutants for new models of motor vehicles (on or after 1 January 1997) are provided in the Second Schedule.[413] For this purpose, 'new motor vehicle' means a motor vehicle imported directly into Malaysia as a completely built-up ('CBU') unit and for the first time registered and assigned a registration number by the Director for Road Transport on or after 1 January 1997; or a motor vehicle imported into Malaysia as a completely knocked down ('CKD') pack and was subsequently manufactured or assembled and

405. *See* First and Second Schedule of the Environmental Quality (Control of Petrol and Diesel Properties) Regulations 2007.
406. Regulation 4(4) of the Environmental Quality (Control of Petrol and Diesel Properties) Regulations 2007.
407. Regulation 6 of the Environmental Quality (Control of Petrol and Diesel Properties) Regulations 2007.
408. P.U. (A) 429/96.
409. Regulation 9 of the Environmental Quality (Control of Emissions from Diesel Engines) Regulations 1996.
410. Regulation 10 of the Environmental Quality (Control of Emissions from Diesel Engines) Regulations 1996.
411. Regulation 4 of the Environmental Quality (Control of Emissions from Diesel Engines) Regulations 1996.
412. Regulation 7 of the Environmental Quality (Control of Emissions from Diesel Engines) Regulations 1996.
413. Regulation 4 of the Environmental Quality (Control of Emissions from Diesel Engines) Regulations 1996.

for the first time registered and assigned a registration number by the Director for Road Transport on or after 1 January 1997.[414]

For the First Schedule, the emission standard for a diesel engine tested at a steady speed is measured by the Economic Commission for Europe ('ECE') Regulation No. 24.03 annexed to the United Nations Agreement which was concluded at Geneva on 20 March 1958 Concerning the Adoption of Uniform Conditions of Approval and Reciprocal Recognition of Approval for Motor Vehicle Equipment and Parts. Whereas for a heavy-duty diesel engine for a vehicle with a Gross Vehicle Weight ('GVW') of over 3.5 tonnes, it is measured by the ECE Regulation No. 49 annexed to the United Nations Agreement which was concluded at Geneva on 20 March 1958 Concerning the Adoption of Uniform Conditions of Approval and Reciprocal Recognition of Approval for Motor Vehicle Equipment and Parts. In addition, for a diesel engine with a GVW not exceeding 3.5 tonnes, it is measured by the ECE Regulation No. 15 annexed to the United Nations Agreement which was concluded at Geneva on 20 March 1958 Concerning the Adoption of Uniform Conditions of Approval and Reciprocal Recognition of Approval for Motor Vehicle Equipment and Parts.

Under the Second Schedule, for a diesel engine having a total mass exceeding 3.5 tonnes, emission is measured by the ECE Regulation No. 49.02 annexed to the United Nations Agreement which was concluded at Geneva on 20 March 1958 Concerning the Adoption of Uniform Conditions of Approval and Reciprocal Recognition of Approval for Motor Vehicle Equipment and Parts. For a diesel engine having a total mass not exceeding 3.5 tonnes, the emission is measured by the Council Directive 93/59/EEC of 28 June 1993 amending Directive 70/220/EEC on the approximation of the laws of the Member States relating to measures to be taken against air pollution by emission from motor vehicles.

234. Under Regulation 19, these standards may be contravened through the grant of licence from the DG if he is satisfied that:

- the motor vehicle is to be used for assessing the durability or emission performance of the motor vehicle, or the motor vehicle is to be used for rallying, with the prior written approval of the DG;
- the motor vehicle has been indented from the manufacturer and consigned for assembly in Malaysia or is already assembled or manufactured prior to the date of the coming into force of the Regulations and has not at any time been registered under the Road Transport Act 1987;[415]
- the motor vehicle is intended for military, combat or tactical purposes; or
- the motor vehicle is in transit through Malaysia.

414. Regulation 2 of the Environmental Quality (Control of Emissions from Diesel Engines) Regulations 1996.
415. Act 333.

II. Petrol Engine

235. The motor vehicle emission from petrol engines is regulated by the Environmental Quality (Control of Emission from Petrol Engines) Regulations 1996.[416] Restrictions and prohibitions under these Regulations are similar to those of the Environmental Quality (Control of Emissions from Diesel Engines) Regulations 1996.

236. Emission standards under the Environmental Quality (Control of Emission from Petrol Engines) Regulations 1996 are as follows:

- First Schedule: Emission Standard of pollutants for the emission from petrol engines;
- Second Schedule: Emission standard of pollutants for new models of motor vehicles (on or after 1 January 1997);
- Third Schedule: Emission standard of pollutants for new models of motor vehicles (on or after 1 January 2000);
- Fourth Schedules: Emission standards for petrol engines in use; and
- Fifth Schedule: Emission test for petrol engines in use.

Vehicles having an engine capacity of 700 cm^3 and below and 1,020 kg and below shall comply with the emission standard of pollutants as prescribed in the First Schedule, whereas emission standard of pollutants for new models of motor vehicles (on or after 1 January 1997) is provided in the Second Schedule. On or after 1 January 2000, any new model of motor vehicle shall comply with the emission standard of pollutants as prescribed in the Third Schedule.[417]

For the Regulations, 'new motor vehicle' means a motor vehicle imported directly into Malaysia as a CBU unit and for the first time registered and assigned a registration number by the Director for Road Transport on or after 1 January 1997; or a motor vehicle imported into Malaysia as a CKD pack and subsequently manufactured or assembled and for the first time registered and assigned a registration number by the Director for Road Transport on or after 1 January 1997.[418]

Under the First Schedule, emission of the gaseous pollutants of Carbon Monoxide and the combination of Hydrocarbons and Nitrogen Oxides is measured by the ECE regulation No. 15.04 annexed to the United Nations Agreement which was concluded at Geneva on 20 March 1958 Concerning the Adoption of Uniform Conditions of Approval and Reciprocal Recognition of Approval for Motor Vehicle Equipment and Parts.

Emission Standard of Pollutant for New Models of Motor Vehicles (on or after 1 January 1997) in the Second Schedule for a petrol engine with a total mass less than 2.5 tonnes is measured by the Council Directive 91/441/EEC of 26 June 1991,

---

416. P.U. (A) 543/96.
417. Regulation 4 of the Environmental Quality (Control of Emissions from Diesel Engines) Regulations 1996.
418. Regulation 2 of the Environmental Quality (Control of Emissions from Petrol Engines) Regulations 1996.

amending Directive 70/220/EEC on the approximation of the Laws of the Members States relating to Measures to be Taken Against Air Pollution by Emissions from Motor Vehicle. Whereas for a petrol engine used for carrying goods and having a maximum weight not exceeding 3.5 tonnes, it is measured by the Council Directive 93/59/EEC of 28 June 1993 amending Directive 70/220/EEC on the approximation of the Laws of the Members States relating to Measures to be Taken Against Air Pollution by Emissions from Motor Vehicle.

For the Third Schedule, Emission Standard of Pollutant for New Models of Motor Vehicles on or after 1 January 1997 for a petrol engine with a total mass less than 2.5 tonnes, is measured by the Directive 94/12/EEC of The European Parliament and the Council of 23 March 1994 relating to Measures to be Taken Against Air Pollution by Emission from Motor Vehicles and amending Directive 70/220/EEC. Whereas for a motor vehicle used for carrying goods and having a maximum weight not exceeding 3.5 tonnes, it is measured by The Council Directive 93/59/EEC of 28 June 1993 amending Directive 70/220/EEC on the approximation of the Member States Relating to Measures to be Taken Against Air Emission from Motor Vehicle.

237. Under Regulation 19, these standards may be contravened through the grant of a licence from the DG if he is satisfied that:

- the motor vehicle is to be used solely for assessing the durability or emission performance of the motor vehicle, or the motor vehicle is to be used for rallying with the prior written approval of the DG;
- the motor vehicle has been indented from the manufacturer and consigned for assembly in Malaysia or is already assembled or manufactured prior to the date of coming into force of these Regulations and has not at any time been registered under the Road Transport Act 1987;
- the motor vehicle is intended for military, combat or tactical purposes; or
- the motor vehicle is in transit through Malaysia.

III. Lead

238. For the control of lead concentration in motor gasoline, the Environmental Quality (Control of Lead Concentration in Motor Gasoline) Regulations 1985[419] provide for restrictions on the following unless licensed:[420]

- import or manufacture of any motor gasoline which contains lead or lead compounds expressed as lead in excess of 0.40 gram per litre;[421]

419. P.U. (A) 296/85.
420. Regulation 11 of the Environmental Quality (Control of Lead Concentration in Motor Gasoline) Regulations 1985.
421. Regulation 3 of the Environmental Quality (Control of Lead Concentration in Motor Gasoline) Regulations 1985.

– possession, offer or exhibit for sale, sale, delivery for use or exchange for use of any motor gasoline which contains lead or lead compounds in excess of 0.40 gram per litre;[422] or
– import, manufacture, possession, offering or exhibition for sale, sale, delivery for use or exchange for use of any motor gasoline which contains lead or lead compounds in excess of 0.15 gram per litre.[423]

239. Offences committed against any of the restrictions above can be compounded by the DG.[424]

IV. Motorcycles

240. Another form of air-pollution-emission control by the EQA 1974 is that of motorcycles under the Environmental Quality (Control of Emission from Motorcycles) Regulations 2003.[425]

241. The gaseous emission limit for motorcycles in the Regulations is provided in the Second Schedule. The standard is based on specific categories,[426] whether it is imported or locally manufactured or assembled; a new model[427] or a current model; and engine type.[428] Under the Regulations, 'new model' means any model of motorcycle manufactured or assembled after 1 January 2004 and equipped with an engine type which was designed after 1 January 2004; whereas 'current model' means any model of motorcycle manufactured or assembled after 1 January 2004 and equipped with an engine type which was designed on or before 1 January 2004.[429]

Under the Regulations, a manufacturer of any current or new model must ensure that the gaseous emission limit of such model in a type approval test[430] complies with the gaseous emission limit prescribed in the Second Schedule.[431] Any person who intends to import any current or new model is also required to submit a report to the DG on the type approval test conducted on such model, as prescribed in the

422. Regulation 4 of the Environmental Quality (Control of Lead Concentration in Motor Gasoline) Regulations 1985.
423. Regulation 5 of the Environmental Quality (Control of Lead Concentration in Motor Gasoline) Regulations 1985.
424. Regulation 13 of the Environmental Quality (Control of Lead Concentration in Motor Gasoline) Regulations 1985.
425. P.U. (A) 464/2003.
426. First Schedule of the Environmental Quality (Control of Emission from Motorcycles) Regulations 2003.
427. *See* the definition of 'new model' in Regulation 2 of the Environmental Quality (Control of Emission from Motorcycles) Regulations 2003.
428. Engine types with two and four stroke.
429. Regulation2 of the Environmental Quality (Control of Emission from Motorcycles) Regulations 2003.
430. 'Type approval test' is a test conducted by the manufacturer as provided in Regulation 7 of the Environmental Quality (Control of Emission from Motorcycles) Regulations 2003.
431. Regulation 5(1) of the Environmental Quality (Control of Emission from Motorcycles) Regulations 2003.

Second Schedule.[432] Any manufacturer who fails to comply with these requirements or fabricates the test commits an offence and may be liable to a fine not exceeding MYR 100,000 or to imprisonment not exceeding five years, or both.[433] For verifying the gaseous emission limits for motorcycle engines as prescribed in the First Schedule, the manufacturer shall conduct type approval gaseous emission tests for every current and new model of motorcycles in accordance with the European Economic Committee ('EEC') Council Directive 97/24/EC of 17 June 1997.[434]

242. Idling gaseous emission limits and tests for motorcycle engines are provided in the Fourth and Fifth Schedules respectively. Any registered owner or rider of any motorcycle in use, the engine type of which is as prescribed in the First Schedule, must ensure that such motorcycles (in use) do not emit gaseous pollutant exceeding the emission limit as prescribed in the Fourth Schedule.[435] Any person who contravenes the provision commits an offence and may be liable to a fine not exceeding MYR 5,000.[436] A person who obstructs any authorized officer conducting an idling gaseous emission test, commits an offence and may be liable to a fine not exceeding MYR 10,000 or to imprisonment not exceeding two years, or both.[437]

243. Regulation 11 prohibits any person riding a motorcycle from allowing the engine of such motorcycle to run while the motorcycle is stationary for more than three minutes in an enclosed or a partially enclosed public place, or parking area or any terminus. Any person who contravenes this provision commits an offence and may be liable to a fine not exceeding MYR 2,000.

244. A contravention licence of acceptable conditions may be granted by the DG for motorcycle emissions for assessing the durability or emission performance of such motorcycles.[438]

---

432. Regulation 5(2) of the Environmental Quality (Control of Emission from Motorcycles) Regulations 2003.
433. Regulations 5(4) and 7(6) of the Environmental Quality (Control of Emission from Motorcycles) Regulations 2003.
434. Regulation 7 of the Environmental Quality (Control of Emission from Motorcycles) Regulations 2003.
435. Regulation 10(1) of the Environmental Quality (Control of Emission from Motorcycles) Regulations 2003.
436. Regulation 10(2) of the Environmental Quality (Control of Emission from Motorcycles) Regulations 2003.
437. Regulation 10(6) of the Environmental Quality (Control of Emission from Motorcycles) Regulations 2003.
438. Regulation 12 of the Environmental Quality (Control of Emission from Motorcycles) Regulations 2003.

§5. PROHIBITION OF OPEN BURNING

245. Another source of air pollution regulated by the EQA 1974, is that involving open burning activities. Section 29A of the Act strictly prohibits any person from causing open burning on any premises, including any land, and imposes the punishment of a fine up to MYR 500,000, and a jail term for five years, or both.

246. Any offence of open burning under section 29A or 29B of the Act is also a compoundable offence as provided by the Environmental Quality (Compounding of Offences) (Open Burning) Rules 2000.[439]

247. Investigation of offence under section 29A is dealt with under the Environmental Quality (Delegation of Powers) (Investigation of Open Burning) Order 2000.[440] Under this Order, the DG is empowered to delegate the powers relating to open burning to the following persons:[441]

- any Superintendent, Probationary Superintendent, Senior Assistant Superintendent, Assistant Probationary Superintendent, Fire Officer Grade I, Fire Officer Grade II and Fire Officer Grade III of the Fire And Rescue Department;
- any police officer in charge of any police station; Any Medical Officer, State Health Director, State Public Health Deputy Director, District Health Officer, Public Health Engineer and Health Inspector of the Ministry of Health;
- any Health Officer, Environment Officer, Enforcement Officer, Health Inspector, Assistant Enforcement Officer, Assistant Public Health Officer, Cleansing Supervisor, City Officer, Town Officer and Assistant Enforcer of any Town Council, City Council or District Council;
- the Director, Deputy Director, Medical and Health Officer, Environment Officer, Senior Health Inspector and Health Inspector of the Health Department of Dewan Bandaraya Kuala Lumpur;
- the Director, Deputy Director, Assistant Director and City Cleansing Superintendent of the City Cleansing Control Department of Dewan Bandaraya Kuala Lumpur;
- the Director, Deputy Director, Senior Assistant Director, Assistant Director, Superintendent, Deputy Superintendent, Chief Inspector, Inspector, Assistant Inspector, Sarjan Major and Sarjan of the Enforcement Directorate of Dewan Bandaraya Kuala Lumpur; The Deputy Director II, Building Surveyor, Engineer, Senior Technician, Technician, Senior Assistant Technician and Assistant Technician of the Building Control Division of Dewan Bandaraya Kuala Lumpur; and
- the Deputy Secretary I, Town Council Officer, Assistant Enforcement Officer and Assistant Enforcer of the Majlis Perbandaran Labuan.

---

439. P.U. (A) 310/2000.
440. P.U. (A) 311/2000.
441. *See* Schedule of the Environmental Quality (Delegation of Powers) (Investigation of Open Burning) Order 2000.

248. In the case of the prohibition of open burning under section 29A, there are some exceptions to the general rules where certain activities, known as 'declared activities' are excluded from the control of this section.[442] These are provided in the Environmental Quality (Declared Activities) (Open Burning) Order 2003.[443]

The Order contains fifteen instances deemed to be declared activities and exempted from the prohibition of section 29A, namely:[444]

- the burning of any diseased plant and noxious plant and agricultural equipment relating to the diseased plant and noxious plant pursuant to a notice or direction under the Plant Quarantine Act 1976;
- the burning of solid or liquid fuels or structures in the course of carrying out research into the causes and control of fires, or for the training of any Fire Officer, Auxiliary Fire Officer, or any personnel in the fire brigades of any private organization, educational institution or voluntary organization or voluntary fire brigades established under the Fire Services Act 1988;
- the burning of plant from a land clearing for the cultivation of food crops or cash crops for the purposes of shifting cultivation;
- the burning of paddy stalks prior to replanting;
- the burning of sugar cane leaves prior to harvesting in an area that does not exceed 20 ha during the harvesting period;
- the burning of plants for land clearing for planting or replanting of any plant crops by smallholders in an area that does not exceed 2 ha/day;
- the burning of pineapple stumps prior to replanting, which is dry prior to burning, in an area that does not exceed 6 ha/day;
- cremation;
- camp fire which is not carried out at any peat soil area;
- outdoor grills, barbecues or fireplaces for the preparation of food which is not carried out at any peat soil area;
- the burning of agricultural plant for land clearing for planting or replanting of plant crops by subsistence farmers in rural areas which is not carried out at any peat soil area;
- the burning of leaves, tree branches and yard trimmings in villages in rural areas which is not carried out at any peat soil area; and
- the burning of flammable gases where the industrial flare is properly operated.

According to the Order, exceptions to open burning of those fifteen activities can be executed only if they are carried out in accordance with the conditions specified by the Order. There are specific conditions imposed on each of the declared activities before the burning takes place. They include the requirement to notify the Director General of the Department of Environment in writing before the burning is carried out; the potential content of the material to be burned; the circumstances of

442. *See* s. 29AA of the Environmental Quality Act 1974.
443. P.U. (A) 406/2003.
444. Order 3 of the Environmental Quality (Declared Activities) (Open Burning) Order 2003.

combustible material generation; the weather condition; the time of the day permitted; type of soil on which the open burning is to be carried out; and prevention of nuisance. The Order prohibits any type of open burning on peat soil.

249. However, for the protection of air quality, the Department of Environment has the right to withdraw this exemption during hazy spells so as to prevent further degradation of environmental quality from the smoke emitted from the open burning activities.[445]

§6. Criminal Provision on Air Pollution

250. Criminal sanction for air pollution is provided in section 22 of the EQA 1974. This section restricts any person from emitting or discharging any waste into the air unless licensed. The restriction also covers the act of burning any waste.[446] Those found guilty may be liable to a fine up to MYR 100,000, five years imprisonment, or both.[447]

251. It is also an offence for any person to emit dark smoke, dust or gases in contravention of Regulations 12 and 13 of the Environmental Quality (Clean Air) Regulations 2014 without a licence issued under section 22(1).[448] The application for such licence need to be accompanied by a report on emission of pollutants characterization; and the licence fee amounting to MYR 1,000.[449]

252. The Regulations also impose a fine not exceeding MYR 100,000 or to imprisonment for a term not exceeding two years or both to any person who provides false or misleading information under these Regulations.[450] In addition, penalty imposed on any person who contravenes or fails to comply with any provisions of the Regulations is a fine not exceeding MYR 100,000 or to imprisonment for a term not exceeding two years or both.[451]

§7. Other Legislation

253. The Occupational Safety and Health Act 1994[452] contains provisions on air pollution control. One of its Regulations, the Occupational Health and Safety (Use and Standard of Exposure of Chemicals Hazardous to Health) Regulations 2000,[453]

445. Clause (2) of s. 29AA of the Environmental Quality Act 1974.
446. Clause (2)(c) of s. 22 of the Environmental Quality Act 1974.
447. Section 22(3) of the Environmental Quality Act 1974.
448. Regulation 25 of the Environmental Quality (Clean Air) Regulations 2014.
449. Regulation 27 of the Environmental Quality (Clean Air) Regulations 2014.
450. Regulation 28 of the Environmental Quality (Clean Air) Regulations 2014.
451. Regulation 29 of the Environmental Quality (Clean Air) Regulations 2014.
452. Act 514.
453. P.U. (A) 131/2000.

provide for a list of chemicals deemed hazardous to workers and the permitted limits on the chemicals' airborne concentration. The Regulations apply to all places of work which are within the jurisdiction of the Act where chemicals hazardous to health are used.[454]

254. The Road Transport Act 1987[455] is another provision on air pollution control under the Motor Vehicle (Control of Smoke and Gas Emission) (Revocation) Rules 1996.[456] These Rules were enacted by virtue of section 66 of the Act, and they empower the Minister to control, in connection with the use of motor vehicles, the emission of smoke, oily substances, ashes, water, steam, visible vapour, noxious fumes, sparks, cinders, gas or grit. The Rules were introduced to control excessive black smoke from diesel vehicles.

255. Under the National Forestry Act 1984, the scope on the regulation of forest burning is confined to permanent reserved forest only. Section 82 of the Act states that no person shall kindle, keep or carry any fire, or leave any fire burning, within a permanent reserved forest in such a manner as to endanger such reserved forest. Penalty imposed on any person who contravenes this section is a fine not exceeding RM 50,000 or to imprisonment for a term not exceeding five years or both.

256. Another statute, the Food Act 1983,[457] gazetted the Control of Tobacco Product Regulations 2004[458] to control air pollution from cigarette smoke in public places.[459]

257. Regulation 11 of the Control of Tobacco Product Regulations 2004 prohibits any person from smoking at the following places, namely in any: entertainment centre or theatre, except any pub, discotheque, night club or casino; hospital or clinic; public lift or toilet; air-conditioned eating place or shop; public vehicle or public transport terminal; building specified by the Minister; airport; government premises; area which is used for any assembly activity in a building other than private or residential building; educational institution or a higher educational institution; nursery; school bus; floor with a service counter in the building; shopping complex; petrol station; stadium, sports complex, fitness centre or gymnasium; building or public place which is used for religious purposes; library; or internet café. The penalty imposed for those who contravene this provision is a fine not exceeding MYR 10,000 or imprisonment for a term not exceeding two years.

258. Under Regulation 12, the proprietor or occupier of the premises or vehicles referred to in Regulation 11 must display a sign as specified in the Third Schedule

454. Regulation 1 of the Occupational Health and Safety (Use and Standard of Exposure of Chemicals Hazardous to Health) Regulations.
455. Act 333.
456. P.U. (A) 421/96, introduced to revoke the Motor Vehicles (Control of Smoke and Gas Emission) Rules 1977, P.U. (A) 414/1977.
457. Act 281.
458. P.U. (A) 324/2004.
459. These Regulations revoked the Control of Tobacco Product Regulations 1993, P.U. (A) 383/ 1993.

with regard to the prohibition of smoking at any conspicuous part of the premises or vehicle. Those who contravene this provision commit an offence and may be liable to a fine not exceeding MYR 3,000 or to imprisonment for a term not exceeding six months.[460]

460. Regulation 12(2) of the Control of Tobacco Product Regulations 2004.

Chapter 3. Water Pollution

§1. Introduction

259. The significance of rivers in Malaysia in the past and present is immense. Currently, rivers are mostly relied on as the main source of water supply for domestic, agricultural and industrial consumption, besides being used for other purposes, such as fishing, transportation, hydroelectric power and recreation. Besides rivers, other types of inland waters in Malaysia include waterfalls, lakes and dams, as well as groundwater.[461]

260. Malaysia receives an annual average of 990 cubic billion metres of rainfall, of which 360 billion returns to the atmosphere through the process of evapotranspiration, 566 billion appears as surface runoff and the remaining 64 billion seeps into groundwater reservoirs. At the moment, river systems as a whole contribute about 97% of the source of raw water supply in the country. Groundwater makes up less than 10% of the total amount of water resources in Malaysia and is not relied upon as the main source of water supply.[462]

261. The growing Malaysian population, and the rapid agricultural and economic development have greatly increased the demand for water. However, the quality of water in these rivers is fast deteriorating, evidently due to pollution.

262. Active pollution of inland waters in Malaysia can be traced back to the early days of the twentieth century with the opening of vast stretches of land for rubber estates causing massive soil erosion and siltation of river channels. Following independence in 1957 and until today, aggressive economic development activities and rapid growth of urbanization and industrialization further threaten the quality of inland waters. Other sources of water pollution include household waste, sewage and discharge from animal husbandry.[463]

§2. The Constitution

263. The competence of the federal and state governments to legislate regarding inland water in Malaysia is provided in the Ninth Schedule of the Federal Constitution.

461. *See* Drainage & Irrigation Dept. Malay., *Rivers of Malaysia* (Design Dimension 1992).
462. Sahabat Alam, Malaysia, *Malaysian Environmental Alert 2001* 50–51 (Sahabat Alam Malay. 2001).
463. *See* Kementerian Sumber Asli dan Alam Sekitar Malaysia, *Environmental Quality Report 2016* (Jabatan Alam Sekitar 2016).

264. Generally, water and rivers come under the jurisdiction of states, as provided by List II State List of the Constitution,[464] allowing states to enact laws on the matter. However, these laws apply only for rivers wholly within one state.

265. Under List I Federal List, the federal government has jurisdiction over rivers and canals, except those wholly within one state, or regulated by an agreement between all the states concerned.[465] Matters pertaining to water supplies and services come under List III, Concurrent List.[466] Thus, both the federal and state governments can make laws on these matters.

§3. Institutional Framework

266. Several agencies have been established to manage various aspects of inland water including the enforcement of related laws, one of which is the Department of Environment, under the Ministry of Environment and Water.[467]

267. Under this Department, the pollution control strategy is implemented through the two principal tasks of river pollution prevention and a water quality programme. Under these tasks, the Department monitors the quality of a number of major rivers in Malaysia by collecting samples from the various monitoring sites. The assessment of water quality is carried out in terms of the physical, biological and chemical characteristics of the water body. From this programme, the Department of Environment is able to provide data about the current state of river water quality in Malaysia, including the number of polluted or clean rivers, as well as the types of pollutants contained in polluted rivers.[468]

268. Another relevant agency is the Department of Drainage and Irrigation, which is also under the Ministry of Environment and Water.[469] This Department is mainly responsible for irrigation, drainage, and construction of public water supply networks, and their supervision, operation and maintenance.

269. Other related agencies include the local government, which is empowered by its legislations and by-laws to control inland water pollution within its locality.

---

464. Item 6(c) of List II State List.
465. Item 11(b) of List I Federal List.
466. Item 9(D) List III Concurrent List.
467. *See* the official website at https://www.doe.gov.my/portalv1/en/.
468. *See* Sharifah Zubaidah & Maizatun Mustafa, *Preventing Pollution in Malaysian Rivers: A Legal and Institutional Perspective*, a paper presented at the *5th Asia Law Institute Conference* (U. Sing. 2008).
469. *See* the official website at https://www.water.gov.my/.

§4. WATER QUALITY

I. Water Quality Index

270. Malaysia has a national monitoring network that was established by the Department of Environment since 1978, which aims to monitor and detect changes in Malaysian river water quality and to identify pollution sources.

271. Water samples are collected at regular intervals from designated stations for in situ and laboratory analysis to determine their physicochemical and biological characteristics. This enables water quality levels violating ambient standards for specific parameters to be reported in real time to the Department of Environment, and immediate inspection will be then be conducted at the suspected sites.

272. The Department of Environment established the Water Quality Index (WQI) to evaluate the status of the river water quality. It consists of six parameters, namely: Dissolved Oxygen, Biochemical Oxygen Demand, Chemical Oxygen Demand, Ammoniacal Nitrogen, Suspended Solids and pH. The WQI also serves as a basis for environmental assessment of a watercourse in relation to pollution load categorization and designation of classes of beneficial uses.[470]

273. The WQI is used to monitor the water quality of the rivers in Malaysia, based on the classification of clean (WQI = 90–100), slightly polluted (WQI = 70–80) and polluted (WQI = 10–60) status. In 2006, a total of 1,064 water quality monitoring stations located within 146 river basins were monitored. Out of these 1,064 monitoring stations, 619 (58%) were found to be clean, 359 (34%) slightly polluted and 86 (8%) polluted.[471]

II. Interim National Water Quality Standards

274. The Department of Environment also categorizes rivers into classes of beneficial uses under the Interim National Water Quality Standards for Malaysia.[472] This system is a preliminary means of assessing a river for compliance with the standards set by the WQI together with a total of seventy-one other chemical and biological parameters to be measured.[473]

470. Kementerian Sumber Asli dan Alam Sekitar Malaysia, *Environmental Quality Report 2012* 28 (Jabatan Alam Sekitar 2012).
471. *Ibid.*, 28–32.
472. *Ibid.*, 28
473. *Ibid.*, 28.

275. The Interim National Water Quality Standards assigns the river to one of five classes, based on usages such as domestic water supply, fisheries and aquaculture, irrigation, livestock, and recreation, each with its own set of biological, chemical and physical parameters. They are as follows:[474]

- Class I: conservation of natural environment;
- Class IIA: conventional treatment required;
- Class IIB: recreational use with body contact;
- Class III: extensive treatment required;
- Class IV: irrigation; and
- Class V: none of the above.

III. Drinking Water Standards

276. In Malaysia, the Ministry of Health is given the responsibility to ensure the quality and safety of all drinking water, and it is the leading agency for water quality monitoring and surveillance. This is done through a programme known as the National Drinking Water Quality Surveillance Programme.[475] The main functions of the programme are to monitor and survey treated water quality and safety, and to protect and control raw water sources and supplies.

277. In 1983, the Ministry of Health established the National Drinking Water Quality Standards which is based on the World Health Organization guidelines. The standards stipulate limits for physical, chemical, microbiological and radiological parameters and serves as the guideline for water operators on the quality of water supplied to consumers.

278. Compliance with the said standards is mandatory for all private water suppliers as provided in Regulation 394 of the Food Regulations 1985[476] on the standard for wholesome water, ice or steam. This regulation stipulates that water shall be clean and free from contamination, objectionable taste and odour, and shall comply with the standard as prescribed in the Twenty-Fifth Schedule. The Twenty-Fifth Schedule set up specific standards for water, including its physical, chemical, and bacteriological content and radioactivity.

474. *Ibid.*, 28.
475. This Programme is undertaken by the Engineering Department of the Ministry of Health Malaysia. *See* further information provided at the official website at http://kmam.moh.gov.my, January 2019.
476. Enacted under the Food Act 1983, Act 281.

§5. The Environmental Quality Act 1974

279. There are four types of inland water pollutants regulated by the EQA 1974 through criminal sanction. They are the discharge of effluent from the palm oil[477] industry, from rubber industries,[478] from other industries and the discharge of sewage.[479]

280. The sanction is stipulated in section 25 of the EQA 1974. Under this section, a person is said to be guilty of an offence if he emits, discharges or deposits any environmentally hazardous substance, pollutant or wastes into any inland waters in contravention of the acceptable conditions specified in section 21, unless licensed.[480]

281. Under subsection (2) of section 25, a person is deemed to discharge wastes into inland waters if he does any of the following:

- places any waste in or on any waters or in a place where it may gain access to any waters;
- places any waste in a position where it falls, descends, drains, evaporates, is washed, is blown or percolated or is likely to fall, descend, drain, evaporate or be washed, be blown or percolated into any waters, or knowingly or through his negligence, whether directly or indirectly, causes or permits any wastes to be placed in such a position; or
- causes the temperature of the receiving waters to be raised or lowered by more than the prescribed limits.

282. Under section 25(3), those who are found guilty of the offence may be subjected to a fine not exceeding MYR 100,000 or imprisonment for a period not exceeding five years, or both. A further fine not exceeding MYR 1,000 a day may also be imposed for every day that the offence is continued after a notice from the DG requiring him to cease the act, has been served upon him.

477. The Environmental Quality (Prescribed Premises) (Crude Palm Oil) Regulations 1977.
478. The Environmental Quality (Prescribed Premises) (Raw Natural Rubber) Regulations 1978.
479. The Environmental Quality (Sewage) Regulations 2009; and the Environmental Quality (Industrial Effluent) Regulations 2009.
480. *See* Maizatun Mustafa, *River and Water Pollution: Are Our Laws Adequate?* (1997) *Infoline* November/December; and Maizatun Mustafa, *Legal Approach towards Water Resources Protection and Pollution Control in Malaysia*, in *Water Environmental Planning* (Alias Abdullah et al. eds, Intl. Islamic U. Malay. 2004).

§6. Other Legislation

I. Water Act 1920

283. The Waters Act 1920 is considered to be the earliest legislation in Malaysia pertaining to inland water.[481] This Act was enacted by the federal legislature in accordance with Article 76(3) of the Constitution, which allows any federal law to come into operation in any state, provided that it has been adopted by the state to become state law, and may thus be amended or repealed by the state legislature. This Act applies to the states of Negeri Sembilan, Pahang, Perak, Selangor, Malacca, Penang and Federal Territory.[482]

284. The relevant state laws enacted based on the Waters Act 1920 are as follows:

- the Negeri Sembilan Waters Enactment 1971;[483]
- the Pahang Waters Enactment 1985;[484]
- the Perak Waters Enactment 1973;[485]
- the Selangor Enactment 1971;[486]
- the Malacca Waters Enactment 1966;[487]
- the Penang Waters Enactment 1967;[488] and
- the Federal Territory Waters Act 1974.[489]

285. The main objective of the Waters Act 1920 is to control rivers and streams including river conservation and pollution control. Under this Act, 'rivers' are defined to include a tributary of a river and any other stream or natural watercourse; and any canal declared by the Minister.[490]

286. The prohibition of the pollution of rivers is provided for in section 7A which prohibits any person from polluting any rivers[491] unless he is authorized by any written law or is issued with a licence by the Commissioner or State Authority. The person is deemed to have caused pollution if he entered or discharged into any river the following:

- any poisonous, noxious or polluting matter;

481. Act 418 (Revised 1989).
482. Section 1(2) of the Waters Act 1920.
483. No. 12 of 1971.
484. No. 8 of 1985.
485. No. 11 of 1973.
486. No. 11 of 1971.
487. No. 5 of 1966.
488. No. 4 of 1967.
489. P.U. (A) 66/1974.
490. Section 2 of the Waters Act 1920.
491. For the purpose of s. 7A, 'river' shall be deemed to further include any inland water; any subterranean water resource; and any water of any estuary or sea adjacent to the coast.

– any matter which, by virtue of its temperature, chemical or biological content, or its effect in discolouring the waters, makes such water difficult to treat; or
– oil of any nature, used, waste or otherwise.

287. This section further provides that, whenever any such entry or discharge has been made, the owner or occupier of the property from which such entry or discharge originates shall, in the absence of proof to the contrary, be presumed to have made the discharge. Only the states of Perak, Melaka and Negeri Sembilan provide a penalty for the contravention of this section, which amounts to a fine of MYR 2,000 for the state of Perak, and MYR 10,000 for the states of Malacca and Negeri Sembilan.

II. Water Services Industry Act 2006

288. Another statute that provides for penalties in cases of water pollution is the Water Services Industry Act 2006.[492]

289. This Act is a federal law and enacted to regulate water supply services and sewerage service to Peninsular Malaysia. It is made pursuant to Articles 74(1) and 80(2) of the Federal Constitution, and it confers executive authority on the Federation for matters relating to water supply systems and water supply services.

290. This Act applies to any 'watercourse' which includes 'rivers, streams and creek including any tributary, distributary or artificial deviation thereof, seas, lakes, groundwater, dams, reservoirs, ditches, drains and passages, other than pipes, through which water flows for the supply of water to any premises'.[493]

291. Section 121 of the Act creates offences with regard to the contamination, or acts causing the contamination, of any watercourse or the water supply system, with the intention to cause death, or with the knowledge that the act would be likely to cause death or endanger a person's life. The punishment for such offences includes death, jail up to twenty years or whipping. If the act does not result in death, but causes the water supply system to contain radioactive or toxic substances, then the punishment is jail up to ten years and fine up to MYR 500,000, or whipping, or all three.

292. Under section 122, any person may also be held liable for committing certain acts such as negligently damaging any part of a public water supply system, or throwing any rubbish into any part of a public water supply system. The sanction imposed for such offence may be a fine up to MYR 50,000, jail for up to six months, or both. When convicted under section 122, apart from having to pay the fine, the person may also be required to pay compensation to the licensee for the damage caused, as provided in section 88.

492. Act 655.
493. Section 2 of the Water Services Industry Act 2006.

III. Drainage Works Act 1954

293. Drainage Areas and Irrigation Areas are areas within the jurisdiction of the Drainage and Irrigation Department, under the Ministry of Environment and Water as provided in the Drainage Works Act 1954.[494] The main objective of this Act is to lay down the rules under which the drainage and irrigated areas will be established for agriculture purposes. The Act concerns the engineering aspects of the operation and maintenance of drainage in a district.

294. The Act defines 'drainage works' as 'the construction and maintenance of drains and water courses, embankments, culverts, sluices, water gates, access paths in drainage reserves and other similar works'.

295. There are several provisions under this Act that are relevant to inland water pollution. However, its provisions are applicable only if such inland water is gazetted to be within the drainage area or irrigation area. Section 11 empowers the state ruler to take action against any person who does the following:

- blocks up or obstructs any drainage work or causes any drainage work to be blocked up or obstructed;
- encroaches on any drainage work;
- places any fish trap in any drainage work;
- breaches or cuts through the banks or sides of any drainage work;
- opens, closes or otherwise tampers with any sluice, water gate, regulator, pipe, bench mark, water gauge or other work forming part of such drainage work;
- suffers or permits fruit, leaves, tree branches, tree trunks or other vegetation to grow across or fall into any drainage work or fails to take adequate steps to prevent the same; or
- leads any animal, or suffers or permits any animal to stray upon the banks or sides of any drainage work.

296. The penalty imposed on any person who is liable under section 11 is imprisonment for up to six months, a fine of MYR 500, or both. The power to arrest for offences committed under section 11 is provided for under section 17. This section authorizes any *penghulu* or *penggawa*,[495] any police officer or any officer of the Drainage and Irrigation Department, not below the rank of Inspector, to arrest without warrant any person found committing such offences.

IV. Irrigation Areas Act 1953

297. Another statute applicable to drainage and irrigation is the Irrigation Areas Act 1953,[496] which is under the Drainage and Irrigation Department. The objective

494. Act 354.
495. Head of village.
496. Act 386.

of this Act is to lay down the rules under which the drainage and irrigated areas are established for agriculture purposes. Specifically, the Act concerns paddy cultivation,[497] and its objective is to ensure successful irrigation among paddy farmers.

298. Under this Act, 'irrigation' means 'the practice of causing water to flow upon, or spread over, or under, the surface of land or of retaining water on or under the surface of land for agricultural purpose and includes drainage for the removal of water which is injurious to agriculture'. 'Irrigation works' is defined to mean 'the construction and maintenance of headworks, main canal, subsidiary canals, distribution channels, drainage channels, banks, bunds, *batas*, water gates, culverts, sluices, drains and other similar works'.

299. Section 11 of the Act is on filling up obnoxious waterways. Under this section, the Drainage and Irrigation Engineer in charge of any irrigation area is empowered to fill up, construct, widen or drain any canal, water course, drain, ditch, pond or swamp, whether it is within or outside an irrigation area, if it will be of benefit to the irrigation works. Thus, this provision is applicable not only to rivers within the irrigation area, but also those outside the area.

300. Obstruction or damage of irrigation is an offence under section 15. This section states that any person who wilfully or maliciously blocks up or obstructs or causes to be in any way blocked up or obstructed; encroaches on or attempts to take fish by means of a fish trap out of any irrigation tank, channel or watercourse; or breaches or cuts through the banks or sides of the same, shall be liable to imprisonment for a period not exceeding six months or to a fine not exceeding MYR 300 or both.

301. A specific provision on water pollution is under section 23. This states that any person who bathes or washes articles in or otherwise pollutes or causes to be polluted any irrigation tank, channel or watercourse shall be liable to imprisonment for a term not exceeding three months, to a fine not exceeding MYR 150, or both.

302. The power of arrest for offences under sections 15, 16 and 23 is provided for in section 25. It empowers any *penghulu* or *penggawa*, any police officer, or any officer of the Drainage and Irrigation Department, not below the rank of Inspector, to arrest without warrant any person found committing such offences.

§7. Legislations on River Conservation

I. Drainage and Irrigation

303. The Drainage and Irrigation Department is charged with the general management and conservation of rivers, including activities that can affect their banks. The law which gives the Department these powers is the Ministerial Functions Act

497. Section 5 of the Irrigation Areas Act 1953.

1969,[498] which provides the Drainage and Irrigation Department a general jurisdiction over planning and management of rivers.[499]

304. Under section 12 of the Irrigation Areas Act 1953, the Drainage and Irrigation Engineer may require the owner or occupier of any lands within such area to clear the banks of any irrigation works from any trees or plants growing thereon, or to remove from any lands adjoining any irrigation works any growth or refuse likely to damage such works or harbour rats or other vermin.[500]

305. Section 21 of the Act prohibits any person from leading any animal or allowing any animal to stray upon the banks or sides of any irrigation works. The penalty provided for under section 21 is imprisonment for a period not exceeding three months, a fine not exceeding MYR 150, or both.

306. Section 22 prohibits unauthorized use of vehicles or boats on the irrigation area. It states that any person who drives, draws or pushes or causes to be driven, drawn or pushed any vehicle along the banks or sides of, or uses or causes to be used any boat, vessel, raft or float or causes to be floated any wood or other material on any irrigation canal or watercourse without consent of the Drainage and Irrigation Engineer shall be liable to imprisonment for a term not exceeding three months, to a fine not exceeding MYR 50, or both.

307. Another relevant law is the Drainage Works Act 1954. Section 11 empowers the officer in charge of any drainage area to require the owner or occupier of any land to take such steps in regard to any tree or other vegetation on such land as may be necessary to ensure that no fruit, leaves, tree branches, tree trunks or other vegetation shall grow across or fall into any drainage work.[501] If there is a default in complying with such notice, the officer in charge may take action, and may recover the cost of, and all expenses incurred in doing any necessary work from the owner or occupier.[502]

II. Waters Act 1920

308. The Waters Act 1920 also contains provisions indirectly relevant to river conservation. Section 4 of this Act prohibits any person from interfering with the bank of any river and empowers the Minister or the State Authority to require such

498. Act 2.
499. *See* Sharifah Zubaidah & Maizatun Mustafa, *Preventing Pollution in Malaysian Rivers: A Legal and Institutional Perspective*, a paper presented at the *5th Asia Law Institute Conference* (U. Sing. 2008).
500. Section 12(1)(a) of the Irrigation Areas Act 1953.
501. Section 11(3) of the Drainage Works Act 1954.
502. Section 11(4) of the Drainage Works Act 1954.

person to restore the same to its original condition. The penalty provided for this offence is a fine of MYR 500, and a daily fine of MYR 10 if the offence is continued.[503]

309. It is also an offence under the Act to fell trees into rivers, as it may cause blockage or obstruction of river waters and possible pollution of the waters, as provided in section 6. Where a bank of a river is interfered with, or where any felling takes place in contravention of this provision, the presumption is that the owner and occupier interfered with the bank or effected the felling, unless it is proven to the contrary.

310. Under section 14, it is a prohibition to erect any building or wall along the bank of any river, or to erect any building within 50 feet of such bank or any flood channel. The main purpose of this section is to ensure that any land abutting rivers are free from any construction, so that in the event of floods, such banks of rivers may be used to channel the flood. The penalty imposed for the contravention of this section is a fine of MYR 2,000.[504]

§8. Groundwater

I. General

311. In Malaysia, groundwater, which makes up less than 2% of the total amount of water resources, is not relied upon as the main source of water supply. The use of groundwater for domestic purposes is mainly confined to rural areas, where there is no piped water supply.

312. Major threats to groundwater quality are from the point sources and non-point sources, such as untreated sewage and other household wastes, industrial wastewaters, fertilizers and pesticides.

313. The Federal Constitution does not specifically provide for 'groundwater' under its legislative lists. Generally, 'water'[505] and 'land'[506] come under the jurisdiction of states, as provided in List II State List of the Constitution. However, the federal government has jurisdiction over mineral resources.[507] Matters indirectly relating to groundwater, such as 'drainage and irrigation',[508] and 'water supply',[509] come under List III Concurrent List whereby both federal and state legislatures can enact law concerning these matters.

503. Section 15 of the Waters Act 1920.
504. Section 14(4) of the Waters Act 1920.
505. Item 6 of List II State List.
506. Item 2 of List II State List.
507. Item 8 of List I Federal List.
508. Item 8 of List II Concurrent List.
509. Item 9D of List II Concurrent List.

314. There is no specific agency specializing in groundwater. However, there are two federal agencies authorized with specific aspects of groundwater management. The Department of Mineral and Geoscience regulates the abstraction and exploitation of groundwater and other minerals, while the Department of Environment controls the pollution of groundwater. The former comes under the Ministry of Energy and Natural Resources,[510] whereas the latter the Ministry of Environment and Water.[511]

315. In 1997, the Department of Environment initiated the National Groundwater Monitoring Programme. By 2012, seventy-nine monitoring wells had been established in Peninsular Malaysia, thirteen wells in Sarawak and fifteen wells in Sabah. The sites were selected and categorized according to the surrounding land use, which were agricultural, urban/suburban, rural, industrial, solid waste landfills, golf courses, radioactive landfill, animal burial areas, municipal water supply and examining areas.[512]

316. In Malaysia, the groundwater quality status is determined based on the National Guidelines for Raw Drinking Water Quality from the Ministry of Health, as the benchmark.[513]

II. Legislation

A. Geological Survey Act 1974

317. The main law applicable to exploitation and abstraction of groundwater is the Geological Survey Act 1974.[514] This law is enforced by the Director General of the Geological Survey, under the Department of Mineral and Geoscience, Ministry of Energy and Natural Resources.[515]

318. Section 13 of the Act requires that any person who bores, drills, digs or otherwise develops a well for searching for or extracting water therefrom notify the DG. In this section, a 'well' does not include a well which is less than 30 feet in depth without reaching bedrock, or a well yielding less than 500 gallons of water per day that is used only for the domestic purposes of the household of the person responsible for its development.

319. The Act further requires any person who bores, drills, digs or otherwise develops a hole, pit, shaft, tunnel, cutting or other excavation exposing bedrock, to

510. *See* the official website at https://www.jmg.gov.my/en/.
511. *See* the official website at https://www.doe.gov.my/portalv1/en/.
512. Kementerian Sumber Asli dan Alam Sekitar Malaysia, *Environmental Quality Report 2012* 52 (Jabatan Alam Sekitar 2012).
513. *Ibid.*, 52–53.
514. Act 129.
515. *See* the official website at https://www.jmg.gov.my/en/.

notify the DG of such details as may be prescribed from time to time.[516] However, this provision does not apply to the following persons:

- any person making an excavation incidental to the erection of a single- or double-storeyed building; or
- any person making an excavation in accordance with the provisions of any law relating to mining for the time being in force.

320. The general penalty for the contravention of the Act is provided in section 18. Under this section, any person who contravenes any provision of the Act or who fails to comply with any lawful direction, notice, condition or restriction imposed thereunder, shall be guilty of an offence. The penalty provided for is a fine not exceeding MYR 10,000 and, in addition, a fine of MYR 50 per day for every day during which the contravention or failure continues.

321. Where no other penalty is specifically provided under this Act, any person who contravenes the provisions, upon conviction, is liable to a fine not exceeding MYR 5,000 and in addition to a fine of MYR 25 a day for every day during which the contravention continues.[517]

B. Environmental Quality Act 1974

322. There is no specific legislation enacted to control groundwater pollution. However, several provisions under existing statutes are relevant. Under the EQA 1974, there is a provision relevant to groundwater.

323. Section 2 of the EQA 1974 defines 'inland waters' to include groundwater, namely, 'spring or well, or any other body of natural or artificial surface or subsurface water'. Thus, section 25 of the Act, on the restriction of inland water pollution, can be used to regulate groundwater pollution. The penalty provided is a fine not exceeding MYR 100,000, imprisonment for a period not exceeding five years, or both. A further fine not exceeding MYR 1,000 a day may also be imposed for every day that the offence is continued after a notice requiring him to cease the act has been served upon him.

324. The requirement of EIA under the EQA 1974 is indirectly relevant to control groundwater pollution.

325. Under section 34A of the Act, and the Environmental Quality (Prescribed Activities) (EIA) Order 2015,[518] specific activities that may directly cause pollution to groundwater must submit an EIA report before the commencement of the project. Activities under the First Schedule are as follows:

---

516. Section 14 of the Geological Survey Act 1974.
517. Section 14(4) of the Geological Survey Act 1974.
518. P.U. (A) 195/2015.

- Item 14(a), the construction of recovery plant, wastewater treatment plant and storage facility of scheduled waste;
- Item 14(b), the construction of composting plant, and recovery plant or recycling plant of solid waste;
- Item 14(c), the construction of sewage treatment plant with 20,000 population equivalent or more, and sludge treatment facilities; and
- Item 21, groundwater development for industrial, agricultural or urban water supply of 4,500 m^3 or more per day.

Relevant activities under the Second Schedule of the Environmental Quality (Prescribed Activities) (EIA) Order 2015 include:

- Item 14(a), in relation to schedule waste, the construction of thermal treatment plant, off-site recovery plant for lead acid battery wastes, and off-site recovery plant or treatment facility that generates significant amount of wastewater which is located at the upstream of public water supply intake; and
- Item 14(b), the construction of thermal treatment plant, sanitary landfill facility and transfer station.

326. The penalty imposed on any person who contravenes section 34A is a fine not exceeding MYR 500,000, jail for a period not exceeding five years, or both, and a further fine of MYR 1,000 for every day that the offence is continued.

§9. Water Supply

I. Introduction

327. In Malaysia, up until 2008, water supply was a state matter under the Federal Constitution. Thus, water services, including water treatment and water distribution, had been provided directly by the states. Apart from that, in order to manage the diverse issues in water supply, the federal and state governments had to rely on the decentralization of responsibilities to various government agencies.

328. Thus, until January 2008, water supply services were conducted in a decentralized manner, with relevant agencies performing their functions, which were either distinct or overlapped with one another. These agencies included:

- Water Services Department under the Ministry of Energy, Water and Communications;
- Department of Engineering, Ministry of Health;
- Public Works Department under the Ministry of Works;
- Department of Environment under the Ministry of Natural resources and the Environment;
- State Public Works Department;
- State Water Supply Department;
- State Water Supply Board; and

– Regulatory bodies.

329. Apart from the existence of a variety of agencies at federal and state levels dealing with water supply, some of the states, such as Selangor, Johor, Pulau Pinang, Kelantan and Terengganu, had either privatized or corporatized their water sectors, while water sectors in others, for example, Perlis, Kedah, Pahang, Negeri Sembilan and Labuan, were operating as government departments.[519]

II. Previous Legal Framework

330. Previously, up until 21 March 2005, under the Federal Constitution, the jurisdiction and control over water, including water supplies, rivers and canals, was enumerated under the State List. Therefore, up to that time, the power to legislate over matters relating to water fell exclusively within the jurisdiction of the states.

331. Up until that time, there was no specific legislation that dealt with water supply. Each state had its own separate legislation pertaining to water, which was only applicable in that particular state. Under the Water Supply Enactment Act 1955, state water supply authorities were empowered to supply water to domestic and trade consumers. It also empowered the authorities to lay water mains and distribute pipes across or under any street and through or under any enclosed land. The Enactment only applied to the states of Negeri Sembilan, Pahang, Perak and Selangor. For the other states, there were similar provisions in the respective state enactments.

332. Under the Waters Act 1920, the entire property in the control of all rivers in any state was vested solely in the Ruler of that state. No person could obstruct or interfere with any river except in accordance with a licence issued under the Act. A licence to divert water from a river in any district could be granted by the district officer with the approval of the State Authority for the following:

– private or domestic purposes;
– use in the cultivation of rice; and
– industrial and other purposes.

333. The Waters Act 1920 only applied to the states of Negeri Sembilan, Pahang, Perak, Selangor, Melaka, Pulau Pinang and the Federal territory. For other states, there were similar provisions in the state enactments.

334. Other legislation relevant to water supply includes the Geological Survey Act 1974. It governs the abstraction of groundwater. It requires that any person who

519. *See* Ministry Energy, Water & Commun., Malay., *The Water Tablet: Malaysian Water Reforms* 24–25 (Ministry Energy, Water & Commun., Malay. 2008).

develops a well for extracting water has to notify the Director General of the Mineral and Geoscience Department, which is under the Ministry of Energy and Natural Resources.[520]

III. Present Framework

A. Amendment of the Federal Constitution

335. The water services industry of Malaysia was reformed in 2007, after the country realized that the existing regulatory structure did not work for water services. The purpose of the reform was to establish a strong and large independent national regulator that would be more efficient. The existing water supply industry was revamped to allow a federal agency to act as a single regulator, as a means to regulate the development of a sustainable water services industry for the country.

336. For this purpose, the Federal Constitution was amended in 2005; 'water supply and services' was deleted from the State List of the Constitution and inserted in the Concurrent List. The amendment came into force on 21 March 2005.

337. The newly amended item in List II State List now reads: 'Subject to the Federal List, water (including rivers and canals but excluding water supplies and services); control of silt; riparian rights.'[521]

338. The newly inserted item of List III Concurrent List reads: 'subject to the Federal List, water supplies and services'.[522]

339. This Constitutional amendment enables the transfer of the powers of water supply treatment, distribution and billing from the State governments to the Federal government. It also serves to enable the consolidation of the water management and the regulatory functions of the water services for the country, except for Sabah and Sarawak.

340. The amendment of the Federal Constitution does not affect water resources of states including rivers, water catchment areas and groundwater. As such, they are still exclusively under the exclusive jurisdiction of the states, whereby the relevant legislation such as the Waters Act 1920 still applies.

341. Pursuant to the amendment, the federal government has enacted the following Acts as means to implement the restructuring of the whole water supply and services:[523]

---

520. See the official website at https://www.jmg.gov.my/en/.
521. *See* the Constitution (Amendment) Act 2005, Act 1239.
522. *Ibid.*
523. *See* Ministry Energy, Water & Commun., Malay., *The Water Tablet: Malaysian Water Reforms* 141–186 (Ministry of Energy, Water & Commun., Malay. 2008).

– Water Services Industry Act 2006; and
– National Water Services Commission Act 2006.

B. Water Services Industry Act 2006

342. The Water Services Industry Act 2006 was enacted in accordance with clause (1) of Article 74 and clause (2) of Article 80 of the Federal Constitution. This Act came into effect on 1 January 2008 and was enacted for the following objectives:

– to ensure uniformity of law and policy to make a law for the proper control and regulation of water supply services throughout Peninsular Malaysia and the Federal Territories of Putrajaya and Labuan;
– to confer executive authority on the Federation for matters relating to water supply systems and water supply services throughout Peninsular Malaysia and the Federal Territories of Putrajaya and Labuan;
– to establish the powers and functions of the National Water Services Commission; and
– to establish powers and procedures for the administration of the Act.

343. Under this Act, 'watercourse' is defined to include 'rivers, streams and creeks, including any tributary, distributary or artificial deviation thereof, seas, lakes, groundwater, dams, reservoirs, ditches, drains and passages, other than pipes, through which water flows for the supply of water to any premises'.

344. 'Water supply services' means 'the treatment of water abstracted from watercourses and the distribution and supply of treated water to consumers and includes the operation and maintenance of the water supply system'.

345. 'Water supply system' means:

> the whole of a system incorporating public mains, pipes, chambers, treatment plants, pumping stations, service or balancing reservoirs or any combination thereof and all other structures, installations, buildings, equipment and appurtenances used and the lands where the same are located for the storage, abstraction, collection, conveyance, treatment, distribution and supply of water.

346. Section 3 of the Act provides that the federal government has executive authority with respect to all matters relating to water supply systems and water supply services throughout Peninsular Malaysia and the Federal Territories of Putrajaya and Labuan.

347. Part II of the Act deals with licensing provisions. Two types of licences are provided under this Act. The first is an individual licence, regulated under section 4 of the Act. Another type of licence is a class licence under section 20. Unlike an individual licence, a class licence is obtained through registration, as provided in sections 25 and 28. Those eligible shall be approved by the Minister, based on pre-determined criteria.

348. Part III of the Act deals with duties and obligations of licensees. Under this part, section 29 sets out the duty of a licensee to provide information to the Commission about the licensee's licensed activities.

349. Licensee's responsibilities towards public health are provided in section 55(4). If a water distribution licensee knows, or has reason to believe that the supply of water is unsafe for the purposes of normal supply to the public, or poses a health risk to the public and fails to cease the supply of water to any premises; or reduces or diverts in part any of its pipe, the water distribution, the licensee commits an offence and shall, on conviction, be liable to a fine not exceeding MYR 500,000, to imprisonment for a term not exceeding five years, or both.

350. Part X is on general offences and penalties. Section 121 states that a person who contaminates or causes to be contaminated any watercourse or the water supply system, or any part of the watercourse or water supply system, with any substance, with the intention to cause death; with the knowledge that he is likely to cause death; or which would likely endanger the life of any person, commits an offence.

351. Section 121(2) provides for three sets of punishment for a person found guilty of an offence under subsection (1) on conviction:

- where death is the result of the act, the person shall be punished with death or imprisonment for a term which may extend to twenty years, and where the punishment is not death, he shall also be liable to whipping;
- where death is not the result of the act but the substance which is used to contaminate the watercourse or water supply system or any part of the watercourse or the water supply system is a radioactive or toxic substance, the person shall be liable to imprisonment for a term not exceeding ten years or to a fine not exceeding MYR 500,000 or to whipping or to all three; or
- in any other case, the person shall be liable to a fine not exceeding MYR 100,000 or to imprisonment for a term not exceeding one year or both.

352. Section 122 further provides for wrongful acts where upon conviction the perpetrator is liable to a fine not exceeding MYR 50,000, to imprisonment for a term not exceeding six months, or both. The wrongful Acts are where a person:

- wilfully, negligently or recklessly damages or causes to be damaged any pipe, channel, conduit or structure, sewer, manhole, chamber, fixture, equipment, reservoir, cistern, pump, hydrant, valve, meter, sub-metre or any part of any public water supply system or public sewerage system;

- flushes, draws off, diverts or takes water from any public water supply system or part of the system, unless the person is otherwise permitted under the Act or any other written law;
- bathes, wastes or throws any rubbish or creature, dead or alive, into any public water supply system or part of the system; or
- trespasses on any area of a service reservoir or booster station of a public water supply system or on any area of a sewage pumping station or sewage treatment works of a public sewerage system.

353. Part XIII of the Act establishes saving and repeal provisions and arrangements and procedures for the transition from the current regulatory regime to the new regime under the Act. The Sewerage Services Act 1993[524] is repealed in respect of its application to Peninsular Malaysia and the Federal Territories of Putrajaya and Labuan; and any subsidiary legislation made under the repealed legislation shall, insofar as it is consistent with this Act, remain in operation until revoked or replaced by any subsidiary legislation made under this Act.

C. Suruhanjaya Perkhidmatan Air Negara Act 2006

354. The Suruhanjaya Perkhidmatan Air Negara Act 2006[525] or the National Water Services Commission Act 2006, came into effect on 1 February 2007, and is enforced by the Ministry of Energy, Water and Communication.

355. This Act was enacted in order to establish a body known as the *Suruhanjaya Perkhidmatan Air Negara*, or the National Water Services Commission, for regulating the Water Services Industry Act 2006.[526]

356. The Commission, which is fully functional since 1 January 2008, is a central regulatory agency to oversee adequate, clean and healthy water supply, including to regulate and oversee the treated water supply. It is also expected to create an integrated system involving all stakeholders.

357. Part III provides for functions and powers of the Commission. Section 15 of the Act states that the Commission shall have all the functions conferred on it under the water supply and sewerage services laws and shall also have the following functions:

- to advise the Minister on all matters in relation to the national policy objectives of the water supply and sewerage services laws and to implement and promote the national policy objectives;

---

524. Act 508.
525. Act 654.
526. *See* Ministry Energy, Water & Commun., Malay., *The Water Tablet: Malaysian Water Reforms* 187–199 (Ministry Energy, Water & Commun., Malay. 2008).

- to implement and enforce the water supply and sewerage services laws and to consider and recommend reforms to the water supply and sewerage services laws;
- to ensure the productivity of the water supply services and sewerage services industry and the monitoring of operator compliance with stipulated service standards, contractual obligations and relevant laws and guidelines;
- to increase concerted efforts towards improving the operational efficiency of the industry and in particular the reduction of non-revenue water through short-term, medium-term and long-term programmes;
- to advise the Minister on a fair and efficient mechanism for the determination of tariffs that is fair both consumers and licensees and to implement tariffs that have been established through appropriate mechanism and tools;
- to ensure the national development goals pertaining to coverage, supply and access to water supply services and sewerage services are achieved;
- to ensure long-term sustainability of quality of water and sewerage services through continued capital works development;
- to formulate and implement a plan so that all reasonable demands for sewerage services are satisfied and, in consultation with the relevant authorities, prepare a sewerage catchment plan formulating the policy and general proposals in respect of the development of any new sewerage system and measures for improvement of any existing sewerage system;
- to carry out any function conferred upon it under any other written law; and
- to advise the Minister generally on matters relating to water supply services and sewerage services.

358. Powers of the Commission are laid down in section 16 and are as follows:

- to utilize all the property of the Commission, movable and immovable, in such manner as the Commission may think expedient, including the raising of loans by mortgaging such property;
- to impose fees or charges for services rendered by the Commission;
- to appoint such agents, experts or consultants as it deems fit to assist the Commission in the performance of its functions;
- to grant loans and scholarships to employees of the Commission for such purposes as may be approved by the Minister;
- to formulate and implement human resource development and funding and cooperation programmes for the proper and effective performance of the functions of the Commission;
- to cooperate with any body corporate or government agency for performing the Commission's functions; and
- to do anything incidental to any of its functions and powers.

359. The previous institutional framework for the water industry in Malaysia provides the federal government agencies with the responsibility for environmental and health regulation under the Department of Environment and the Health Department, respectively. Within the present setup, the administrative and legislative functions of these two agencies would remain the same. The Commission's scope covers the social and economic aspects of the water services industry.

§10. Marine Pollution

I. General

360. Malaysia's coastal and marine waters are subject both land- and vessel-based pollution. The land-based marine pollution originates from industrial, domestic and agricultural sources, while vessel-based pollution is predominantly from oil and grease, suspended solids and spillages of oil from tankers and platforms. Major marine environmental degradation is mainly on the west coast of Peninsular Malaysia, at the Straits of Malacca.

361. The Straits of Malacca cover an area of 45,882 square nautical miles and approximately 500 miles long. The greater part of the waterway runs through the territorial waters of Indonesia, Malaysia and Thailand, with the much shorter part of Singapore. The Straits are rich in natural resources and ecological diversity. They supply myriads of marine resources and support the economy of the littoral states including Malaysia.[527]

362. Other economic activities within the Straits of Malacca include tourism, recreation and maritime industry, and it is an important site for archaeological resources. The Straits are also a major commercial shipping route between the Indian Ocean and the Pacific Ocean, with an average of two hundred ships passing per day.

II. Jurisdiction Over the Marine Environment

A. The Constitution

363. The legislative list of the Federal Constitution does not provide for any direct provision on marine environment. However, matters indirectly concerning the marine environment come mainly within the jurisdiction of the federal government. They are Item 9 on shipping, navigation and fisheries; and Item 1 on external affairs, including implementation of treaties, agreements and conventions with other countries. However, turtles come under the jurisdiction of the state.[528]

---

527. *See* Abdul Haseeb Ansari, *Prevention, Abatement and Control of Pollution of Straits: An Appraisal with Special Reference to the Straits of Malacca,* 3 MLJ xxxvii (2005).
528. Item 12 of List II State List.

B. Department of Environment

364. The main agency established for monitoring and enforcement of marine pollution law is the Department of Environment. The Department started the marine monitoring programme in 1978 for Peninsular Malaysia, and in 1985 for Sabah and Sarawak. The parameters for the Interim Marine Water Quality Standards applied by the Department are *Escherichia coli*; oil and grease; total suspended solid; arsenic; cadmium; total chromium, copper; lead and mercury.[529]

365. Apart from marine pollution monitoring, the Department is also empowered to enforce laws on marine pollution through provisions under the EQA 1974. The scope of the Act on marine pollution is confined to that of 'Malaysian waters'. This term is defined in the Act to mean 'the territorial waters of Malaysia as determined in accordance with the Emergency (Essential Powers) Ordinance, No. 7 of 1969'. Under this Ordinance, the breadth of the territorial waters of Malaysia is twelve nautical miles.[530]

366. The power of the Director General of the Department of Environment is within this limit of the territorial sea. For enforcement purposes, the DG is empowered to delegate his powers to investigate offences under sections 27 and 29 of the Act. For this purpose, the Environmental Quality (Delegation of Powers on Marine Pollution Control) Order 1993[531] empowered the DG to delegate the power to the following public officers:

- any port officer and deputy port officer appointed under the Merchant Shipping Ordinance 1952;[532]
- any port officer, ship surveyor and inspector appointed under the Merchant Shipping Ordinance (Sarawak) 1960;[533]
- any port officer appointed under the Merchant Shipping Ordinance (Sabah) 1960;[534]
- any fisheries' officer appointed under the Fisheries Act 1985;[535]
- any officer commanding a vessel of the Royal Malaysian Navy; and
- any officer of customs commanding a vessel of the Customs and Excise Department.

367. Another instrument of delegated legislation regarding marine pollution is the Environmental Quality (Delegation of Powers on Marine Pollution Control)

529. Kementerian Sumber Asli dan Alam Sekitar Malaysia, *Environmental Quality Report 2012* 60–61 (Jabatan Alam Sekitar 2012).
530. Section 1 of the Emergency (Essential Powers) Ordinance, No. 7 of 1969, and in accordance with the Geneva Convention on the Territorial Sea and the Contiguous Zone 1958.
531. P.U. (A) 276/93. This Order revoked the Environmental Quality (Delegation of Powers) Order 1976, P.U. (A) 51/76.
532. 70/1952.
533. Sarawak 2/60.
534. Sabah 11/60.
535. Act 317.

Order 1994.[536] This Order authorizes the DG to delegate his powers to investigate offences under sections 27 and 29 of the EQA 1974 to any police officer commanding a vessel, or any appointed police officer, or the Royal Malaysia Police.[537]

C. Marine Department

368. Another agency empowered to enforce law on marine pollution is the Marine Department, Malaysia, established under the Merchant Shipping Ordinance 1952,[538] and the Merchant Shipping (Oil Pollution) Act 1994.[539]

369. The scope of the Merchant Shipping Ordinance 1952 is confined to the territorial Malaysian waters determined in accordance with the Emergency (Essential Powers) Ordinance, No. 7 of 1969.[540] The scope of the Merchant Shipping (Oil Pollution) Act 1994 is[541] the territorial sea of Malaysia as well as the exclusive economic zone of Malaysia, and references to any area of any other Liability Convention country include the territorial waters of that Liability Convention country.

D. Malaysian Maritime Enforcement Agency

370. The Malaysian Maritime Enforcement Agency is a newly established agency set up under the Prime Minister's Department. The Agency is employed in the Malaysian Maritime Zone for the maintenance of law and order, the preservation of the peace, safety and security, the prevention and detection of crime, the apprehension and prosecution of offenders, and the collection of security intelligence.[542]

371. This Agency is headed by a DG, as provided by the Malaysian Maritime Enforcement Agency Act 2004.[543] The main tasks of this Agency are the maintenance of law and order and the preservation of the peace, safety and security in the Malaysian Maritime Zone. The 'Malaysian Maritime Zone' is defined as 'the internal waters, territorial sea, continental shelf, exclusive economic zone and the Malaysian fisheries' waters and includes the air space over the Zone', and thus it covers all the maritime areas of Malaysia.

536. P.U. (A) 537/94.
537. Regulation 2 of the Environmental Quality (Delegation of Powers on Marine Pollution Control) Order 1994.
538. Federation of Malaya Ordinance No. 7 of 1952.
539. Act 515.
540. P.U. (A) 307A/69.
541. Section 2 of the Merchant Shipping (Oil Pollution) Act 1994.
542. For details, *see* the Department's official website at https://www.mmea.gov.my, January 2014.
543. Act 633.

372. The functions of this Agency are provided in section 7 of the Act as follows:

- to enforce law and order under any federal law;
- perform maritime search and rescue;
- prevent and suppress the commission of an offence;
- lend assistance in any criminal matters on request by a foreign state as provided under Mutual Assistance in Criminal Matters Act 2002;[544]
- carry out air and coastal surveillance;
- provide platform and support services to any relevant agency;
- establish and manage maritime institutions for the training of officers of the Agency; and
- perform any other duty for ensuring maritime safety and security or do all matters incidental thereto.

373. The Agency is also responsible, among other things, for the control and prevention of maritime pollution on the high seas as provided in section 7 of the Act.

374. In relation to environmental protection, section 6(1) empowers the Agency to be responsible for controlling and preventing maritime pollution on the high seas. Furthermore, section 7, which lists activities considered to be prejudicial to the peace, good order and security of Malaysia, includes pollution and any fishing activities.

III. Legislations on Marine Pollution

A. Environmental Quality Act 1974

375. There are two separate provisions under the EQA 1974 on marine pollution. Under section 27, no person is permitted to discharge or spill any oil or mixture containing oil into Malaysian waters, in contravention of the acceptable conditions, unless licensed under section 21.

376. Another provision is section 29, which prohibits any person from discharging environmentally hazardous substances, pollutants or wastes into the Malaysian waters in contravention of the acceptable conditions specified under section 21, unless licensed.

377. The distinction between these two sections is that the EQA 1974 provides special defences for offences committed under section 27, in section 28. Under this section, where any person is charged for any offence under section 27, it shall be a defence that such discharge or spillage was:

---

544. Act 621.

- for securing the safety of the vessel;
- for saving human life;
- the result of damage to the vessel and that all reasonable steps were taken to prevent, to stop or to reduce the spillage;
- the result of a leakage, which was not due to want of care, and that all reasonable steps had been taken to stop or reduce the leakage; or
- the result of an effluent produced by operation for the refining of oil, and that all reasonable steps had been taken to eliminate oil from the effluent and that it was not reasonably practicable to dispose of the effluent otherwise than by discharging or spilling it into the Malaysian waters.

378. The penalty imposed for any person who contravenes sections 27 and 29 is a fine not exceeding MYR 500,000, imprisonment for a period not exceeding five years, or both.[545]

B. Merchant Shipping Ordinance 1952

379. The Merchant Shipping Ordinance 1952 is an Ordinance that consolidates and amends the law with respect to merchant shipping in Malaysia and enforces the International Convention for the Safety of Life at Sea 1974 and the International Convention on Load Lines 1966. Part VA of the Merchant Shipping Ordinance 1952[546] deals with pollution from ships and applies throughout Malaysia.[547] In the context of Part VA, 'ship' applies to:[548]

- registered Malaysian ships;
- vessels licensed under this Ordinance or under the Merchant Shipping Ordinance 1960 of Sabah or Sarawak;
- foreign ships while in Malaysian waters;
- pleasure crafts in Malaysian waters;
- fishing vessels; and
- such vessels or class of vessels as the Minister may prescribe.

The term 'discharge' in Part VA means any release of oil or harmful substances from a ship, including any escape, disposal, spilling, leaking, pumping, emitting or emptying. However, it does not include release of harmful substances or chemicals for legitimate scientific research into pollution abatement or control; dumping within the meaning of the Convention on the Prevention of Marine Pollution by Dumping of Wastes and Other Matter 1972, or dumping with the consent of the Government; or release of harmful substances directly arising from the exploration, exploitation and associated offshore processing of sea-bed mineral resources.[549]

---

545. Subsection (2) of ss 27 and 29, respectively.
546. No. 70 of 1952.
547. Amendment 792/91.
548. Section 306B(1) of the Merchant Shipping Ordinance 1952.
549. Section 306C of the Merchant Shipping Ordinance 1952.

380. Under this Ordinance, 'oil' means any persistent or non-persistent hydrocarbon mineral oil in any form, including any mixture with any oil content, whether carried on board a ship as cargo in bulk or in the bunkers of the ship; whereas 'oily mixture' means a mixture with any oil content.[550] Section 306 CA prohibits the discharge of oil or harmful substance into any part of Malaysian waters, any Malaysian coast or Malaysian reef. The term 'harmful substance' here means any substance which, if introduced into the sea, is liable to create hazards to human health, to harm living resources and marine life, to damage amenities or to interfere with other legitimate uses of the sea. Prohibition of Section 306CA shall not apply to any discharge of oil-related harmful substances on the following situations:

- which is necessary for securing the safety of the ship or saving life at sea;
- resulting from damage, other than intentional damage, to a ship or its equipment and, all reasonable precautions have been taken after the occurrence of the damage or discovery of the discharge for preventing or, if it could not be prevented, stopping or minimizing the discharge; or
- which is for combating specific pollution incidents in order to minimize damage from pollution and is approved by the Director of Marine and, where the discharge occurred within the jurisdiction of the government of the country other than Malaysia, by that government.

Any person who contravenes Section 306CA shall be liable for each offence to a fine not exceeding MYR 50,000 or to imprisonment for a term not exceeding two years or both.

According to section 306D, where oil or harmful substance is escaping from, or where the Director of Marine is satisfied that oil or harmful substance is likely to escape from a ship, then, for preventing or reducing the extent of the pollution or likely pollution by the oil or harmful substance of any Malaysian waters, any part of the Malaysian coast or any Malaysian reef, the Director of Marine, in consultation with the Director General of Environmental Quality, may, by notice in writing address to the owner of the ship to do all or any of the following:

- require such action to be taken in relation to the ship or its cargo as is specified in the notice;
- prohibit the removal of the ship from a place specified in the notice except with his approval; and
- prohibit the removal from the ship of any cargo, or any cargo specified in the notice, except with his approval.

381. In such cases, the Director of Marine may require action to be taken to prevent the escape of oil or harmful substance from the ship; action to be taken on the removal of oil or harmful substance from the ship; and action to be taken on the removal of the ship to a place specified by the Director of Marine.

550. Section 306C of the Merchant Shipping Ordinance 1952.

382. The penalty for offences under Part VA is provided in section 306F. This section states that where a notice is served and a requirement specified in the notice is not complied with, the owner and master of the ship shall be guilty of an offence and shall be liable on conviction to a fine not exceeding MYR 50,000 in respect of each period of twenty-four hours within the default period.

383. Matters pertaining to the escape of oil or harmful substance from two or more ships are provided in section 306H. Under this section, where oil or harmful substance has escaped or is likely to escape from two or more ships, and it is not reasonably practical to identify the oil or harmful substance that had escaped from a particular ship, then all the oil or harmful substance that had escaped from those ships shall, for the purpose of this Part, be deemed to have escaped from each of those ships.

384. Section 306I deals with action to be taken in cases of maritime casualty. Where, as a result of a maritime casualty or in consequence of any act resulting therefrom, there is or is likely to be, in the opinion of the Director of Marine, an escape of oil or harmful substance or any other threat of pollution in Malaysian waters, any Malaysian coast or Malaysian reef, the Director of Marine, in consultation with the Director General of Environmental Quality, may take such actions as he deems necessary and issue the notice under the provisions of section 306D.

C. The Merchant Shipping (Oil Pollution) Act 1994

385. The Merchant Shipping (Oil Pollution) Act 1994[551] is another statute that contains provision on marine oil pollution. This Act was enacted to give legal effect to the Civil Liability Convention 1969 and Fund Convention 1971.

386. 'Pollution damage' under this Ordinance means loss or damage caused outside a ship by contamination resulting from the discharge or escape of oil from the ship, wherever such discharge or escape may occur. Compensation for impairment of the environment, other than loss of profit from such impairment, shall be limited to costs of reasonable measures of reinstatement actually undertaken or to be undertaken; or the costs of preventive measures and further loss or damage caused by preventive measures. However, the term 'oil', except in Part III, means any persistent hydrocarbon mineral oil such as crude oil, fuel oil, heavy diesel oil and lubricating oil, whether carried on board a ship as cargo or in the bunkers of such a ship.[552]

387. For the purposes of this Act, references to any area of Malaysia include the territorial sea of Malaysia and exclusive economic zone of Malaysia, and references to any area of any other Liability Convention country include the territorial sea and the exclusive economic zone of that Liability Convention country. References to the exclusive economic zone of a country are references to the exclusive economic zone

551. Act 515.
552. Section 2 of the Merchant Shipping (Oil Pollution) Act 1994.

of that country established in accordance with international law, or, if such a zone has not been established, such area adjacent to the territorial sea of that country determined by that country in accordance with international law, extending not more than 200 nautical miles from the baselines from which the breadth of the territorial sea is measured.[553]

388. Civil liability for oil pollution is provided in Part II of the Act which requires that the owner of a ship at the time of an incident, or where the incident consists of a series of occurrences, at the time of the first occurrence, shall, except as otherwise provided for by this Act, be liable for any pollution damage caused by the ship as a result of the incident in any area of Malaysia. The section further states that the owner of the ship shall be liable for any pollution damage caused to any area of any other Liability Convention country as a result of any incident specified.[554] For the purpose of this Act, 'ship' means any sea-going vessel and seaborne craft of any type constructed or adapted for the carriage of oil in bulk as cargo, provided that a ship capable of carrying oil and other cargoes shall be regarded as a ship only when it is actually carrying oil in bulk as cargo and during any voyage following such carriage unless it is proved that it has no residues of such carriage of oil in bulk aboard.[555]

389. Under subsection (3) of section 3, where an incident involving two or more ships occurs and pollution damage results from the incident, the owners of all the ships concerned shall, unless exonerated under section 4, be jointly and severally liable for all such pollution damage which is not reasonably separable. Section 5 provides for the restriction of liability for oil pollution damage in situations; where an incident occurs and pollution damage results from the incident, the owner of the ship shall not be liable for such pollution damage otherwise than under that section. Under section 6, the owner of a ship who incurs a liability under section 3 may limit his liability in accordance with this Act as set out in Part I of the First Schedule. However, the owner will not be entitled to limit his liability if it is proved that the pollution damage resulted from an act or omission of the owner of the ship, committed with the intent to cause such damage, or recklessly and with the knowledge that such damage would probably result. Where the owner of a ship has or is alleged to have incurred a liability under section 3, section 7 allows him to apply to the Court for the limitation of that liability to an amount determined in accordance with section 6. Compulsory insurance against liability for pollution is a requirement under section 11. This section is applicable to any ship carrying in bulk a cargo of more than two thousand tonnes of oil; any such ship shall not enter or leave a port in Malaysia or arrive at or leave a terminal installation area in any area of Malaysia or, if the ship is registered in Malaysia, it shall not enter or leave a port in any other country or a terminal installation in the territorial sea of any other country. Requirements pertaining to the international oil pollution compensation fund are provided in Part III of the Act.

553. *Ibid.*
554. Section 3 of the Merchant Shipping (Oil Pollution) Act 1994.
555. Section 2 of the Merchant Shipping (Oil Pollution) Act 1994.

390. Any claim made in respect of liability incurred under the Act is within the jurisdiction of the High Court[556] in relation to matters of admiralty under paragraph 24(b) of the Courts of Judicature Act 1964.[557] Where any oil is discharged or escapes from a ship but does not result in any pollution damage in any area of Malaysia, and no preventive measures are reasonably taken to prevent or minimize such damage in that area, no Court in Malaysia shall consider an action to enforce a claim arising from any pollution damage caused in any area of another Liability Convention country resulting from the discharge or escape.[558]

D. Exclusive Economic Zone Act 1984

391. Another statute relevant to marine pollution is the Exclusive Economic Zone Act 1984.[559] According to section 3 of the Act, the exclusive economic zone of Malaysia, as proclaimed by the King vide P.U. (A)115/80, is an area beyond and adjacent to the territorial sea of Malaysia and subject to subsections (2) and (4), and it extends to a distance of two hundred nautical miles from the baselines from which the breadth of the territorial sea is measured.

Section 4 provides that in the exclusive economic zone Malaysia has sovereign rights for exploring and exploiting, conserving and managing the natural resources, whether living or non-living, of the seabed and subsoil and the superjacent waters, and with regard to other activities for the economic exploitation and exploration of the zone, such as the production of energy from the water, currents and winds; jurisdiction with regard to the establishment and use of artificial islands, installations and structures; marine scientific research; the protection and preservation of the marine environment and such other rights and duties as are provided for by international law.

The prohibition of activities in the exclusive economic zone or on the continental shelf except where authorized is stated in section 5, namely to explore or exploit any natural resources, whether living or non-living; to carry out any search, excavation or drilling operations; to conduct any marine scientific research: or to construct or authorize and regulate the construction, operation and use of any artificial island, any installation or structure for any of the purposes provided for in section 4 or for any other economic purpose; or any installation or structure which may interfere with the exercise of the rights of Malaysia in the zone or on the continental shelf.

392. Part IV of the Act deals with the protection and preservation of the marine environment. This Act is enforced by the Director General of the Department of Environment. Section 9 emphasizes Malaysia's sovereign right to exploit her natural resources in the exclusive economic zone pursuant to her environmental policies and in accordance with her duty to protect and preserve the marine environment in

556. Section 23 of the Merchant Shipping (Oil Pollution) Act 1994.
557. Act 91.
558. Section 23(2) of the Merchant Shipping (Oil Pollution) Act 1994.
559. Act 311.

the zone. It is an offence under section 10 of this Act to discharge any oil, mixture containing oil or pollutant into the exclusive economic zone from any vessel, land-based source, installation, device or aircraft, from or through the atmosphere or by dumping.[560]

Interpretation of some of the terms of section 10 is provided in section 2 as follows:

> 'mixture containing oil' means a mixture with an oil content of one hundred parts or more in one million parts of the mixture; or a mixture with such oil content as is prescribed by the Minister charged with responsibility for the environment by order in the Gazette to be a mixture containing oil for the purposes of this Act.
>
> 'oil' means crude oil, diesel oil, fuel oil or lubricating oil; or any other description of oil which is prescribed by the Minister charged with responsibility for the environment by order in the Gazette to be oil for the purposes of this Act;
>
> 'pollutant' means any substance which, if introduced into the sea, is liable to create hazards to human health or to harm living resources in the sea or other marine life, or to damage amenities or interfere with other legitimate uses of the sea and, without limiting the generality of the foregoing, includes any substance that is prescribed by the Minister charged with responsibility for the environment by order in the Gazette to be a pollutant for the purposes of this Act;
>
> 'waste' includes: any matter, whether liquid, solid, gaseous or radioactive, which is discharged, emitted, deposited or dumped in the marine environment in such volume, composition or manner as to cause an alteration of the environment; or any matter which is prescribed by the Minister charged with responsibility for the environment by order in the Gazette to be waste for the purposes of this Act;
>
> 'dumping' means: any deliberate disposal of wastes or other matter from vessels, aircraft, platforms or other man-made structures at sea; or any deliberate disposal of vessels, aircraft or other man-made structures at sea, but 'dumping' does not include:
>
> - the disposal of wastes or other matter incidental to, or derived from, the normal operations of vessels, aircraft, platforms or other man-made structures at sea and their equipment, other than wastes or other matter transported by or to vessels, aircraft, platforms or other man-made structures at sea, operating for the purpose of disposal of such matter or derived from the treatment of such wastes or other matter on such vessels, aircraft, platforms or structures; or
> - placement of matter for a purpose other than the mere disposal thereof, provided that such placement is not contrary to the aims of this Act, any applicable written law or international law.

560. Section 10(1) of the Exclusive Economic Zone Act 1984.

393. Section 10 is applied to the following persons who, upon conviction, shall each be liable to a fine not exceeding MYR 1,000,000. They are:

- the owner or master of the vessel, if the discharge or escape is from a vessel;
- the owner or occupier of the place on land, if the discharge or escape is from land;
- the owner or person in charge of the installation or device, if the discharge or escape is from an installation or a device; or
- the owner or pilot of the aircraft, if the discharge or escape is from an aircraft.

Where a person is charged with an offence under section 10, section 11 provides for defences in situations where discharge or escape of the substance was caused for securing the safety of the vessel, the place on land, the installation, device or aircraft concerned, or for saving life. However, a defence under this section shall not operate if the court is satisfied that the discharge or escape was not necessary for the alleged purpose or was not a reasonable step to take in the circumstances.

394. Section 12 of the Act requires the discharge or escape of certain substances to be reported. If any oil, mixture containing oil or pollutant is discharged or escapes into the exclusive economic zone from any vessel, land-based source, installation, device or aircraft, the owner or master of the vessel, the owner or occupier of the place on land, the owner or person in charge of the installation or device, or the owner or pilot of the aircraft, as the case may be, must immediately report the occurrence of such discharge or escape to the DG. The penalty imposed on the failure to comply with this section is a fine not exceeding MYR 10,000.[561] By virtue of section 14, where Malaysia's coastline or any segment or element of the environment or related interests, including fishing in the exclusive economic zone is damaged or threatened to be damaged as a result of any discharge or escape of any substance mentioned in section 10, the DG may issue such directions to remove, disperse, destroy or mitigate the damage or threat of damage. Failure to comply with the direction shall be guilty of an offence and shall be liable to a fine not exceeding MYR 10,000.

395. Section 15 empowers the DG to detain any vessel from which the oil, mixture containing oil or pollutant escaped or was discharged in the circumstances. The DG may release any vessel detained upon the owner depositing such sum of money or furnishing such security as would be adequate to meet all costs and expenses incurred in carrying out the work required to remove, disperse, destroy or mitigate the damage or threat of damage caused by such escape or discharge. However, if any vessel which has been detained proceeds to sea without being released, the owner or master of the vessel or any other person who causes the vessel to proceed to sea shall be guilty of an offence and shall be liable to a fine not exceeding MYR 1,000,000.

The power relating to hot pursuit is provided by section 25 in situations where an authorized officer has reason to believe that a foreign vessel has contravened any

561. Section 12(2) of the Exclusive Economic Zone Act 1984.

provision of this Act or any applicable written law, to undertake the hot pursuit of such vessel with a view to stopping, arresting and bringing it within the exclusive economic zone in accordance with international law. Except as otherwise provided by any regional or bilateral agreement to which Malaysia is a party, the right of hot pursuit shall cease as soon as the vessel pursued enters the territorial sea or exclusive economic zone of its own State or any third State.

396. Damage to the environment in the exclusive economic zone or on the continental shelf is addressed in section 40. Where, by reason of any act or omission in contravention of this Act or any applicable written law, damage is caused to the environment within, the exclusive economic zone or continental shelf, the following person from which any oil, mixture containing oil or pollutant was discharged or escaped may be liable for the damage:[562]

- the owner and the master of the vessel;
- the owner and the occupier of the place on land;
- the owner and the person in charge of the installation or device; or
- the owner and the pilot of the aircraft.

Section 29 provides for the general penalty for any offences under this Act, which is a fine not exceeding MYR 1,000,000.

IV. International Law on Marine Pollution

397. Malaysia has acceded to several international conventions relevant to the protection of the marine environment.[563] However, these conventions do not have domestic effect until parliament enacts legislation to implement their content, by virtue of Article 76(1)(a) of the Federal Constitution.

398. Under this constitutional provision, Malaysia enacted several statutes in order to implement international treaties relevant to the marine environment. For example, the enabling of Malaysian legislations for the United Nations Convention on the Law of the Sea 1982[564] are the Exclusive Economic Zone Act 1984[565] and the Fisheries Act 1985.[566]

---

562. Section 40(1) of the Exclusive Economic Zone Act 1984.
563. For detail, *see* Abdul Ghafur Hamid, *Malaysia's Commitments Under International Conventions and the Need for a Harmonized Legal Regime Regulating Marine Pollution,* 6 MLJ cxxiv (2007); Maizatun Mustafa & Mariani Ariffin, *Protection of Marine Biodiversity from Pollution: Legal Strategies in Malaysia,* 1 Intl. J. Bioscience, Biochemistry & Bioinformatics (2011); and Maizatun Mustafa, *The Application of Law on Pollution Control towards Marine Biodiversity Conservation in Malaysia,* in *International Conference on Environment and BioScience IPCBEE,* 21 IACSIT Press (2011).
564. Accessed by Malaysia on 14 Oct. 1996.
565. Act 311.
566. Act 317.

399. The Exclusive Economic Zone Act 1984 is a mirror of Part V of the Convention, which governs state jurisdiction in the exclusive economic zone over marine pollution prevention and other matters. Whereas the Fisheries Act 1985 regulates the various provisions of the Convention pertaining to fisheries' management.

400. There are two other international conventions ratified by Malaysia and subsequently applied through the enabling law of the Merchant Shipping (Oil Pollution) Act 1994. These conventions are the International Convention for the Prevention of Pollution from Ships 1973;[567] and the International Convention on the Establishment of an International Fund for Compensation for Oil Pollution Damage, 1992.[568]

401. Other conventions ratified by Malaysia include the International Convention on Oil Pollution Preparedness, Response and Cooperation 1990;[569] and the International Convention on Civil Liability for Oil Pollution Damage, 1992.[570] Other international conventions pertaining to marine pollution relevant to Malaysia are the:

- United Nations Convention on the Law of the Sea 1982;
- International Convention for the Prevention of Pollution from Ships 1973;
- International Convention on Oil Pollution Preparedness, Response and Cooperation 1990;
- International Convention on Civil Liability for Oil Pollution Damage 1992;
- International Convention on the Establishment of an International Fund for Compensation for Oil Pollution Damage 1992; and
- Basel Convention on the Control of Transboundary Movements of Hazardous Wastes and Their Disposal 1989.

567. Ratified by Malaysia on 1 May 1997.
568. Ratified on 9 Jun. 2005.
569. Ratified on 30 Oct. 1997.
570. Ratified on 9 Jun. 2005.

Chapter 4. Waste

§1. Introduction

402. In Malaysia, the EQA 1974 adopts the 'impact' concept for describing waste. The Act defines 'waste' to include any matter prescribed to be scheduled waste, or any matter whether in a solid, semi-solid or liquid form, or in the form of gas or vapour which is emitted, discharged or deposited in the environment in such volume, composition or manner as to cause pollution.[571]

403. The impact concept emphasizes the impact of a substance before it can be considered as waste. Thus, under the EQA, before a material is considered as 'waste', it must not only be discharged or deposited into the environment, but it must also cause pollution as well. The applicability of environmental law is based on different categories of waste discharged.[572]

§2. Legal Framework

I. Industrial Waste

404. Industrial waste in the context of the EQA 1974 includes, specifically, waste generated from the palm oil and raw rubber industries, and more generally, sewage and industrial effluents. The relevant regulations are:

- Environmental Quality (Prescribed Premises) (Crude Palm Oil) Regulations 1977;
- Environmental Quality (Prescribed Premises) (Raw Natural Rubber) Regulations 1978; and
- Environmental Quality (Industrial Effluent) Regulations 2009.

405. Pollution control strategy under these Regulations is through the application of effluent standards, whereby discharge exceeding these standards is considered an offence. The four types of industrial waste above are regulated through the issuance of specific licences.

A. *Crude Palm Oil*

406. Premises that discharge waste in the form of crude palm oil are prescribed as prescribed premises under the Environmental Quality (Prescribed Premises)

571. *See* s. 2 of the EQA.
572. *See* Maizatun Mustafa & Mariani Ho, *Agriculture Wastes and Role of Environmental Law in Malaysia*. Paper presented at the *International Conference of Agricultural Wastes* (Universiti Putra Malaysia 2006).

(Crude Palm Oil) Order 1977.[573] This Order requires that all premises occupied or used for the processing of oil-palm fruit or oil-palm fresh-fruit bunches into crude palm oil, whether as an intermediate or final product, be prescribed as prescribed premises. Owners of these premises must obtain a licence[574] from the Department of Environment; otherwise, it would be an offence.

407. The Environmental Quality (Prescribed Premises) (Crude Palm Oil) Regulations 1977[575] require that every occupier of prescribed premises shall[576] submit to the DG a quarterly return for that quarter in respect of the prescribed premises. The limits for parameters of effluents to be discharged into a watercourse are provided in Regulation 12, whereas Regulation 13 provides for limits for parameters of effluent to be discharged onto land.

408. Every licence issued must contain a condition or conditions limiting the parameters of the effluent discharged as provided in the Second Schedule of the Regulations. Once the licence is given, the occupier must obtain written approval from the DG whenever there are going to be any changes to the effluent.[577]

B. Raw Natural Rubber

409. For industrial waste in the form of raw natural rubber, the Environmental Quality (Prescribed Premises) (Raw Natural Rubber) Order 1978[578] requires the following premises to be prescribed as prescribed premises:

- all premises occupied or used for the production or processing of raw natural rubber in technically specified form, latex form including pre-vulcanized or the form of modified and special purpose rubber; and
- all premises occupied or used for the production or processes of conventional sheet, skim, crepe or any other form of raw rubber not already described in quantities of five tonnes or more per day, or with a production or processing capacity of a similar quantity.

410. Once prescribed as prescribed premises, the occupation or use of these premises would be an offence unless a prescribed premises licence[579] is obtained. The

573. P.U. (A) 199/77.
574. License for Prescribed Premises as required by s. 18.
575. P.U. (A) 342/77.
576. For the purposes of the Environmental Quality (Prescribed Premises) (Crude Palm Oil) Regulations 1977, a 'quarter' means a period of three months commencing on 1 January, 1 April, 1 July, or 1 October.
577. Regulation 6 of the Environmental Quality (Prescribed Premises) (Crude Palm Oil) Regulations 1977.
578. P.U. (A) 250/78.
579. Section 18 of the EQA 1974.

discharge holder of these prescribed premises is regulated by the Environmental Quality (Prescribed Premises) (Raw Natural Rubber) Regulations 1978.[580]

411. Under Regulation 10 of the Regulations, every occupier of prescribed premises shall, within fourteen days after the end of each quarter, submit to the DG a quarterly return[581] for that quarter in respect of the prescribed premises.[582]

412. The Environmental Quality (Prescribed Premises) (Raw Natural Rubber) Regulations 1978 provide for acceptable conditions for the discharge of effluents as follows:

- acceptable conditions for the discharge of effluent from prescribed premises occupied or used for the production of concentrated latex or its associated products into a watercourse;[583]
- acceptable conditions for the discharge of effluent from prescribed premises occupied or used for the production of concentrated latex or its associated products onto land;[584]
- acceptable conditions for the discharge of effluent from prescribed premises occupied or used for the production of products other than concentrated latex or its associated products into a watercourse;[585] and
- acceptable conditions for the discharge of effluent from prescribed premises occupied or used for the production of concentrated latex or its associated products onto land.[586]

413. For all the acceptable conditions above, the DG has the power to impose conditions and more stringent limits on the individual licence limiting the parameters of the effluents.[587] Once the licence is given, the occupier of the prescribed premises has the responsibility to obtain the written approval of the DG if there is going to be any change to the effluent, by way of altering the quality of effluent or

580. P.U. (A) 338/78.
581. For the purposes of the Environmental Quality (Prescribed Premises) (Raw Natural Rubber) Regulation 1978, 'quarter' means a period of three months commencing on 1 January, 1 April, 1 July or 1 October.
582. *See* First Schedule of the Environmental Quality (Prescribed Premises) (Raw Natural Rubber) Regulations 1978.
583. Regulation 12 of the Environmental Quality (Prescribed Premises) (Raw Natural Rubber) Regulations 1978.
584. Regulation 13 of the Environmental Quality (Prescribed Premises) (Raw Natural Rubber) Regulations 1978.
585. Regulation 14 of the Environmental Quality (Prescribed Premises) (Raw Natural Rubber) Regulations 1978.
586. Regulation 15 of the Environmental Quality (Prescribed Premises) (Raw Natural Rubber) Regulations 1978.
587. *See* Second, Third and Fourth Schedule of the Environmental Quality (Prescribed Premises) (Raw Natural Rubber) Regulations 1978.

diluting it.[588] The point of discharge will be specified by the DG in every licence for the prescribed premises to which the licence relates.[589]

C. *Other Forms of Industrial Effluents*

414. Other types of industrial wastes are regulated by the EQA 1974 under the Environmental Quality (Industrial Effluent) Regulations 2009. Under the Regulations, 'sewage' is defined as 'any liquid waste or wastewater discharge containing human, animal, domestic, or putrescible matter in suspension or solution, and includes liquids containing chemicals in solution either in the raw, treated or partially treated form'.[590] Whereas 'industrial effluent' means 'any waste in the form of liquid or wastewater generated from manufacturing process including the treatment of water for water supply or any activity occurring at any industrial premises'.[591]

415. However, provisions under the Environmental Quality (Industrial Effluent) Regulations 2009 do not apply to effluents discharged from prescribed premises or those in the First Schedule[592] that is:

(a) processing of oil-palm fruit or oil-palm fresh-fruit bunches into crude palm oil, whether as an intermediate or a final product;
(b) processing of natural rubber in technically specified form, latex form including pre-vulcanized or the form of modified and special purpose rubber, conventional sheet, skim, crepe or scrap rubber;
(c) mining activities;
(d) processing, manufacturing, washing, or servicing of any other products or goods that produce effluent of less than 60 m^3;
(e) processing, manufacturing, washing, or servicing of any other products or goods that the effluent of which does not contain those contaminants listed as parameters (vi)–(vii) in the first column of the Fifth Schedule;
(f) processing, manufacturing, washing, or servicing of any other products or goods where the total load of biochemical oxygen (BOD) at 20C or suspended solids or both, shall not exceed 6 kg/day (concentration of 100 mg/l).

588. Regulations 6 and 8 of the Environmental Quality (Prescribed Premises) (Raw Natural Rubber) Regulations 1978.
589. Regulation 19 of the Environmental Quality (Prescribed Premises) (Raw Natural Rubber) Regulations 1978.
590. Regulation 2 of the Environmental Quality (Industrial Effluent) Regulations 2009.
591. *Ibid.*
592. Regulation 3 of the Environmental Quality (Industrial Effluent) Regulations 2009.

416. The control of industrial effluent under the Environmental Quality (Industrial Effluent) Regulations 2009 is based on parameter limits of effluent to be discharged into inland waters.[593] This is done through the application of licences known as contravention licences.[594]

417. Written permission from the DG is required before a person can carry out activities that may cause the discharge of industrial effluent.[595] If there has been any spill or accidental discharge, then the DG must be informed immediately. The person responsible for the spill or accidental discharge bears the responsibility to contain, cleanse or abate it. The DG has the power to recover all costs and expenses from the person responsible for the occurrence of any damage that it caused.[596]

418. The control of the discharge of industrial effluent and sludge onto the environment is also provided by the Environmental Quality (Industrial Effluent) Regulations 2009. Specifically, an owner or occupier of any premises that discharge industrial effluent or mixed effluent onto or into any soil, or into any inland waters or Malaysian waters are required, at his own expense, to monitor the discharge and submit the record of the discharge to the DG.[597] In addition, no person shall discharge any sludge that is generated from any production or manufacturing processes or from any industrial effluent treatment system or water treatment plant into any soil, or surface of any land, or into any inland waters or Malaysian waters without the prior written permission of the DG.[598]

II. Scheduled Wastes

A. *Cradle-to-Grave Concept*

419. Under the EQA 1974, regulations pertaining to industrial toxic and hazardous wastes[599] were formulated based on the 'cradle-to-grave' concept[600] where such wastes would be regulated and monitored from the time of its generation to the time of its disposal.[601]

---

593. Regulations 11, 12, and 13 of the Environmental Quality (Sewage and Industrial Effluent) Regulations 2009.
594. *See* s. 21 of the EQA 1974.
595. Regulation 4 of the Environmental Quality (Sewage and Industrial Effluent) Regulations 2009.
596. Regulation 20 of the Environmental Quality (Sewage and Industrial Effluent) Regulations 2009.
597. Regulation 7 of the Environmental Quality (Sewage and Industrial Effluent) Regulations 2009.
598. Regulation 13 of the Environmental Quality (Sewage and Industrial Effluent) Regulations 2009.
599. For scheduled wastes pollution sources, *see* Kementerian Sumber Asli dan Alam Sekitar Malaysia, *Environmental Quality Report 2006* 64 (Jabatan Alam Sekitar 2007).
600. *See* Kementerian Sumber Asli dan Alam Sekitar Malaysia, *Environmental Quality Report 1989* 4 (Jabatan Alam Sekitar 1990).
601. These requirements were formulated in a set of Regulations and Order, that is, Environmental Quality (Scheduled Wastes) Regulations 1989, P.U. (A) 139/1989; and Environmental Quality (Prescribed Premises) (Scheduled Wastes Treatment and Disposal facilities) Order 1989, P.U. (A) 140/1989.

420. The Act defines 'scheduled waste' as 'any waste prescribed by the Minister in the regulations as scheduled wastes'.[602] The regulations here refer to the Environmental Quality (Scheduled Wastes) Regulations 2005.[603]

421. With regard to the regulation of scheduled wastes, it is a requirement under the Environmental Quality (Scheduled Wastes) Regulation 2005[604] for waste producers to notify the DG of any generation of scheduled waste in their premises.[605] This notification requirement is followed by the requirement on storage procedures.[606] Every waste producer has to ensure that his scheduled wastes are properly stored in containers which are durable and able to prevent spillage.[607]

422. In the case of spillage, the DG may take such action as is necessary to remove, disperse, destroy or mitigate the pollution and may recover from that person all costs and expenses incurred in connection therewith under section 47 of the EQA.

423. It is also a requirement that scheduled waste containers must be clearly labelled in accordance with the Third Schedule of the Environmental Quality (Scheduled Wastes) Regulations 2005[608] and marked with the scheduled waste code as specified in the First Schedule of the Regulations.[609] Incompatible scheduled wastes[610] should be stored in separate containers and placed in separate secondary containment areas.[611]

---

602. *See* Regulation 2 of the Environmental Quality (Scheduled Wastes) Regulation 2005.
603. P.U. (A) 294/2005. The First Schedule of the Regulations contains a list of items considered as scheduled wastes including that of metal and metal bearing wastes; wastes containing principally inorganic constituents which may contain metals and organic materials; wastes containing principally organic constituents which may contain metals and inorganic materials; wastes which may contain either inorganic or organic constituents; and other wastes.
604. The Regulations were introduced to repeal the Environmental Quality (Scheduled Wastes) Regulations 1989, P.U. (A) 139/1989.
605. Regulation 3 of the Environmental Quality (Scheduled Wastes) Regulations 2005.
606. Regulation 9 of the Environmental Quality (Scheduled Wastes) Regulations 2005.
607. Incidents of spillage and accidental discharge are provided in Regulation 14 of the Environmental Quality (Scheduled Wastes) Regulations 2005.
608. Regulation 10 of the Environmental Quality (Scheduled Wastes) Regulations 2005.
609. Regulation 10 of the Environmental Quality (Scheduled Wastes) Regulations 2005.
610. 'Incompatible scheduled wastes' is defined in Regulation 2 of the Environmental Quality (Scheduled Wastes) Regulations 2005 to mean 'scheduled wastes specified in the Fourth Schedule which when mixed, will produce hazardous situations through heat generation, fires, explosions or the release of toxic substances'.
611. Regulation 9(2) of the Environmental Quality (Scheduled Wastes) Regulations 2005.

424. Another aspect of monitoring is the transportation of the scheduled wastes.[612] Every waste generator must provide information in accordance with the Seventh Schedule of the Regulations, in respect of each category of scheduled waste to be delivered.[613]

425. The final aspect of monitoring is the treatment and disposal of scheduled wastes. It is a legal requirement that scheduled wastes have to be treated and disposed of at prescribed premises only.[614] As far as practicable, prior to disposal the scheduled wastes should be rendered innocuous.[615] Scheduled wastes can only be disposed of by the waste generator at prescribed premises.[616]

B. Licence for Scheduled Wastes

426. Under the EQA 1974, schedules waste is regulated through licensing requirements under section 18 the Act and the Environmental Quality (Prescribed Premises) (Scheduled Wastes Treatment and Disposal Facilities) Order 1989.[617] Six toxic and hazardous waste facilities are considered as prescribed premises under this Order, namely:

- off-site storage facilities;
- off-site treatment facilities;
- off-site recovery facilities;
- scheduled waste incinerators;
- land treatment facilities; and
- secure landfills.

427. The regulations pertaining to licences for prescribed premises on scheduled wastes are the Environmental Quality (Prescribed Premises) (Scheduled Wastes Treatment and Disposal Facilities) Regulations 1989.[618] These Regulations require that when a person is a holder of a licence, he must keep an accurate and up-to-date inventory of the types and quantities of scheduled wastes received.[619]

612. Regulation 13 of the Environmental Quality (Scheduled Wastes) Regulations 2005.
613. The requirements in the Seventh Schedule include information pertaining to its properties, handling manners, precautions in case of spills or accidents, and steps to be taken in case of spill or accident discharge causing material damage.
614. Regulation 4 of the Environmental Quality (Scheduled Wastes) Regulations 2005.
615. Regulation 4(2) of the Environmental Quality (Scheduled Wastes) Regulations 2005.
616. In the case of Malaysia, it is the Kualiti Alam waste management centre at Bukit Nanas, Negeri Sembilan, Malaysia.
617. P.U. (A) 140/1989.
618. P.U. (A) 141/1989.
619. Regulation 6 of the Environmental Quality (Prescribed Premises) (Scheduled Wastes Treatment and Disposal Facilities) Regulations 1989.

428. Being a prescribed premises for scheduled wastes, its occupation and use is an offence unless the person is a holder of the licence.[620] Any person who is found guilty of operating prescribed premises without licence is liable to a fine up to MYR 50,000, imprisonment for a period not exceeding two years, or both, and can be further fined MYR 1,000 for every day that the offence is continued after a notice to quit is served on him.[621] One decided case on a prescribed premises for scheduled waste is *P.P. v. Lohtra Enterprise*.[622] In this case, a premises was found to be operating silver metal recovery from discharged spent aqueous[623] without a licence for prescribed premises. On this basis, the owner was charged with committing an offence under section 18 of the EQA 1974.

C. Prescribed Conveyance

429. Vehicles and ships used to transport scheduled wastes are also prescribed as prescribed conveyances under section 18(1A)[624] of the EQA 1974, together with the Environmental Quality (Prescribed Conveyance) (Scheduled Wastes) Order 2005.[625]

430. Under this Order, prescribed conveyances are any vehicle or ship of the following description:

– propelled by a mechanism contained within itself;
– constructed or adapted to be used on land or water; and
– used for the movement, transfer, placement or deposit of scheduled wastes.

D. Legal Provisions

431. General prohibition on the deposit of schedules wastes is provided in section 34B of the EQA 1974. Under this section, no person is allowed to do the following without prior written approval from the DG:

620. *See* Regulation 3 of the Environmental Quality (Prescribed Premises) (Scheduled Wastes Treatment and Disposal Facilities) Order 1989. *See also* Kementerian Sains, Teknologi dan Alam Sekitar, Malaysia, *Malaysian Integrated Scheduled Wastes Collections, Treatment and Disposal Project: Environmental Impact Assessment* (Jabatan Alam Sekitar 1992).
621. Section 18(3) of the EQA 1974.
622. Petaling Jaya Session's Court, Case No. 63-1-2004.
623. 'Spent aqueous' has been listed as scheduled waste with code N161 under the First Schedule of the Environmental Quality (Scheduled Wastes) Regulations 1989.
624. Subsection (1A) of s. 18 states that the Minister, after consultation with the Council may by order prescribe the vehicle or ship used for the movement, transfer, placement or deposit of wastes (hereinafter referred to as 'prescribed conveyance') the use of which by any person shall, unless he is the holder of a licence issued in respect of the prescribed conveyance, be an offence under this Act.
625. P.U. (A) 293/2005.

- place, deposit or dispose of, or cause or permit to place, deposit or dispose of, except at prescribed premises only, any scheduled wastes on land or into Malaysian waters;
- receive or send, or cause or permit to be received or sent any scheduled wastes in or out of Malaysia; or
- transit or cause or permit the transit of scheduled wastes.

432. One decided case pertaining to section 34B is *P.P. v. LK Metal (M) Sdn. Bhd.*[626] In this case, an accused person was found guilty for allowing aluminium dross[627] to be placed within his premises without a written approval from the DG in contravention of section 34B. Thus, he was fined MYR 25,000 for the offence.

433. Under section 34B, it is also an offence to receive, send or transit any scheduled wastes with an approval obtained through falsification, misrepresentation or fraud or which does not conform in a material way with the relevant documents in such form as may be prescribed.[628] The penalty imposed upon conviction under section 34B is a fine not exceeding MYR 500,000 or imprisonment for a period not exceeding five years or both.

III. International Law

434. Provisions on scheduled wastes under Part IVA of the EQA 1974 were introduced in order to implement the Basel Convention on the Control of Transboundary Movements of Hazardous Wastes and their Disposal.[629]

435. To further facilitate implementation of the Convention, Malaysia has formulated two Orders under the Customs Act 1967.[630] They are:

- the Customs (Prohibition and Exports) Order 1998;[631] and
- the Customs (Prohibition of Imports) Order 1998.[632]

436. These Orders are being enforced together by the Malaysian Royal Customs and Excise Department and the Department of Environment. They require that any exporter and importer of toxic and hazardous wastes out of or into Malaysia obtain prior written consent from the DG, who is the designated competent authority and focal point for Malaysia.

626. In the Session Court at Kelang, Case No. SS2-63-88-00.
627. Scheduled Waste code N201, First Schedule of the Environmental Quality (Scheduled Wastes) Regulations 1989.
628. Section 34B(3) of the EQA 1974.
629. Malaysia became a party to the Convention in October 1993.
630. Act 235.
631. P.U. (A) 211/98.
632. P.U. (A) 210/98.

§3. Sewerage

I. Previous Framework

437. Previously, up until January 2008, the main laws that applied to deal with the discharge of sewage in Malaysia were the Sewerage Services Act 1993[633] and the Local Government Act 1976.[634] These laws were implemented by the Sewerage Department under the Ministry of Energy, Water and Communications, and the Local Authority.

438. The sewerage services were previously provided by the local authority under the state government and the cost was borne by the rates charged by the local authority to the property owner. In 1993, with the enactment of the Sewerage Services Act 1993, the federal government was empowered to privatize the sewerage services. The enactment of the Act also allowed the federal government to take over the executive authority on matters relating to sewerage services throughout Malaysia and to remove all jurisdictions of the local authority over sewerage matters.[635]

439. Apart from that, the sewerage services was privatized by the federal government. This privatization was carried out through an agreement between the government and a concessionaire, which is a private entity known as the *Indah Water Konsortium Sdn. Bhd.* However, the Consortium, which holds the concession to the privatized sewage services, has been operating at a deficit. The company was originally owned by a private sector entity. Since it remained unprofitable, it had to be taken over by the federal government.[636]

440. Despite attempts to improve the level of service, a large amount of sewage produced daily in Malaysia remained untreated and discharged into the rivers. Problems that exist with the sewerage services in Malaysia require a radical reform through an integration of sewage services with the water services.

II. Previous Legislation

A. Sewerage Services Act 1993

441. Up until January 2008, the main legislation that applied to matters relating to public or private sewerage systems and services was the Sewerage Services Act 1993.[637] This Act dealt with the regulation of public and private sewerage systems

633. Act 508.
634. Act 171.
635. *See* Ministry Energy, Water & Commun., Malay., *The Water Tablet: Malaysian Water Reforms* 27–35 (Ministry Energy, Water & Commun., Malay. 2008).
636. *Ibid.*, 35–42.
637. (Act 508), deleted by Act 655.

to ensure proper management of the sewerage system. The Act also provided guidelines for how a sewerage system is to be constructed, operated and maintained.

442. This Act was regulated by the Sewerage Services Department. The DG of this department was responsible to ensure that the sewerage system was properly managed and maintained.[638] He also had the power to give notice requiring the owner or occupier to take the necessary measures for the draining of sewage from the building.[639] Under this Act, the sewerage system was only meant for sewage. Industrial effluents could only enter the system with the prior written permission of the DG.[640] Non-compliance would result in a fine not exceeding MYR 50,000, and a further fine of MYR 5,000 for each day the offence continued after conviction.[641] Perpetrators could also be required to pay compensation for any damage caused.[642]

B. The Local Government Act 1976

443. The Local Government Act 1976 is another statute that had been relied upon for sewerage regulation as provided in section 70.

444. This section empowers the local government to prosecute any person who causes to fall or flow any solid or liquid sewage matter into any stream, either within the limit of the local government area or otherwise. In this case, the local government can impose a fine up to MYR 5,000, jail up to two years, or both on the person, if found guilty.[643]

III. Present Framework

A. Introduction

445. For effective and comprehensive regulation of sewerage services in Malaysia, the federal government revamped the water services industry and established a federal agency to act as a single regulator of sewerage services. For this purpose, the Federal Constitution was amended to transfer water services from the State List to the Concurrent List.

446. The Constitution (Amendment) Act 2005 includes the items 'water supplies and services' under the Concurrent List to enable the federal government to regulate sewerage services through the enactment of the Water Services Industry Act 2006 and the Water Services Industry Corporation Act 2006.

---

638. Section 15 of the Sewerage Services Act 1993.
639. Section 17 of the Sewerage Services Act 1993.
640. Section 19(1) of the Sewerage Services Act 1993.
641. Section 19(2) of the Sewerage Services Act 1993.
642. Section 20 of the Sewerage Services Act 1993.
643. Relevant by-laws here are the Penang Sewage and Sanitary Installation By-Laws 1970, and the Municipal Council of Penang Island (Public Lavatories) By-Laws 1993.

B. Water Services Industry Act 2006

447. Section 2 of the Water Services Industry Act 2006[644] provides for the definitions of relevant terms. 'Sewerage services area' means 'an area within which a service licensee is authorized to provide sewerage services'.

448. This Act defined 'sewage' as:

> any liquid discharges containing human excreta, animal or vegetable matters in suspension or solution derived from domestic activities and being generated from household, commercial, institutional and industrial premises including liquid discharges from water closets, basins, sinks, bathrooms and other sanitary appliances but excluding rain water and prohibited effluent.

449. 'Sewerage services' means 'the collection, conveyance, treatment and disposal of sewage or sewage sludge, and includes the operation and maintenance of a sewerage system and the de-sludging of septic tanks'.

450. 'Sewerage system' means:

> a system incorporating sewers, disposal pipes, pumping stations or sewage treatment works or any combination thereof and all other structures, equipment and appurtenances (other than individual internal sewerage piping, common internal sewerage piping or septic tanks) used or intended to be used for the collection, conveyance, pumping or treatment of sewage and sewage sludge or the disposal of treated sewage effluent or sewage sludge.

451. Part III of the Act deals with duties and obligations applicable to licensees providing sewerage services. Section 43 of the Act requires every service licensee operating and maintaining a public sewerage system to:

- manage, operate, maintain, inspect, repair, alter, arch over or otherwise improve the public sewerage system and to treat and dispose of the contents thereof; and
- properly de-sludge the public sewerage system;

and for such purposes the service licensee may cause the construction or placing, either above or underground, of such sewers, pumps and other works as are necessary.

452. Section 61 is on the prohibition of the discharge of effluent or noxious matter into a public sewer. It states that no person shall discharge into or allow to be discharged into any public sewer or public-sewage-treatment works the following matters:

- any prohibited effluent, without the approval of the Commission;

644. Act 655.

- any noxious, volatile or inflammable substance or any other matter likely to damage or impair the functioning of any public sewer or public-sewage-treatment works or to interfere with the free flow of its contents or to affect prejudicially the treatment or disposal of its contents; or
- any effluent, matter or substance from a garbage grinder or such other device determined by the Commission, without the approval of the Commission.

453. Under section 61, a person who contravenes this section commits an offence and shall, on conviction, be liable to a fine not exceeding MYR 100,000, to imprisonment for a term not exceeding one year, or both.

454. The penalty in respect of nuisance caused by private sewerage systems or septic tanks is provided in section 66. Here, the owner of or management corporation responsible for any private sewerage system or septic tank which is so foul, is in such a state, or is so situated as to be a nuisance or a danger to health; or any premises which are not ventilated in such manner as to render harmless as far as practicable any gas, vapour, dust or other impurity that is harmful to health generated from that private sewerage system or septic tank, commits an offence and shall, on conviction, be liable to a fine not exceeding MYR 50,000, to imprisonment for a term not exceeding six months, or both.

455. Other wrongful acts for sewerage are provided in section 122(1) which includes a person who performs any of the following:

- wilfully, negligently or recklessly damages or causes to be damaged any pipe, channel, conduit or structure, sewer, manhole, chamber, fixture, equipment, reservoir, cistern, pump, hydrant, valve, metre, sub-metre or any part of any public water supply system or public sewerage system;
- flushes, draws off, diverts or takes water from any public water supply system or part of the system, unless the person is otherwise permitted under this Act or any other written law;
- bathes, wastes or throws any rubbish or creature, dead or alive, into any public water supply system or part of the system; or
- trespasses on any area of a service reservoir or booster station of a public water supply system or on any area of a sewage pumping station or sewage treatment works of a public sewerage system.

456. In such situations, the person commits an offence and shall, on conviction, be liable to a fine not exceeding MYR 50,000, to imprisonment for a term not exceeding six months, or both.

457. Part XIII of the Act provides for repeal, savings and transitional provisions. Regarding previously existing sewerage services, under section 189(1), all local authorities who were, prior to the coming into operation of this Act, authorized under any written law to own a sewerage system or provide sewerage services, continue to be authorized under this Act to own or provide the aforesaid facilities and services for a period of one year from the appointed date or such other period as may be extended by the Commission, if such local authority registered with the Commission within three months or such other period as may be extended by the Commission after the appointed date.

§4. SULLAGE

458. Sullage water is effluent discharged into the drainage system without any treatment and can come from various sources such as trade and commercial activities, domestic sullage, wet markets and slaughterhouses. The main agency that has the power and responsibility over sullage water is the local government through the enforcement of the Street Drainage and Building Act 1974.[645]

459. Under this Act, 'sullage' is defined to include 'any household waste liquids discharged from any bath, shower, lavatory, basin, floor gully, laundries or sink but excludes faecal water and urine'. The control of sullage is provided under section 56 of the Act which disallows pipes used for the carrying off of rain water from any roof to be used for carrying off the soil or drainage from any privy or water closet or any sullage water. Any person who contravenes this section can be fined up to MYR 500.

460. Section 55 of this Act can be applied to regulate the discharge of both domestic and commercial sullage by prohibiting any water closet[646] or privy from connecting with any river, canal, stream, pond, lake, sea or with any public surface or storm water drain without permission from the Local Authority or State Authority. Under this section, any person who contravenes any condition imposed on the permission may be liable to a fine up to MYR 1,000 for each offence.

461. The discharge of sullage water from wet markets and slaughterhouses is provided in section 47(1)(d). Here, the local authority has the power to sanction any person who throws, places, spills, or scatters any blood, brine, swill, noxious liquid or other offensive or filthy matters of any kind in such manner as to run or fall into any public place, including a riverbank. Any person who commits such offence can be arrested without warrant and can be fined up to MYR 500.

462. There are other provisions that can be used indirectly to deal with the problem of sullage. Under the Street, Drainage and Building Act 1974, the local authority can take proactive measures to prevent the discharge of sullage directly into the drain or river as provided in section 58(2) and (3). Here, when a person submits a plan for the erection of a house or building to the local authority, the local authority

645. *See* Sharifah Zubaidah & Mustafa Maizatun, *Preventing Pollution in Malaysian Rivers: A Legal and Institutional Perspective*, a paper presented at the *5th Asia Law Institute Conference* (U. Sing. 2008).

646. 'Water Closet' is defined in s. 58 of the Street Drainage and Building Act 1974 as a 'closet communication used or adapted or intended to be used in connection with water carriageway system and comprising provision for the flushing of the receptacle by means of a fresh water supply, and having proper communication with a sewer'.

can require such house or building to be provided with a proper number of water closets, urinals, sinks and bathrooms, which must be connected to the sewer.

§5. Agricultural Waste

463. In Malaysia, agricultural waste in the form of the discharge from animal husbandry contributes towards environmental pollution. One livestock activity that has become a major contributor towards water pollution is pig farming, through the discharge of pig waste into water resources.[647]

464. Generally, the regulation of pig farming, including the issuance of a licence, is under the jurisdiction of the state government through its respective State Veterinary Services Department. These also have the power to pass law on piggery farm management and the control of the discharge of piggery waste into inland water. The relevant state legislation on pig farming activities are as follows:

- the Control of Rearing Pigs Enactment of Negeri Sembilan 1980;[648]
- the Rearing of Pigs Enactment of Johor 1975;[649]
- the Rearing of Pigs Enactment of Malacca 1980;[650]
- the Rearing of Pigs Enactment of Perlis 1987;[651]
- the Rearing of Pigs Enactment of Terengganu 1976;[652]
- the Control of Pigs Farming Enactment of Selangor 1991;[653] and
- the Control of Pigs Enactment of Perak 1992.[654]

465. These Enactments are applied only in the relevant states, but they are not strictly uniform. Generally, they contain similar provisions on matters such as the planning and siting of pig farms and the hygienic control of animal wastes and pig farming licensing.

466. Under these enactments, the power to issue licences lies with the 'licensing officer' who is the State Director of Veterinary Services for the respective states.[655]

467. One general provision under these Enactments is the prohibition on the rearing, breeding or keeping of any pig within the state, unless a licence is obtained

647. *See* Maizatun Mustafa & Mariani Ho, *Agriculture Wastes and Role of Environmental Law in Malaysia.* Paper presented at *International Conference on Agriculture Wastes* (Universiti Putra Malay 2006).
648. No. 9 of 1980.
649. No. 5 of 1975.
650. No. 3 of 1980.
651. No. 7 of 87.
652. No. 3 of 1991.
653. No. 3 of 1991.
654. No. 5 of 1992.
655. Section 2 of the respective Enactments.

from the licensing officer. Any person who fails to produce a licence without a reasonable excuse may be liable to a fine not exceeding MYR 500,[656] except for in the state of Perak, where the penalty is a fine of up to MYR 15,000, jail for up to three years, or both.

468. All the enactments, under their respective section 4, make it a prohibition for a person to rear, breed or keep any pig for any purpose otherwise than in a properly fenced enclosure, or within a pig farming zone, as provided in section 7 of Perak's Enactment.

469. Certain enactments also make a requirement that pig farming cannot cause any pollution to any well, river, stream, waterway, inland water, irrigation canal or any subterranean water resources, the water of which is likely to be used for human bathing or drinking purposes. The Malacca Enactment provides a penalty amounting to a fine not exceeding MYR 500 for such offences.

470. Under section 21 of the Selangor Enactment, a licensee shall be guilty of an offence if any untreated pig waste is discharged or disposed of into or onto any river, lake or sea; public drain; pool or pond or land situated outside the boundaries of the pig farm. The punishment imposed under section 21 for the contravention of this provision is a fine of up to MYR 10,000 or one-year imprisonment. Whereas section 21 of Perak's Enactment imposes a fine of up to MYR 15,000, a jail sentence of up to three years, or both for the same offence.

§6. Solid Waste

I. Introduction

471. Solid waste has been identified to be one of the main contributors of soil and inland water pollution in Malaysia. Based on the population size of 27 million in 2007, the total solid waste generated in Malaysia was about 21,600–27,000 tonnes per day. The sharp rise in waste generation is very characteristic of a fast developing country like Malaysia and needs to be managed properly to avoid adverse environmental pollution.

472. Prior to the enactment of the Solid Waste and Public Cleansing Management Act 2007, the regulation and control of solid waste and public cleansing management came under the various local authorities through their respective by-laws. Unfortunately, the lack of uniformity in the laws hindered a more efficient management of solid waste.

656. Section 8 of the respective Enactments.

II. Solid Waste: Previous Framework

473. Up until 2008, the regulation of solid waste was under the local government through the Local Government Act 1976. This Act contained provisions on public nuisance;[657] pollution of streams from solid refuse or any rubbish or waste matter;[658] and cleanliness and sanitary services, such as removal of rubbish, litter, solid or liquid refuse and effluent within the local government's area.[659]

474. Another local government legislation on solid waste was the Street, Drainage and Building Act 1974. Section 47, which empowered the local authority to take action against any person who, among other things:

- places, deposits or throws refuse, boxes, barrels, bales or other articles or things in public places;
- drops, spills, scatters garden refuse, stable refuse, trade refuse, manure, garbage or any other things in any public places; or
- throws or leaves behind bottles, glass, cans, food wrappers or particles of food in any public place.

III. Present Framework

A. Introduction

475. In order to ensure uniformity of solid waste services throughout Malaysia, the federal government enacted the Solid Waste and Public Cleansing Management Act 2007. This enactment was passed in accordance with clause (1) of Article 74 and clause (2) of Article 80 of the Federal Constitution.

476. For implementing this Act, a new body has been set up, known as the National Water Services Corporation, which was established under the Solid Waste and Public Cleansing Corporation Act 2007. This Corporation comes under the National Solid Waste Management Department of the Ministry of Housing and Local Government. The main functions of this Department are mainly focusing on the law, setting up strategies, action plans and policies. The Department is also empowered to approve licences to those who will do the collection, transportation of solid wastes and public cleansing.

657. Section 69 Local Authority Act 1976.
658. Section 70 Local Authority Act 1976.
659. Sections 72 and 73 Local Authority Act 1976.

B. Solid Waste and Public Cleansing Act 2007

477. The Solid Waste and Public Cleansing Management Act 2007 was enacted in accordance with clause (1) of Article 74 and clause (2) of Article 80 of the Federal Constitution. It was passed by the Malaysian Parliament in August 2007 but has yet to come into force.

478. The main purpose of its introduction is to ensure uniformity of law and policy, and to provide for proper control and regulation of matters relating to the management of controlled solid waste and public cleansing throughout Peninsular Malaysia and the Federal Territories. The Act also provides executive authority to the federal government on matters relating to the management of controlled solid waste and public cleansing.

479. The definitions of relevant terms are provided in section 2 of the Act. Under this section, 'solid waste' includes:

> any scrap material or other unwanted surplus substance or rejected products arising from the application of any process; any substance required to be disposed of as being broken, worn out, contaminated or otherwise spoiled; or any other material that according to this Act or any other written law is required by the authority to be disposed of for Solid Waste and Public Cleansing Management but does not include scheduled wastes as prescribed under the EQA 1974; sewage as defined in the Water Services Industry Act 2006; or radioactive waste as defined in the Atomic Energy Licensing Act 1984.

480. 'Public solid waste' means 'any solid waste generated by public places, which are under the supervision or control of any local authority'.

481. 'Imported solid waste' means 'any solid waste generated in other countries and imported to Malaysia for processing or disposal'.

482. 'Household solid waste' means 'any solid waste generated by a household, and of a kind that is ordinarily generated or produced by any premises when occupied as a dwelling house, and includes garden waste'.

483. 'Institutional solid waste' means 'any solid waste generated by any premises approved under any written law or by the State Authority for use wholly or mainly for religious worship or for charitable purposes; any premises occupied by any Federal or State Government department, any local authority or any statutory body; any educational premises; any healthcare facilities including hospitals, clinics and health centres; or any premises used as public zoos, public museums, public libraries and orphanages'.

484. 'Special solid waste' means 'any kind of controlled solid waste as may be prescribed which is or may be dangerous to public health; or is difficult to treat, keep or dispose of, so that special provisions are required to deal with it'.

485. 'Commercial solid waste' means 'any solid waste generated from any commercial activity'.

486. 'Construction solid waste' means 'any solid waste generated from any construction or demolition activity, including improvement, preparatory, repair or alteration works'.

487. 'Industrial solid waste' means 'any solid waste generated from any industrial activity'.

488. 'Controlled solid waste' means 'any solid waste falling within any of the following categories: commercial solid waste; construction solid waste; household solid waste; industrial solid waste; institutional solid waste; imported solid waste; public solid waste; or solid waste which may be prescribed from time to time'.

489. 'Recyclable solid waste' means 'controlled solid waste which is suitable for recycling as may be prescribed'.

490. 'Public cleansing management services' means the following services: the cleansing of public roads, public places, public toilets and public drains; the cleansing of hawker centres excluding privately owned and maintained food courts; and markets excluding privately owned and maintained markets; the clearing of illegally dumped controlled solid waste on public roads and in public places; beach cleansing; kerbside grass cutting on public roads; grass cutting in public places; and removal of carcasses, but excludes landscaping and the maintenance of public roads and public places.

491. Section 3 provides that the Federal Government shall, upon the coming into operation of this Act, have executive authority with respect to all matters relating to the management of solid waste and public cleansing throughout Peninsular Malaysia and the Federal Territories of Putrajaya and Labuan.

492. Part II of the Act contains provisions on administration. Under section 5, the Minister is empowered to appoint a Director General of Solid Waste and Public Cleansing Management, who shall head a department, from among members of the public service for such period and on such terms and conditions as may be specified in the instrument of appointment. Functions and powers of the DG are provided in section 6(1), namely:

- to propose, after taking into consideration the recommendation from the Corporation, policies, plans and strategies in respect of solid waste and public cleansing management to the Minister;
- to formulate, after taking into consideration the recommendation from the Corporation, plans for solid waste management including the location, type and size of new treatment facilities, the coverage areas of the solid waste management

facilities, the solid waste management schemes to supply controlled solid waste to the solid waste management facilities and the timescale for the implementation of the plans;

- to set, after taking into consideration the recommendation from the Corporation, standards, specifications and codes of practice relating to any aspect of solid waste management services and public cleansing management services;
- to exercise the regulatory functions specified in this Act and any regulations made under this Act;
- to grant licences and approvals under this Act; and
- to carry out such other activities for carrying out, or in connection with, the performance of his functions under this Act.

493. Part IV is on licensing provisions. The requirement of holding a licence is stated in section 14; no person shall undertake or provide any solid waste management services unless he holds a licence. Under section 14(3), a person who is liable may be fined not less than MYR 50,000 and not exceeding MYR 100,000, imprisoned for a term not exceeding five years, or sentenced to both, and in the case of a continuing offence, may be liable to a fine not exceeding MYR 5,000 for every day or part of a day during which the offence continues after conviction.

494. Part VIII deals with control of solid waste generators and persons in possession of controlled solid wastes. Under section 71, no person shall deposit, separate, store, keep, collect, transfer, transport, treat or dispose of or cause to be or permit to be deposited, separated, stored, kept, collected, transferred, transported, treated or disposed of any controlled solid waste otherwise than in accordance with this Act.

495. Part IX contains enforcement provisions including the power of enforcement and investigation. Power of investigation is provided in section 80(1) which empowers an authorized officer to investigate the commission of any offence under this Act.

496. A general penalty is provided in section 107. Any person who commits an offence under this Act for which no penalty is expressly provided shall, on conviction, be liable to a fine not exceeding MYR 10,000, to imprisonment for a term not exceeding one year, or both.

C. Solid Waste and Public Cleansing Corporation Act 2007

497. Another statute relevant to solid waste and public cleansing management is the Solid Waste and Public Cleansing Corporation Act 2007[660] for establishing a body known as the Solid Waste Management Corporation. However, this Act is yet to come into force.

660. Act 673.

498. Once established, this Corporation will be the enforcement arm of the National Solid Waste Management Department to coordinate and manage collection of wastes from households, institutions and industries, including commercial and construction wastes.

499. Specifically, the Department and Corporation are taking over public cleansing, previously under the local authority areas, cleaning-up roads, public places, public toilets, drains, markets, hawker centres, beaches and grass cutting. Their other responsibilities include managing landfills, incinerators and transportation of solid wastes.

500. Part II of the Act is on the establishment of the Corporation. Section 3(1) provides for a body corporate by the name of the 'Solid Waste and Public Cleansing Management Corporation' to be established.

501. Under section 5, the Corporation shall consist of the following members who shall be appointed by the Minister:

- the Chairman;
- a representative of the Ministry charged with the responsibility for solid waste and public cleansing management;
- a representative of the Treasury;
- a representative of the Economic Planning Unit;
- a representative of the ministry related to the environment;
- the Chief Executive Officer; and not more than three other members who shall have relevant knowledge and experience.

502. As the enforcement arm, the Corporation has powers delegated from the Department to ensure that its laws, policies, strategies and action plans on solid waste and public cleansing are carried out by those involved. The Corporation has the power to grant licences to concessionaires to undertake solid waste and public cleansing management services in local authority areas. It is expected that the Urban Services Department in all local authorities will be privatized and will be given such licence under the new law.

§7. Leachate

503. Leachate is a potentially polluting liquor which accumulates beneath a landfill site resulting from the infiltration and percolation of rainfall, groundwater, runoff or floodwater into and through an existing or abandoned solid waste landfill site.[661]

661. Jaffar Y.M. Alkassasbeh et al., *Toxicity Testing and the Effect of Landfill Leachate in Malaysia on Behavior of Common Carp (Cyprinus carpio L., 1758; Pisces, Cyprinidae)*, 5 Am. J. Envtl. Sci. 209–217 (2009).

In 2009, the EQA 1974 has gazetted another new Regulation applicable to solid waste transfer stations and landfills which discharge or release leachate.[662] The Regulations, known as the Environmental Quality (Control of Pollution from Solid Waste Transfer Station and Landfill) Regulations 2009, also revoked the Environmental Quality (Sewage and Industrial Effluents) Regulations 1979.[663] By virtue of the new Regulations, the control of the discharge or release of leachate from solid waste transfer stations and landfills is within the jurisdiction of the Department of Environment Malaysia.

The definitions of relevant terms are provided in Regulation 2 of the Environmental Quality (Control of Pollution from Solid Waste Transfer Station and Landfill) Regulations 2009. Under this regulation, 'leachate' means 'liquid that has percolated through solid waste and has been extracted or dissolved, or suspended materials from the solid waste, or liquid discharged or released from a solid waste transfer station and landfill'.

'Solid waste' is meant to have the same meaning assigned to it in the Solid Waste and Public Cleansing Management Act 2007. Whereas 'solid waste transfer station' means 'a facility where solid waste is received for the purpose of subsequent transfer to another facility for further processing, treatment, transfer or disposal'.

'Landfill' means 'a waste disposal site for the deposit of solid waste onto or into land'.

Under Regulation 4 of the Regulations, no person shall carry out any work on any solid waste transfer station or landfill,[664] or construct on any land any facility or building that may result in a new source of leachate discharge or release without prior written notification to the DG.

It is a requirement under Regulation 5 that an owner or occupier of a solid waste transfer station or landfill to operate the solid waste transfer station or landfill in such a manner that the following are strictly controlled namely: noise, dust or odours; air pollution; pollution of the soil, surface water or groundwater; and entry and disposal of scheduled wastes.

The same owner or occupier of a landfill that discharges leachate onto or into any soil, or into any inland waters or Malaysian waters is also required, at his own expense, to monitor the concentration of ammoniacal nitrogen[665] and other parameters[666] in the leachate discharged from the landfill. He is also required to conduct performance monitoring of the components of the leachate treatment system,[667] namely the routine monitoring of certain characteristics to provide an indication that a treatment process is functional and capable of treating leachate.

---

662. Regulation 3 of the Environmental Quality (Control of Pollution from Solid Waste Transfer Station and Landfill) Regulations 2009.
663. [P.U. (A) 12/1979]. Regulation 30 of the Environmental Quality (Control of Pollution from Solid Waste Transfer Station and Landfill) Regulations 2009.
664. First Schedule, the Environmental Quality (Control of Pollution from Solid Waste Transfer Station and Landfill) Regulations 2009.
665. Regulation 8(a) of the Environmental Quality (Control of Pollution from Solid Waste Transfer Station and Landfill) Regulations 2009.
666. Regulation 8(b) of the Environmental Quality (Control of Pollution from Solid Waste Transfer Station and Landfill) Regulations 2009.
667. Regulation 11 of the Environmental Quality (Control of Pollution from Solid Waste Transfer Station and Landfill) Regulations 2009.

One of the prohibitions imposed by the Regulations is the discharge or release of leachate onto or into any soil, or into any inland waters to Malaysian waters through a bypass.[668] It is also a prohibition for a person to dilute[669] any leachate at any time after it is produced at any solid waste transfer station or landfill.[670]

The control of the discharge of leachate under the Environmental Quality (Control of Pollution from Solid Waste Transfer Station and Landfill) Regulations 2009 is based on specified acceptable conditions as provided in the Second Schedule of the Regulations.[671]

No person is allowed to discharge leachate which contains substances in concentration greater than those specified as acceptable conditions into or into any soil, or into any inland waters or Malaysian waters.[672] However, any person may apply licence to contravene the acceptable conditions for the discharge of leachate under subsection 25(1) of the EQA 1974.[673]

Specific penalty is imposed on any person who contravenes the Regulations whereby, on conviction, shall be liable to a fine of up to MYR 100,000 or a jail for up to five years or both. A further fine not exceeding MYR 1,000 a day will be imposed for every day that the offence continues after the notice by the DG requiring him to cease the act as specified in the notice has been served upon him.

---

668. Regulation 16 of the Environmental Quality (Control of Pollution from Solid Waste Transfer Station and Landfill) Regulations 2009.
669. Under Regulation 18(2), leachate becomes diluted when it undergoes a process to make it less concentrated by adding water or other liquids from external sources other than liquids or materials used for treating leachate.
670. Regulation 17(1) of the Environmental Quality (Control of Pollution from Solid Waste Transfer Station and Landfill) Regulations 2009.
671. Regulation 13 of the Environmental Quality (Control of Pollution from Solid Waste Transfer Station and Landfill) Regulations 2009.
672. *Ibid.*
673. Regulation 14(1) of the Environmental Quality (Control of Pollution from Solid Waste Transfer Station and Landfill) Regulations 2009.

Chapter 5. Soil Pollution

§1. Introduction

504. Under the Federal Constitution, land and soil conservation in general comes under the jurisdiction of the state government as provided in List II, State List.[674] However, the federal government has jurisdiction over mineral resources[675] and matters pertaining to public health.[676]

505. In Malaysia, the main agency dealing with matters relating to soil pollution is the Department of Environment under the Ministry of Environment and Water.[677] However, land matters involving soil erosion come under the respective state and local governments.

§2. Legal Framework

I. Environmental Quality Act 1974

506. Under the EQA 1974, 'soil' is defined in section 2 to include 'earth, sand, rock, shale, minerals and vegetation in the soil'. Restrictions on the pollution of soil are provided in section 24 of the Act. This section prohibits any person from 'polluting or causing or permitting to be polluted any soil or surface of any land in contravention of the acceptable conditions specified under section 21 unless licensed'.

507. Subsection (2) of section 24 further states that a person shall be deemed to pollute any soil or the surface of any land if he does any of the following:

- places in or on any soil or in any place where it may gain access to any soil, any matter whether liquid, solid or gaseous; or
- establishes on any land a refuse dump, garbage tip, soil and rock disposal site, sludge deposit site, waste-injection well or otherwise used land for the disposal of or a repository for solid or liquid wastes so as to be obnoxious or offensive to human beings or interfere with under groundwater or be detrimental to any beneficial use of the soil or the surface of the land.

508. The penalty for offences committed under section 24 is provided in subsection (3) of section 24. It states that any person who contravenes the section shall be guilty of an offence and shall be liable to a fine not exceeding MYR 100,000, to imprisonment for a period not exceeding five years, or both, and to a further fine

674. Item 2 of List II State List.
675. Item 8 of List I Federal List.
676. Item 14 of List I Federal List.
677. See the official website at https://www.doe.gov.my/portalv1/en/

not exceeding MYR 1,000 a day for every day that the offence is continued after a notice by the DG requiring him to cease the act specified therein has been served upon him.

II. Environmental Quality (Sewage) Regulations 2009

509. Another relevant provision on soil pollution under the EQA 1974 is the Environmental Quality (Sewage) Regulations 2009.

510. These Regulations concern the control of sewage into the environment including the control of the discharge of industrial effluent and sludge onto land.

511. Regulation 15 of the Regulations restricts any person from discharging any without the prior written permission of the DG.

512. The Environmental Quality (Sewage) Regulations 2009 must be read together with section 24 of the EQA 1974 which imposes a penalty for offences committed under the Regulations. Subsection (3) of section 24 states that those who are found guilty of the offence may be subject to a fine not exceeding MYR 100,000, imprisonment for a period not exceeding five years, or both.[678]

III. Environmental Impact Assessment

513. The requirement of EIA under the EQA 1974 is another provision relevant to soil pollution.

514. Under section 34A of the Act, and the Environmental Quality (Prescribed Activities) (EIA) Order 2015,[679] persons carrying out specific activities that may cause pollution to soil must submit an EIA report before the commencement of the activity. Activities relevant to soil pollution under the First Schedule are as follows:

- Item 14(a), the construction of recovery plant, waste water treatment plant and storage facility of scheduled waste;
- Item 14(b), the construction of composting plant, and recovery plant or recycling plant of solid waste;
- Item 14(c), the construction of sewage treatment plant with 20,000 population equivalent or more, and sludge treatment facilities; and
- Item 21, groundwater development for industrial, agricultural or urban water supply of 4,500 m^3 or more per day.

678. A further fine not exceeding MYR 1,000 a day may also be imposed for every day that the offence is continued after a notice from the Director General requiring him to cease the act has been served upon him.
679. P.U. (A) 195/2015.

Relevant activities under the Second Schedule of the Environmental Quality (Prescribed Activities) (EIA) Order 2015 include:

- Item 14(a), in relation to schedule waste, the construction of thermal treatment plant, off-site recovery plant for lead acid battery wastes, and off-site recovery plant or treatment facility that generates significant amount of wastewater which is located at the upstream of public water supply intake; and
- Item 14(b), the construction of thermal treatment plant, sanitary landfill facility and transfer station.

515. The penalty imposed on any person who contravenes section 34A is a fine not exceeding MYR 500,000, jail for a period not exceeding five years, or both, and a further fine of MYR 1,000 for every day that the offence is continued.

IV. Street Drainage and Building Act 1974

516. There is a specific provision under the Street Drainage and Building Act 1974 that empowers the local authority to control soil pollution due to earthworks. 'Earthworks' under this Act includes 'any act of excavation, levelling, filling with any material, piling, the construction of foundations, or felling of trees, on any land, or any other act of dealing with or disturbing any land'.[680]

517. Section 70A(1) specifies that no person shall commence or carry out or permit to be commenced or carried out any earthworks without having first submitted to the local authority plans and specifications in respect of the earthworks and obtained the approval of the local authority thereto.

518. Subsection (2) of section 70A further states that where the earthworks are to be commenced or carried out for the construction of any building, street, drain, sewer, or embankment, or for the laying of any cable or pipe, the plans and specifications relating to such construction or work required to be submitted under this Act shall be submitted to the local authority at the same time as the plans and specifications in respect of the earthworks.

519. The penalty for the contravention of section 70A is provided in subsection (9). It states that any person who fails to comply with any direction or order given under this section or does any act to obstruct the entry or the execution of any work by or on behalf of the local authority shall upon conviction be guilty of an offence and shall be liable to imprisonment for a term not exceeding five years, to a fine not exceeding MYR 50,000, or both, and in the case of a continuing offence to a fine which may extend to MYR 500 for every day during which the offence is continued.

680. Section 70A(18) of the Street Drainage and Building Act 1974.

520. In exercising this power, section 70A(12) empowers the local authority to recover any expenses and costs incurred by it from the owner of the land on which the earthworks were carried out.

V. Land Conservation Act 1960

521. The Land Conservation Act 1960, revised 1989, is another statute relevant to the control of soil pollution. Part III of this Act deals with control of silt and erosion.

522. The power to control silt and erosion is conferred to the Land Administrator. Under section 11 of the Act, the Land Administrator may issue a notice on the owner or occupier of land, requiring him to show cause if:

- the owner causes earth, mud, silt, gravel or stone from such land to cause, or to be likely to cause damage to other land, whether alienated or not, or to any watercourse, whether natural or artificial, or to interfere or to be likely to interfere with the due cultivation of other land, whether alienated or not; or
- by reason of the steepness of the slope of such land, damage has been or is likely to be caused to such land by erosion or displacement of earth, mud, silt, gravel or stone upon or from such land.

523. The Land Administrator's power to make orders is specified in section 14. Under this section, if an owner or occupier of land who is required to show cause fails to attend at the time and place mentioned in the notice, or, having so attended, fails to show cause to the satisfaction of the Land Administrator, the Land Administrator may do any of the following:

- make an order prohibiting interference with, destruction or removal of any trees, plants, undergrowth, weeds or grass within or from such parts of the said land as are specified in the order;
- with the sanction of the State Secretary, make an order requiring the making on the said land of drains and watercourses, and the construction thereon of dams and retaining walls, of such character and dimensions and in such positions as are specified in the order; or
- with the sanction of the State Secretary, make an order requiring any act likely to prevent, and prohibiting the doing of any act or thing which facilitates the passage of earth, mud, silt, sand, gravel or stone from the said land to other land, whether owned by any person or not, or to any river, canal or drain.

524. The penalty for failure to comply with the prohibition order is provided in section 18. It states that, any person who without reasonable excuse fails to comply with any order made under, or any provision of this Act, shall be liable to a fine of not exceeding MYR 5,000 and in default of payment thereof to imprisonment for a term which may, subject to section 283 of the Criminal Procedure Code,[681] as the circumstances may require, extend to six months.

VI. Contaminated Soil

525. In Malaysia, there is no specific legislation governing contaminated soil. Although section 24 of the EQA 1974 provides powers to the DG to prohibit pollution of any soil or surface of any land, it does not specify the acceptable conditions for deposition of wastes into this medium of the environment.

526. However, several sections of the EQA 1974 address soil contamination indirectly. Section 34B on scheduled wastes prohibits the placing of any waste on land or surface waters without prior written approval from the DG. Under subsection (4) of section 34B, any person who contravenes this section shall be guilty of an offence and shall on conviction be punished with imprisonment for a term not exceeding five years and shall also be liable to a fine not exceeding MYR 500,000.

527. Under the Environmental Quality (Schedules Wastes) Regulations 2005, 'scheduled wastes' is defined in the First Schedule of the Regulations, to include, under Schedules Wastes 408, contaminated soil, debris or matter resulting from cleaning-up of a spill or chemical, mineral oil or scheduled waste. In such instances, contaminated soil will be treated by the Environmental Quality (Schedules Wastes) Regulations 2005 in a similar way to any other scheduled waste.

681. Act 593.

Chapter 6. Noise Pollution

§1. Introduction

528. Noise has been a perennial environmental problem in Malaysia, but less prominent than other forms of pollution. This is due to the nature of the pollutant, which is indiscernible, in addition to noise being accepted as the inevitable consequence of progress.[682]

529. Noise as a form of environmental pollution comes mainly within the jurisdiction of the Department of Environment, which also carries out the monitoring programme.[683] This programme is mainly to gauge the noise levels in residential areas of Malaysia based on values recommended by the World Health Organization, that is, 55 dB(A) during day time and 45 dB(A) during night time.

530. In Malaysia, there is no single statute that comprehensively deals with noise pollution, However, there are several provisions under the EQA 1974 on the control of noise pollution from mobile sources, specifically that of motor vehicles. Apart from that, local government legislation, which contains provisions on nuisance, is also relevant for noise pollution control.

§2. Legal Framework

I. Environmental Quality Act 1974

A. *Environmental Quality (Motor Vehicle Noise) Regulations 1989*

531. The EQA's jurisdiction on noise pollution concerns the control of noise in streets from moving vehicles. The main sources of road traffic noise are the power and transmission units, that is, engine and gearbox, exhaust noise and tyre noise.

532. For this purpose, section 51(j) of the EQA 1974 authorizes the Minister to make regulations defining objectionable noise and prescribing standards for tolerable noise. By virtue of this section, a Regulation was introduced under the Act to control noise pollution through the application of noise pollution standards.

533. The emission of noise from individual new vehicles is controlled by the Department of Environment through the provision in the Environmental Quality (Motor Vehicle Noise) Regulation 1987 requiring motor vehicle assemblers to conduct noise level tests on new vehicles of each model assembled in Malaysia as provided in Regulation 6. The Third and Fourth Schedules of the Regulations provide

682. *See The Encyclopedia of Malaysia: Volume 1: The Environment* 114–115 (Sham Sani ed., Archipelago Press 1998).
683. *See* Kementerian Sumber Asli dan Alam Sekitar Malaysia, *Annual Report 2011* 111–114 (Jabatan Alam Sekitar 2011).

for methods of measuring the noise emission from vehicles. The test method attempts to simulate a driving condition similar to the noisiest type of urban driving.

534. There are three Maximum Sound Level Standards, Standard A, Standard B and Standard C that are applied to regulate the sound levels of different types of motor vehicles. Specifically, Standards A and B are the standards for the maximum sound level permitted for motor vehicles having two wheels or three wheels but with different categories of vehicle. Standard C provides for the maximum sound level permitted for motor vehicles having more than three wheels.

535. The Third and Fourth Schedules of the Environmental Quality (Motor Vehicle Noise) Regulation 1987 provide for the method of measuring the noise emission from vehicles. The test method is to simulate a driving condition similar to the noisiest type of urban driving.

B. Section 23 of the Environmental Quality Act 1974

536. Section 23 of the EQA 1974 makes it an offence to emit or permit to be emitted without licence, noise over and above the acceptable standards.

537. In situations where provisions under the Environmental Quality (Motor Vehicle Noise) Regulation 1987 have been infringed, a penalty is provided for under section 23 of the EQA. Specifically, subsection (1) of this section on the restrictions on noise pollution states that no person shall, unless licensed, emit or cause or permit to be emitted any noise greater in volume, intensity and quality, in contravention of the acceptable conditions specified under section 21.

538. Acceptable conditions in the context of section 23(1) refers to the maximum noise levels in Standards A, B and C of the Environmental Quality (Motor Vehicle Noise) Regulation 1987. Subsection (2) of section 23 states that, any person who contravenes subsection (1) shall be guilty of an offence and shall be liable to a fine not exceeding MYR 100,000, to imprisonment for a period not exceeding five years, or both. A further fine not exceeding MYR 500 a day for every day would further be imposed if the offender continued with the act after the issuance of a notice to cease the act.

C. Section 48A of the Environmental Quality Act 1974

539. Section 48A is on the jurisdiction of the DG to test and prohibit the use of vehicles and relates to noise pollution.

540. Subsection (1) of section 48A authorizes the DG to enter and inspect any vehicle in use and to require any vehicle to be stopped. He may detain any vehicle for inspection. If, on such inspection, it appears to the DG that such vehicle is or is likely to contravene this Act or any regulations, he may prohibit the use of such vehicle.[684]

II. Local Government Act 1976

541. The Local Government Act 1976 also contains provisions enabling action to be taken against owners or occupier of premises, whether public or private, emitting noise that is deemed to be a nuisance. The Act defines 'nuisance' as 'any act, omission or thing occasioning or likely to occasion injury, annoyance, offence, harm, danger or damage to the sense of sight, smell or hearing or which is or is likely to be injurious or dangerous to health or property or which affects the safety or the rights of the inhabitants at large'.

542. Section 80 empowers the local government to abate the nuisance through issuance of an abatement notice. Once the notice has been served, any person who defaults in complying with the notice shall be guilty of an offence and shall, on conviction, be liable to a fine not exceeding MYR 1,000, to a term of imprisonment not exceeding six months, or both.

543. A provision on nuisance is also provided in the Street, Drainage and Building Act 1974, which defines the term as 'any act, omission or thing occasioning or likely to occasion injury, annoyance, offence, harm, danger or damage to the sense of sight, smell or hearing, or which is or is likely to be injurious or dangerous to health or property'.[685]

544. Where nuisance happens, section 87 empowers the local authority to serve notice to the person who causes the nuisance to require him to abate such nuisance. In the case of default, and upon conviction, such person shall be liable to a fine not exceeding MYR 500 for each offence.

III. The Civil Aviation Act 1969

545. The Civil Aviation Act 1969[686] is another statute in Malaysia relating to noise pollution from aircrafts. Generally, this Act was enacted by virtue of the Chicago Convention on International Civil Aviation 1944, to which Malaysia is one of the contracting states. Malaysia is bound by the Convention Agreement. This Act is enforced by the Director General of Civil Aviation of Malaysia.[687]

684. Section 48A(2) of the Environmental Quality Act 1974.
685. Section 2 of the Street, Drainage and Building Act 1974.
686. Act 3.
687. Section 2A Civil Aviation Act 1969.

546. Part V of the Act deals with liability for damage caused by aircrafts. Section 20 states that regulations made under section 3 may provide for the conditions under which noise and vibration may be caused by aircrafts on aerodromes, and may provide that subsection (2) shall apply to any aerodrome concerning which provision as to noise and vibration caused by aircrafts is so made.

547. With regard to noise pollution from aircrafts, subsection (2) of section 20 states that no action shall lie in respect of nuisance by reason only of the noise and vibration caused by aircrafts on an aerodrome to which this subsection applies by virtue of regulations under section 3, so long as any such regulations are duly complied with. 'Aerodrome' is defined in section 2 to mean any area of land or water designed, equipped, set apart or commonly used for affording facilities for the landing and departure of aircraft.

IV. Civil Aviation Regulations 1996

548. By virtue of section 3 of the Act, the Minister gazetted the Civil Aviation Regulations 1996.[688] The relevant part on noise pollution under these Regulations is Part XI on aerodromes, aeronautical lights and radio stations. Aircraft noise is provided in Regulation 102, which specifies the noise levels that an aircraft can cause.

549. Subregulation (1) of Regulation 102 requires that an aircraft shall not land or take-off in Malaysia unless the following conditions exist:

- there is in force in respect of that aircraft a noise certificate which is deemed to be used by the DG, issued or validated by the competent authority of the state in which the aircraft is registered, or issued or validated by the competent authority of the state in which the aircraft is registered; and
- all conditions subject to which the certificate was issued are complied with.

550. Subregulation (4) of Regulation 102 provides for situations where noise and vibration may be caused by an aircraft, provided that any such noise or vibration does not exceed the levels specified in Annex 16 of the Chicago Convention, when:

- the aircraft is taking off or landing;
- the aircraft is moving on the ground or water; or
- the engines are being operated in the aircraft for ensuring their satisfactory performance; for bringing them to a proper temperature in preparation for, or at the

688. P.U. (A) 139/96. It revoked the following Regulations: Civil Aviation (Aerodromes) Regulations 1979 P.U. (A) 177/79; Flight Calibration Service Charge Regulations 1977 P.U. (A) 130/ 77; and Landing, Parking and Housing Passenger Service and Air Navigation Facility Charges Regulations, 1975 – P.U. (A) 427/75.

end of, a flight; or for ensuring that the instruments, accessories or other components of the aircraft are in satisfactory condition.

551. Under section 102(5), subject to proof of compliance with the conditions specified in Annex 16 of the Chicago Convention, a noise certificate may be issued to an airplane registered in Malaysia on application to the DG by the operator concerned.

V. Factories and Machinery Act 1989

552. The Factories and Machinery Act 1967[689] was enacted to provide for the control of factories with respect to matters relating to the safety, health and welfare of persons therein, the registration and inspection of machinery and for matters connected therewith. This Act is enforced by the Chief Inspector of Factories and Machinery[690] which is under the Department of Occupational Safety and Health[691] of the Ministry of Human Resources.

553. Matters pertaining to noise exposure are regulated by the Factories and Machinery (Noise Exposure) Regulations 1989,[692] gazetted by virtue of section 56(1) of the Factories and Machinery Act 1967. Regulation 3 states that the Regulations shall apply to all factories in which persons are employed in any occupation involving exposure to excessive noise levels in the workplace.

554. Under Regulation 4, it is the duty of every employer involved in such an occupation to comply with the Regulations, and in pursuance of the Regulations, every employee must do the following:

- cooperate with the employer by wearing a noise dosimeter during employee exposure monitoring;
- wear and make full and proper use of the hearing protection device provided for his use;
- attend and undergo audiometric testing or any medical examination or test arranged by the occupier; and
- attend employee information and training programmes conducted by the occupier.

555. Regulation 5 is on permissible exposure limits. It states that no employee shall be exposed to noise levels exceeding the equivalent of a continuous sound level of 90 dB(A) or exceeding the limits specified in the First Schedule or exceeding the daily noise dose of unity; and no employee shall be exposed to a noise level

689. Act 139, revised 1974.
690. Section 4 of the Factories and machinery Act 1967.
691. Previously Department of Factory and Machinery.
692. P.U. (A) 106/89.

exceeding 115 dB(A) at any time. Regulation 6 further prohibits any employee from being exposed to impulsive noise exceeding a sound pressure level of 140 dB.

556. Where provisions under the Regulations have been contravened, the penalty is provided for in Regulation 34, which is a fine not exceeding MYR 1,000.

Chapter 7. Radiation and Vibrations

§1. THE LEGAL FRAMEWORK

I. The Atomic Energy Licensing Act 1984

557. The Malaysian legislation relating to radiation and vibrations is mainly laid down in the Atomic Energy Licensing Act 1984.[693] The authority to enforce the Act is the Director General of Health, under the Ministry of Health Malaysia.

558. The objectives of the enactment of this Act were to provide for the regulation and control of atomic energy, and for the establishment of standards on liability for nuclear damage. Under this Act, 'environment' is given the same meaning assigned to that expression in section 2 of the EQA 1974 and includes the marine environment.[694]

559. The control of ionizing radiation is through licensing under Part III of the Act. Section 3 of the Act provides for the establishment of the Atomic Licensing Board to regulate matters pertaining to licensing. The licensing authority is provided for in section 15. This section provides that the licensing authority under this Act shall be the Atomic Licensing Board.

560. The main objective of licensing is to licence and register all applications for the use of ionizing radiation in medicine. Section 12 is on licensing of nuclear installations and activities. It states that no person shall do the following unless he is the holder of a valid licence issued under subsection 16(5) by the appropriate authority for such purpose and as specified in the licence:

- site, construct or operate a nuclear installation; and
- deal in, possess or dispose of any radioactive material, nuclear material, prescribed substance or irradiating apparatus.

561. Subsection (2) of section 15 further authorizes the Board to grant a general licence to the Director General of Health to issue separate licences on behalf of the Board to any person applying for a licence to undertake any of the activities referred to in the classification of licences under this Act where such activities are in respect of medical purposes.

562. Part VI is on the disposal of radioactive waste. Under section 26, no person is allowed to dispose of or cause to be disposed of any radioactive waste without the prior authorization in writing of the DG, where the activity to be licensed is in respect of a medical purpose, or by the Atomic Energy Licensing Board where the purpose is other than a medical purpose.

---

693. Act 304. This Act repealed the Radioactive Substances Act 1968, Act 17.
694. Section 2 of the Atomic Energy Licensing Act 1984.

563. Under section 29, where any situation or condition endangering life, health, property or the environment is found to exist in or on any premises, nuclear installation, conveyance or site, the appropriate authority may direct the licensee or any other person, who in its opinion is responsible for such premises, nuclear installation, conveyance or site, to adopt such measures as would eliminate or protect against such a situation or condition.

564. For the purpose of Part VI of the Act, section 31 provides that in the performance of its functions under this part, the Director General of Health or the Atomic Energy Licensing Board may, if it thinks it fit so to do, consult the Director General of Environmental Quality appointed under subsection 3(1) of the EQA 1974 on any matter under this part.

565. Part IX of the Act is on liability for nuclear damage. Section 48 deals with claims for compensation for nuclear damage to the environment. Under this section, where there is any nuclear damage to the environment, a claim for compensation shall be made by the Government of Malaysia, the Government of a State in Malaysia or by both, as the case may be, according to whether the segment of the environment that is damaged is within the jurisdiction of the Government of Malaysia, of a State in Malaysia, or of both.

566. The penalty for offences committed under the Act is provided in section 40. Under this section, where no penalty is expressly provided, a person who contravenes the Act shall be liable to imprisonment for a term not exceeding ten years, a fine not exceeding MYR 100,000, or both.

II. The Environmental Quality (Clean Air) (Regulations) 2014

567. The EQA 1974 does not have a provision that is directly concerned with radiation and vibrations. However, Regulations issued under the Act indirectly relevant to radiation and vibrations are the Environmental Quality (Clean Air) Regulations 2014.[695]

568. These Regulations deal with the control of air pollution from the following premises or processes that are used for any industrial or trade purposes, or on which matter is burnt in connection with any industrial or trade purposes, including burning of waste; any other premises or process that discharges or is capable of discharging air pollutants into the open air; any industrial plant; and any fuel burning equipment, which include any furnace, boiler, fireplace, oven, retort, internal combustion engine, vessel, or any other apparatus, device, mechanism, stack, chimney or structure used in connection with the burning of any combustible material.[696]

695. P.U. (A) 151/2014.
696. Regulation 3 of the Environmental Quality (Clean Air) Regulations 2014.

569. Under the Regulations, the term 'air pollutants' is interpreted to mean 'smoke, cinders, solid particles of any kind, gases, fumes, mists, odours and radioactive substances or any other substances which the Minister may by notification in the Gazette declares to be air pollutants for the purposes of these Regulations'. Whereas the term 'process' is interpreted to mean:

> any action, operation, conversion or treatment embracing chemical, industrial, manufacturing or processing factors, methods or forms, including furnaces, ovens, retorts, kettles, converters, cupolas, kilns, crucibles, stills, dryers, roasters, separator filters, reboilers, columns, classifiers, screens, quenchers, cookers, digesters, towers, washers, scrubbers, mills, condensers or absorbers.[697]

570. Activities that are directly or indirectly concerned with radiation and vibration are listed in the First Schedule of the Regulations and subjected to specific limit values and technical standards.[698] These activities include fuel burning, including heat and power generation in boilers, combustion turbines or generator; production and processing of ferrous and non-ferrous metals; oil and gas industries; non-metallic industry in cement production; all stationary asphalt mixing plants in the form of liquid, solid or gas; pulp and paper industry; chemical and petrochemical industry; production of pharmaceutical products, plant health products and biocides, and mixing and packaging of chemicals, pesticides, pharmaceutical products; solvent use in industry for dressing, printing, coating, degreasing, waterproofing, painting; and waste incinerators.

571. Second Schedule provides for limit values and technical standards for the control of activities or processes not covered by the First Schedule. They are the fuel burning equipment, incinerators and crematoria; Non-methane Volatile Organic Compound emissions; and fugitive emissions.

572. In the Third Schedule of the Regulations, limit values and technical standards are provided based on activity or industry. They include:

- heat and power generation that comprised boilers, combustion turbines; and generator sets for combined heat and power production with a total thermal output ≥ 3 MWe;
- production and processing of ferrous metals (Iron and steel mills);
- ferrous metal foundries with a capacity ≥1 tonne molten metal per day;
- production and processing of non-ferrous metals with a capacity >0.5 tonnes per day for lead or cadmium or >2 tonnes per day for other metals;
- Oil and gas industries including refineries, natural gas processing and storage, and storage and handling of petroleum products;
- non-metallic (mineral) industry: cement production (all sizes); manufacture of glass including glass fibre with a melting capacity ≥ 1 tonne of product per day;

697. Regulation 4 of the Environmental Quality (Clean Air) Regulations 2014.
698. Regulation 13 of the Environmental Quality (Clean Air) Regulations 2014.

manufacture of ceramic products by firing, roofing tiles, bricks, refractory bricks, tiles, ceramic glass, stoneware or porcelain, with a production capacity ≥10 tonnes of product per day;
- asphalt mixing plants;
- pulp and paper industry including paper recycling facilities in all sizes;
- chemical and petrochemical industry in all sizes;
- solvent use in industry: facilities for the surface treatment of substances, objects or products using organic solvents, in particular for dressing, printing, coating, degreasing, waterproofing, sizing, painting, cleaning or impregnating, fat extraction, with a solvent consumption capacity of more than 200 tonnes per year; and
- waste incinerators in all sizes.

573. The Fourth Schedule prescribed for limit values and technical standards for emission of dioxin and furan. They are expressed as 2, 3, 7, 8 tetrachlorinated dibenzo-para-dioxin toxicity equivalent which is calculated by summing the concentration of each 2, 3, 7, 8 congener in the sample multiplied by the appropriate TEFs as provided in clause (5) of Regulation 13.

574. It is an offence for any person to contravene regulations 12 and 13 of the Environmental Quality (Clean Air) Regulations 2014 without a licence issued under section 22(1).[699] Penalty imposed on any person who contravenes or fails to comply with any provisions of the Regulations is a fine not exceeding MYR 100,000 or to imprisonment for a term not exceeding two years or both.[700]

699. Regulation 25 of the Environmental Quality (Clean Air) Regulations 2014.
700. Regulation 29 of the Environmental Quality (Clean Air) Regulations 2014.

Chapter 8. Other Sectors

§1. Noxious Substances

I. The Legal Framework

575. In Malaysia, matters pertaining to noxious substances generally come within the jurisdiction of the federal government, as provided in the Federal Constitution. There are several items under List I Federal List that provide for these, namely:

- Item 8 on trade, commerce and industry, including: factories, boilers and machinery, dangerous trades, and dangerous and inflammable substances;
- Item 14 on medicine and health, including sanitation in the federal capital, and including poisons and dangerous drugs; intoxicating drugs and liquors; manufacture and sale of drugs; and
- Item 20 on control of agricultural pests, protection against such pests, and prevention of plant diseases.

576. In addition, List III of the Concurrent List, which provides for the competency of both federal and state governments, includes Item 7 on public health, sanitation (excluding sanitation in the federal capital) and the prevention of diseases.

577. There are several agencies entrusted with powers pertaining to noxious substances including pesticides and poison. They are the:

- Department of Agriculture, Ministry of Agriculture and Food Industry;
- Department of Health, Ministry of Health;
- Department of Occupational Safety and Health, Ministry of Human Resources; and
- Department of Environment, MNRE.

II. Pesticides Act 1974

578. The Pesticides Act 1974[701] was enacted in order to ensure the registration of pesticides before these are marketed in Malaysia. It is enforced by the Department of Agriculture under the Ministry of Agriculture and Food Industry.

579. The Act defines 'pesticide' to mean 'any substance that contains an "active ingredient"; or any preparation, mixture or material that contains any one or more of the "active ingredients" as one of its constituents'.

701. Act 149.

580. Under this Act, 'active substances' in the pesticides are evaluated according to an environmental assessment, health assessment and efficacy specifications.

- A pesticide registration has to be renewed every three years and new scientific knowledge and/or strengthened criteria can result in a de-registration.

581. Part II of the Act relates to the Pesticides Board. This Board is established under section 3 of the Act and consists of the following members:

- the Director General of Agriculture, who shall be the Chairman;
- a senior officer of the Department of Agriculture, West Malaysia, who shall be appointed by the Minister and shall be the Secretary;
- the Deputy Director General of Health;
- the Director General of Chemistry;
- the Director General of the Malaysian Agricultural Research and Development Institute;
- the Director General of the Malaysian Rubber Board;
- the Director General of the Department of Standards, Malaysia;
- the Director General of Veterinary Services;
- the Director of Pharmaceutical Services of the Ministry of Health;
- the Director General of Forestry, West Malaysia;
- the Director of Agriculture, Sabah;
- the Director of Agriculture, Sarawak;
- the Director General of Environmental Quality; and
- the Director General of the Malaysian Palm Oil Board.

582. Apart from the establishment of a Pesticides Board, the Act also provides for the appointment of Pesticides Licensing Officers under the Department of Agriculture for specified areas.[702]

583. Part III of the Act deals with the control of importation and manufacture of pesticides by registration and permit. Section 13 is on the penalty imposed on importation and manufacture of a misbranded or unregistered pesticide. Any person who contravenes this section, on a first conviction, may be sentenced to imprisonment for five years, or a fine of MYR 50,000, and on second or subsequent conviction, to imprisonment for ten years, to a fine of MYR 100,000, or both.

584. Part IV of the Act is on the control of manufacture, sale and storage of pesticides by licensing. Section 15 requires that a licence must be obtained from the Board for the manufacture of pesticides.

585. Part V is on the control of the presence of pesticides in food. For this purpose, section 21 of the Act empowers the Minister to make regulations to prohibit the use of pesticide in food of any specified kind; or the treatment of such food. The selling of contaminated food is an offence under section 25 of the Act.

702. Section 16 of the Pesticides Act 1974.

586. The general penalty for offences committed under the Act is provided in section 56. It states that a person who commits an offence against this Act, or breaches the rules or regulations issued under it, for which no other penalty is specifically provided thereby, is liable, on a first conviction, to imprisonment for six months, or to a fine of MYR 5,000 and, on a second or subsequent conviction, to imprisonment for one year, to a fine of MYR 10,000, or both.

III. Poisons Act 1952

587. The Poisons Act 1952[703] was enacted to regulate the importation, possession, manufacture, compounding, storage, transport, sale and use of poisons. This Act comes under the jurisdiction of the Department of Health under the Ministry of Health.

588. Section 3 provides for the establishment of a Poisons Board for the purpose of the Act and to advise the Minister generally. This advisory board consists of the following members:

- the Director General of Health, who shall be an ex-officio member;
- one pharmacist holding office in the service of the Government, to be appointed by the Minister;
- one officer of the Department of Chemistry to be appointed by the Minister;
- one officer of the Department of Agriculture to be appointed by the Minister;
- one officer of the Veterinary Department holding office in the service of the Government, to be appointed by the Minister.

589. Apart from the above members, section 3 provides for another eight persons ordinarily resident in Malaysia and not in the service of any government in the Federation, to be appointed by the Minister, who shall be nominated as follows:

- one by the Malaysian Medical Association;
- one by the Malaysian Medical Council established under the Medical Act 1971;
- one by the Malaysian International Chambers of Commerce and Industry;
- one by the Associated Chinese Chambers of Commerce and Industry of Malaysia;
- one by the Malay Chambers of Commerce;
- one by the Associated Indian Chambers of Commerce, Malaysia;
- one by the Malaysian Pharmaceutical Association; and
- one by the Malaysian Rubber Producers' Council.

590. The Control of imports of poisons is provided in section 8, whereas section 9 is on packaging, labelling and storing of poisons. Under section 13 of the Act, it is an offence to possess poison for sale, unless licensed. Any person who contravenes this section shall be guilty of an offence under this Act.

---

703. Act 366, revised 1989.

591. The penalty for offences committed under the Act is provided for in section 32. Under this section, any person who does any of the acts listed shall be guilty of an offence and liable to a fine not exceeding MYR 5,000, imprisonment for a term not exceeding two years, or both. A person commits an offence if he:

- wilfully fails to keep any book required to be kept under this Act; or
- wilfully fails to make any entry required by the Act; or
- knowingly or recklessly makes any false entry in such book which he knew to be false, or which he did not believe to be true.

IV. Occupational Safety and Health Act 1994

592. Another statute relevant to the regulation of noxious substances is the Occupational Safety and Health Act 1994,[704] enforced by the Department of Occupational Safety and Health, under the Ministry of Human Resources Malaysia.

593. The objectives of the enactment of this Act were to make further provisions for securing the safety, health and welfare of persons at work, for protecting others against risks to safety or health in connection with the activities of persons at work and to establish the National Council for Occupational Safety and Health. This Act is applicable throughout Malaysia, except on board ships governed by the Merchant Shipping Ordinance 1952,[705] the Merchant Shipping Ordinance 1960, the Sabah Ordinance 1960,[706] the Sarawak Ordinance 1960[707] or the armed forces.

594. The relevant part of this Act is Part VIII on notification of accidents, dangerous occurrences, occupational poisoning and occupational diseases. Section 32 of the Act requires any employer to notify the nearest occupational safety and health office of any accident, dangerous occurrence, occupational poisoning or occupational disease which has occurred or is likely to occur at the place of work.[708]

595. Section 32 further requires a registered medical practitioner or medical officer attending to a patient whom he believes to be suffering from any of the diseases listed in the third schedule of the Factories and Machinery Act 1967[709] or under the Occupational Safety and Health Act 1994, to report the matter to the DG.[710] Under section 33, the DG may direct an enquiry to be held.

596. The third schedule of the Factories and Machinery Act 1967 provides for a list of notifiable industrial diseases including:

704. Act 514.
705. Order 70 of 1952.
706. Sabah Order No. 11 of 1960.
707. Sarawak Order No. 2 of 1960.
708. Section 32(1) of the Occupational Safety and Health Act 1994.
709. Act 139.
710. Section 32(2) of the Occupational Safety and Health Act 1994.

- dust diseases of the lungs;
- systematic intoxication by specified metals or their compounds;
- intoxication resulting from the use of solvents;
- pulmonary irritation;
- intoxication resulting from handling of insecticides, or herbicides or fungicides as organic phosphate compounds, nitrogenous and chlorinated compounds;
- conditions of occupational dermatosis resulting from handling of mineral oils, acids, alkalis, dusts and other irritants;
- occupational infections, such as anthrax;
- malignant disease resulting from handling or inhalation or contact with carcinogenic tars, or radioactive dusts; and
- toxic jaundice resulting from nitro or amino derivatives of benzene or other substances.

V. Environmental Quality Act 1974

597. The EQA 1974 is indirectly relevant to controlling noxious substances, specifically under the Environmental Quality (Scheduled Wastes) Regulations 2005. These Regulations concern the management of scheduled waste and toxic and hazardous wastes, which also include noxious substances.

598. Under Regulation 3, waste producers are required to notify the DG of any generation of scheduled waste in their premises, followed by the storage procedures as provided in Regulation 9. Every waste producer has to ensure that his scheduled wastes are properly stored in containers which are durable and able to prevent spillage.[711] In the case of spillage, the DG may take such action as is necessary to remove, disperse, destroy or mitigate the pollution and may recover all costs and expenses incurred.[712]

599. Regulation 10 further requires that scheduled waste containers must be clearly labelled in accordance with the Third Schedule of the Environmental Quality (Scheduled Wastes) Regulations 2005. Regulation 13 requires monitoring of the transportation of scheduled wastes. The final aspect is the treatment and disposal of scheduled wastes, whereby they have to be treated and disposed of at prescribed premises only.[713]

---

711. Incidents of spillage and accidental discharge are provided in Regulation 14 of the Environmental Quality (Scheduled Wastes) Regulations 2005.
712. Section 47 of the Environmental Quality Act 1974.
713. Regulation 4 of the Environmental Quality (Scheduled Wastes) Regulations 2005.

Part II. Nature Conservation and Management

Chapter 1. Nature Conservation and Management

§1. General Information

I. Biodiversity

600. Malaysia's humid tropical location provides excellent conditions for thousands of plant species to thrive and evolve[714] and places Malaysia among the seventeen countries internationally recognized as possessing megadiversity.[715] These seventeen countries act as an index for species richness around the world. Countries with a high number of endemic species, such as Malaysia, are globally important in terms of conservation, because loss of these species locally would signal their worldwide extinction.[716]

601. Malaysia's biodiversity is one of the most important ones in the world. It has at least 15,000 species of the known flowering plants, 3,000 species of orchids, 306 species of mammals, 742 species of birds, 242 species of amphibians and reptiles, 742 species of birds, 150 species of coral and at least 4,000 species of marine fish and 449 species of freshwater fish. Moreover, Malaysia has about 700 species of fungi and 832 species of mosses.[717]

602. Like other countries, Malaysia is also suffering from biodiversity erosion. In the course of development, many of its plants and animals are threatened with extinction. Thus, biodiversity protection is necessary to stop species from becoming

---

714. *See Conservation and Faunal Biodiversity in Malaysia* (Zainal Abidin & Zubaid Akbar eds, Penerbitan Universiti Kebangsaan Malay. 1996).
715. *See* the official portal of the Ministry of Water, Land and Natural Resources, http://www.nre.gov.my/en-my/Biodiversity/Pages/default.aspx, July 2018.
716. *See* Grace Wong (compiler), *Assessment of Biological Diversity in Malaysia* (Ministry Sci., Tech. Envt. Malay. 1997).
717. Sham Sani (ed.), *The Encyclopedia of Malaysia: Volume I: The Environment* 99 (Archipelago Press 1998).

extinct and to preserve them for future generations. Various efforts have been made by Malaysia to conserve the existing biodiversity, including through the application of law.[718]

603. One method of conserving the biodiversity and preventing habitat loss through legal intervention is by setting aside protected areas. According to the Second National Communication to the UNFCCC, in 2000, 18,195,554 million ha or 56% of Malaysia was covered in forests.[719] In 2007, the forest area was reduced to 17,712,894 million ha. However, the latest data by the Ministry of Water, Land and Natural Resources shows that in 2014 the total land under natural forest in Malaysia has increased to 18,277,602 million ha.[720] From the total area of forested land, about 11% or 2,757,362 million ha are designated as protected areas, whereas another 11,671,853 million ha cover permanent reserved forest or permanent forest estate(s). The remaining land uses comprise agricultural crops, rubber plantations, oil-palm plantations, urban and other uses. Protected areas which include nature parks, wildlife reserves, bird sanctuaries and marine parks are protected by law. Other methods of conservation are in the form of botanical gardens and zoological parks. Since Malaysia shares common forested borders with a number of neighbouring countries, the governments of Malaysia, Indonesia and Brunei implemented the Heart of Borneo Initiative which aims to conserve 20 million ha of forest within these three participating countries. The initiative is undertaken for the purpose of conservation and sustainable management of the largest transboundary tropical forest expanse remaining in Borneo and South East Asia which covers more than 22 million ha of forest land.[721]

II. Legal Framework

604. Generally, matter relevant to biodiversity such as land, river, turtles, riverine fishing and forests come under the jurisdiction of state government as provided in List II, State List of the Federal Constitution. However, matters such as preservation of heritage, protection of wild animals and wild birds, and national parks are within List II, Concurrent List, which allows both the federal and state government to enact laws on the matter.

605. List I, Federal List also contains items that are relevant to biodiversity conservation. One of these is Item 1 on treaties, agreements and conventions with other countries, and all matters which bring the Federation into relations with any other

718. *See* Wan Izatul Asma Wan Talaat et al. *The Laws on Policies for the Sustainable Management of Biodiversity in Malaysia.* Journal of Sustainability and Science Management (2013). *See also* the official portal of the Ministry of Water, Land and Natural Resources, http://www.nre.gov.my/en-my/Biodiversity/Pages/default.aspx, July 2018.
719. Ministry of Natural Resources and Environment. *Second National Communication to UNFCCC.* (MNRE. 2001).
720. *See* the official portal of the Ministry of Water, Land and Natural Resources, http://www.nre.gov.my/en-my/Forestry/Pages/Statistics-Forest.aspx, July 2018.
721. *See* the ASEAN Portal https://asean.usmission.gov/innovasean_20151028/, July 2018.

country; and implementation of treaties, agreements and conventions with other countries. The effect of this provision is that it is possible for the federal government to enact laws for implementing international treaties on biodiversity, even though the subject matter may come under the State List.

606. For the purpose of biodiversity conservation, the protected areas in Malaysia are classified into two:

- 'totally protected areas' which contain national state parks, wildlife reserves, sanctuaries, virgin forests and marine parks; and
- 'permanent reserve forests', encompassing productive, protective and amenity forests.

607. There is no specific legislation in Malaysia on biodiversity conservation. However there are a number of statutes in Malaysia relevant to the matter. These statutes, either in the form of federal or state legislations, are as follows:

- Protection of Wildlife Act of 1972 (Revoked);
- National Parks Act of 1980;
- Waters Act 1920;
- Land Conservation Act 1960;
- National Land Code 1965;
- National Forestry Act 1984;
- EQA 1974;
- Exclusive Economic Zone Act 1984;
- Fisheries Act 1985;
- Merchant Shipping (Oil Pollution) Act 1984;
- Town and Country Planning Act 1976;
- Animals Act 1953;
- National Forestry Act 1994;
- Sabah Park Enactment 1984;
- Sarawak Wildlife Protection Ordinance 1998;
- Sarawak National Parks and Nature Reserves Ordinance 1998;
- Sabah Forest Enactment 1968;
- Sarawak Forests Ordinance 2015;
- International Trade in Endangered Species Act 2008;
- Wildlife Conservation Act 2010;
- Malaysian Quarantine and Inspection Services Act 2011;
- Biosafety Act 2007;
- Pesticides Act 1974;
- Plant Quarantine Act 1976;
- Continental Shelf Act 1966;
- Customs (Prohibition of Exports Amendment No. 4) Order 1993;
- Aboriginal Peoples Act 1954;
- Protection of New Plant Varieties Act 2004;
- Food Act 1983.

In 2017 Malaysia passed a legislation which is relevant to biodiversity conservation namely the Access to Biological Resources and Benefit Sharing Act 2017.[722]

608. This Act which came into operation on 18 December 2020 was enacted for the purpose of implementing the Convention on Biological Diversity and any protocol to the Convention dealing with access to biological resources and traditional knowledge associated with biological resources and the sharing of benefits arising from their utilization. This Act contains 63 sections which are divided into 10 parts dealing with the regulation of access to all biological resources and traditional knowledge associated with biological resource, and the benefit arising from the utilization of research and development for commercial or non-commercial purposes. It also provides a framework or system for access which includes the application of permit, the mechanics of obtaining prior informed consent and the establishment of benefit sharing agreement.

609. According to section 5 of the Act, a person is said to have access to a biological resource under the following situations[723]: the taking of a biological resource from its natural habitat or place where it is kept, grown or found including in the market for the purpose of research and development; or there is a reasonable prospect as determined by the Competent Authority that a biological resource taken by the person will be subject to research and development. However, under section 5, the following activities are not included as access to a biological resource:[724]

- fishing for commerce, recreation or game;
- taking animals or plants for food;
- taking biological resource that has been cultivated or tended for any purpose other than the purpose of research and development;
- taking natural produce, including oils and honey, for any purpose other than the purpose of research and development;
- collecting plant reproductive material for propagation;
- carrying out commercial forestry;
- in relation to indigenous community and local community, for the use and exchange of the biological resource among themselves in the exercise of their traditional and customary practices;
- taking of a biological resource by any person that is (i) a living modified organism as defined in the Biosafety Act 2007 for which intellectual property rights have been granted and subsist; or (ii) a plant variety for which a breeder's right has been granted and subsists under the Protection of New Plant Varieties Act 2004; and
- access to a biological resource exempted under section 60.

610. The definition of relevant terms is provided in section 4, including as follows:

722. Act 795.
723. Section 5(1) of the Access to Biological Resources and Benefit Sharing Act 2017.
724. Section 5(2) of the Access to Biological Resources and Benefit Sharing Act 2017.

- 'animal' includes: (a) any mammal (other than man), bird, reptile, amphibian, arthropod, or other vertebrate or invertebrate, whether alive or dead, and the egg, young or immature form derived from them; (b) any readily recognizable part or derivative of an animal; (c) wildlife as defined under the Wildlife Conservation Act 2010; and (d) fish as defined in the Fisheries Act 1985;
- 'biological resource' includes: (a) the genetic resources, organisms, microorganisms, derivatives and parts of the genetic resources, organisms, microorganisms or derivatives; (b) the populations and any other biotic component of an ecosystem with actual or potential use or value for humanity; and (c) any information relating to paragraphs (a) and (b);
- 'plant' includes: (a) any species of plant or any part of such species whether alive or dead and includes the stem, branch, tuber, bulb, corm, stock, budwood, cutting, layer, slip, sucker, root, leaf, flower, fruit, seed or any other part or product whatsoever of a plant whether severed or attached; and (b) any readily recognizable part or derivative of a plant;
- 'take' includes: (a) in relation to an animal, to harvest, catch, capture, trap and kill or obtain in any other way; (b) in relation to a plant specimen, to collect, harvest, pick, gather and cut or obtain in any other way; (c) in relation to other biological resources including microorganisms, to collect, pick or obtain in any other way; or (d) to obtain a biological resource in any other way.

611. One of the most important features of the Act is the establishment of relevant authorities, namely National Competent Authority and Competent Authorities as provided in Part II.[725] Generally Competent Authority consists of statutory bodies specified in the First Schedule of the Act[726], with one Competent Authority designated for each state and a National Competent Authority overseeing the general implementation of the Act. Specifically, section 7 provides for the establishment of National Competent Authority which has the following functions:[727]

- to coordinate the implementation and enforcement of the provisions of this Act by the Competent Authorities;
- to determine the fees payable upon consultation with the Competent Authorities;
- to communicate with other countries and the secretariat established under any treaty, agreement, convention or protocol relating to access and benefit sharing in relation to a biological resource, as appropriate, on matters under this Act;
- to implement and to fulfil the requirements under any treaty, agreement, convention or protocol relating to access and benefit sharing in relation to a biological resource to which Malaysia is a party where such treaty, agreement, convention or protocol relates to the purposes of this Act;
- to create awareness and to provide training, education and information relating to access and benefit sharing in relation to a biological resource;
- to keep and maintain a register of permits issued by the Competent Authorities and information relating to the permit;

725. Sections 7–11 of the Access to Biological Resources and Benefit Sharing Act 2017.
726. Section 4 of the Access to Biological Resources and Benefit Sharing Act 2017.
727. Section 8 of the Access to Biological Resources and Benefit Sharing Act 2017.

- to establish measures under subsection 30(1) with the aim of monitoring and tracking a biological resource or traditional knowledge associated with a biological resource accessed;
- to support customary laws and practices of indigenous community and local community, and the development of community protocols and procedures by the indigenous community and local community, as the case may be;
- to establish and maintain a clearing house mechanism under section 32;
- to act as Competent Authority for all *ex situ* collections where the origin of the biological resource cannot be ascertained with due diligence and which do not come within the jurisdiction of any other Competent Authority; and
- to do such other things as it deems fit to enable it to perform its functions effectively or which are incidental to the performance of its functions.

612. In addition to National Competent Authority, the Act also established Competent Authorities as specified in the First Schedule which are given jurisdiction over all matters relating to access to a biological resource in the region as specified in the First Schedule.[728] The Competent Authorities would be required to establish an advisory body to deal with matters relating to indigenous community and local community and traditional knowledge associated with the biological resource comprising representatives of indigenous community and local community whose advice shall be sought and taken into account. Among the functions of the Competent Authorities as provided by the Act includes:[729]

- to deal with all the applications for access to a biological resource or traditional knowledge associated with a biological resource within its jurisdiction and the sharing of benefits arising from the utilization of the biological resource or traditional knowledge associated with a biological resource;
- to maintain a record of all access applications and decisions relating to such applications, including the permits issued;
- to prepare an annual report concerning such access applications and decisions relating to such applications including permits issued and to submit the report and copies of the permits to the National Competent Authority on or before such date as the National Competent Authority may determine; and
- to do such other things as it deems fit to enable it to perform its functions effectively or which are incidental to the performance of its functions.

613. Part III of the Act deals with requirements for permit to access biological resources.[730] The Act requires any person who intends to access a biological resource or traditional knowledge associated with a biological resource to apply for a permit. There are two types of permits under the Act: one for commercial or potential commercial purposes as provided in section 12, and another for non-commercial purposes only (section 15). Both permits are to be applied from, and issued by, the relevant Competent Authority.

728. Section 9 of the Access to Biological Resources and Benefit Sharing Act 2017.
729. Section 10 of the Access to Biological Resources and Benefit Sharing Act 2017.
730. Sections 12–23 of the Access to Biological Resources and Benefit Sharing Act 2017.

614. Under section 12(6), any person who accesses a biological resource or traditional knowledge associated with a biological resource without a permit or contravenes any condition imposed on the permit commits an offence and shall, on conviction, be liable: (a) where such person is an individual, to a fine not exceeding MYR 500,000 or to imprisonment for a term not exceeding ten years or to both; or (b) where such person is a body corporate, to a fine not exceeding MYR 5 million. Whereas in the case of the issue of permit for non-commercial purposes, the penalties are provided in section 15(7) which states that any person who accesses a biological resource or traditional knowledge associated with a biological resource without a permit or contravenes any condition imposed on the permit commits an offence and shall, on conviction, be liable: (a) where such person is an individual, to a fine not exceeding MYR 100, 000 or to imprisonment for a term not exceeding seven years or to both; or (b) where such person is a body corporate, to a fine not MYR 1 million.

615. There are, however, three circumstances where permit is not required as provided in section 18, namely:

(1) by any person employed or studying and carrying out research for non-commercial purpose in or under the authority of a public higher education institution, public research institution or Government agency within Malaysia, subject to such conditions as may be prescribed and subject to prior informed consent of the relevant indigenous community and local community has been obtained for any access to a biological resource and traditional knowledge associated with a biological resource referred to in subsection 23(1);
(2) for the exchange of biological resources between persons within a public higher education institution, public research institution or Government agency within Malaysia or between such institutions or agencies within Malaysia for non-commercial purpose, unless otherwise required by a Competent Authority and subject to such conditions as may be prescribed; or
(3) by any person or institution in or outside Malaysia who accesses a biological resource from a permit holder under subsection 15(1) or the person or institution under paragraph (a), at the request of such permit holder or the person or institution, for the purpose of carrying out or continuing any research for non-commercial purpose.

616. For the purpose of the application of permit, section 22 of the Act requires the application to be accompanied by a document known as Benefit Sharing Agreement which is entered into with the resource provider who gave access to the biological resources or traditional knowledge. The term 'resource provider' is defined by section 4 to include, *inter alia*, the Federal Government or State Authority possessing bio-resources in *in situ* conditions; and the indigenous and local communities where the resource is on land to which they have a right or where they are the holders of the traditional knowledge. However, no such agreement is required if the access is purely for a non-commercial purpose.

617. Under section 23, prior informed consent of the relevant indigenous community must be obtained for access to a bio-resource on land to which they have a right and to associated traditional knowledge held by them. The requirement of obtaining the Prior Informed Consent is based on the Nagoya Protocol's main thrusts by providing that an applicant must have obtained from any relevant indigenous and local community for access to biological resources on land to which the community has a right as established by law and traditional knowledge associated with the resources held by the community.

618. Notwithstanding the impact on researchers and corporations generally, the Act has a number of provisions which would affect patent holders specifically. For example, under section 31, any person applying for a patent, whether in or outside Malaysia, in relation to a biological resource or traditional knowledge associated with a biological resource accessed shall notify to the National Competent Authority in writing within thirty days from the date of the application. Section 31 further states that any person who contravenes the section commits an offence and shall, on conviction, be liable: (a) where such person is an individual, to a fine not exceeding MYR 100,000 or to imprisonment for a term not exceeding seven years or to both; and (b) where such person is a body corporate, to a fine of not exceeding MYR 500,000.

619. The Act does not have a retroactive effect on current owners of patents which are derived from access to bio-resources or traditional knowledge. However, section 63 on transitional provision would be applied. According to section 63, any person who, on the date on which the Act comes into operation, is accessing a biological resource or traditional knowledge with the consent of the resource provider is required to apply for a permit within 12 months of the Effective Date. After the Effective Date, any person in possession of a bio-resource or traditional knowledge without a benefit sharing agreement must enter into such an agreement if there is new use of the bio-resource or traditional knowledge; or there is development of a new product arising therefrom.

620. By virtue of section 62 which confers the Minister, after consultation with the National Competent Authority and Competent Authority, the power to make regulations in relation to the provisions of this Act, the following Regulations have been gazetted in December 2020: The Access to Biological Resources and Benefit Sharing Regulations 2020 (the Regulations). Main objectives of these Regulations are as follows:

- Regulation 2: The establishment of an Advisory Committee by virtue of section 11 of the Access to Biological Resources and Benefit Sharing Act 2017;
- Regulation 3: The establishment of an Advisory Body under section 9 of the Act which requires the Competent Authority to appoint representatives of the indigenous community and local community nominated by the respective communities to be members of the Advisory Body;

Reg. 4: The setting of procedures and forms to be used for an application for a permit for commercial or potential commercial purpose under section 12 of the Act or for non-commercial purpose under section 15 of the Act based on form 1 of the First Schedule;

- Regulation 5: The issuance of permit under sections 13 and 15 based on form 2 of the First Schedule of the Regulations;
- Regulation 8: Report of disposal of biological resources based on section 27 of the Act;
- Regulation 9: Details relating to the benefit sharing agreements based on section 22;
- Regulation 10: Requirements on prior informed consent based on section 23;
- Regulation 11: Matters relating to subsequent claim based on section 23(7);
- Regulation 12: Measures for monitoring and tracking based on section 30(2);
- Regulation 13: Notification of application of patent under section 31(1);
- Regulation 14: Measures for preventing use or commercialisation without permit based on section 34(2);
- Regulation 15: Duty to maintain register; and
- Regulation 16: Duty of researchers to record particulars.

621. Apart from that, several agencies have been established relating to biodiversity conservation. They include:

- Department of Environment;
- Department of Wildlife and National Parks;
- Forestry Department of Peninsular Malaysia;
- Sabah Forestry Department;
- Forest Department Sarawak;
- Fisheries Department;
- Marine Department; and
- Department of Malaysian Quarantine and Inspection Services.

622. Legal and institutional frameworks on biological conservation in Malaysia are discussed in this monograph under separate headings and parts. Matters related to quarantine and inspection and biosafety are discussed here.

623. In 2011, Malaysia enacted the Malaysian Quarantine and Inspection Services Act[731] which is meant to provide for quarantine and inspection services in terms of providing integrated services relating to quarantine, inspection and enforcement at the entry points, quarantine stations and quarantine premises and certification for import and export of plants, animals, carcasses, fish, agricultural produce, soils and microorganisms and includes inspection of and enforcement relating to food and for matters connected to it. This Act is to be read together with the relevant written laws[732] as provided in the Third Schedule,[733] namely:

731. Act 728.
732. Section 2 of the Malaysian Quarantine and Inspection Services Act 2011.
733. Section 3 of the Malaysian Quarantine and Inspection Services Act 2011.

- Animals Act 1953;
- Plant Quarantine Act 1976;
- Lembaga Kemajuan Ikan Malaysia Act 1971;
- Food Act 1983;
- Federal Agricultural Marketing Authority Act 1965; and
- Fisheries Act 1985.

For the purpose of the enforcement of the Act, section 4 provides for the appointment of the DG, whereas functions and powers are provided in sections 7 and 8 respectively. In addition, the Act provides for the establishment of Coordination Committee for Quarantine and Inspection[734] with the main functions to coordinate technical, scientific, procedural and other relevant matters to facilitate the implementation of this Act. Regulations of import and export of any plant, animal, carcass, fish, agricultural produce, soil or microorganism are done through permit, licence and certificate as provided in Part V of the Act. The term import for the purpose of the Act is interpreted to mean to bring or by being a cause to bring into Malaysia by land, sea, inland waters or air any plant, animal, carcass, fish, agricultural produce, soil, microorganism, or food.[735] Whereas the term export means to take or by being a cause to take out of Malaysia by land, sea, inland waters or air any plant, animal, carcass, fish, agricultural produce, soil, microorganism, or food.[736] Interpretation of other relevant terms for the purpose of the Act is as follows:

> 'Plant' means any species of plant or any part thereof whether living or dead and includes the stem, branch, tuber, bulb, corn, stock, budwood, cutting, layer, slip, sucker, root, leaf, flower, fruit, seed or any other part or product of a plant whether severed or attached;
>
> 'Animal' has the same meaning assigned to it under the Animals Act 1953 and includes bird;
>
> 'Carcass' means the dead body of an animal or fish, and includes the meat, bones (whether whole, broken or ground), offal, hide, skin, wool, hair, feathers, hoof, horns or other part of the dead animal or fish, separately or otherwise;
>
> 'Fish' has the same meaning assigned to it under the Fisheries Act 1985;
>
> 'Agricultural produce' means any product from plant, animal, carcass or fish, whether processed or otherwise;
>
> 'Soil' includes earth, ground or other naturally occurring or processed organic and mineral material; and
>
> 'microorganism' means any microorganism other than plant and animal and includes fungus, bacteria and virus.
>
> Under section 11, any person who is involved in the importation and exportation of any plant, animal, carcass, fish, agricultural produce, soil or microorganism who contravenes this section commits an offence and shall, on

734. Section 10 of the Malaysian Quarantine and Inspection Services Act 2011.
735. Section 3 of the Malaysian Quarantine and Inspection Services Act 2011.
736. *Ibid.*

conviction, be liable to a fine not exceeding MYR 100,000 or jail up to six years or both and, for a second or subsequent offence to a fine not exceeding MYR 150,000 or jail for a term not exceeding seven years or both. Under section 13 it is an offence to furnish false information pertaining to permit, licence and certificate whereas under section 14, the importation of any pests, diseases or contaminants from any plant, animal, carcass, fish, agricultural produce, soil or microorganism is also an offence. Penalty imposed is a fine not exceeding MYR 100,000 or to imprisonment for a term not exceeding six years or both and, for a second or subsequent offence to a fine not exceeding MYR 150,000 or to imprisonment for a term not exceeding seven years or both.

624. Malaysia is a party to the Convention of Biological Diversity and the Cartagena Protocol on Biosafety which regulates the transboundary movement of genetically modified organisms. The Biosafety Act 2007[737] was passed into national framework to implement the obligations to both the Convention and Protocol to derive maximum benefit from the potential of modern biotechnology, while minimizing the possible risks posed.

The Biosafety Act 2007 is meant to establish the National Biosafety Board to regulate the release, importation, exportation and contained use of living modified organisms (LMO) in order to protect *inter alia* human, plant and animal health as well as the environment and biological diversity. The Act is to be read together with any other written law relating to import and export, human, plant and animal health, the environmental and biological diversity.[738]

The Act uses the term 'living modified organism' instead of genetically modified organisms. The term 'living modified organism' under the Act means any living organism that possesses a novel combination of genetic material obtained through the use of modern biotechnology. The term 'living organism' means any biological entity capable of transferring or replicating genetic material, including sterile organisms, viruses and viroids. Whereas the term 'biological diversity' means the variability among living organisms from all sources, including, *inter alia*, terrestrial, marine and other aquatic ecosystems and the ecological complexes of which they are part of; it also includes diversity within species, between species and of ecosystems.[739]

The Act regulates the release, importation, exportation and contained use of LMOs, and the release of products of such organisms and requires that the risks posed by, or as a result of modern biotechnology, are identified and managed through regulating activities involving LMOs. The term 'modern biotechnology' in the Act means the application of in vitro nucleic acid techniques, including recombinant deoxyribonucleic acid (DNA) and direct injection of the nucleic acid into cells or organelles; or fusion of cells beyond the taxonomic family that overcome natural physiological reproductive or recombination barriers and that are not techniques used in traditional breeding and selection.

737. Act 678.
738. Section 2(1) of the Biosafety Act 2007.
739. Section 3 of the Biosafety Act 2007.

The Act establishes the National Biosafety Board to administer and make decisions relating to approval for release and import, notification for export, contained use and import for contained use, as well as monitoring, promoting research and establishing mechanisms on matters relating to LMO and biosafety.[740] According to section 4, members of the board consist of members appointed by the minister. They are Secretary General of Ministry of Environment and Water as chairman and one representative each from the Ministry of Health, Ministry of Agriculture and Food Industry, Ministry of Plantation Industries and Commodities, Ministry of International Trade and Industry, Ministry of Science, Technology and Innovation, Ministry of Domestic Trade and Consumer Affairs and four other members who are expert in biosafety. In addition, section 6 provides for the establishment of the Genetic Modification Advisory Committee (GMAC) to provide advice to the Minister or the Board on scientific, technical and related matters.

Another relevant committee is the Institutional Biosafety Committee set up under the Biosafety (Approval and Notification) Regulations 2010. The Regulations empower the Board to direct any organization that undertakes modern biotechnology research and development to establish an institutional biosafety committee for the following purposes: to provide guidance for safe use of modern biotechnology; to monitor activities dealing with modern biotechnology; to establish and monitor the implementation of policies and procedures for handling LMOs; and to determine the classes of Biosafety Levels for contained use activity for modern biotechnology research and development undertaken within a facility where the institutional biosafety committee is established.[741]

The Department of Biosafety[742] was established in 2010 by the MNRE (which was replaced by the Ministry of Land, Water and Natural Resources in 2018, and currently under the Ministry of Environment and Water) to serve as the main referral centre for all biosafety activities. Among the main functions of the Department are to enforce the Biosafety Act 2007; to be the secretariat of the National Biosafety Board; to be the secretariat of the GMAC; and to be the secretariat of the subcommittees established under the Board and GMAC.

The Act prohibits any persons from carrying out activities involving release, importation, exportation, contained use of LMOs or products of such organisms unless they have obtained prior approval or provided notification in accordance with the Act. Specifically, section 5 prohibits any person from undertaking any release activity, or any importation of LMOs without prior approval of the Board. The term 'release activity' means any intentional introduction of LMOs or products of such organisms into the environment through the activities or for the purposes specified in the Second Schedule.[743] These activities are: research and development purposes in all field experiments; supply or offer to supply for sale or placing on the market; offer as gift, prize or free item; disposal; remediation purposes; and any other activity which does not amount to contained use. The term 'contained use' under the Act

740. Section 5 of the Biosafety Act 2007.
741. Regulation 5 of the Biosafety (Approval and Notification) Regulations 2010.
742. *See* the official website at https://www.biosafety.gov.my/en/.
743. Section 3 of the Biosafety Act 2007.

means any operation, including research and development, production or manufacturing operation involving LMOs, or storage of LMOs, undertaken within a facility, installation or other physical structure such that it prevents the contact and impact of the LMOs on the external environment.[744] Under section 12, any person who contravenes the Act commits an offence and shall, on conviction, be liable to a fine not exceeding MYR 250,000 or to imprisonment exceeding five years or both and, in the case of a continuing offence, to a further fine not exceeding MYR 10,000 for each day during which the offence continues after conviction. Where such person is a body corporate, the penalty is a fine not exceeding MYR 500,000 and, in the case of a continuing offence, to a further fine not exceeding MYR 20,000 for each day during which the offence continues after conviction.

An application for the approval of any release activity or any importation of LMOs, or both needs to be submitted to the DG, accompanied by a risk assessment and a risk management report and an emergency response plan.[745] Upon the submission of application, the DG will refer the application to the Advisory Committee for its recommendations. Reference will also be made to any relevant government department or agency on specific matters, and for the purposes of public disclosure, to invite public participation for their views on the application.[746] The Advisory Committee will make its recommendations on application for approval based on section 15 and will forward its recommendation to the Board. After having considered such recommendations, the Board may grant the application by issuing a certificate of approval and imposing terms and conditions.[747] Any approved person who contravenes any terms and conditions imposed on the approval or fails to furnish the information, particulars or documents required commits an offence and shall, on conviction, be liable to a fine not exceeding MYR 100,000 or to imprisonment not exceeding four years or both and, in the case of a continuing offence, to a further fine not exceeding MYR 10,000 for each day during which the offence continues after conviction. Where such person is a body corporate, to a fine not exceeding MYR 250,000 and in the case of a continuing offence, to a further fine not exceeding MYR 20,000 for each day during which the offence continues after conviction.

The Board may review any approval at any time upon obtaining new information or evidence on the LMO or products of such organisms. If the Board is satisfied that there is a risk posed to human, plant or animal health, the environment or biological diversity, the Board may take any of the following actions: revoke the approval; make a temporary cessation order; impose additional terms and conditions; order the approved person to make rectifications; or make any other order as the Board thinks fit in the interest of biosafety.[748] Any person who contravenes any order made under section 18, upon conviction, may be liable to a fine not exceeding MYR 250,000 or jail up to five years or both, and to a further fine not exceeding MYR 10,000 for each day during which the offence continues after conviction. Where

744. *Ibid.*
745. Section 13 of the Biosafety Act 2007.
746. Section 14 of the Biosafety Act 2007.
747. Section 16 of the Biosafety Act 2007.
748. Section 18 of the Biosafety Act 2007.

such person is a body corporate, the penalty is a fine up to MYR 500,000 and a further fine up to MYR 20,000 for each day during which the offence continues after conviction. Section 19 provides further power to the Board to revoke the approval, make a temporary cessation order, impose any additional terms and conditions, order the approved person to make rectifications, or make any other order as the Board thinks fit in the interest of biosafety in the following circumstances:

- where there is a risk posed to human, plant or animal health, the environment or biological diversity;
- where the approved person fails to comply with any terms and conditions imposed on the approval;
- where the approved person fails to comply with any order made by the Board;
- where the approved person has contravened any of the provisions of the Act, whether or not prosecution has been instituted against him; or
- where the approved person has been convicted of an offence under this Act.

Any approved person who contravenes any order made under section 19 commits an offence and, on conviction, be liable to a fine not exceeding MYR 250,000 or to imprisonment for a term not exceeding five years or both. In the case of a continuing offence, to a further fine not exceeding MYR 10,000 for each day during which the offence continues after conviction. Where such person is a body corporate, to a fine not exceeding MYR 500,000 and, in the case of a continuing offence, to a further fine not exceeding MYR 20,000 for each day during which the offence continues after conviction.

All persons conducting exportation, contained use or importation for contained use involving LMOs must notify the Board as provided in section 22. Any person who contravenes this section commits an offence and shall, on conviction, be liable to a fine not exceeding MYR 250,000 or to imprisonment for a term not exceeding five years or both and, in the case of a continuing offence, to a further fine not exceeding MYR 10,000 for each day during which the offence continues after conviction. Where such person is a body corporate, to a fine not exceeding MYR 500,000, in the case of a continuing offence, to a further fine not exceeding MYR 20,000 each day during which the offence continues after conviction. Section 23 requires that any person who intends to export LMOs to comply with the requirements of the importing country on the importation of LMOs and to inform the Board of such requirement. When submitting the notification to the DG, it must be accompanied by the emergency response plan, and in relation to activities involving LMOs, the specific measures to be taken.[749] Specific measures are also required upon any approved person who undertakes a contained use activity as provided in section 26. Any approved person who contravenes the section commits an offence and on conviction may be liable to a fine not exceeding MYR 250,000 or to imprisonment for a term not exceeding five years or both and, in the case of a continuing offence, to a further fine up to MYR 10,000 for each day during which the offence continues after conviction. Where such person is a body corporate, to a fine not exceeding MYR 500,000 and, in the case of a continuing offence, to a further fine

749. Section 24 of the Biosafety Act 2007.

not exceeding MYR 20,000 for each day during which the offence continues after conviction. Under section 29, Advisory Committee will assess the notification for making recommendations to the Board. Upon having considered the recommendations of the Advisory Committee may make no order, issue a cessation order, impose such terms and conditions, order the approved person to make rectifications or make any other order as the Board thinks fit in the interest of biosafety. Decision of the Board will be made within ninety days from the date of receipt of the notification. Where the Board issues a cessation order, the approved person must cease all activities involving LMOs immediately and shall, within seven days from the date of the notification of the cessation order, and surrender the acknowledgement of receipt of a notification issued. Any approved person who contravenes any order made by the Board under this section may be liable to an offence and fined up to MYR 100,000 or to imprisonment for a term not exceeding four years or both, and, in the case of a continuing offence, to a further fine not exceeding MYR 10,000 for each day during which the offence continues after conviction. Where such person is a body corporate, to a fine not exceeding MYR 250,000 and, in the case of a continuing offence, to a further fine not exceeding MYR 20,000 for each day during which the offence continues after conviction. Section 31 provides that the Board may require the approved person to furnish any additional information, and upon obtaining the new information on the LMOs to review the notification. Upon review, where there is a risk posed to human, plant or animal health, the environment or biological diversity, the Board may take any of the following actions: make a cessation order; impose additional terms and conditions; order the approved person to make rectifications; or make any other order as the Board thinks fit in the interest of biosafety.[750] Penalty imposed on any approved person who fails to furnish any information under section 31, or who contravenes any order made by the Board under section 32 is a fine not exceeding MYR 100,000 or to imprisonment for a term not exceeding four years or both and, in the case of a continuing offence, to a further fine not exceeding MYR 10,000 for each day during which the offence continues after conviction. Where such person is a body corporate, the fine not exceeding MYR 250,000 and, in the case of a continuing offence, to a further fine not MYR 20,000 for each day during which the offence continues after conviction. In addition to the Board's power under section 32, the Board may further make a cessation order, impose any additional terms and conditions, order the approved person to make rectifications, or make any other order in the interest of biosafety in the following circumstances:[751]

- where there is a risk posed to human, plant or animal health, the environment or biological diversity;
- where the approved person fails to comply with any terms and conditions imposed on the notification;
- where the approved person fails to comply with any order made by the Board;
- where the approved person has contravened any of the provisions of this Act; or
- where the approved person has been convicted for an offence under this Act.

750. Section 31 of the Biosafety Act 2007.
751. Section 33 of the Biosafety Act 2007.

Another measure taken by the Biosafety Act 2007 is to establish a scheme to assess the risks to human, plant and animal health, the environment and biodiversity associated with various activities involving LMOs. Under section 36, risk assessment refers to an assessment of the risk and adverse effect that such LMOs and products of such organisms will have or are likely to have on the human, plant and animal health, the environmental and biological diversity. Whereas risk management refers to the proposed measures that shall be undertaken to prevent, reduce or control the risks and adverse effect that such LMOs and their products will have or are likely to have on human, plant and animal health, the environment and biological diversity. Section 36 requires that both risk assessment and risk management to be submitted for the application of release, import or contained use of the LMOs. Penalty provided to those who contravene the section is a fine not exceeding MYR 250,000 or to imprisonment for a term not exceeding five years or both and, in the case of a continuing offence, to a further fine not exceeding MYR 10,000 for each day during which the offence continues after conviction. Where such person is a body corporate, the fine imposed is up to MYR 500,000 and, in the case of a continuing offence, to a further fine not exceeding MYR 20,000 for each day during which the offence continues after conviction.

Section 37 imposes the requirements of emergency response plan, which are safety measures and procedures for the protection of human, plant and animal health, the environmental and biological diversity against harm or damage caused directly or indirectly by LMOs or products of such organisms and all necessary measures to be taken in the event of an emergency. The type and amount of penalty imposed on any approved person or body corporate who fails to take the necessary measures in accordance with the emergency response plan are similar to that of section 36.

Under section 38, powers under the Biosafety Act 2017 may be exercised by the enforcement officers of the Board as well as the following officers as provided in the Third Schedule, namely:

- Any police officer not below the rank of Inspector as provided for in the Police Act 1967;
- Any Inspecting Officer of the Department of Agriculture as defined in section 2 of the Plant Quarantine Act 1976;
- Any authorized officer as defined in section 2 of the Food Act 1983;
- Any Officer of customs as defined in section 2 of the Customs Act 1967;
- Any port officer as defined in section 2 of the Merchant Shipping Ordinance 1952;
- Any fisheries officer as defined in section 2 of the Fisheries Act 1985;
- Any authorized officer as defined in section 2 and appointed under section 53 of the Protection of New Plant Varieties Act 2004; and
- Any veterinary authority as defined in section 2 of the Animals Act 1953.

Procedural matters relating to enforcement, including investigations, are provided within sections 40–57 of the Act. Section 58 provides that no prosecution in respect of any offence under the Act shall be instituted except by, or with the written consent of, the Public Prosecutor. Offence by body corporate is covered by section 64 whereas section 65 deals with offence by partner, agent or servant.

Chapter 2. Monuments and Landscapes

§1. Monuments

I. Legal Framework

625. Under the Federal Constitution of Malaysia, state government is conferred with legislative jurisdiction on matters pertaining to museums, ancient and historical monuments, records, and archaeological sites and remains.[752] However, List III Concurrent List, which allows for both federal and state government legislative competence, contains Item 9B on culture and sports, and 9E on preservation of heritage.

626. The main agency dealing with matters pertaining to heritage and monuments is the National Department of Heritage, under the Ministry of Culture, Arts and Heritage Malaysia. The objectives of the establishment of this Department were to implement the formulation of related acts, to collect documentation, and to preserve and develop heritage efficiently and in an orderly manner.

627. Under this Department, there is a specific office established for monuments, known as the Monuments and Natural Environment Office. The functions of this Office are to identify and preserve the authenticity of Malaysia's cultural heritage and to plan for the monitoring and protection of cultural heritage, such as old buildings and historical sites. Another main function of the National Department of Heritage is to enforce the relevant law, the National Heritage Act 2005.

II. The National Heritage Act 2005

628. The National Heritage Act 2005[753] came into force on 1 March 2006. This Act was enacted to provide for the conservation and preservation of national heritage, natural heritage, tangible and intangible cultural heritage, underwater cultural heritage, treasure trove and for related matters. The enactment of this Act also repealed[754] the Antiquities Act 1976[755] and the Treasure Trove Act 957.[756]

629. There are several relevant terms defined by the National Heritage Act 2005. The term 'monument' is defined to mean 'architectural works, works of monumental sculpture and painting, elements or structures of an archaeological nature, inscriptions, cave dwellings and combinations of features, which are of outstanding universal value from the point of view of history, art or science'.

752. Item 12A of List II, State List of the Constitution.
753. Act 654.
754. Section 125 of the National Heritage Act 2005.
755. Act 168.
756. Act 542. 'The Treasure Trove Act 1957 shall continue to apply to those states which do not adopt the provisions of Part XI of this Act on treasure trove by a law made by the legislature of the relevant states in accordance with Clause (3) of Art. 76 of the Federal Constitution.'

630. The term 'natural heritage' is defined to include 'natural features of any area in Malaysia which may consist of earthly physical or biological formations or groups of such formations, geological or physiographical features, mountains, rivers, streams, rock formations, sea shore or any natural sites of outstanding value from the point of view of nature, science, history conservation or natural beauty including flora and fauna of Malaysia'.

631. Part II of the Act is on conservation and preservation of heritage. Under this part, section 3 deals with policy in relation to conservation and preservation of heritage. Under section 3(1), the Minister shall be responsible for providing or issuing policies, statements or directives in respect of any matter, business, strategy or conduct on the conservation and preservation of heritage. However, under section 3(2), the Minister shall not provide or issue any policies, statements or directives under subsection (1) where the matter, business, strategy or conduct on the conservation and preservation of heritage concerns the power or jurisdiction of a state.

632. Part III is on the administration of the Act. Section 4 provides for the appointment of a Commissioner of Heritage for carrying out the powers and functions assigned to the Commissioner under this Act. Functions of the Commissioner as provided in section 6 are as follows:

- to determine the designation of sites, registration of objects and underwater cultural heritage;
- to establish and maintain the Register and to determine and specify the categories of heritage to be listed in the Register;
- to supervise and oversee the conservation, preservation, restoration, maintenance, promotion, exhibition and accessibility of heritage;
- to promote and facilitate any research relating to heritage;
- to authorize, monitor and supervise excavations for heritage purposes;
- to maintain documents relating to any excavation, exploration, finding or search for heritage;
- to establish and maintain liaison and cooperation with the State Authority in respect of conservation and preservation of heritage matters;
- to advise and coordinate with the local planning authority, the Council and other bodies and entities at all levels for safeguarding, promoting and dealing with any heritage;
- to promote and regulate that best standards and practices are applied in the conservation and preservation of heritage;
- to advise the Minister with regard to any matter in respect of conservation and preservation of heritage;
- to perform such other functions under this Act as the Minister may assign from time to time; and
- to do all such things as may be incidental to or consequential upon the discharge of his powers and functions.

633. Apart from the establishment of the Commissioners, the Act also provides for the establishment of a National Heritage Council under Part IV of the Act. Section 9 provides for the functions of the Council, namely to advise the Minister and the Commissioner on all matters relating to heritage, and the due administration and enforcement of laws relating to heritage; and to advise the Minister and the Commissioner on any matter referred to it by the Minister or the Commissioner.

634. Membership of the Council is provided in section 10 as follows:

- a Chairman, to be appointed by the Minister;
- the Secretary General of the Ministry of Culture, Arts and Heritage or his representative;
- the Secretary General of the Ministry of Tourism or his representative;
- the Director General of Town and Country Planning or his representative;
- the Director General of the Museums and Antiquity Department or his representative;
- the Commissioner; and
- not more than six other members, at least one of whom shall be a public officer, who possess experience or expertise in relation to the management, conservation or preservation of sites and objects of natural or cultural heritage significance, to be appointed by the Minister.

635. Under section 32 of the Act, it is a requirement that the Commissioner notifies the local planning authority for the area of the local authority where the heritage site is situated of the designation of the heritage site, so that the local planning authority shall take into consideration any matter, policy, strategy or plan of action pertaining to the interest of the heritage site in preparing any development plan in that local authority area under the Town and Country Planning Act 1976.

636. Section 41 pertains to the monument preservation order. Under section 41(1), where the Commissioner, with the concurrence of the State Authority, is satisfied that any monument regarded as suitable to be registered as a heritage site is in dilapidation or in imminent danger of demolition, destruction, damage or alteration, the Commissioner shall serve on the owner of the monument a Monument Preservation Order pending approval of its registration.

637. Offences in respect of heritage sites are provided in section 112. This states that no person shall do the following, without written approval from the Commissioner:

- dig, construct, excavate, build, plant trees, quarry, irrigate, burn lime or deposit earth or refuse, on or in the heritage site or conservation area;
- demolish, disturb, obstruct, modify, mark, pull down or remove any monument in any heritage site;
- erect any building or structure abutting upon a monument in any heritage site;
- destroy the relationship of a building and its environment that is incompatible with the character of the neighbourhood in any heritage site;

– clear any area or interfere with, destroy or remove any tree, plant undergrowth, weed, grass or vegetation in any heritage site; or
– do any activities or actions that would likely cause damage to the adjacent and surrounding land which have been registered as a heritage site.

638. Under section 112(2), any person who, without lawful authority, contravenes subsection (1) shall be guilty of an offence and shall on conviction be liable to imprisonment for a term not exceeding five years, a fine not exceeding MYR 50,000, or both.

§2. Landscapes

I. General Information

639. Before independence, there already existed several gardens all around Malaysia to cater for the recreational and amenity needs of the public. Among the oldest public gardens established was the Taiping Lake Gardens in the state of Perak. They cover an area of approximately 64 ha of rehabilitated ex tin mining land and have been operational since 1880.

640. In Penang, the Penang Botanical Gardens, which are 29 ha in size, were set up in 1884 by a British officer, Charles Curtis, for recreational and botanical purposes. Whereas the Kuala Lumpur Lake Gardens were initiated in 1888 based on the idea of A.R. Venning, the Chairman of the Sanitary Board of Kuala Lumpur, to create a place for healthy activity, recreation and relaxation for the public. The Kuala Lumpur Lake Gardens were built around an artificial lake and encompass about 91.6 ha of undulating greenery interspersed with flowering shrubs, shady trees, exceptional botanical gardens and other notable features.

641. After independence, the first well-planned greening programme in Malaysia began in the Federal Territory of Kuala Lumpur in 1973 with the establishment of the Beautification Unit under the Beautification Programmes of Kuala Lumpur. The unit was upgraded into a department. Today it is known as the Landscape and Urban Cleansing Control Department under the Ministry of Housing and Local Government.

II. Legal Framework

A. National Landscape Department

642. At the federal level, the National Landscape Department under the Ministry of Housing and Local Government was established in 1996 as a landscape development referral centre for the entire country. The Department's functions are more administrative in nature, with no specific legislation on landscape being enforced by the Department.

643. Among its functions are to regulate landscape development in Malaysia; to undertake the functions of implementing landscape development including the development of public parks, and landscape development programmes; and to provide technical services in landscape development to other government departments, public sector and State Authority agencies. Other services provided by the Department include evaluation of the landscape development requirements, landscape design works and an advisory service in landscape development.

644. Since its inception in 1996, the Department has implemented the preparation of landscape development master plans for several state capitals, cities and tourism towns, undertaken several studies for the Design Guidelines, initiated the formation of a national landscape policy and undertaken the formation of a Landscape Development Act (which is yet to be enacted). The landscape areas identified by the Department for developing a comprehensive landscape for Malaysia are as follows:

- roadsides and highways;
- train routes;
- riverbanks, lakes and beaches;
- housing areas;
- recreational Parks;
- public Building;
- parking Areas;
- basic Facilities;
- burial Grounds;
- rural Areas; and
- walkways and bicycle lanes.

B. Local Government

645. In Malaysia, local authority is given certain powers under the Local Government Act of 1976 and the Town and Country Planning Act 1976 to provide discretionary functions such as amenities and recreational parks. The local authority is also required to provide maintenance and improvement of the environment within the area of jurisdiction, including providing beautification programmes.

646. Specifically, the local authority's function pertaining to developing and maintaining landscaped areas is guided by what is known as the National Landscape Guidelines, published in 1995 by the Department of Town and Country Planning.[757]

647. These guidelines serve as a reference for developing and maintaining landscaped areas, providing standards for tree and shrub planting, tree conservation in

757. Ministry Housing & Loc. Govt., *National Landscape Guidelines* (Dept. Town & Country Planning 1995).

urban development, etc. The guidelines include details on site preparation and planting techniques for trees, palms, shrubs, ground cover, climbers, grass and plants in planter boxes. Appropriate management procedures, such as fertilizer application, mulching, watering, pest and disease control and pruning are also covered.

Chapter 3. Parks and Reserves

§1. The Physical Context

648. National Parks, State Parks, Wildlife Sanctuaries, Wildlife Reserves and Marine Parks are collectively known as protected areas under Malaysian law. Protected areas are crucial for the conservation of natural habitats, wildlife, plants and highly valuable natural resources. They provide a range of ecological services, from watershed protection and climate regulation to soil protection.

649. There are currently about twenty-five terrestrial National and State Parks, and forty Marine Parks in Malaysia. These Parks are managed by the federal government through the Department of Wildlife and National Parks, and the Marine Parks Section of the Department of Fisheries Malaysia.[758]

650. At the state level, state agencies that regulate the protected areas are state forestry departments and state wildlife departments. However, some states have corporatized their parks agencies. This includes the Sabah Foundation for the state of Sabah, the Sarawak Parks Corporation for the state of Sarawak and the Johor National Parks Corporation for the state of Johor.

§2. National and State Parks

651. Under the Federal Constitution, land matters, including matters relating to parks and reserves that are situated within state land, come under List II, Federal List, which allows state governments to have legislative jurisdiction over the matter.

652. At the federal level, the main agency dealing with parks and reserves is the Department of Wildlife, which was previously under the MNRE and currently under the Ministry of Energy and Natural Resources. The main functions of this Department are to plan and implement policies and activities in the national parks in accordance with the existing legislation, guidelines and conventions leading towards the conservation of biodiversity resources.

653. The Department is also entrusted to protect and manage several forests which are gazetted as National Parks. At the moment, there are two national parks managed by this Department, namely Taman Negara National Park and Penang National Park.

654. The Taman Negara Park was established in 1938. The rainforest within this park is estimated to be 130 million years old and with an area of 4,343 sq. km This park is administered by a park superintendent. It is a combination of three protected

758. *See* the official website at https://www.dof.gov.my/en/corporate-info/divisions-units/marine-park-resource-management-division/.

areas, Taman Negara Pahang National Park, Taman Negara Kelantan National Park and Taman Negara Terengganu National Park.[759]

655. In the state of Penang, the Penang National Park is created under the National Parks Act 1980 to conserve and protect wildlife, marine life and plants. The park covers an area of 2,563 ha and is bordered by the Georgetown metropolitan area and the sea. The 1,182 ha of land includes beaches and hills and is rich in flora and fauna while the remaining 1,381 ha are made up of sea.

656. In the state of Sabah, the Sabah Ministry of Tourism and Environmental Development, through its wildlife section, is responsible for the environmental aspects of development and environmentally related projects. This section is responsible for the conservation of mammals, birds and other large vertebrate animals throughout Sabah, except in the State and National Parks. It is also responsible for enforcement of the wildlife protection laws and is involved in public education. Another Sabah state agency, the Sabah Forest Department, is empowered to manage the Forest Reserves.

657. For the state of Sarawak, the Sarawak Forest Department is responsible for the management of forestry and of Forest Reserves. The Department established an office known as the National Parks and Wildlife Office for the development and protection of wildlife sanctuaries and national parks, enforcement of wildlife laws and conducting wildlife research. Another agency is the Marine Fisheries Department, Sarawak, which is involved in the research and management of marine resources, and the Department of Agriculture, which is involved in research into soil types and agricultural capability classification.

§3. LEGAL FRAMEWORK

I. The National Parks Act 1980

658. The Taman Negara Act 1980[760] or the National Parks Act 1980 was enacted to provide for the establishment and control of National Parks or *Taman Negara*. Section 4 provides that the establishment of National Parks is for the preservation and protection of wildlife, plant life and objects of geological, archaeological, historical and ethnological and other scientific and scenic interest, and through their conservation and utilization to promote the education, health, aesthetic values and recreation of the people.

659. The National Parks Act 1980 is applicable throughout Malaysia. However, it does not apply to Sabah and Sarawak and the State Parks of Kelantan, Pahang and Trengganu, which together constitute the Taman Negara as described in the

759. Ibrahim Komoo, *Taman Negara, Conserving Our National Heritage* (Inst. Envt. & Dev., Universiti Kebangsaan Malay. 1996).
760. Act 226.

Schedule to the Taman Negara (Kelantan) Enactment 1938,[761] in the First Schedules to the Taman Negara (Pahang) Enactment 193[762] and the Taman Negara (Terengganu) Enactment 1958.[763]

660. The establishment of the National Park is provided in section 3 of the Act. It empowers the Minister to request the State Authority of any state to reserve any state land within the State (including any marine area) for a National Park. The area so reserved shall be placed under the control of a National Park committee established under section 7.[764]

661. Power to enforce this Act is under the jurisdiction of the DG as provided in section 8. Under this Act, 'Director General' means the Director General of Wildlife and National Parks appointed under the Protection of Wildlife Act 1972.[765]

662. The Act provides for the establishment of the National Parks Advisory Council under section 5, which consists of the following members:[766]

- a chairman to be appointed by the Minister;
- the State Secretary of each of the states in which there is a National Park or part thereof;
- three representatives nominated by the State Authority from each of the states in which there is a National Park or part thereof;
- the DG;
- a representative of the Treasury;
- a representative of the Economic Planning Unit of the Prime Minister's Department;
- a representative of the Tourist Development Corporation;
- a representative of the Department of Forestry; and
- not more than six other persons to be appointed by the Minister.

663. The Act also provides for the establishment of National Park committees, to be responsible for the conservation, utilization, care, control, management and development of the National Parks.[767] The committees consist of the following members:[768]

- the State Secretary of each state within which the National Park is situated;
- the Director of Lands and Mines of each of the states in which there is a National Park or part thereof;

761. No. 14 1938.
762. No. 2 1939.
763. No. 6 1958.
764. Section 3(2) of the Taman Negara Act 1980.
765. Section 8(2) of the Taman Negara Act 1980.
766. Section 5(1) of the Taman Negara Act 1980.
767. Section 7(3) of the Taman Negara Act 1980.
768. Section 7(1) of the Taman Negara Act 1980.

- a representative each of such departments of the Federal Government and, after consultation with the State Authority, of the State Governments as the Minister may consider necessary to be represented; and
- such other persons, not exceeding three in number, as the Minister may appoint after consultation with the State Authority, and subsection 5(2) shall *mutatis mutandis* apply in the case of an appointment under this paragraph.

664. Section 9, on the occupation of land within National Parks, authorizes the State Authority, in accordance with the National Land Code 1965,[769] to lease or permit the use or occupation of any land within a National Park for the following purposes only:

- the construction and maintenance of roads;
- the construction and maintenance of airstrips;
- the construction and maintenance of dams and reservoirs;
- the construction and maintenance of hotels, rest houses, dwelling houses; and
- buildings and works of public utility.

II. The Aboriginal Peoples Act 1954

665. The Aboriginal Peoples Act 1954[770] was enacted to provide for the protection, well-being and advancement of the aboriginal peoples of West Malaysia. Certain provisions in this Act are also relevant for parks and reserves.

666. Section 3 of the Act defines 'aborigine' as:

- 'any person whose male parent is or was a member of an aboriginal ethnic group, who speaks an aboriginal language and habitually follows an aboriginal way of life and aboriginal customs and beliefs, and includes a descendant through males of such persons';[771]
- 'any person of any race adopted when an infant by aborigines who has been brought up as an aborigine, habitually speaks an aboriginal language, habitually follows an aboriginal way of life and aboriginal customs and beliefs and is a member of an aboriginal community';[772] or
- 'the child of any union between an aboriginal female and a male of another race, provided that the child habitually speaks an aboriginal language, habitually follows an aboriginal way of life and aboriginal customs and beliefs and remains a member of an aboriginal community'.[773]

769. Section 9(3) of the Taman Negara Act 1980.
770. Act 134, revised 1974.
771. Section 3(1)(a) of the Aboriginal Peoples Act 1954.
772. Section 3(1)(b) of the Aboriginal Peoples Act 1954.
773. Section 3(1)(c) of the Aboriginal Peoples Act 1954.

667. Protection of aboriginal areas is provided in section 6 where the State Authority may declare any area predominantly or exclusively inhabited by aborigines to be an 'aboriginal area'.

668. Section 6(2) further provides that the following activities are prohibited within an aboriginal area:

- to declare any land as a Malay Reservation under any written law relating to Malay Reservations;
- to declare any land as a sanctuary or reserve under any written law relating to the protection of wild animals and birds;
- to alienate, grant, lease or otherwise dispose of any land to persons not being aborigines normally resident in that aboriginal area or to any commercial undertaking without consulting the DG; and
- to issue licences for the collection of forest produce under any written law relating to forests to persons not being aborigines normally resident in that aboriginal area or to any commercial undertaking without consulting the DG, and in granting any such licence it may be ordered that a specified proportion of aboriginal labour be employed.

669. Section 7 gives the power to the state authorities to declare any area exclusively inhabited by aborigines to be 'an aboriginal reserve'. Section 2 interprets 'aboriginal inhabited place' to mean 'any place inhabited by an aboriginal community but which has not been declared to be an aboriginal area or aboriginal reserve'. However, no land can be declared an aboriginal reserve when it appears unlikely that the aborigines will remain permanently in that place; it shall not be declared an aboriginal reserve but shall form part of an aboriginal area.[774] An aboriginal reserve may be constituted within an aboriginal area. Other restrictions imposed within an aboriginal reserve include the prohibition of declaring, under any written law, the land as Malaysia Reservation, sanctuary or reserved forest.[775] However, the State Authority is empowered to revoke or vary any declaration of an aboriginal reserve made under the Act.[776]

III. National Forestry Act 1984

670. At the state level, states are also empowered to establish 'state park forest' as provided by the National Forestry Act 1984.[777] State park forest is regulated by the state forestry department under the respective states. At the federal level, previously, the forestry department of Peninsular Malaysia came under the MNRE. The administration of environment-related matters has been reorganized many times at the federal level which has seen the forestry department of Peninsular Malaysia to

774. Section 7(1) of the Aboriginal Peoples Act 1954.
775. Section 7(2) of the Aboriginal Peoples Act 1954.
776. Section 7(3) of the Aboriginal Peoples Act 1954.
777. Act 313.

come under the Ministry of Water, Land and Natural Resources in 2018. Whereas from 2019 until presently, the department comes under the Ministry of Energy and Natural Resources.

671. The National Forestry Act 1984 was enacted to provide for the administration, management and conservation of forests and forestry development within the states of Malaysia. This Act was enacted by virtue of clause (1)(b) of Article 76 of the Federal Constitution, for the purpose only of promoting uniformity of the laws of the States of Malaysia.

672. The relevant part pertaining to state parks is Part III on permanent reserve forests. Section 7 empowers the state government to declare any land a permanent reserved forest. Specific areas within state forest land may be gazetted as a state park by the Director of Forests, with the approval of the State Authority, through section 10. Under this section, the Director is empowered to classify every permanent reserved forest under one or more of the following classifications:

- timber production forest under sustained yield;
- soil protection forest;
- soil reclamation forest;
- flood control forest;
- water catchment forest;
- forest sanctuary for wildlife;
- virgin jungle reserved forest;
- amenity forest;
- education forest;
- research forest; and
- forest for federal purposes.

673. Apart from the classification under section 10 of the Act, state governments, through their respective forestry enactments, have inserted an additional classification known as 'state park' to the existing section 10(1), such as that introduced by the state of Perlis under the National Forestry Act 1984 (Amendment) (Perlis) Enactment 2001.

674. Several states have gazetted state parks through the National Forestry Act 1984. In Johor, the Endau-Rompin State Park was gazetted in 1996 by the State Government, based on the Act and the Johor National Park Enactment 1989. This Park is managed by the Johor National Park Corporation, established in 1989.

675. In the state of Kelantan, the Stong State Park was gazetted in 2005 by virtue of the National Forestry Act 1984. For the state of Perak, the Royal Belum State Park was officially gazetted under the Act, together with the Perak State Park Corporation Enactment 2001. In Selangor, the Selangor State Park was gazetted in January 2007 under the National Forestry Act 1984, which has since been adopted and amended by the Selangor state government.

IV. State Legislations

676. In Sabah, the principal laws concerning wildlife in Sabah are the Parks Enactments 1984, Forests Enactment 1968, Forests (Amendment) Enactment 1984, Fauna Conservation Ordinance 1963 and its amendments, and Fisheries Act 1985. All are state legislation, except for the last-named, which is Federal. The Forests (Amendment) Enactment 1984 classifies forests on a scale of 1–7:

(1) Protection Forest, for soil and water conservation.
(2) Commercial Forest, for commercial exploitation.
(3) Domestic Forest, for local traditional use.
(4) Amenity Forest, for recreation, research, etc.
(5) Mangrove Forest, subdivided for different uses.
(6) Virgin Jungle Reserve, for genetic conservation, but often logged.
(7) Wildlife Reserve.

677. Commercial Forests can be selectively logged under licence, but other areas cannot be logged without State Authority. The amended Act strengthens legislation regarding existing Forest Reserves by requiring de-gazettement or excision to be effected by enactment, except for conversion to a Park, Game Sanctuary or Bird Sanctuary.

678. The Parks Enactment 1984 describes the procedure by which the State Assembly may establish parks. Under separate legislation, all National Parks within Sabah have been amended to state parks to ensure that they remain under state rather than federal legislation. Bird Sanctuaries were gazetted under legislation which was repealed in 1963. They are still legally Bird Sanctuaries, but are not managed.

679. For the state of Sarawak, the Natural Resources Ordinance 1949[778] and its subsequent amendments require that a Natural Resources Board be established to give overall direction to the conservation of Sarawak's natural resources. The National Parks Ordinance 1956[779] provides for the constitution, maintenance and control of National Parks in Sarawak.

680. In Sarawak, wildlife Sanctuaries are gazetted under the Wildlife Protection Ordinance 1958[780] to provide totally protected areas of particular natural interest, protected against all forms of exploitation, including tourism. The Ordinance also includes provision for the protection of wild species and their habitats. Both Ordinances are administered by the National Parks and Wildlife Office of the Sarawak Forest Department.

778. Cap. 84.
779. Cap. 127.
780. Cap. 128.

§4. MARINE PARK

I. General Information

681. Malaysia is endowed with a large maritime realm covering sea areas of over 600,000 km and continental shelf areas of about 476,761 km and contains invaluable mangroves, atolls and coastal areas surrounded by resource-rich seas.

682. However, mangrove forests and coral reefs have been exploited by commercial and tourism development for activities such as reclamation, sand mining and direct discharge of wastewater. Moreover, siltation and sedimentation, due to development projects concerned with infrastructure preparation, cause degradation of the marine ecosystem and a decrease of fishery landing sources.[781]

II. Institutional Framework

A. Federal Level

683. Malaysia's marine parks are governed through a three-tiered system which involves the federal government, state government and the local authorities. However, policies are formulated by the federal government.

684. At the federal level, the agency responsible for the management of the marine parks is the Department of Marine Park Malaysia, officially established in July 2007. This Department was formerly under the Department of Fisheries Malaysia and has been transferred to the MNRE in 2004.[782] In 2018, after the general election, the new government had returned of the Department of Marine Park Malaysia from the then MNRE to the Ministry of Agriculture. At present, the Marine Park & Resource Management Division is created under the Department of Fisheries Malaysia, which is part of the Ministry of Agriculture and Food Industry.[783]

685. The task of the Department of Marine Park is to establish, administer and manage the Marine Parks. Each Marine Park has a Marine Park Unit that oversees the day-to-day running of the Marine Park Centres, and carries out general administration and management duties. The functions of the Department of Marine Park include:

- to preserve and rehabilitate the habitat for marine organisms;
- to conserve and protect marine natural resources;
- to manage funding for the management and development of the marine parks;

---

781. *See* Jabatan Taman Laut Malaysia, *Laporan Tahunan Jabatan Taman Laut Malaysia* (JTLM 2012).
782. *See* at the Department of Marine Parks' official website at http://www.dmpm.nre.gov.my/, January 2014.
783. See at the Department of Fisheries Malaysia's official website at https://www.dof.gov.my/en/corporate-info/divisions-units/marine-park-resource-management-division/

– to plan, implement and develop educational and public awareness programmes;
– to manage development of aquatic recreational activities suitable to the island's carrying capacity;
– to carry out enforcement activities;
– to implement research and monitoring programmes on the marine flora and fauna; and
– to formulate and revise a marine park management plan.

686. At the federal level, besides the Department of Marine Park, a council known as the National Advisory Council for Marine Parks and Reserves was established. Its main tasks are to determine guidelines for the implementation at the national level with respect to the protection, conservation, utilization, control, management and development of marine parks and marine reserves; coordinate the development of any area of a marine park or marine reserve with the federal government and any body corporate; and provide technical advice to state governments regarding development projects on any island situated within marine parks or reserves.

B. State Level

687. At the state level, state government has control over land matters of the marine park islands and has the authority to develop and decide matters pertaining to land usage of the islands. These developments are then implemented and supervised by the local government.

688. Additionally, the State Economic Planning Units play the lead role in policy and project planning, coordination and development in each state. Any land-based development proposals for marine park islands need approval by the state through the State Economic Planning Unit.

689. Other important state institutions are the local Land and District Authorities which are empowered to administer and develop land within their districts. Some states have also developed specific agencies to deal with island development. For example, in the state of Johor, the Johor National Parks Corporation has the power to gazette land areas adjacent to marine waters as state conservation areas.

C. Consultative Level

690. To resolve any conflicts which may arise from the different tiered governing system, the National Advisory Council for Marine Park and Marine Reserve was formed at the federal level.[784]

784. Further information on the National Advisory Council for Marine Park can be found at the Department of Marine Parks official website at http://www.dmpm.nre.gov.my/history_of_establishment.html?&lang=en, January 2014.

691. The Council provides an opportunity for consultative decision-making on policies pertaining to marine parks. Its members consist of representatives from federal and state governments, environmental NGOs, local universities and relevant commercial firms. Its functions include:[785]

- to determine the guidelines for the implementation at the national level with respect to protection, conservation, utilization, control management and progress of the marine park and marine reserve areas;
- to coordinate the development of any area of a marine park or marine reserve with the Federal Government and any body corporate; and
- to give technical advice to the State Government with respect to any development projects on any island which is situated in a marine park or marine reserve area.

III. Fisheries Act 1985

A. *The Constitution*

692. The Fisheries Act 1985[786] is the main legislation enacted for the establishment and management of marine parks. It was enacted to consolidate and amend the written law relating to fisheries, including the conservation, management and development of maritime and estuarine fishing and fisheries in Malaysian fisheries' waters and to turtles and riverine fishing in Malaysia.

693. This Act was enacted by virtue of clause (1)(b) of Article 76 of the Federal Constitution allowing the Parliament to make laws with respect to any matter enumerated in the State List for promoting uniformity of the laws of two or more States.

B. *Marine Parks and Reserves*

694. The setting up of marine parks is provided for under sections 41 through 45 of the Fisheries Act 1985. The principal goal of establishing Marine Parks is to protect, conserve and manage in perpetuity representative marine ecosystems of significance, particularly coral reefs and their associated flora and fauna. The objectives of the marine parks are as follows:

- to conserve and protect coral reefs to sustain fisheries resources;
- to upgrade and conserve natural habitats for endangered species of marine life;
- to establish specific management zones for the conservation of marine life; and
- to establish zones for recreational use consistent with the carrying capacity of each area.

---

785. *See* Jabatan Taman Laut Malaysia, *Laporan Tahunan Jabatan Taman Laut Malaysia* (JTLM 2012).
786. Act 317. It repealed the Fisheries Act 1963, Act 210.

695. Until now, the Marine Parks Malaysia Order 1994 gazetted under the Act has included forty islands in Malaysia as protected areas.

696. Part IX of the Act deals with marine parks and reserves. Section 41 of the Act empowers the Minister to establish a marine park or marine reserve for the following purposes:[787]

- to afford special protection to the aquatic flora and fauna of such area or part thereof and to protect, preserve and manage the natural breeding grounds and habitat of aquatic life, with particular regard to species of rare or endangered flora and fauna;
- to allow for the natural regeneration of aquatic life in such area or part thereof where such life has been depleted;
- to promote scientific study and research in respect of such area or part thereof;
- to preserve and enhance the pristine state and productivity of such area or part thereof; and
- to regulate recreational and other activities in such area or part thereof to avoid irreversible damage to its environment.

C. The National Advisory Council for Marine Park and Marine Reserve

697. Under section 41, the Minister is empowered to establish the National Advisory Council for Marine Park and Marine Reserve, and it consists of the following members:[788]

- the Secretary General of the Ministry of Agriculture;
- a representative of the State Government concerned;
- a representative of the Ministry charged with the responsibility for finance;
- a representative of the Ministry charged with the responsibility for science, technology and environment;
- a representative of the Fisheries Department;
- a representative of the Department of Wildlife and National Park;
- a representative of the Implementation and Coordination Unit of the Prime Minister's Department;
- a representative of the Malaysia Tourism Promotion Board;
- a representative of the Malaysian Society of Marine Sciences;
- a representative of the World Wide Fund for Nature Malaysia;
- a representative of the Malaysian Nature Society; and
- any other member to be appointed from time to time.

698. The function of the National Advisory Council for Marine Park and Marine Reserve is provided in section 41B, which is to advise the Minister on any matter relating to a marine park or marine reserve area, and in particular:

787. Section 41(1) of the Fisheries Act 1985.
788. Section 41(2) of the Fisheries Act 1985.

- to determine the guidelines for the implementation at the national level with respect to protection, conservation, utilization, control, management and progress of the marine park and marine reserve areas;
- to coordinate the development of any area of a marine park or marine reserve with the Federal Government and anybody corporate; and
- to give technical advice to the State Government with respect to any development project on any island which is situated in a marine park or marine reserve area.

699. Section 42 empowers the Director General of Marine Park to supervise and direct the responsibility of coordination in respect of all matters relating to marine parks and marine reserves in Malaysian fishery waters.

D. Offences

700. Under section 43, it is an offence for any person who is in any marine park or marine reserve in Malaysia fisheries waters to do certain acts without written permission of the DG, namely, if that person:

- fishes or attempts to fish;
- takes, removes or is in possession of any aquatic animal or aquatic plant or part thereof, whether dead or alive;
- collects or is in possession of any coral, dredges or extracts any sand or gravel, discharges or deposits any pollutant, alters or destroys the natural breeding grounds or habitat of aquatic life, or destroys any aquatic life;
- constructs or erects any building or other structure on or over any land or waters within a marine park or marine reserve;
- anchors any vessel by dropping any kind of weight on, or by attaching any kind of rope or chain to, any coral, rock or other submerged object; or
- destroys, defaces or removes any object, whether animate or inanimate, in a marine park or marine reserve.

701. Section 44 is an absolute prohibition of certain weapons. Subsection (1) of this section prohibits any person from carrying, using or possessing within a marine park or marine reserve in Malaysian fisheries waters the following weapons, namely any spring-gun, spear gun, spearfishing equipment, harpoon or suction gun; or any other kind of weapon potentially harmful to any aquatic plant life, aquatic animal life or to the coral reef structure.

702. The Fisheries Act 1985 gazetted the Fisheries (Prohibited Areas) Regulations 1994, to provide conservation of marine resources by declaring certain areas as prohibited areas. Therefore, no collection of shells, molluscs or corals is permitted. The killing or capture of any fish in this area must be in accordance with a licence. The Act also gazetted the Fisheries (Control of Endangered Species of Fish) Regulations 1999 which provide protection to species of whales, dolphins, whale sharks and giant clams.

§5. Fish and Other Marine Life

I. General Information

703. The fisheries sector is an important sub-sector in Malaysia and plays a significant role in the national economy. Basically, the fisheries sector is divided into three: marine capture fisheries, aquaculture and inland fisheries.

704. The marine capture fisheries can be categorized into two main types, coastal or inshore fisheries, and deep-sea fisheries. The coastal or inshore fishery is where the fishing vessels operate within 30 nautical miles from the coastline, whereas the deep-sea fishing vessels operate beyond 30 nautical miles from the shoreline:

– The marine capture fisheries are also categorized by various types of fishing gear used by the fishermen to harvest the large diversity of marine species found in Malaysian waters.[789]

705. Besides marine fisheries, inland fisheries and inland aquaculture add to the stock of fisheries. The aquaculture industry is made up of freshwater culture, brackish-water systems, ornamental fish and fingerling production. Malaysian rivers exhibit very diverse riverine fishery resources which support inland fisheries especially in remote rural areas. However, riverine fishing is small compared to marine fishing.

706. Fisheries are interdependent with coastal management and marine related activities. Thus, deteriorating environmental conditions through factors such as overfishing, coastal pollution, disruption of mangrove areas, coastal erosion and disruption of coral can affect the fishing industry.

II. Legal Framework

707. The main agency relevant to matters relating to fisheries is the Department of Fisheries, under the Ministry of Agriculture and Food Industry. This Department is entrusted with the roles of developing, managing and regulating the fisheries sector.

708. The objectives of the Department of Fisheries are to increase the national fish production, manage the fisheries resources on a sustainable basis, develop a dynamic fisheries industry, intensify the development of fish-based industries and to maximize the income of the fishing industry. The functions of the Department of Fisheries include:[790]

789. *See* Jabatan Taman Laut Malaysia, *Laporan Tahunan Jabatan Taman Laut Malaysia* (JTLM 2006).
790. Refer to the Department of Fisheries official website at http://www.dof.gov.my/August 2016.

- to formulate policies and strategies for the development and development planning for the fisheries industry in general;
- to enforce the Fisheries Act 1985 and the Exclusive Economic Act 1984;
- to manage and conserve and rehabilitate fisheries resources;
- to conduct fisheries research;
- to promote sustainable aquaculture;
- to provide fisheries extension services;
- to train fishermen, farmers and downstream industry entrepreneurs;
- to control fish diseases and provide quarantine services;
- to promote recreational fisheries;
- to monitor pollution affecting the fisheries resources;
- to provide basic fishery data;
- to establish standards; and
- to inspect fisheries products with the cooperation of other related agencies.

709. The Department of Fisheries is headed by the Director General of Fisheries. There are also twelve state fisheries offices in charge of all the district fisheries offices throughout the country. Each of these state fisheries offices is headed by a State Fisheries Director.

710. At the state level, the state Fisheries Department of each state is vested with powers to develop marine and inland farming and to consult with the relevant state authorities on inland fisheries and aquaculture regulations.

III. Fisheries Act 1985

A. *Historical Development*

711. Historically, the first legislation on fisheries enacted in Malaysia was the Fisheries Ordinance 1909. This Act was later repealed by the Fisheries Rules of 1951. During this time there were also seven Fisheries Ordinances or Enactments introduced by the various States. However, in the 1960s and 1970s, the introduction of trawling in coastal waters created much conflict between traditional fishermen and trawlers.

712. This led to the formulation of the Fisheries Act 1963, which provided a more comprehensive legal framework to manage the fisheries in Malaysian waters. This Act was formulated to integrate and strengthen the legal framework relating to marine and inland fisheries; to protect the natural living resources; to protect the interests of the fishermen; to ensure equitable allocation of fisheries resources; and to strengthen administrative activities to reduce conflict among the fishing communities. This Act was subsequently replaced by the Fisheries Act 1985.[791]

791. For further details on the historical development of laws on fisheries in Malaysia, *see* the Department of Fisheries' official website at http://www.dof.gov.my/index.php/pages/view/318, August 2016.

713. The preamble of the Fisheries Act 1985 states that the Act relates to fisheries, including the conservation, management and development of maritime and estuarine fishing and fisheries, in Malaysian fisheries waters, to turtles and riverine fishing in Malaysia and to matters connected therewith or incidental thereto. The preamble continues that it was expedient to consolidate and amend the written law relating to fisheries, including the conservation, management and development of maritime and estuarine fishing and fisheries, in Malaysian fisheries waters and to turtles and riverine fishing in Malaysia.

714. The Fisheries Act 1985 is an expansion of an improvement on the previous act, incorporating the Exclusive Economic Zone, and it is consistent with relevant provisions in the 1982 United Nations Convention on the Law of the Sea, to which Malaysia acceded on 14 October 1996.

B. Administration

715. The Fisheries Act 1985 provides for the establishment of Fisheries Protected Areas and Fisheries Prohibited Areas. Its objective is to ensure the protection of marine ecosystems, specifically, coral reefs around islands, and to guarantee the availability of nursing and feeding grounds for fisheries and endangered species. As an added measure, the amendment also prohibits fishing activity of any kind within the confines of the marine parks.

716. There are several relevant terms defined in this Act. The term 'fish' means 'any aquatic animal or plant life, sedentary or not, and includes all species of finfish, crustacea, mollusca, aquatic mammals, or their eggs or spawn, fry, fingerling, spat or young, but does not include any species of otters, turtles or their eggs'.

717. The term 'fishery' means 'any one or more stocks of fish which can be treated as a unit for the purposes of their conservation, management and development and includes fishing for any such stocks, and aquaculture'. The Act defines 'fishing' as:

- the catching, taking or killing of fish by any method;
- the attempted catching, taking or killing of fish; and
- engaging in any activity which can reasonably be expected to result in the catching, taking or killing of fish.

718. Part II of the Act deals with the administration aspect. Section 3 empowers the Minister to be responsible for all matters relating to fisheries, including the conservation, management and development of maritime and estuarine fishing and fisheries, in Malaysian fisheries water, to turtles and inland fisheries in the Federal Territories of Kuala Lumpur and Labuan and to turtles in waters outside the jurisdiction of any state in Malaysia.

719. Part III deals with fisheries plans. Section 6 provides that the DG is empowered to prepare and keep under continual review fisheries plans based on the best scientific information available and designed to ensure optimum utilization of fishery resources, consistent with sound conservation and management principles, with the avoidance of overfishing, and in accordance with the overall national policies, development plans and programmes.

C. *Offences*

720. Section 25 on offences under the Act, contained in Part VI, provides that:

> Under this section, any person who contravenes or fails to comply with any provision of this Act shall be guilty of an offence and where no special penalty is provided in relation thereto, such person shall be liable, where the vessel concerned is a foreign fishing vessel or the person concerned is a foreign national, to a fine not exceeding RM 1,000,000 each in the case of the owner or master, and RM 100,000 in the case of every member of the crew. In all other cases, the fine is not exceeding RM 20,000 or a term of imprisonment not exceeding two years or both.

721. It is also an offence under this Act to fish with explosives or poisons. Under section 26, any person who does the following commits an offence:

- uses or attempts to use any explosive, poison or pollutant, or any apparatus utilizing an electric current, or any prohibited gear, for killing, stunning, disabling or catching fish, or in any other way rendering such fish more easily caught;
- carries or has in his possession or under his control any explosive, poison or pollutant, or any apparatus utilizing an electric current, or any prohibited gear, with the intention of using such explosive, poison or pollutant, or apparatus, or prohibited gear, for any of the purposes referred to; or
- knowing or having reasonable cause to believe that any fish is a prohibited species or has been taken in contravention of the provisions of this Act, receives or is found in possession of such fish.

722. Section 27 deals with offences against aquatic mammals or turtles in Malaysian fisheries waters. Under this section, no person shall fish for, disturb, harass, catch or take any aquatic mammal or turtle which is found beyond the jurisdiction of any state in Malaysia. Section 27(20) further provides that the provisions of the relevant state law shall apply in respect of aquatic mammals and turtles which are found within such jurisdiction.

D. Inland Fisheries

723. Provisions on inland fisheries are provided in Part VII of the Act. Under section 37, the DG may, in consultation with the State Authority concerned, promote the development and rational management of inland fisheries through the following activities:

– the conduct or coordination of research;
– the provision and maintenance of experimental and demonstration aquaculture stations, fish-breeding stations and training centres;
– the provision of advice and technical assistance to the appropriate authorities of the state;
– the provision of publicity and demonstration facilities and other connected services; and
– the provision of advice on measures for the prevention of fish diseases.

724. The power of state authorities and Ministers to make rules concerning inland fisheries is provided in section 38. Section 38(1) states that the State Authority or, in respect of the Federal Territories of Kuala Lumpur and Labuan, the Minister, may make rules specifically or generally for the proper conservation, development, management and regulation of inland fisheries in any state in Malaysia or in the Federal Territories of Kuala Lumpur and Labuan.

725. Matters pertaining to aquaculture are provided in Part VIII of the Act. Section 39 authorizes the DG, in consultation with the State Authority, to promote the development of aquaculture in Malaysia.

726. Under the Fisheries Act 1985, the Minister of Agriculture is empowered to make regulations for the management and conservation of marine resources. A number of fisheries regulations have been made under the Fisheries Act.

E. Regulations under the Fisheries Act 1985

727. Until now, a number of Regulations have been gazetted under the Fisheries Act 1985 and earlier legislations on fisheries. They are as follows:

– Fisheries (Cockles Conservation and Culture) Regulations 2002;[792]
– Fisheries (Prohibition of Method of Fishing for Kerapu Fry) Regulations 1996;[793]
– Fisheries (Closed Season to Catch Kerapu Fry) Regulations 1996;[794]
– Fisheries (Prohibited Areas) (Rantau Abang) Regulations 1991;[795]

792. P.U. (A) 405/2002.
793. P.U. (A) 620/96.
794. P.U. (A) 619/96.
795. P.U. (A) 277/91.

- Fisheries (Prohibition of Import, etc. of Fish) Regulations 1990;[796]
- Fisheries (Marine Culture System) Regulations 1990;[797]
- Fisheries (Maritime) (Licensing of Local Fishing Vessel) Regulations 1985;[798]
- Fisheries (Prohibition of Method of Fishing) Regulations 1980;[799]
- Fisheries (Maritime) (Sarawak) Regulations 1976;[800]
- Fisheries (Maritime) Regulations, 1967;[801]
- Fisheries (Kelantan and Perlis) Regulations 1964;[802]
- Fisheries (Johore) (No. 2) Regulations 1964;[803]
- Fisheries (Johore) Regulations 1964;[804]
- Fisheries (Perak) (Fees) Regulations 1963;[805]
- Prohibition of Set Barrier Fishing Gear (Perak) Rules, 1962;[806] and
- Fisheries Rules, 1952 – Kelantan Government *Gazette* Notification.[807]

796. P.U. (A) 441/90.
797. P.U. (A) 131/90.
798. P.U. (A) 567/85.
799. P.U. (A) 314/80.
800. P.U. (A) 401/76 as amended by P.U. (A) 216/2000.
801. P.U. 49/67.
802. L.N. 161/64.
803. J.L.N. 77/64.
804. J.L.N. 76/64.
805. L.N. 87/63.
806. L.N. 221/62.
807. No. 276 1952.

Chapter 4. Wildlife Protection

§1. General Information

728. In Malaysia, wildlife is protected through the establishment of Wildlife Sanctuaries, Wildlife Reserves and Marine Parks as protected areas.

729. There are currently about twenty-five terrestrial National and State Parks, and forty Marine Parks in Malaysia, including the Wildlife Sanctuaries and Wildlife Reserves.

§2. Institutional Framework

I. Historical Development

730. In Malaysia, the main agency responsible for the conservation of terrestrial fauna biodiversity and its habitats is the Department of Wildlife and National Parks under the Ministry of Energy and Natural Resources.[808]

731. Historically, the Department of Wildlife and National Parks was known as the Game Department and was created in stages since 1896, during the time of the British. The designation of protected areas started in 1903 with the gazettement of Chior Wildlife Reserve at Kuala Kangsar District in the state of Perak. It was also the first protected area designated in Malaysia.[809]

732. Efforts to create a federal wildlife agency to coordinate conservation activities of the states' Department of Wildlife and National Parks started in 1930 with the formation of the Wildlife Commission of Malaya. Two major actions were undertaken by the colonial government based on the recommendations of the Wildlife Commission of Malaya Report of 1932 namely, to establish the headquarters of the Department of Wildlife and National Parks in 1936, and to form the Taman Negara National Park in 1938.

733. In 1955, the Federal Government introduced new legislation, known as the Wild Animals and Wild Birds Protection Ordinance 1955, to strengthen the enforcement of wildlife protection in Peninsular Malaysia. During that time, the administration of states' Department of Wildlife and National Parks was still under the respective state governments.

808. See the official website at https://www.wildlife.gov.my/index.php/en/
809. Further details on the historical development and the establishment of the Department of Wildlife and National Parks can be found in the Department's official website at http://www.wildlife.gov.my, August 2013.

734. Between 1972 and 1976, the federal government, after consulting with the state governments, federalized the administration of the states' Department of Wildlife and National Parks, following the enactment of the Protection of Wildlife Act in 1972.

II. Present Framework

735. At present, The Department of Wildlife and National Parks is responsible for the management of national parks and wildlife reserves in Peninsular Malaysia.

736. The mandate to execute the Department's role is derived from legislation passed by the Parliament, government gazettements and the policy decisions that were made at higher levels. These mandates are entrusted to the Department, whose policies are then implemented at state, district and protected area levels.

737. Due to high value and high demand from the international market, wildlife has become the main target by poachers with special interest. Hence, the Department has strengthened its effort in enforcing the laws to conserve biodiversity resources effectively. The enforcement of the law is implemented at all levels: the headquarters, states and districts.

§3. Federal Legislation

I. The Wildlife Conservation Act 2010

A. General Information

738. In Malaysia, the main legislation on wildlife protection, except for the states of Sabah and Sarawak, is the Wildlife Conservation Act 2010.[810] Prior to the enactment of the Act, the main law applicable was the Protection of Wildlife Act 1972[811] which was enacted to consolidate the laws relating to the protection of wildlife and for purposes connected with it and to repeal the Wild Animals and Birds Protection Ordinance 1955.[812] The new 2010 Act represents the first major revamp of the national wildlife law in over thirty years. It is also meant to overcome weaknesses within the outdated 1972 Act, including to provide for stiffer penalties for poaching and other wildlife-related crimes, such as punishments for wildlife cruelty and zoos that operate without licence.

739. Under the Act, the term 'wildlife' is defined to mean 'any species of wild animal or wild bird, whether totally protected or protected, vertebrate or invertebrate, live or dead, mature or immature and whether or not may be tamed or bred

810. Act 716.
811. Act 76. Revoked by Act 716.
812. Order 2 1955.

in captivity'.[813] Whereas the term 'part of derivative' in relation to wildlife is defined to mean any substantially complete or part or derivative of wildlife, in natural form, stuffed, chilled, preserved, dried, processed or otherwise treated or prepared which may or may not be contained in preparations, and includes: (a) meat, bone, hide, skin, leather, tusk, horn, antler, gland, feathers, hair, teeth, claw, shell, scale, nest and eggs; (b) tissue, blood, fat, oil, milk, venom, saliva, urine and faeces; any compound derived from anything mentioned in paragraph (a) or (b); or (d) anything which is claimed by any person, or which appears from an accompanying document, the packaging, a label or mark or from any other circumstances, to contain any part or derivative of wildlife. The term 'taxidermy business' under the Act means a business involving the carrying out of the following activities: preparing, preserving, stuffing or mounting any wildlife or any part or derivative of any wildlife; or manufacturing or creating an article or thing from any wildlife or any part or derivative of any wildlife.[814]

740. Part II is on administration. Section 4 provides for the appointment of a Director General for Wildlife and National Parks and his deputies for the proper carrying out of the provisions of this Act. Among the DG's powers as provided in section 7 include to issue administrative orders, consistent with the provisions of this Act, in respect of the general control, training, duties and responsibilities of officers and for such other matters as may be necessary or expedient for carrying out the provisions of this Act.

B. Protected and Totally Protected Wildlife

741. Main strategy applied by the Act for the protection and conservation of wildlife is through its classification into two categories, namely 'protected wildlife' and 'totally protected wildlife'.

742. The term 'protected wildlife' is defined by the Act to mean 'any wildlife specified in the First Schedule'.[815] Species included in this Schedule are referred to either by the name of the species or as being all of the species included in a higher taxon or designated part thereof. The common names included after the scientific names of families are for reference only. They are intended to indicate the species within the family concerned that are included in this Schedule. Where there is conflict between a scientific term and a common term in the use of the name of any species in this Schedule, the scientific term shall prevail. Under the First Schedule, protected wildlife is divided into two parts namely Part 1 for hunted species which include mammals and birds; and Part 2 for other which includes mammals, birds, reptiles, amphibians, spiders, insects, leeches, and snails and conches.

---

813. Section 3 of the Wildlife Conservation Act 2010.
814. *Ibid.*
815. *Ibid.*

743. The term 'totally protected wildlife' means 'any wildlife specified in the Second Schedule'.[816] Similar to the First Schedule, species included in the Second Schedule are also referred to either by the name of the species or as being all of the species included in a higher tax on or designated part thereof. The common names included after the scientific names of families are for reference only. They are intended to indicate the species within the family concerned that are included in this Schedule. Where there is conflict between a scientific term and a common term in the use of the name of any species in this Schedule, the scientific term shall prevail. Under the Second Schedule, totally protected wildlife is classified according to the following categories, namely mammals, reptiles, amphibians, insects, and snails and conches.

744. Other relevant schedules are Third Schedule which provides for standard of maturity for totally protected wildlife and protected wildlife, and Sixth schedule for the list of wildlife for aborigine's consumption.

C. Licence and Permits

745. Part III of the Act is on licensing provisions involving protected wildlife and totally protected wildlife. Under section 9, licence is required for the following activities: to hunt or keep any protected wildlife; to take or keep any part or derivative of any protected wildlife; to collect birds' nests; to carry on the business of dealing; to carry on the taxidermy business; or to import, export or re-export any protected wildlife or any part or derivative of any protected wildlife. Under subsection (3) of section 9, any person who intends to carry on the business of dealing or taxidermy business at more than one place of business shall apply for a separate licence for each of the place of business.

746. Section 10 deals with permit which is required upon the following activities, namely: operating a zoo, operating a commercial captive breeding; operating a circus or wildlife exhibition; and carry out research or study on any protected wildlife. Under subsection (2) of section 10, where the zoo, commercial captive breeding, circus or wildlife exhibition operation involves any totally protected wildlife, the person shall obtain a special permit pursuant to section 11 in respect of the totally protected wildlife.

747. Section 11 deals with special permit which is imposed on any person for the following activities: (a) hunting or keeping any totally protected wildlife or take or keep any part or derivative of any totally protected wildlife; (b) importing, exporting or re-exporting any totally protected wildlife or any part or derivative of any totally protected wildlife; (c) hunting any protected wildlife during the close season; (d) carrying on research or study on any totally protected wildlife; or (e) using any totally protected wildlife for his zoo, circus or wildlife exhibition operation or commercial captive breeding.

---

816. *Ibid.*

748. Matters relating to the application for licence are provided in sections 12–35 of the Act. Specifically application for a licence or permit is through the submission of an application form to the licensing officer, whereas application for a special permit is through the submission of a written submission to such officer.[817] On the part of the licensing officer, he may require the additional information on the application[818] before he approves or refuses the application. In the case of an application for a special permit, the approval is obtained from the Minister.[819] The licensing officer may impose any conditions when approving any licence, permit or special permits.[820] The licence officer may also suspend or revoke a licence, permit or special permit if he is satisfied the holder of the licence, permit or special permit had committed any of the following acts: breached any specified conditions; failed to comply with the Act; convicted of an offence under the Act; or induced on his behalf, by a false representation of facts, the granting of such licence, permit or special permit.[821]

749. On the part of the holder of a licence, permit or special permit holder, he must carry the licence or special permit while hunting any wildlife or taking any part or derivative of any wildlife. He must also display the licence at a conspicuous place at his place of business, if he is a licensed dealer or licensed taxidermist. Otherwise, it would be an offence, and upon conviction shall be liable to a fine not exceeding MYR 10,000 or jail of up to six months or both.[822] The licence holder must lodge a police report, inform the licensing officer and stop any authorized activities when the licence, permit or special permit is lost,[823] and must return the licence upon the expiry date.[824]

750. Under the Act, no licence shall be granted during close season,[825] and the DG is given the power under section 35 to prescribe the following: (a) the open season and close season in respect of protected wildlife; (b) the number of wildlife which may be hunted, and part or derivative of wildlife which may be taken; (c) the methods or means by which any wildlife may be hunted, including the type of arm or trap to be used; (d) the times during which, and the places where, any wildlife may be hunted, or the nest or egg of any wildlife may be taken; (e) the quota of licences and permits to be granted for each of the activities specified under sections 9 and 10, each year or open season, and each state, in respect of each protected wildlife or any part or derivative of wildlife; and (f) the standard of maturity of wildlife which may be hunted.

817. Section 12 of the Wildlife Conservation Act 2010.
818. *Ibid.*
819. Section 13 of the Wildlife Conservation Act 2010.
820. Section 15 of the Wildlife Conservation Act 2010.
821. Section 23 of the Wildlife Conservation Act 2010.
822. Section 17 of the Wildlife Conservation Act 2010.
823. Section 19 of the Wildlife Conservation Act 2010.
824. Section 22 of the Wildlife Conservation Act 2010.
825. Section 27 of the Wildlife Conservation Act 2010.

751. Duties and obligations of licensed holders are provided in sections 36–46 of the Act. Under section 36, the licensed hunter who hunts any protected wildlife or a holder of a special permit who hunts any totally protected wildlife, shall record the following: (a) the number, sex and species of the wildlife which was hunted; (b) the date on which, and the locality in which, the wildlife was hunted; (c) the methods or means by which the wildlife was hunted; and (d) the methods and date of disposal, including the licence, permit or special permit number of the purchaser should the wildlife be sold. For the licensed dealer, section 37 requires him to keep and maintain a record consisting of the following particulars: (a) the number and species of wildlife (live or dead), the number of parts or derivatives of wildlife and the number of articles manufactured from any wildlife or part or derivative of any wildlife, which were purchased, acquired or sold; (b) the name, address and licence number of the person from whom the wildlife, parts or derivatives of wildlife or articles were purchased or acquired; (c) the name, address and licence number, if any, of the person to whom the wildlife, parts or derivatives of wildlife or articles were sold; (d) the receipt number issued for any sale or purchase; and (e) the date of any purchase, acquisition or sale. Whereas for the licensed taxidermist, he is required under section 38 to keep and maintain a record consisting of the following particulars: (a) the date, time and person from whom the wildlife or part or derivative of the wildlife was received; (b) the name, address and licence number of the owner of the wildlife or part or derivative of the wildlife; and (c) the date and time the wildlife or part or derivative of wildlife is returned to the owner. Any licensed hunter, dealer or taxidermist who commits an offence under sections 36–38 respectively, on conviction, will be liable to a fine not exceeding MYR 10,000 or to jail not exceeding six months or both.

752. The Act requires that the licensed hunter and the birds' nest collector to sell hunted protected wildlife or collected birds' nest respectively only to the licensed dealer or licensed taxidermist.[826] It is also a requirement on the part of licensed dealer or licensed taxidermist to purchase protected wildlife from a licensed hunter, licensed dealer or licensed taxidermist, as otherwise it would be an offence.[827]

753. There is also a wildlife tagging requirement under the Act. Section 45 states that a holder of a licence, permit or special permit who keeps, sells, imports, exports, re-export or breeds any wildlife, as the case may be, shall tag or label such wildlife in the following manner: (a) implantation of a scannable device in the wildlife; (b) placement of a band on any part of the wildlife; (c) placement, whether by piercing or otherwise, of a tattoo or ring on any part of the wildlife; or (d) labelling or marking of a container in which the wildlife is kept. Any person who contravenes this section commits an offence and shall, on conviction, be liable to a fine not exceeding MYR 20,000 or to imprisonment for a term not exceeding one year or both.

---

826. Sections 40 and 41 of the Wildlife Conservation Act 2010.
827. Section 42 of the Wildlife Conservation Act 2010.

D. Wildlife Reserves and Sanctuaries

754. The protection of wildlife through wildlife reserves and sanctuaries is provided in Part V of the Act. Section 47 empowers the State Authority to do the following:

– declare any state land to be a wildlife reserve or a wildlife sanctuary and designate the officer for the time being having the control of such reserve or sanctuary;
– define and alter the boundaries of the wildlife reserve or wildlife sanctuary;
– in the case of a wildlife reserve, specify certain animals and birds (which are not wildlife in this Act) as protected wildlife or totally protected wildlife (as the case may require) which shall be in addition to the lists of any wildlife specified in the Schedules to this Act.

755. Under section 48, permits are required for entering wildlife reserves and wildlife sanctuaries. Section 49 prohibits certain actions within a wildlife reserves and wildlife sanctuaries, namely: in a wildlife reserve, to disturb cut, remove or take any soil, timber or vegetation; and in a wildlife sanctuary, to hunt any animal or bird; to take, disturb, damage or destroy the nest or egg of any animal or bird; or to disturb, cut, remove or take any soil, timber or vegetation.

E. Exceptions

756. Despite prohibitions pertaining to wildlife, the Act provides for general exceptions and presumptions to such prohibitions under Part VI of the Act. Under section 50, for carrying any conservation activity, the DG may breed, keep, hunt, import, export, sell or purchase any wildlife.

757. Another exception is given to the aborigines as provided in section 51. It states that, an aborigine may hunt any protected wildlife as specified in the Sixth Schedule for his sustenance or the sustenance of his family members. Any protected wildlife hunted under this section shall not be sold or exchanged for food, monetary gains or any other thing. Any aborigine who contravenes this section commits an offence and shall, on conviction, be liable to a fine not exceeding MYR 10,000 or to imprisonment for a term not exceeding six months or both.

758. Under section 52, an officer may hunt wildlife if it is a danger to human life or property; or if it is necessary to prevent undue suffering on the part of the wildlife. On the part of an owner or occupier of land, section 53 allows him with the written approval of the Director, use birdlime for the good faith destruction of grain-eating birds found damaging or destroying growing cereals during the period when the crop is ripe or ripening.

759. An exception is also granted in cases of the capturing or killing of wildlife for protection of crops. Section 54 provides that, where any wildlife is causing, or there is reason to believe that it is about to cause serious damage to crops, vegetables, fruits, growing timber, domestic fowls or domestic animals in the possession of an owner or occupier of land, the owner or occupier or any servant of the owner or occupier or any officer may capture or kill the wildlife after first using reasonable efforts to frighten away the wildlife and failing to do so. Under subsection (2) of section 54, where any wildlife has caused serious damage but has ceased to do so, it shall not be captured or killed. It is a requirement under subsection (3) of section 54 for the owner or occupier of land, without unnecessary delay, to report to any officer the details of the occurrence, including the species of the wildlife, the damage and weapon which has been used (if any) and whether the wildlife has been captured or killed. Any owner or occupier of land or servant of owner or occupier of land who contravenes this section commits an offence and shall, on conviction, be liable to a fine not exceeding MYR 10,000 or to imprisonment for a term not exceeding six months or both. Any wildlife captured or killed under this section shall be the property of the state and shall without delay be handed to an office.

760. Under section 55, if a wildlife constitutes an immediate danger to human life, any person may kill that wildlife. Under subsection (2) of section 55, where the immediate danger to human life is a result of provocation or wounding of the wildlife by the person who kills the wildlife, the person shall be absolved from guilt only in respect of killing the wildlife but he may be charged in respect of such provocation or wounding under section 88. Any person who kills any wildlife pursuant to this section shall, without unnecessary delay, report to any officer the details of the occurrence, including the species of the wildlife which has been killed and the weapon which has been used.[828] Any person who contravenes this section commits an offence and shall, on conviction, be liable to a fine not exceeding MYR 10,000 or to imprisonment for a term not exceeding six months or both. Any wildlife captured or killed under this section shall be the property of the state and shall without delay be handed to an office.

F. Offences and Penalties

761. Offences and penalties are provided in Part VII of the Act. This Part divides offences according to chapters, namely that relating to licence, permit and special permit.

762. Chapter 1 of Part VII deals with offences relating to licence. Under section 60, it is an offence to hunt or keep any protected wildlife, or take any part of any protected wildlife without a licence. Similarly, it is an offence under section 63 to carry out taxidermy business without a licence. Penalties imposed for both sections are a fine not exceeding MYR 50,000 or jail for up to two years, or both. Higher penalty is imposed for hunting or keeping immature protected wildlife or female of protected wildlife without a licence as provided in sections 61 and 62 respectively. Penalties imposed for both sections are a fine not exceeding MYR 100,000, or jail

828. Subsection (3) of s. 55 of the Wildlife Conservation Act 2010.

for up to five years or both. Under section 64, any person who collects birds' nests without a licence commits an offence, whereas in section 65, it is an offence to import, export or re-export any protected wildlife or any of its part without a licence. Any person who commits an offence under either section 64 or 65 shall, on conviction, be liable to a fine of not less than MYR 20,000 and not more than MYR 50,000 or to imprisonment for a term not exceeding two years or both.

763. Chapter 2 of Part VII deals with offences relating to permit. Section 66 provides that any person who operates a zoo, commercial captive breeding, circus or wildlife exhibition without a permit commits an offence and shall, on conviction, be liable to a fine not exceeding MYR 70,000 or to imprisonment for a term not exceeding three years or both. Whereas in section 67, any person who carries out a research or study on any protected wildlife without a permit commits an offence and upon conviction shall be liable to a fine not exceeding MYR 50,000 or jail for up to two years or both.

Chapter 3 of Part VII covers offences relating to special permit as provided in sections 68–73. Under subsection (1) of section 68, it is an offence to hunt or keep any totally protected wildlife, or take any part of any protected wildlife without a special permit. Penalty imposed for offences committed under this subsection are a fine not exceeding MYR 100,000, or jail for up to three years or both. Whereas, subsection (2) of section 68 imposes different penalties for offences committed under subsection (1) involving the following totally protected wildlife: (a) Pangolin, Blood Python, Harlequin Monitor, Dumeril's Monitor, or Clouded Monitor exceeding twenty heads, the penalties are a fine of not less than MYR 50,000 and not more than MYR 100,000 or with imprisonment for a term not exceeding three years or both; (b) Crested Argus, Mountain Peacock, Great Argus, Green Peafowl, Straw-headed Bulbul, Rhinoceros Hornbill, Great Hornbill, Plain-pouched Hornbill, or Helmeted Hornbill, the penalties are a fine of not less than MYR 30,000 and not more than MYR 100,000 and with imprisonment for a term not exceeding two years; or (c) Serow, Gaur, Javan Rhinoceros, Sumatran Rhinoceros, Tiger, Leopard, Clouded Leopard or False Gharial, the penalties are a fine of not less than MYR 100,000, and not more than MYR 500,000 with imprisonment for a term not exceeding five years.

764. Under subsection (1) of section 69, any person who hunts or keeps any immature totally protected wildlife without a special permit commits an offence and shall, on conviction, be liable to a fine not exceeding MYR 200,000 or to imprisonment for a term not exceeding ten years or both. Subsection (2) of section 69 further states that any person who commits an offence under subsection (1) and which offence involves wildlife specified in paragraph 68(2)(c), shall, on conviction, be punished with a fine of not less than MYR 150,000 and not more than MYR 500,000 and with imprisonment for a term not exceeding five years.

765. Hunting of female totally protected wildlife without a special permit is an offence under subsection (1) of section 70 which imposes a fine not exceeding MYR 300,000 or to imprisonment for a term not exceeding ten years or both. Additionally, subsection (2) of section 70 states that any person who commits an offence under subsection (1) and which offence involves wildlife specified in paragraph 68(2)(c), shall, on conviction, be punished with a fine of not less than MYR 200,000 and not more than MYR 500,000 with imprisonment for a term not exceeding five years.

766. Section 71 deals with penalty for the imports, exports or re-exports of totally protected wildlife, or any of its parts without permit, which is a fine of not less than MYR 30,000 and not more than MYR 100,000 and a jail term not exceeding three years. Subsection (1) of section 72 imposes penalty to any person who uses any totally protected wildlife for his zoo, circus or wildlife exhibition operation; or uses any totally protected wildlife for his commercial captive breeding operation, which is a fine not exceeding MYR 100,000 or to imprisonment for a term not exceeding three years or both. In addition, subsection (2) of section 72, imposes a different penalty on any person who commits an offence under subsection (1), and which offence involves wildlife specified in paragraph 68(2)(b) which is a fine of not less than MYR 30,000 and not more than MYR 100,000 and with imprisonment for a term not exceeding two years. Whereas subsection (3) of section 72 imposes a fine not less than MYR 100,000 and not more than MYR 500,000 and jail not exceeding five years for any person who commits an offence under subsection (1) and which offence involves wildlife specified in paragraph 68(2)(c).

767. Under section 73, it is an offence to carry out research or study on any totally protected wildlife without special permit. Any person who commits an offence under this section may be liable to a fine not exceeding MYR 70,000 or jail for up to three years or both.

768. Chapter 4 of Part VII, which covers sections 74–88, deals with miscellaneous matters relating to offences and penalties. Section 74 imposes penalty on any person who damages or destroys the nest or egg of a protected wildlife which is a fine not exceeding MYR 20,000 or jail for up to one year or both. Damaging the nest or egg of a totally protected wildlife is an offence under section 75 and shall, on conviction, be liable to a fine not exceeding MYR 50,000 or to imprisonment for a term not exceeding two years or both.

769. There are various miscellaneous offences relating to hunting, including that under section 76 involving hunting of wildlife or taking the nest or egg of any wildlife in a wildlife reserve or a wildlife sanctuary which carries the penalty of a fine not exceeding MYR 50,000 or jail for up to two years or both. Under sections 77 and 78, hunting of wildlife during prohibited hours, or hunting of protected wildlife during close season is also an offence within the respective section. Other offences include hunting of wildlife with poison;[829] hunting wildlife with arms or traps;[830] hunting of wildlife within 400 m of salt lick;[831] and hunting wildlife from conveyance.[832]

770. Another penalty provided in Chapter 4 is that of section 85 on the disturbing of salt lake or its vicinity which, on conviction, be liable to a fine not exceeding MYR 50,000 or to imprisonment for a term not exceeding two years or both. For the purposes of this section, 'disturb' includes to remove or agitate any soil, mineral, water, tree, shrubs, undergrowth or other vegetation in or on the salt lick or in or on the land in the immediate vicinity of the salt lick. Another provision, section 86 deals with cruelty to wildlife which provides that any person who: (a) beats, kicks, infuriates, terrifies, tortures, declaws or defangs any wildlife; (b) neglects to supply sufficient food or water to any wildlife which he houses, confines or breeds; (c) keeps, houses, confines or breeds any wildlife in such manner so as to cause it unnecessary pain or suffering including the housing, confining or breeding of any wildlife in any premises which is not suitable for or conducive to the comfort or health of the wildlife; (d) uses any wildlife for performing or assisting in the performance of any work or labour which by reason of any infirmity, wound, disease or any other incapacity is unfit to perform; (e) uses, provokes or infuriates any wildlife for baiting it or for fighting with any other wildlife or animal, or manages any premises or place for any of these purposes; or (f) wilfully does or wilfully omits to do anything which causes any unnecessary suffering, pain or discomfort to any wildlife, commits an offence and shall, on conviction, be liable to a fine of not less than MYR 5,000 and not more than MYR 50,000 or to imprisonment for a term not exceeding one year or both.

G. Powers Relating to Enforcement

771. Powers relating to enforcement are provided in Part VIII of the Act which covers sections 89–116. Section 89 states that every offence under this Act shall be a seizable offence for the purposes of the Criminal Procedure Code,[833] and under section 90, the DG may authorize any public officer to exercise the powers of enforcement under this Act. Power of investigation is vested upon the enforcement officer by virtue of section 92, whereas section 93 provides that an enforcement officer may arrest without warrant any person whom he reasonably believes has committed or is attempting to commit an offence under this Act. The enforcement officer making an investigation may examine any persons acquainted with the case as provided in section 107.

829. Section 79 of the Wildlife Conservation Act 2010.
830. Section 80 of the Wildlife Conservation Act 2010.
831. Section 81 of the Wildlife Conservation Act 2010.
832. Section 82 of the Wildlife Conservation Act 2010.
833. According to s. 92(2), for the purposes of this Act, an enforcement officer shall have all or any of the powers of a police officer of whatever rank in relation to police investigations in seizable cases as provided for under the Criminal Procedure Code, and such powers shall be in addition to the powers provided for under this Act and not in derogation thereof.

772. Under the Act, search and seizure can be done either with or without warrant. The former is provided in section 94(1) where, if it appears to a Magistrate, upon written information on oath from an enforcement officer, that there is reasonable cause to believe that: (a) any premises has been used; or (b) there is in any premises evidence necessary to the conduct of an investigation into, the commission of an offence under this Act, the Magistrate may issue a warrant authorizing the enforcement officer to enter the premises and if need be by force. Under section 94(2), the Magistrate may authorize the enforcement officer to do the following: (a) search the premises for, and to seize or remove from the premises, any wildlife, part or derivative of any wildlife, snare, trap, bait, poisoned bait, arms, conveyance, book, record, document or thing that is reasonably believed to furnish evidence of the commission of such offence; (b) take samples of any wildlife, part or derivative of any wildlife or thing found in the premises for the purposes of ascertaining, by testing or otherwise, whether the offence has been committed; and (c) make copies of or take extracts from any book, record, document or thing found in the premises. Section 94(5) authorizes the enforcement officer making a search of person under to seize or take possession of, and place in safe custody all things, other than the necessary clothing found upon the person, and any of those things, which there is reason to believe were the instruments or other evidence of the offence may be detained until the discharge or acquittal of the person. Whereas in section 94(6), an enforcement officer may, in the exercise of his powers under this section, if it is necessary so to do: (a) break open any outer or inner door or window of the premises or any fence, enclosure, gate or other obstruction to the premises in order to effect entry into the premises and every part thereof; (b) remove by force any obstruction to entry, search, seizure and removal as he is empowered to effect under this section; and (c) detain any person found in the premises until the search has been completed.

773. Search and seizure without warrant is provided in section 95 of the Act. It states that, if an enforcement officer is satisfied upon information received that he has reasonable cause to believe that by reason of delay in obtaining a search warrant under section 94 the investigation would be adversely affected or evidence of the commission of an offence is likely to be tampered with, removed, damaged or destroyed, the enforcement officer may enter the premises and exercise in, upon and in respect of the premises all the powers referred to in section 94 in as full and ample a manner.

774. Under section 99, an enforcement officer conducting a search shall be given access to computerized data whether stored in a computer or otherwise. For the purposes of this section, 'access' includes being provided with the necessary password, encryption code, decryption code, software or hardware and any other means required to enable comprehension of the computerized data; and has the meaning assigned to it by the Computer Crimes Act 1997.[834] The enforcement officer is also

834. Act 563.

empowered by section 101 to stop, search and seize any conveyance carrying any wildlife or any of its parts, and to prepare, according to section 103 a list of wildlife or its part seized.

775. The court under section 104 may allow temporary return of conveyance to its owner, and under section 105, the Magistrate has the power to order any seized wildlife or its parts to be released or disposed of. Requirements relating to the released and forfeiture of seized wildlife or related matters are provided in sections 109 and 110 respectively.

776. The final part of the Act is Part IX on general matters covering sections 117–136 prohibitions relating to controlled species in sections 117 and 118, and prohibition on hybridization activity in section 119. Offences committed by body corporate, including offences committed by his employee or agent in the case of neglect or default are provided in section 124, whereas general offence relating to the Act is provided in section 125, and compounding of offences is covered by section 126. Under the Act, protection of informers is covered by section 130, and in section 131, the DG is empowered to reward any person for services rendered in connection with the detection of any offence under the Act. Matters relating of repeal and saving provisions in relation to the Protection of Wildlife Act 1972 are provided in section 135, whereas section 136 deals with transitional provision for activity to which the Act applies.

777. The power to make regulations by the Minister is provided in section 132 in relation to the following matters: (a) disseminating information on wildlife including their breeding habits, habitat, species and ways or means of helping to conserve them; (b) the administration and management of wildlife reserves and wildlife sanctuaries; (c) the conditions under which totally protected wildlife or protected wildlife may be kept and bred; (d) the means of disposing any wildlife; (e) regulating the operation of zoo, commercial captive breeding, circus or wildlife exhibitions; (f) the specifications of containers for importing and exporting live wildlife; (g) the fees payable under this Act; and (h) the offences which may be compounded.

II. Legislation Regarding Zoos in Malaysia

778. There are several zoological parks and mini zoos in Malaysia, including the *Zoo Negara* or National Zoo. Zoological parks come under the Department of Wildlife and National Parks and receive an annual grant from the related ministry besides their own sponsors and gate collection, whereas the mini zoos are private zoos and self-funding. Requests for permission to operate a zoo must be made in writing to the Director General of the Department of Wildlife and National Parks.

779. Prior to the enactment of the Wildlife Conservation Act 2010, Malaysia did not have any specific zoo management legislation or guidelines. For the purposes of wildlife protection within a zoo, the relevant law applied was the Protection of Wildlife Act 1972, which contains general provisions on totally protected or protected wild animals and birds.

780. With the passing of the Wildlife Conservation Act 2010, new provisions and regulation relating to zoo are introduced. Section 10 of the Act specifically requires any person who shall operate a zoo to hold a permit granted under the Act, whereas under section 11 a special permit is required for any person who shall use any totally protected wildlife for his zoo. Under section 66, any person who operates a zoo, commercial captive breeding, circus or wildlife exhibition without a permit commits an offence and shall, on conviction, be liable to a fine not exceeding MYR 70,000 or to imprisonment for a term not exceeding three years or both. Additional prohibition is provided in section 72 on any person who uses any totally protected wildlife for his zoo without a special permit, whereby upon conviction shall be liable to a fine not exceeding MYR 100,000 or to imprisonment for a term not exceeding three years or both.

781. The prerequisites to operate a zoo is provided in section 28 which states that the licensing officer shall not grant a permit to operate a zoo unless he is satisfied that: (a) the establishment or continuity of the establishment of the zoo … will not bring ill effects to the health or safety of any person or community in the surrounding area; (b) there is prepared an emergency plan relating to plague, natural disaster and accidental release of any wildlife; and (c) the person has never been previously convicted of an offence under this Act or any of its subsidiary legislation or any other written law related to cruelty to animals.

782. Section 34 empowers the DG, by rules published in the Gazette, to prescribe the methods and means of disposal, disease control or quarantine of, any wildlife, to be complied with by an operator of a zoo. On the part of the Minister, he is empowered by section 132 to make such regulations as may be expedient or necessary for the better carrying out the provisions of this Act or for prescribing anything that may be, or is required to be, prescribed under this Act. Regulations may be made in respect of various matters including that relating to the operation of zoo. Subsection (3) of section 132 provides that the Regulations made under this section may prescribe any act or omission in contravention of the regulations to be an offence and may prescribe penalties of a fine not exceeding MYR 100,000 or imprisonment for a term not exceeding five years or both.

783. By virtue of section 132, the Minister has made the Wildlife Conservation (Operation of Zoo) Regulations 2012.[835] The Regulations defined the term 'zoo' to mean 'any area or premises which keeps or places fifty or more wildlife species which the total number is 100 or more whether for the purposes of conservation, education, research or recreation, and is open to the public'. Whereas the term 'zoo operator' is defined to mean 'any individual, statutory bodies, companies, associations or local authorities that own or operate the zoo'.

835. P.U. (A) 36/12.

784. The requirement for permit is provided in Regulation 3(1) which states that no person shall operate a zoo unless he holds a permit issued under paragraph 10(1)(a) of the Act., and under Regulation 3(2), no person shall use any totally protected wildlife for zoo operation unless he holds a special permit issued under paragraph 11(e) of the Act. Regulation 6 requires any zoo operator to provide an appropriate enclosure for each wildlife species according to the sizes as specified in the Schedule, and to submit the design of the enclosure to the DG for an approval. The zoo operator is also required under Regulation 7 to provide a quarantine area for the placement or temporary isolation of any newly acquired wildlife for preventive or treatment purposes of any diseases that the wildlife may have.

785. Other requirements under the Regulations include Regulation 8 on diet which requires the zoo operator to ensure that any food and water provided for the wildlife: (a) contain all the necessary nutrients, uncontaminated and is given in sufficient quantities as determined by the veterinary surgeon; and (b) correspond with the natural diet of the species, physiological condition and sex of the wildlife. Regulation 9(1) is on wildlife healthcare which imposes responsibility on the zoo operator for ensuring the healthcare of the wildlife at the zoo under his control. For the purpose of subregulation (1), the zoo operator shall do the following: (a) employ a veterinary surgeon to be stationed at the zoo full time or to appoint a veterinary surgeon as a consultant for the zoo, subject to subregulation (4); (b) provide a veterinary clinic and hospital in the zoo; (c) ensure that post mortem to be conducted on all dead wildlife and recorded by the veterinary surgeon; (d) tag and record all births of the wildlife in the zoo; (e) maintain and keep records of all matters relating to the management of each wildlife in the zoo; and (f) report to the veterinary authority if any wildlife is infected or suspected to be infected with diseases or died or suspected to have died of diseases, in accordance with the requirements of under the Animals Act 1953.[836]

786. Under Regulation 10, the zoo operator shall maintain the cleaning activities of the enclosure of the wildlife at the zoo and keep all records in relation to the cleaning of each enclosure of the wildlife at the zoo, and under Regulation 11, the zoo operator shall ensure that any vaccination to the wildlife is to be conducted by the veterinary surgeon or any other person under the supervision of the veterinary surgeon. Regulation 12(1) deals with euthanasia on any wildlife at the zoo whereby it can only be conducted by a veterinary surgeon or any other person under the supervision of the veterinary surgeon. According to Regulation 12(2), euthanasia on any wildlife can be conducted if the veterinary surgeon finds that upon examination, the wildlife is injured or suffering from an incurable illness or for any other reasons which he thinks necessary to terminate the life of the wildlife.

787. Under Regulation 13(1), any zoo operator who wants to hold a wildlife show activity in the zoo under his control shall submit a written application to the DG. The DG may approve the application under subregulation (1) provided that the wildlife show (a) is performed based on the wildlife natural behaviour; (b) does not

836. Act 647.

involve any force, abuse or any element of force to the wildlife; and (c) does not cause distress, pain and fear to the wildlife. According to Regulation 13(3), the wildlife used for the wildlife show activity shall not be placed in the transfer cage for more than one hour in a day.

788. Regulation 14 empowers the DG to require the zoo operator to deposit a sum of money as a deposit as determined by the DG for financing any costs incurred by the Government in seizing, keeping and maintaining any wildlife seized from the zoo operator in accordance with the Act. Regulation 15 provides that any person who contravenes any provisions of these Regulations shall be guilty of an offence and shall, on conviction, be liable to a fine not exceeding MYR 100,000 or imprisonment for a term not exceeding five years or both.

III. Fisheries Act 1985

A. Endangered Species

789. Apart from the Protection of Wildlife Act 1972, there are several statutes relevant to wildlife conservation in Malaysia. One of these is the Fisheries Act 1985[837] which concerns fisheries, including the conservation, management and development of maritime and estuarine fishing and fisheries in Malaysian waters, including turtles.

790. For the purpose of marine wildlife protection, by virtue of section 61 of the Act, the Minister gazetted the Fisheries (Control of Endangered Species of Fish) Regulations 1999.[838]

791. Under the Fisheries (Control of Endangered Species of Fish) Regulations 1999,[839] no person shall fish for, disturb, harass, catch, kill, take, possess, sell, buy, export or transport any endangered species of fish or any part of it specified in the Schedule except with the written permission of the DG.[840]

792. Under Regulation 2(3), where any endangered species of fish specified in the Schedule is caught or taken unavoidably during fishing, such endangered species of fish shall, if it is alive, be released immediately or, if it is dead, the catching or taking thereof shall be reported to a fisheries officer and the endangered species of fish shall be disposed of in accordance with his directions. Any person who contravenes this provision or any of the conditions imposed by the DG commits an offence.

837. Act 317.
838. P.U. (A) 409/99.
839. P.U. (A) 409/99.
840. Regulation 2 of the Fisheries (Control of Endangered Species of Fish) Regulations 1999.

793. The schedule to the Regulations provides for the list of endangered species of fish, which include species under the Dugong group, species under the Whale group, species under the Dolphin group, species under the Whale Shark group, species under the Clam group and species under the Sawfish group.

794. This regulation lists all the species of fish and mammals that are protected, and includes the dugong, whale, dolphin, whale shark and the giant clam, which are included in the list of endangered species in the Convention on International Trade of Endangered Species (CITES). It is an offence to fish for, harass, catch, kill, possess, sell, buy, export or transport any endangered fish as specified in these regulations. Any of the listed endangered fish species caught unintentionally shall be released immediately, or disposed of as directed by a Fisheries Officer.

795. Apart from protecting endangered species, the Fisheries Act 1985 also covers 'fisheries prohibited areas', under the Fisheries (Prohibited Areas) Regulations 1994.[841] Regulation 3 of the Regulations prohibits any person from collecting shells, molluscs or corals within the fisheries prohibited area, whereas Regulation 4 prohibits any person from killing or capturing any fish within the fisheries prohibited area unless he holds a licence issued under the Act.

B. *Turtles*

796. Provisions on turtles are provided in Part VII of the Act. Under section 37, the DG may promote the development and rational management of inland fisheries through the following activities:

- the conduct or coordination of research;
- the provision and maintenance of experimental and demonstration aquaculture stations, fish-breeding stations and training centres;
- the provision of advice and technical assistance to the appropriate authorities of the state;
- the provision of publicity and demonstration facilities and other connected services; and
- the provision of advice on measures for the prevention of fish diseases.

797. The power of the State Authority and the Minister to make rules concerning turtles is provided in section 38 for the purposes of proper conservation, development, management and regulation of turtles and inland fisheries in any state in Malaysia or in the Federal Territories of Kuala Lumpur and Labuan.

841. P.U. (A) 402/94.

IV. Animals Act 1953

798. The Animals Act 1953[842] was enacted for amending and consolidating the laws for preventing the introduction into and the spreading within Malaysia of diseases of animals; for the control of the movement of animals into, within and from Malaysia; for the control of the slaughter of animals; for the prevention of cruelty to animals; and for measures pertaining to the general welfare and conservation and improvement of animals in Malaysia.

799. The Act provides for the definition of relevant terms. 'Bird' is defined to include 'domestic fowls, ducks, geese, turkeys, guinea fowls and pigeons of any age or sex and their eggs'. 'Cattle' means 'bulls, cows, oxen, heifers and calves and includes buffaloes of any age or sex'.

800. Part II of the Act is on the importation and exportation of animals and birds. Section 6 prohibits any person from importing any animal or bird except in accordance with a licence as may be prescribed. Any person who imports an animal or bird contrary to this section shall be liable to a fine of MYR 5,000, to imprisonment for a term of two years, or both.

801. For every animal or bird imported or about to be imported, section 7 requires it to undergo an examination by a veterinary authority if any such animal or bird is considered likely to have been exposed to infection with any disease.

802. Part III is on the prevention of the spread of disease. Section 18 empowers the veterinary authority to examine or test any animal, bird or carcass which may be infected with any disease. Under section 19, a veterinary authority may order the immediate isolation or destruction of any animal, bird or carcass found or reasonably believed to be infected with disease or suspected to have been in contact with a diseased animal or bird, or infected carcass or material.

803. Part IV is on the prevention of cruelty to animals. For the purpose of this part, 'animal' means 'any living creature other than a human being and includes any beast, bird, fish, reptile or insect, whether wild or tame'.

804. Under section 44, any person who does the following is guilty of an offence of cruelty and shall be liable to a fine of MYR 200, to imprisonment for a term of six months, or both, namely:

- cruelly beats, kicks, ill-treats, overrides, overdrives, overloads, tortures, infuriates or terrifies any animal;
- causes or procures or, being the owner, permits any animal to be so used; or
- being in charge of any animal in confinement or in the course of transport from one place to another neglects to supply such animal with sufficient food or water; or

842. Act 647, revised 2006.

- by wantonly or unreasonably doing or omitting to do any act, causes any unnecessary pain or suffering, or, being the owner, permits any unnecessary pain or suffering to any animal; or
- causes, procures or, being the owner, permits to be confined, conveyed, lifted or carried any animal in such manner or position as to subject it to unnecessary pain or suffering; or
- employs or causes or procures or, being the owner, permits to be employed in any work or labour, any animal which in consequence of any disease, infirmity, wound or sore, or otherwise is unfit to be so employed; or
- causes, procures or assists in the fighting or baiting of any animal, or keeps, uses, manages, or acts or assists in the management of any premises or place for the purpose, or partly for the purpose, of fighting or baiting any animal, or permits any premises or place to be so kept, managed or used, or receives or causes or procures any person to receive money for the admission of any person to such premises or place.

805. A general penalty is provided in section 72. Under this section, any person guilty of an offence against this Act shall, where no other penalty is specified, be liable to a fine of MYR 2,000. Under section 73, any person convicted of any offence under the Act, who is within a period of twelve months from the date of such conviction convicted of a second or subsequent like offence against this Act, shall, where no penalty of imprisonment is otherwise provided for such offence, be liable to imprisonment for two months, in addition to, or in lieu of any fine.

V. Aboriginal Peoples Act 1954

806. The Aboriginal Peoples Act 1954[843] was enacted for the protection, well-being and advancement of the aboriginal peoples of West Malaysia. However, in a situation where there is a conflicting need between aboriginal protection and wildlife protection over a specified area, then the former will prevail.

807. Specifically, section 6 on aboriginal areas empowers the State Authority, by notification in the Gazette, to declare any area predominantly or exclusively inhabited by aborigines to be an aboriginal area and may declare the area to be divided into one or more aboriginal cantons, provided that where there is more than one aboriginal ethnic group there shall be as many cantons as there are aboriginal ethnic groups.

808. Subsection (2) of section 6 further states that within an aboriginal area no land shall be declared a sanctuary or reserve under any written law relating to the protection of wild animals and birds.

809. Under section 7 on aboriginal reserves, the State Authority is empowered to declare any area exclusively inhabited by aborigines to be an aboriginal reserve,

843. Act 134, revised 1974.

provided that, when it appears unlikely that the aborigines will remain permanently in that place, it shall not be declared an aboriginal reserve, but shall form part of an aboriginal area. An aboriginal reserve may be constituted within an aboriginal area.

810. Under section 7(2), within an aboriginal reserve, no land shall be declared a sanctuary or reserve under any written law relating to the protection of wild animals and birds.

VI. International Trade in Endangered Species Act 2008

811. The International Trade in Endangered Species Act[844] was enacted in 2008 to implement the Convention on International Trade in Endangered Species of Wild Fauna and Flora 1973 (CITES). This Act aims to enforce the import, export and re-export activities of CITES-listed species at entry and exist points according to the CITES rules and regulations. According to section 2, this Act is to be read together with any other written law relating to import and export, conservation of plants, forests and animals and trade in scheduled species, and the provisions of this Act shall be in addition to, and not in derogation of, the provisions of such other written laws.

There are three different authorities being set up for the purpose of the Act. Under section 4, Lead Management Authority for the Act is the Ministry of Energy and Natural Resources. Its main functions, as provided in section 5, include to coordinate the implementation and enforcement of the provisions of this Act by the Management Authorities and Scientific Authorities; to communicate with all other countries and the secretariat of the Convention on all matters under this Act; to cause national obligations under the Convention to be fulfilled; to create awareness and to provide training, education and information relating to the Convention; and to do such other things as it deems fit to enable it to perform its functions effectively or which are incidental to the performance of its functions.

Another authority set up for the purpose of the Act is the Management Authority which has jurisdiction over the plant, animal or any combination of plant and animal including the readily recognizable part or derivative of the plant or animal in the region.[845] The list of Management Authority is provided in the First Schedule of the Act which include: Department of Wildlife and National Parks, Ministry of Energy and Natural Resources; Department of Fisheries, Ministry of Agriculture and Food Industry Malaysia; Malaysian Timber Industry Board; Department of Agriculture, Ministry of Agriculture and Food Industry Malaysia; Sabah Wildlife Department; Sabah Fisheries Department; Forests Department Sarawak, and Sarawak Forestry Corporation. Under section 7, functions of the Management Authority include: to maintain records of international trade in scheduled species and prepare annual and biennial reports concerning such trade, and to submit the reports to the Lead Management Authority; to establish Rescue Centres; to inform the Lead Management Authority offences committed under this Act; and to do such

844. Act 686.

845. Section 6 of the International Trade in Endangered Species Act 2008.

other things as it deems fit to enable it to perform its functions effectively. In addition, a Management Authority is given the power to issue a permit or certificate, or allow registration under this Act.[846]

Other authorities established for the Act are Lead Scientific Authority and Scientific Authority. The former is the Ministry of Energy and Natural Resources Malaysia which is empowered to appoint such number of Scientific Authorities as may be necessary to provide advice on international trade in scheduled species.[847] Under section 9, the Scientific Authority shall provide advice to the Lead Management Authority and Management Authority on international trade in scheduled species on matters including the impact of the trade on the survival of the scheduled species; the quotas for the export of the scheduled species; the appropriate care of any live scheduled species to be imported or to be kept in Malaysia; the measures to be taken when the harvest of the scheduled species threatens its survival; the appropriate treatment of any seized or confiscated scheduled species; the method of disposal of any seized or confiscated scheduled species; and any other matters as it deems fit to enable it to perform its functions effectively.

Part IV of the Act provides for methods of regulation applied by the Act, namely permit to import or export any scheduled species; certificate to re-export or introduce from the sea any scheduled species; and the registration to reproduce captive bred animals or artificially propagated plant or animal of any scheduled species for commercial trade purposes.[848] Penalties for undergoing any of these activities without specific authorization are specified in the text. Part V of the Act further provides for powers of enforcement officers to investigate, search, seize and enter any premises. According to section 19, the list of enforcement officers is provided in the Second Schedule, namely any officer as defined in section 3 of the Protection of Wildlife Act 1972; any fisheries officer as defined in section 2 or appointed under section 5 of the Fisheries Act 1985; the DG as defined in section 2 and any officer of the Board appointed under subsection 9(2) of the Malaysian Timber Industry Board (Incorporation) Act 1973; the Director and any Inspecting Officer as defined in section 2 of the Plant Quarantine Act 1976; any authorized officer as defined in section 2 of the Wildlife Conservation Enactment 1997;[849] any fisheries officer as defined in section 2 or appointed under section 5 of the Fisheries Act 1985 and the Director and authorized officer as defined in section 2 of the Sabah Inland Fisheries and Aquaculture Enactment 2003;[850] any Wildlife Officer as defined in section 2 of the Wildlife Protection Ordinance 1998;[851] and any forest officer as defined in section 2 of the Forests Ordinance.[852]

The Act provides for penalties for those who conduct any of the specified activities without specific authorization, including penalties in relation to import and export of scheduled species without a permit;[853] re-exports or introduces from the

846. Section 7(2) of the International Trade in Endangered Species Act 2008.
847. Section 8 of the International Trade in Endangered Species Act 2008.
848. Section 16 of the International Trade in Endangered Species Act 2008.
849. Sabah En. 61/1997.
850. Sabah En. 21/2003.
851. Sarawak Cap. 26.
852. Sarawak Cap. 126.
853. Section 10 of the International Trade in Endangered Species Act 2008.

sea any scheduled species without a certificate;[854] and possession of scheduled species.[855] It is also an offence if a person transits any scheduled species without a valid export or re-export permit, licence, certificate or written permission, in accordance with the Convention;[856] or to breed or propagate any scheduled species without being registered with the Management Authority.[857] Other offences include that pertaining to procedures relating to permit, certificate or registration,[858] as well as relating to enforcement procedures.[859] The Act further provides for compounding of offences under section 42, and the protection of informers under section 50.

Animal Welfare Act 2015.[860]

The Animal Welfare Act 2015 that came into force on 1 July 2017 is a federal legislation enacted to provide for the establishment of the Animal Welfare Board, to set out the functions of the Board, to promote the welfare and responsible ownership of animals, and for related matters. The term 'animal' in this Act means any living creature other than a human being and includes any beast, bird, aquatic animals, reptile or insect but does not include wildlife under the Wildlife Conservation Act 2010.[861]

Section 3 of the Act provides for the establishment of the Animal Welfare Board. Functions of the Board are as follows:

- to monitor the work of associations or bodies established for preventing trauma, pain or suffering to animals;
- to monitor the work for the protection of animals, including animals in rescue homes, animal shelters or sanctuaries;
- to monitor the situation of the place where the animals may find a shelter when the animals are infirmed or in need of protection;
- to impart education in relation to the humane treatment of animals and to encourage the formation of public opinion relating to the infliction of trauma, pain or suffering to animals;
- to promote the animal welfare by means of lectures, books, posters, cinematographic exhibitions and others;
- to advise the Minister on any matter relating to animal welfare, the prevention of infliction of trauma, pain or suffering on animals, the prevention of unnecessary killing and to provide for the welfare and well-being of the animal;
- to administer, enforce and ensure the effective implementation of this Act; and
- to discharge all such functions as authorized under this Act or subsidiary legislation made under this Act, including those functions that may be entrusted to the Board under the direction of the Minister.

---

854. Section 11 of the International Trade in Endangered Species Act 2008.
855. Section 12 of the International Trade in Endangered Species Act 2008.
856. Section 13 of the International Trade in Endangered Species Act 2008.
857. Section 14 of the International Trade in Endangered Species Act 2008.
858. Sections 17 and 18 of the International Trade in Endangered Species Act 2008.
859. Sections 23, 28, 30, 34 and 40 of the International Trade in Endangered Species Act 2008.
860. Act 772
861. Section 2 of the Animal Welfare Act 2015.

List of the Board's membership is provided in section 6 which consist of the following members:

- the Director General of the Department of Veterinary Services, as Chairman;
- a senior officer of the Department of Veterinary Services, who shall be appointed by the Minister as Deputy Chairman;
- the Director General of the Department of Wildlife and National Parks of Peninsular Malaysia or his representative;
- the Director General of the Department of Fisheries or his representative;
- the Director General of the Department of Local Government or his representative;
- the dean of faculty in relation to veterinary, from a public institution of higher learning to be appointed by the Minister;
- a senior officer of the Ministry of Agriculture and Food Industry to be appointed by the Minister;
- a senior officer of the Ministry of Education to be appointed by the Minister; and
- a senior officer of the Ministry of Health to be appointed by the Minister.

In addition, the Minister may appoint any person to be a member of the Board whereas the Director of the Department of Veterinary Services and Animal Industry Sabah and the Senior Assistant Director (Veterinary) of the Department of Agriculture Sarawak shall be ex-officio members of the Board.[862]

Matter pertaining to animal welfare under this Act is regulated through licensing as provided in Part III. According to section 15, no person is allowed to carry on the activities involving animals as specified in the Schedule unless he holds a valid licence under the Act. Penalty imposed for the contravention of section 15 is a fine not less than MYR 15,000 and not more than MYR 75,000 or jail for a term not more than two years or both. However licence is not required for the activity of slaughtering animals for religious and customary purposes. Specific activities provided in the Schedule for the purpose of section 15 are as follows:

- animal boarding;
- animal riding and spelling;
- performing animal;
- breeding of animals;
- research, testing and teaching on animals;
- animal rescue and rehabilitation;
- activities relating to animal pound and animal shelters;
- quarantine of animals;
- animal training;
- captivity of live animal for sale activities;
- slaughtering of animals;
- animal disposing; and
- strays controlling by any individual, organization or body corporate.

862. Section 6(3) of the Animal Welfare Act 2015.

Matters pertaining to application, renewal, suspension and revocation of licence are provided in sections 16–21 of the Act. Under section 23, where a person has been convicted of an offence under the Act, he may be barred from holding any licence for a period not exceeding five years from the date when the proceeding of the conviction is finally concluded.

Matters relating to animal welfare are provided in Part IV which include duties of the owner or licensee pertaining to animal welfare;[863] requirements pertaining to using of animals in research, testing or teaching;[864] transportation of animals;[865] and selling of animals to persons who are under the age of 12 years.[866] Part V of the Act provides for matters relating to cruelty to animals. Section 29 provide for the list of actions that constitute cruelty offences which on conviction will be liable to a fine not less than MYR 20,000 and not more than MYR 100,000 or to imprisonment for a term not more than three years or both. They include the followings:

- cruelly beats, kicks, overloads, tortures or terrifies any animals;
- overrides or overdrives any animal, except for activities in relation to equestrian sports listed in the Sports Development Act 1997;
- causes, procures or, being the owner, permits any animal to be so used;
- being the owner of any animal or, being the person in charge of any animal in confinement, fails or neglects to provide such animal with sufficient food, drink or shelter;
- by wantonly or unreasonably doing or omitting to do any act, causes any unnecessary pain or suffering, or, being the owner, permits any unnecessary pain or suffering to any animal;
- causes, procures or, being the owner, permits any animal to be confined, conveyed, lifted or carried in such manner or position as to subject such animal to unnecessary pain or suffering;
- employs, causes, procures or, being the owner, permits to be employed at any work or labour, any animal which in consequence of any disease, infirmity, wound or sore, or otherwise is unfit to be so employed;
- mutilates any animal in any manner, including ear cropping, tail docking, defanging, declawing, branding, piercing or debarking unless in the manner as determined and certified by a veterinary authority or a registered veterinary surgeon;
- skins, roasts or kills any live animals for superstitious belief through a procedure which causes pain and suffering to the animals;
- extracts any parts of any live animals through a procedure which causes pain and suffering to the animals for getting skins, oils or other animal products;
- dynamites, electrifies or poisons any streams, rivers or other water bodies for killing, harvesting or catching animals;
- keeps any animal chained or tethered by using a short or heavy chain or cord, or hobbles the legs of animal;

863. Section 24 of the Animal Welfare Act 2015.
864. Section 26 of the Animal Welfare Act 2015.
865. Section 27 of the Animal Welfare Act 2015.
866. Section 28 of the Animal Welfare Act 2015.

– keeps or confines any animal in any cage or other receptacle which does not measure sufficiently in height, length and width to permit the natural movement of the animal;
– offers for sale any animal which is suffering in pain by reason of mutilation, starvation, thirst, overcrowding or other ill-treatment;
– possesses, without reasonable cause, any animal which is suffering in pain by reason of mutilation, starvation, thirst, overcrowding or other ill-treatment;
– abandons any animal in circumstances which the animal is likely to suffer trauma, pain or suffering by reason of relocation, starvation, thirst, injury or illness;
– being the owner of any animal, wilfully or negligently, causes any animal to go out unattended in any place while the animal is infected with infectious disease;
– being the owner of animal, wilfully or negligently, causes any diseased, disabled or injured animal to die in any place;
– causes, obtains or assists at the fighting or baiting of any animal, or keeps, uses, manages, or acts or assists in the management of any premises or place for fighting or baiting any animal, or permits any premises or place to be so kept, managed or used, or receives or causes or obtains any person to receive money for the admission of any person to such premises or place; promotes or takes part in any shooting match or competition of which animals are released from captivity for such shooting; or
– organizes, participates, promotes or in any manner is associated with any sport or activity involving the use of animals, where such animals are subjected to cruelty, either during the sport or activity itself or while in training.

The act of killing of any dog, cat or any other animal by way of shooting with firearms is an offence under section 30 unless it is authorized by the veterinary authority during emergency or for the purposes of disease control. Other exceptions provided in section 30 are the killing of the animal is for human consumption; the animal is incurably ill as determined by the veterinary authority; the killing of the animal is deemed necessary to end the suffering of such animal as determined by a veterinary authority; the killing is done to prevent an imminent danger to the life or limb of a human being; the killing is done for animal population control by any authorized authority under any written law; the killing is approved by the animal ethics committee at the end of any research, testing and teaching procedures; or the killing is for any other reasons as determined by a veterinary authority.

Other actions that constitute offences under Part V are administration of poisons to any animal without lawful authorization or reasonable excuse[867] and involvement in animal fighting venture which refers to any event that involves a fight between at least two animals and is conducted for the purposes of sport, wagering or entertainment except where the animals are expressing their natural behaviour.[868] Part VI deals with animals in distress. According to section 34, if a registered veterinary surgeon certifies in writing that an animal shall be destroyed, an animal welfare officer may destroy or arrange for the animal to be destroyed. Section 35 empowers the court to make an order in relation to animals taken into possession

867. Section 31 of the Animal Welfare Act 2015.
868. Section 34 of the Animal Welfare Act 2015.

and to appoint any person to carry out the order. Powers relating to enforcement is provided in Part VII, including the appointment of animal welfare officer;[869] power of investigation,[870] search[871] and seal of premises;[872] and power to apply to the court for orders in relation to the seized animals.[873] Ancillary power of the court is covered in Part VIII which include the following: to impose penalty up to twice the original sum on second and subsequent offences;[874] to deprive ownership of owner or licensee who was convicted under the Act;[875] to disqualify a convicted person from owning or keeping animals;[876] to seize animals in connection with disqualification;[877] to order destruction of animal;[878] and to forfeit items used in relation to the offences.[879]

§4. State Legislation

812. In Sabah, the principal laws concerning wildlife in Sabah are the Parks Enactment 1984, Forests Enactment 1968, Forests (Amendment) Enactment 1984, Fauna Conservation Ordinance 1963 and its amendments, and Fisheries Act 1985.

813. In Sarawak, wildlife Sanctuaries are gazetted under the Wildlife Protection Ordinance 1958[880] to provide totally protected areas of particular natural interest, protected against all forms of exploitation, including tourism. The Ordinance also includes provision for the protection of wild species and their habitats. This Ordinance and the Fauna Conservation Ordinance are administered by the National Parks and Wildlife Office of the Sarawak Forest Department.

814. The following are Sabah and Sarawak state enactments directly or indirectly relevant to wildlife conservation and management:

- the Sarawak Forest Ordinance 1954;
- the Natural Resources and Environmental Ordinance 1994;
- the National Parks and Nature Reserve Ordinance 1998;
- the Wildlife Protection Ordinance 1998 of Sarawak;

869. Section 36 of the Animal Welfare Act 2015.
870. Section 37 of the Animal Welfare Act 2015.
871. Section 40 of the Animal Welfare Act 2015.
872. Section 43 of the Animal Welfare Act 2015.
873. Sections 45 and 46 of the Animal Welfare Act 2015.
874. Section 50 of the Animal Welfare Act 2015.
875. Section 51 of the Animal Welfare Act 2015.
876. Section 52 of the Animal Welfare Act 2015.
877. Section 53 of the Animal Welfare Act 2015.
878. Section 54 of the Animal Welfare Act 2015.
879. Section 55 of the Animal Welfare Act 2015.
880. Cap. 128.

- the Sarawak Biodiversity Ordinance 1998;
- the Kinabalu Park Ordinance 1962;
- the Wildlife Conservation Enactment 1997 of Sabah;
- the Sabah Biodiversity Enactment 2001.

Chapter 5. Agricultural Resources

§1. General Information

815. Among the main impacts of agricultural activities on Malaysia's environment are surface runoff, floods and sedimentation. Sedimentation by clearing of large tracts of land either for plantation development, road construction or urban expansion is a major cause of flash floods, as rivers are quickly choked under the intense tropical rainstorms experienced in Malaysia.

816. Soil loss also occurs during clear cutting operations before the establishment of a stable cover crop following replanting. The clearing of land particularly through opening of jungle leads to marked changes in the hydrological balance.

817. The establishment of a plantation from forested or cleared areas often involves modifications to the terrain in addition to the establishment of estate roads and drainage systems. This results in considerable soil disturbance and loss of relatively nutrient rich top soil which is already very thin in a tropical forest environment.[881]

§2. Institutional Framework

818. At present, there are a number of agencies in Malaysia with specific and overlapping functions in matters relevant to agricultural resources. However, the main agency on agricultural development is the Department of Agriculture, under the Minister of Agriculture and Food Industry.

819. This Ministry is guided by the National Agricultural Policy of Malaysia. This policy, promulgated in 1984, emphasized the achievement of balanced development between the agricultural and manufacturing sectors. Other objectives of this Policy include maximizing income through the efficient use of agriculture resources, and increasing farm productivity by choosing remunerative crops and employing the most efficient technologies.

820. Among the objectives of the Department of Agriculture are the following:

- to provide consultancy, technical support and advisory services in various agricultural fields, particularly in food crops and agro-processing industries, to ensure sufficient food production;
- to guide and develop successful agricultural entrepreneurs in order to increase farm productivity and national agricultural production;

881. A detailed study on the link between agricultural resources and their impact on the environment in Malaysia can be found in Amitabha Guha, *Environmental Constraints to Agriculture in Malaysia* (Agric. Research & Advisory Bureau 1995), in http://www.arabis.org/documentation/whitepaper/MSIA_Environment.shtml, January 2014.

- to develop trained and skilled manpower in the agricultural sector;
- to protect agricultural crops from pests and diseases through crop protection programmes and plant quarantine services;
- to ensure the production of food crops which are safe for consumption and to protect the environment through the control of pesticides; and
- to control plant and germ-plasm materials of economic importance from being freely taken out of the country.

§3. Legislation

821. There are several statutes which are enforced by the Department of Agriculture, one of which is the Pesticides Act 1974. This Act authorizes the Department to:

- issue pesticide import permits for research and education purposes;
- issue licences for premises to sell pesticides and to store pesticides for sale;
- carry out the registration of imported and manufactured pesticides for sale;
- grant approval for aerial spraying of pesticides; and
- grant approval of pesticide advertisements.

822. Another statute enforced by the Department is the Plant Quarantine Act 1976. Through this Act, the Department is authorized to issue import permits for plants, plant products and organisms/microorganisms; and to issue Phytosanitary Certificates for plant materials and agricultural products for export and post-entry quarantine.

823. Under the Plant Variety Protection Act 2004, the Department is empowered to protect plant propagation rights for new varieties of plants created or discovered; to recognize and protect the farmers, local people and the natives who discover the existence of a new variety; and to encourage investment towards the development of new varieties. Apart from that, the Department is also authorized to issue permits for the export of endangered wild plant species, based on the CITIES.

824. Another statute relevant to agricultural resources is the EQA 1974, through its provision on EIA under section 34A. This section makes assessment a mandatory requirement for particular projects or 'prescribed activities'. Such activities include agriculture (of or more than 500 ha), drainage and irrigation, land reclamation, fisheries, forestry, housing, industry, infrastructure, airports, ports, mining, petroleum, dams and man-made lakes, power generation, quarries, railways, transportation, resort and recreational development, waste treatment and disposal, and water supply.

825. Other legislation which contains provisions relating to the control of run-off, sedimentation of rivers and other natural resources and their impact on the environment are the following:

- the Land Conservation Act of 1960;
- the National Forest Act 1984;
- the Waters Act 1920; and
- the Street, Drainage and Building Act 1974.

Chapter 6. Forests

§1. General Information

826. The tropical rainforest of Malaysia is a repository of genetic resources for both flora and fauna, and Malaysia, with 20.56 million ha of forest, plays host to a wide variety of plant and animal species.[882]

827. The forested area in Peninsular Malaysia is divided into four major forest types, namely the Inland Dipterocarp Forest, Mangrove Swamp Forest, Peat Swamp Forest and Plantation Forest.[883] The forested areas cover 59.5% of the total land area in the country.[884]

§2. Legal Framework

828. Forestry in Malaysia is predominantly a state matter, and the thirteen state governments have complete jurisdiction over their forest resources, as provided in Article 74(2) and List II State List of the Federal Constitution. As such, each state is empowered to enact laws on forestry, formulate forest policy and undertake corresponding forest management responsibilities independently.

829. The executive authority of the federal government only extends to the provision of advice and technical assistance to the states, the maintenance of experimental and demonstration stations, training and the conducting of research. The federal government also provides technical advice on forest management and development of wood-based industries and trade.

830. However, a close relationship between the states and the federal government is essential regarding all land and forestry issues. To facilitate coordination between the federal and state governments, a National Forestry Council was established in 1971 by the National Land Council.

831. Under the Malaysian Constitution, the National Land Council is empowered to formulate national policies relating to land utilization in agriculture, forestry and mining.[885] The establishment of the National Forestry Council under the National Land Council provides a forum between the federal and state governments on policies and other issues. Members of the National Forestry Council include Chief Ministers from all the states, ministers responsible for forestry, agriculture,

882. *See* Maizatun Mustafa, *Urban Forest Protection from the Perspective of Environmental Law in Malaysia: Issues and Challenges*, a paper presented at the *COBRA- The RICS Construction and Building Research Conference* (U. Cape Town 2009).
883. *See Tropical Peat Swamps: Safe-Guarding a Global Natural Resources* (Mashhor Mansor, et al. eds, Penerbitan Universiti sains Malay. 2004); and *Sustainable Development of Matang Mangroves* (Mohamad Ismail Sharuddin et al. eds, Forestry Dep. Peninsular Malay. 2005).
884. *See* the report from the WWF Malaysia at http://www.wwf.org.my/, January 2014.
885. Article 91 of the Constitution.

environment and trade, and the Council is chaired by the Deputy Prime Minister. The National Forestry Policy was introduced in 1978 which provides guidance on the development of the forestry sector with the main objective of conserving and managing of forest based on the principles of sustainable management. In 1992, the Policy was revised in order to incorporate matters relating to biological diversity conservation and sustainable utilization of genetic resources, as well as relating to the role of local communities in forest development.[886]

832. The Forestry Department in Malaysia was first formed in 1883 during the time of the British. During that time and until the period of independence, each state had its own legislation on forest management. It was only in 1984 that Malaysia enacted uniform legislation on forestry through the National Forestry Act 1984.

§3. National Forestry Act 1984

I. Introduction

833. The National Forestry Act 1984[887] was enacted to provide for the administration, management and conservation of forests and forestry development within the States of Malaysia; and for promoting uniformity of the laws of the States of Malaysia. This Act was enacted pursuant to clause (1)(b) of Article 76 of the Federal Constitution and consequently does not come into force in a state unless it has been adopted by a law made by the legislature of the state pursuant to clause (3) of Article 76 of the Federal Constitution. As a federal legislation, the Act has subsequently been adopted by the legislatures of all states except Sabah and Sarawak, as the law on forestry in the respective states, including for the Federal Territories of Kuala Lumpur and Labuan. Sabah and Sarawak have not adopted the National Forestry Act 1984. Each of these states has its own forestry legislation.

834. Upon the coming into force of the Act in the various states, the following state forest enactments were repealed:[888]

- F.M.S. Forest Enactment 1934;[889]
- Johor Forest Enactment;[890]
- Kedah Forest Enactment;[891]
- Kelantan Forest Enactment;[892]
- Perlis Forest Enactment;[893]

---

886. *See* the official website, Forestry Department Peninsular Malaysia, https://www.forestry.gov.my/index.php/en/about-us/national-forestry-policy, July 2018.
887. Act 313.
888. Section 112, National Forestry Act 1984.
889. Cap. 153.
890. J. En. No. 58.
891. K. En. 15/1357.
892. Kn En. 4/1939.
893. Ps En. 3/1370.

– S.S. Forest Ordinance;[894] and
– Terengganu Forest Enactment.[895]

835. The National Forestry Act 1984 provides a legal basis for defining and recognizing forest areas according to a range of uses and services that they provide. The Act was reviewed and amended in 1993 to include measures aimed at improving and strengthening capacity in forest management and biodiversity conservation in Malaysia.

836. Under this Act, 'forest management plan' is defined as 'an operating plan relating to silvicultural, economic or conservation activity or programmes prescribed for a particular permanent reserved forest or part thereof to secure the orderly taking, renewal and conservation of trees in accordance with the principle of sustained yield'.

837. The term 'forest produce' for the purpose of the Act includes the following when found in or brought from a permanent reserved forest:

(a) guano, peat, rock, sea-sand, river-sand, sea-shells, shell-sand and surfaces oil;
(b) the following when found in or brought from a permanent reserved forest or state land:
  – trees and all parts or produce not hereinafter mentioned of trees;
  – plants including climbers, creepers and grasses, and all parts or produce of such plants;
  – silk, cocoons, honey and wax and edible bird's nests; and
  – fuel wood, charcoal, *getah*, *getah taban* leaves, wood oil, bark, extracts of bark, *damar* and *atap*, whether found in or brought from a permanent reserved forest, state land, mining land, reserved land or alienated land timber.

838. Part II of the Act deals with administration. For the purposes of this Act, the State Authority may appoint a State Director of Forestry and his deputies.[896] Section 4 provides for duties of the Director, namely:

– to be responsible to the State Authority for the due administration within the state of the provisions of this Act;
– to implement state forest management plans;
– to prepare and implement reforestation plans;
– to review the state forest management plans and reforestation plans;
– to prepare and implement programmes relating to amenity forests;
– to prepare an annual report on the activities of the State Forestry Department during the preceding financial year and submit such report to the State Authority and the Director General of the Federal Forestry Department;

894. Cap. 147.
895. Tr No. 44/1356.
896. Section 3 of the National Forestry Act 1984.

- to prepare and submit to the State Financial Authority an annual budget; and
- to perform such other duties as the State Authority may from time to time determine.

II. Permanent Reserved Forest

839. Part III contains provisions on permanent reserved forest. For this purpose, section 7 of the Act authorizes the State Authority to constitute any land a permanent reserved forest, specifying the situation and extent of such land and declaring that such land shall be a 'permanent reserved forest' from a date fixed by the notification.

840. Under section 9, if the State Authority considers it expedient to constitute any land a permanent reserved forest, it may cause such land to be acquired for a public purpose.

841. Under section 10(1), the State Director of Forestry, with the approval of the State Authority, is empowered to classify every permanent reserved forest under one or more of the following classifications which shall be descriptive of the purpose or purposes for which the land is being or is intended to be used:

- timber production forest under sustained yield;
- soil protection forest;
- soil reclamation forest;
- flood control forest;
- water catchment forest;
- forest sanctuary for wildlife;
- virgin jungle reserved forest;
- amenity forest;
- education forest;
- research forest; and
- forest for federal purposes.

842. For the purposes of subsection (1), any permanent reserved forest may be divided into several parts and each part, the situation and extent of which shall be specified in the notification, may be classified under one or more of the classifications enumerated in subsection (1).[897]

843. However, under section 11, the State Authority may excise land from a permanent reserved forest if satisfied that any land in a permanent reserved forest is no longer required for the purpose for which it was classified under section 10, and is required for economic use higher than that for which it is being utilized. Where any

897. Section 10(2) of the National Forestry Act 1984.

land is excised under section 11, the State Authority shall, wherever possible and if it is satisfied that it is in the national interest so to do, have regard to:[898]

- the need for soil and water conservation, biodiversity and other environmental considerations;
- the need to sustain timber production in the state in order to meet the requirements of the forest industry;
- the economic development of the state; and
- the availability of suitable land.

Chapter 8 of the Act provides for provisions on forest development fund. The State Authority has the power to establish this fund as provided in section 56. According to section 58, the Fund is established for the purposes of the preparation of the State forest management plans; the preparation and implementation of reforestation plans; the reviewing of the State forest management plans and reforestation plans; the preparation and implementation of programmes relating to amenity forests; and any expenses incurred by the State Authority in effecting a reforestation plan under section 24. Moneys to be paid into the Fund come from a number of resources, which are:[899]

- sum which is annually appropriated by the State Legislative Assembly necessary for the purposes of the Fund for the following financial year;
- the forest development cess collected under section 60;
- any loan or grant given to the State Authority by the Federal Government for the purposes of the Fund;
- any money paid to the State Authority under subsection 24(2); and
- all money collected under any previous forest law by the State Authority for financing research on forestry, silviculture works, forest surveys, inventory and other related operations connected with forest development in the State, which remains unexpended.

III. Licences and Permits

844. Another relevant part in this Act is Part IV on forest management and development. Section 14 under this part specifies that all forest produce situated, lying, growing or having its origin within a permanent reserved forest or state land shall be the property of the State Authority.

845. Under section 15(1), no person shall take any forest produce from a permanent reserved forest or state land except under the authority of a licence, minor licence or use permit; or in accordance with any other written law. The penalty provided for any person who contravenes this section is a fine not exceeding MYR

898. Section 12 of the National Forestry Act 1984.
899. Section 57 of the National Forestry Act 1984.

500,000, to imprisonment for a term which shall not be less than one year but shall not exceed twenty years, or both such a fine and imprisonment.[900]

846. Under section 32, no person shall occupy or carry out any activity upon any land within a permanent reserved forest, unless he is the holder of a use permit. Any person who contravenes this provision shall be guilty of an offence and shall, on conviction, be liable to a fine not exceeding MYR 50,000, to imprisonment for a term not exceeding five years, or both such a fine and imprisonment.

847. Use permits are provided for in section 34. The State Authority may issue use permits for the following activities:

- research;
- education or training;
- recreation;
- use of water resources except the construction or operation of hydroelectric dams;
- cultivation of vegetables and fodder crops;
- the establishment of conversion plants; and
- the establishment of logging infrastructures.

848. Requirements for removal licences are provided in section 40. Under this section, no person shall remove any forest produce from any alienated land; land held under a temporary occupation licence; mining land; or reserved land, unless he is the holder of a removal licence. Any person who contravenes this section shall be guilty of an offence and shall, on conviction, be liable to a fine not exceeding MYR 500,000, to imprisonment for a term which shall not be less than one year but shall not exceed twenty years, or both such a fine and imprisonment.[901]

849. For offences concerning removal licences, section 40(2A) further provides that any person convicted of an offence under this section may, in addition to any penalty imposed, be ordered to pay to the State Authority a sum not exceeding ten times the royalty, premium and cess in respect of any forest produce unlawfully taken, and a sum not exceeding ten times the value of such forest produce. Any other charges payable, and any sum ordered to be so paid, shall be recoverable as if it were a fine so imposed.

850. Section 45 provides for the power of the State Authority to declare permanent reserved forest as open forest or closed forest. Until a permanent reserved forest or part thereof has been so declared to be an open forest, it shall be deemed to be a closed forest. Apart from that, under section 46, it is a requirement that in exercising the powers under section 45, the State Authority shall give due consideration to the necessity of protecting the forest and the environment, and to the recreational and other needs of the public.

900. Section 15(2) of the National Forestry Act 1984.
901. Section 40(2) of the National Forestry Act 1984.

IV. Offences and Penalties

851. Under section 81(2), any person who contravenes subsection (1) shall be guilty of an offence and shall, on conviction, be liable to a fine between MYR 10,000 and MYR 50,000, and jail not exceeding three or five years.

852. Offensive littering in a permanent reserved forest is also an offence, under section 83 of the Act. Those found guilty under this Act may be liable to a fine not exceeding MYR 10,000, to imprisonment for a term not exceeding three years, or both such a fine and imprisonment.

853. Under section 83(3), offensive littering in a permanent reserved forest includes:

- creating an objectionable stench;
- degrading the beauty or the appearance of property; or
- detracting from the natural cleanliness or safety of property;
- by intentionally:
- discarding or depositing any rubbish, trash, garbage, debris or other refuse;
- draining, or causing or permitting to be drained, mining sludge, industrial effluent, sewage or the drainage from a cesspool, septic tank, recreational or camping vehicle waste holding tank or other contaminated source; or
- permitting any rubbish, trash, garbage, debris or other refuse to be thrown from a vehicle which he is operating or which is under his control.

854. Section 87 contains a general penalty whereby whoever commits a breach of any rules for the breach of which no penalty is expressly provided, they shall, on conviction, be liable to a fine not exceeding MYR 50,000, to imprisonment for a term not exceeding five years, or both such a fine and imprisonment.

§4. Other Legislation

855. The EQA 1974 is another statute relevant to forest protection through the requirement of an EIA under section 34A and the Environmental Quality (Prescribed Activities) (EIA) Order 2015.

856. Under this Order, activities involving certain forest land uses that require an EIA, can be found in both First and Second Schedules. Under the First Schedule, the relevant activities include the followings:

(1) agriculture, involving land development schemes covering an area of 20 ha or more but less than 500 ha to bring forest into agricultural production;
(2) forestry, involving:
   - conversion of forest at 300 m or more above mean sea level to other land use covering an area of 20 ha or more but less than 100 ha;

- logging, or cutting or taking of timber for the purpose of conversion from forest to other land use covering an area of 100 ha or more but less than 500 ha;
- logging, or cutting or taking of timber from forest at less than 300 m above mean sea level covering an area of 100 ha or more, outside permanent reserved forest;
- conversion of an area of mangrove forest; peat swamp forest; or fresh water swamp forest;
- for industrial, housing or agricultural use covering an area of 20 ha or more but less than 50 ha; and
- development of planted forest covering an area of 100 ha or more but less than 500 ha.

(3) development in costal and hill area involving the construction of hill-station resort or hotel at 300 m or more above mean sea level covering an area of 20 ha or more; and
(4) development in slope area, involving the development or land clearing less than 50% of an area with slope greater than or equal to 25° but less than 35°.

Whereas, under the Second Schedule, activities relating to forest land uses that require EIA include:

(1) agriculture involving land development schemes covering an area of 500 ha or more to bring forest into agricultural production;
(2) aerodrome, involving the construction of aerodrome in or adjacent or near to any state park, national park, national marine park, island surrounding marine park or environmentally sensitive area;
(3) drainage and irrigation involving the construction of man-made lakes and artificial enlargement of lakes with surface areas of 50 ha or more in or adjacent or near to environmentally sensitive area; or any drainage of wetland, wildlife habitat or of dry inland forest covering an area of 20 ha or more;
(4) fisheries, involving land-based aquaculture projects accompanied by clearing of mangrove forest, peat swamp forest or fresh water swamp forest covering an area of 50 ha or more;
(5) forestry, involving:
- conversion of forest at 300 m or more above mean sea level to other land use covering an area of 100 ha or more;
- logging or conversion of forest to other land use within a catchment area of reservoirs used for municipal water supply, irrigation or hydropower; an area adjacent or near to any state park, national park or national marine park; any state park, national park or national marine park; or an area gazetted as water catchment forest under the National Forestry Act 1984;
- logging, or cutting or taking of timber from forest at 300 m or more above mean sea level covering an area of 100 ha or more, outside permanent reserved forest;
- logging, or cutting or taking of timber covering an area of 500 ha or more.
- development of planted forest covering an area of 500 ha or more.

- conversion of an area of mangrove forest; peat swamp forest; or fresh water swamp forest, for industrial, housing or agricultural use covering an area of 50 ha or more; and
- clearing of mangrove forest, peat swamp forest or fresh water swamp forest on islands adjacent to any national marine park.

(6) land reclamation along riverbanks within or adjacent or near to environmentally sensitive areas;
(7) mining of minerals within or adjacent or near to environmentally sensitive area;
(8) development in coastal area, national park and state park;
(9) development in slope area relating to land clearing of 50% or more of an area with slope greater than or equal to 25° but lesser than 35°; and
(10) construction of dam or impounding reservoir for irrigation, flood mitigation, control of siltation, recreational, water supply or any other reason with a surface area of 100 ha or more; or dam and hydroelectric power scheme with either dam of 15 m or more in height and ancillary structures covering a total area of 40 ha or more; or reservoir with a surface area of 100 ha or more.

857. Other enactments which are considered of major importance to the forestry sector are the Land Conservation Act 1960, the National Land Code 1965, the Protection of Wildlife Act 1972, the Malaysian Timber Industry Board Act 1973, the EQA 1974, the National Park Act 1980, and the Malaysian Forestry Research and Development Board Act 1985.

858. For the state of Sabah, the main legislation on forest is the Sabah Forest Enactment 1968[902] which was enacted by the Legislature of the state of Sabah. Similar to the National Forestry Act 1984 which applies to all states in Peninsular Malaysia, the Sabah Forest Enactment 1968 also contains administrative and criminal strategies relating to forest conservation and forest offences for the state of Sabah. Provisions pertaining to forest reserves are provided in Part II of the Enactment. Under section 5, the Yang di-Pertua Negeri may constitute any State land, other than land reserved for a public or special purpose under any written law, to be a Forest Reserve of specific class of one or more of the following Classes:

- Class I – Protection Forest – Maintenance of forest essential on climatic or physical grounds;
- Class II – Commercial Forest – For supply of timber and other produce to meet the general demands of trade;
- Class III – Domestic Forest – For supply of timber and other produce for local consumption;
- Class IV – Amenity Forest – For local amenity and aboretum work;
- Class V – Mangrove Forest – For supply of mangrove timber or other produce to meet the general demands of trade and for eco-tourism activities;
- Class VI – Virgin Jungle Reserve – For forest research purpose; and
- Class VII – Wildlife Reserve – For protection of wildlife.

902. Sabah En.2/68.

In addition, under section 5A, the Yang di-Pertua Negeri may declare any area in a Forest Reserve or on State land which may require special protection for reasons of soil, wildlife, ecological or water conservation to be a protected area and may, at any time, in like manner vary or revoke such declaration. Section 5A further added that notwithstanding the terms of any licence or licence agreement to the contrary, no logging, land clearing, cultivation, grazing or other exploitation of any kind can be undertaken in a protected area except as provided in the declaration of the protected area or as specially authorized in writing by the Minister. When an area has been proposed to become a forest reserve, the following are not permitted during the period between the publication of a notice of intention and the terminal date in respect of the proposal:[903] issuing new titles; acquiring of new right or privilege; erecting new buildings or forming new plantations; clearing for cultivation; cutting of trees or taking forest produce.

Section 20 of the Enactment provides for a list of prohibited acts in Forest Reserves. Under section 20(1)(a) the penalty of seven years of imprisonment and a fine is imposed on the following acts: girdling, marking, loping, taping or injuring by fire or otherwise of any forest produce; negligently causes any damage in felling any tree or in cutting, extracting or removing any forest produce; kindling or causing to be kindled or carrying any fire, or throwing down any lighted match or other lighted material. Under section 20(1)(b) a person shall be guilty of an offence for committing the following acts in any forest reserve, namely to erect or construct any building or livestock enclosure; to depasture livestock or causes or permits any livestock to be; or to cultivate any land or clear or dig up any land for cultivation or for any other purpose. Whereas under section 20(1)(c), the penalty of a fine not exceeding MYR 50,000 or jail not exceeding three years or both fine and imprisonment will be imposed on any person who enters any part of a Forest Reserve which has been closed by or under the rules; or damages, alters, shifts, removes, or interferes in any way whatsoever with any fence or notice board in a Forest Reserve.

Additional penalty is provided by section 20(2) on any person who cuts, collects, converts, fells, or removes any forest produce in a Forest Reserve with the penalty imposed is a fine not exceeding MYR 500,000 and to imprisonment for a term which shall not be less than one year but shall not exceed twenty years. Any person convicted of an offence under section 20 may, in addition to any penalty imposed on the conviction, be ordered to pay, in respect of any forest produce unlawfully taken, to the Government a sum not exceeding ten times the royalty, fee and other sum due; a sum not exceeding ten times the value of such forest produce; and any other charges payable, and any sum ordered to be so paid shall be recoverable as if it were a fine so imposed.

Provisions pertaining to forest produce are provided in Part III of the Enactment. Under this section 'forest produce' is interpreted to mean:

- timber, converted timber, wood chip, saw dust, oil, carving, firewood, charcoal, getah, gaharu, wood oil, bark, extracts of bark, copal, dammar and atap found in or brought from a Forest Reserve, State land or alienated land;

903. Section 7 of the Sabah Forest Enactment 1968.

- the following when found in or brought from a Forest Reserve or State land namely trees and any produce thereof, silk, cocoons, honey and wax; or carbon stored in trees or plants;
- all vegetable and animal matters and products other than animals and animal products which are subject to the provisions of the Wildlife Conservation Enactment 1997 (Enactment No. 6/1997), and all minerals and mineral substances other than mineral oil which are subject to the provisions of the Mining Ordinance 1960 (Ordinance No. 20/1960) found in or brought from a Forest Reserve or State land; and
- imported timber.

Section 23 imposes penalty of a fine not exceeding MYR 50,000 or to imprisonment for a term not exceeding five years or both such fine and imprisonment on any person who girdles, marks, lops, taps or injures by fire, or otherwise any forest produce on any State land; or removes any forest produce found on any alienated land beyond the boundaries of that land. In addition, any person who cuts, collects, converts, fells or removes any forest produce on any State land shall be guilty of an offence and on conviction shall be punished with a fine not exceeding MYR 500,000 and to imprisonment for a term which shall not be less than one year but shall not exceed twenty years. Any person convicted of an offence under section 23 may, in addition to any penalty imposed on conviction, be ordered to pay, in respect of any forest produce unlawfully taken, to the Government a sum not exceeding ten times the royalty, fee and other sum due; a sum not exceeding ten times the value of such forest produce; and any other charges payable, and such sum ordered to be so paid shall be recoverable as if it were a fine so imposed.

Prohibited acts of sections 20 and 23 are allowed to be committed through the issuance of licence by the Chief Conservator as provided in section 24. Such issuance is subject to conditions and the payment of fees or royalties. A licence relating to the doing of any act in a Forest Reserve shall not be expressed as being valid for a period exceeding five years. Notwithstanding any provisions of this Enactment, under section 24A, the Minister may revoke or cancel a licence or licences or vary the conditions or impose such additional conditions upon such licence or licences entered into or issued under the Enactment. Before any licence for an area exceeding one thousand hectares in a Forest Reserve or on State land is issued or before a licence agreement is entered into, section 28A empowers the Chief Conservator to require the prospective holder thereof to prepare a forest management plan or forest harvesting plan, as the case may be – and a reforestation plan. The holder of a licence who has been required to prepare a forest management plan, or forest harvesting plan and reforestation plan, must carry them into effect to the satisfaction of the Chief Conservator. Under section 28B, where the holder of licence fails to carry into effect a reforestation plan, the Chief Conservator may, in addition to revoking the licence or recommending to the Minister to terminate the licence agreement, require the holder thereof to pay a sum equivalent to the amount which would be incurred by the Government if it were to undertake or to engage any person to carry the plan into effect.

Similar to the National Forestry Act 1984 which provides for certain exceptions to the native people on matters relating to forest procedure, exceptions are provided by the Enactment relating to native rights. Under section 41, subject to any provisions prohibiting or regulating the cutting or removing of forest produce in any specified locality, no prohibition is imposed on the cutting and removing from state land or alienated land, by any native of forest produce for the following purposes: for the construction or repair of a dwelling house for himself and his family; for the construction of fences and temporary huts on any land lawfully occupied by him; for the construction or repair of native boats; for the upkeep of his fishing stakes and landing places; for firewood to be consumed for domestic purposes; or for the construction and upkeep of clinics, schools, community halls, places of worship, bridges and any work for the common benefit of the native inhabitants of his kampung (village).

859. For the state of Sarawak, the main legislation on forest is the Sarawak Forests Ordinance 2015[904] which repealed the Sarawak Forests Ordinance 1958.[905] Similar to the National Forestry Act 1984 which is applicable to all states in Peninsular Malaysia, the Sarawak Forests Ordinance 2015 also contains comparable administrative and criminal strategies relating to forest conservation and forest offences for the state of Sarawak. Provisions relating to forest reserves, protected forests and communal forests are provided in Part III of the Ordinance. According to section 7, a forest reserve or protected forest may be constituted over any state land. Section 10 provides that the rights or privileges that may be claimed in an area to be constituted a forest reserve or protected forest shall be only those rights or privileges which have been enjoyed or exercised by or accrued to a native or his forefathers or a native community for an uninterrupted period beginning from a date prior to 1 January 1954 to the date of the notification. Any person who fails to submit a claim to any right or privilege over the land to be constituted a forest reserve or protected forest within the period stipulated in the notification shall be deemed to have abandoned or waived such right or privilege and shall not be entitled to any payment of compensation.[906] Factors to be taken in assessing compensation payable include nature and extent of the right or privilege claimed; whether such right or privilege is still exercised or enjoyed by the claimant at the date of the notification; the degree of actual dependency of the claimant on such right or privilege as a means of his livelihood; if the right or privilege relates to the planting of any crop, whether an alternative site or area has been provided by the Government for the person or the community to which he belongs, for farming; and any other relevant factors or circumstances pertaining to the enjoyment or exercise of such right or privilege.

860. Under section 18, the Minister may publish a proclamation to constitute in the area specified in the notification a forest reserve or protected forest. Such proclamation shall provide a name for the forest reserve or protected forest; specify the limit of the forest reserve or protected forest; declare the date on which the proclamation shall take effect; declare that all rights or privileges in the forest reserve or

904. Sarawak Cap. 71.
905. Sarawak Cap. 126.
906. Section 11 of the Sarawak Forests Ordinance 2015.

protected forest have been extinguished; and stipulate the special conditions governing the reservation or protection. Effects of proclamation as stipulated in section 20 would be that the forest reserve or protected forest and all the forest produce therein belong absolutely to the Government. Such forest will be managed, administered and controlled by the Director and no person whose rights or privileges have been extinguished can exercise such rights without written approval of the Director. Within the forest reserve or protected forest, following acts are prohibited, namely:[907] trespass; pasture cattle or permit cattle to trespass; fell, cut, ring, mark, lop or tap any tree, or injure by fire or otherwise any tree or timber; cause any damage by negligence in felling any tree or cutting or dragging any timber; quarry stone, burn lime or charcoal or search for, collect or remove any forest produce or minerals; erect any building, or clear or break up any land for cultivation or for any other purpose; or kindle, keep or carry any fire or leave any fire burning.

861. One special feature of the Sarawak Forests Ordinance 2015 is the provisions on Communal Forests which is interpreted by section 2 as a communal forest constituted over state land under Part III of the Ordinance. Section 30 of the Ordinance empowers the Minister, at the request of a community, to constitute any State land, not being a forest reserve, protected forest or other Government reserve, a communal forest. The constitution of a communal forest is through notification. Under section 31, when the Resident is satisfied that it is the desire of majority of the members of a community that a communal forest shall be constituted, he shall, with the written approval of the Minister, publish a notification. Such notification will specify the situation and limits of the communal forest and declare that it is proposed to constitute a communal forest. The notification will also call upon any person desirous of making a claim to any rights or privileges to lodge such claim. The proclamation of the communal forest which is published in the Gazette contains a name for the communal forest; specifies the limits of the forest; and rights and privileges admitted or conceded in respect of the forest.[908] From the date so fixed, the area will be a communal forest and together with all the produce therein and all things found thereon will be set aside for the sole use of the native community, by whom the forest will be maintained and controlled.[909] Maintenance of the communal forest is undertaken by the native community as provided in section 36 in a condition of sustained yield. Requirements pertaining to the removal of forest produce from the communal forest are provided in section 37. The section permits a member of the native community to remove, free of royalty or fee, any forest produce for his own use and not for sale, barter or profit. However, no other person shall remove any forest produce from a communal reserve for any purpose whatsoever. Under section 37, it is a presumption that a member of the native community takes forest produce for sale, barter or profit unless he can prove that he requires the forest produce as firewood or for the construction, repair or extension of his dwelling house or for the making of any boat, furniture or any other household goods or utensils for the use of himself or his immediate family, and that the forest produce was

907. Section 26 of the Sarawak Forests Ordinance 2015.
908. Section 35 (2) of the Sarawak Forests Ordinance 2015.
909. Section 35 (3) of the Sarawak Forests Ordinance 2015.

taken by himself or a member of his family. Any person who contravenes section 37 shall, upon conviction, be punished with a fine of not less than MYR 5,000 and not exceeding MYR 50,000 or imprisonment for a term not exceeding two years or both, and for a subsequent offence, shall be punished with a fine of not less than MYR 10,000 and not exceeding MYR 100,000 or imprisonment for a term not exceeding five years or both.

862. Part IV of the Ordinance relates to the management and development of forests. According to section 39, all forest produce situated, lying, growing or having its origin within a permanent forest or state land shall be the property of the state except where the rights to such forest produce have been specifically disposed of in accordance with the provisions of the Ordinance or any other written law. Under section 2, timber is defined to include trees when they have fallen or been felled, and all woods whether or not cut up, fashioned or hollowed out for any purpose, but it does not include firewood. The Ordinance prohibits the use of timber tree as fuel as stated in section 53 where any person, except with the written approval of the Director, is prohibited to cut for conversion into firewood or charcoal any timber other than branchwood and timber which has been declared to be unserviceable. However, an exception is granted in section 60 to any resident of Sarawak to allow without a licence, collection and removal from State land which is not a forest reserve or protected forest, any forest produce other than timber which is required exclusively for his own domestic use and not for sale, barter or profit. The penalty for those who contravene the provision of section 60 is a fine of no less than MYR 5,000 or not exceeding MYR 50,000 or jail for up to two years or both. Section 61 empowered the Director to declare any tree or species of tree found on any permanent forest or alienated land, as a protected tree or species of tree, on account that the tree or the species thereof has medicinal compound or properties upon which research could be carried out for the development or production of medicinal or pharmaceutical products. Penalty in the form of fine and jail term will be imposed on any person who contravenes section 61. The control and regulation of the taking of forest produce is within the power of the Director through the issuance of licences, calling for tenders and collection of fees or other payments, including the payment for ecosystem services in respect of forest produce.[910] It is a requirement under section 44 that before a licence is issued the applicant must deposit as a security certain amount as determined by the Director. Under section 45, the payment of royalty is required on forest produce taken from any permanent forest or alienated land. However, the same section provides that in the case of timber, no royalty is payable on such portions of a tree as may be declared to be unserviceable. No royalty is also payable on forest produce taken under a licence issued by the Director for any work of public utility, or other purposes to be specified in such licence. In addition to the payment of royalty, another type of payment required is the charge premium in respect of any forest produce taken under licence. According to section 46, any premium received on hill timber is to be credited to the State Consolidated Fund and accounted in the State Consolidated Revenue Account to be applied for the benefit of the natives in Sarawak. Other types of payment that are imposed under

910. Section 40 of the Sarawak Forests Ordinance 2015.

the Ordinance are the payment of cess which is credited into the State Consolidated Fund,[911] and payment of fees on forest produce based on rates specified in the Second and Third Schedules.[912] Different types of licence are required for the establishment of planted forests. Section 65 empowers the Director to grant a licence to any person to establish, maintain and harvest a crop of trees on land together with any ancillary rights of constructing thereon and using such roads, tracks, culverts, bridges and buildings and other facilities as may be necessary to establish, maintain and harvest the crop. All planted forests established under licence issued under section 65 will form part of the permanent forests.[913] However no licence for planted forests is granted over state land which native customary rights have been lawfully claimed by the natives.

§5. Logging

I. General Information

863. In Malaysia, timber is a source of income of the country and timber extraction is controlled by each state through a licensing mechanism under the National Forestry Act 1984. Under this Act, removal of forest produce is regulated by licences issued by the State Forest Departments. Information recorded in the licence includes serial number, name and address of the holder, the date of issue and expiry, a map and boundary description, logging prescriptions, the name and location of the checking station where the produce is to be measured, payment conditions and road standards.

864. As the sources of log production data, District Forest Offices keep records of all issued forest products harvesting licences. In addition, individual licence files contain data on production, forest charges, renewals and termination of licences. A removal pass, which carries a record of the type and volume of produce and the royalties and forest development cess, is issued for each consignment of forest products.

II. Illegal Logging

865. One main problem faced by Malaysia in managing its forest resources is illegal logging which happens in deep forests, where enforcement is difficult. However, specific provisions are available under the National Forestry Act 1985 to combat problems relating to illegal logging.

866. Under this Act, section 15 provides for severe punishments for illegal logging, imprisonment for up to twenty years and a maximum fine of 500,000 with a

911. Section 47 of the Sarawak Forests Ordinance 2015.
912. Section 48 of the Sarawak Forests Ordinance 2015.
913. Section 66 of the Sarawak Forests Ordinance 2015.

mandatory jail sentence of one year. This increased penalty was brought in by section 15(2) of the National Forestry (Amendment) Act 1993, with the prime object that the enhanced penalty would have sufficient deterrent effect to control illegal logging activities in the country.

867. Section 16 of the Act states that the timber rights in both permanent forest estates and state land forests may be transferred by the State Authority in any of three ways, namely, tendering, negotiation and other processes, such as grant or status.

868. Section 86 provides for a penalty for counterfeiting or defacing, or possessing implements for counterfeiting, marks on trees and timber and altering boundary marks. They include the following acts:

- knowingly counterfeiting upon any tree or timber, or having possession of any implement for counterfeiting, any mark used by forest officers;
- unlawfully or fraudulently affixing to any tree or timber any mark used by forest officers or any property mark;
- altering, defacing or obliterating any mark placed on any tree or timber by or under the authority of a forest officer; or
- altering, removing, destroying or defacing, any boundary mark of a permanent reserved forest or of any land proposed to be included in a permanent reserved forest.

869. Any person who commits offences under section 86, upon conviction, shall be liable to a fine not exceeding MYR 500,000 and to imprisonment for a term which shall not be less than one year but shall not exceed twenty years.

III. Environmental Quality Act 1974

870. Another relevant statute that can control illegal logging is the EQA 1974, through the application of EIAs under section 34A and the Environmental Quality (Prescribed Activities) (EIA) Order 2015.

871. Under the First and Second Schedule of this Order, clearing of forests requires the submission of the EIA report, whereby activities that fall under the Second Schedule require public display and public comment obtained in relation to that report. Under the First Schedule, EIA is required on land that comes under the following categories:

- forest area of 20 ha or more but less than 500 ha to turn it into agricultural production;
- conversion of forest at 300 m or more above mean sea level to other land use covering an area of 20 ha or more but less than 100 ha;
- logging, or cutting or taking of timber for the purpose of conversion from forest to other land use covering an area of 100 ha or more but less than 500 ha;

- logging, or cutting or taking of timber from forest at less than 300 m above mean sea level covering an area of 100 ha or more, outside permanent reserved forest;
- mangrove forest, peat swamp forest or fresh water swamp forest area of 20 ha or more but less than 50 ha to turn it into industrial, housing or agricultural use;
- forest covering an area of 100 ha or more but less than 500 ha for the development of planted forest; and
- coastal and hill area of 20 ha or more involving the construction of hill-station resort or hotel at 300 m or more above mean sea level.

Under the Second Schedule, the relevant land categories include:

- 500 ha or more of forest area to turn it into agricultural production;
- any state park, national park, national marine park, island surrounding marine park or environmentally sensitive area; involving the construction of aerodrome;
- 50 ha or more land adjacent or near to environmentally sensitive area; or any drainage of wetland, wildlife habitat or of dry inland forest covering an area of 20 ha or more involving the construction of man-made lakes and artificial enlargement of lakes with surface areas;
- mangrove forest, peat swamp forest or fresh water swamp forest covering an area of 50 ha or more involving land-based aquaculture projects;
- conversion of forest at 300 m or more above mean sea level to other land use covering an area of 100 ha or more;
- logging or conversion of forest to other land use within a catchment area of reservoirs used for municipal water supply, irrigation or hydropower; an area adjacent or near to any state park, national park or national marine park; any state park, national park or national marine park; or an area gazetted as water catchment forest under the National Forestry Act 1984;
- forest area of 100 ha or more, outside permanent reserved forest for logging, or cutting or taking of timber from forest at 300 m or more above mean sea level;
- forest area of 500 ha or more for logging, or cutting or taking of timber;
- forest area of 500 ha or more development of planted forest;
- mangrove forest; peat swamp forest; or fresh water swamp forest area of 50 ha or more for industrial, housing or agricultural use;
- clearing of mangrove forest, peat swamp forest or fresh water swamp forest on islands adjacent to any national marine park; and
- mining of minerals within or adjacent or near to environmentally sensitive area;
- development in coastal area, national park and state park.

IV. International Law

872. Malaysia is a member of the International Tropical Timber Organization (ITTO) and adopts the ITTO's Guidelines for Sustainable Forest Management of Natural Tropical Forests, and its criteria for the measurement of sustainable tropical forest management.[914]

873. For implementing the ITTO guidelines, the Ministry of Primary Industries has formulated the Malaysia Criteria and Indicators for Sustainable Forest Management, based on the ITTO Criteria and Indicators.

874. The Malaysia Criteria and Indicators for Sustainable Forest Management are formulated for two levels of operations, one at the national level, and the other at the forest management level. In 1998, the federal government established the Malaysian Timber Certification Council to implement the timber certification scheme in Malaysia.

914. Refer to Abdul Haseeb Ansari, *Legal Issues in Forest Management in India and Malaysia: A Critical Appraisal*, 2 MLJ xxi (2004).

Chapter 7. Subsoil and Minerals

§1. General Information

875. The significance of minerals in contributing towards the economic development of Malaysia from the early years of the twentieth century is immense.[915]

876. One of the most important mineral resources is tin. Malaysia has a long-established mining tradition, based on the production of alluvial tin deposits in the coastal plain areas of Peninsular Malaysia. Malaysia was the world's biggest tin exporter. The collapse of the world tin markets in the 1980s led to the decline in Malaysia's tin mining industry. Apart from tin, Malaysia is endowed with a wide range of other minerals, such as gold, copper and iron.[916]

§2. The Constitution

877. Under the Federal Constitution, matters pertaining to mineral resources can be found in all the legislative lists. Under List I, Federal List, relevant matters include development of mineral resources such as mines, mining and minerals. However, matters such as permits and licences for prospecting for mines come under List II, State List. Under List III, Concurrent List, relevant matter is the rehabilitation of mining land which has suffered soil erosion.

878. Under the Federal Constitution, ownership of mineral resources is based on the position of land matters, and this comes under List II, State List of the Federal Constitution. Thus, all minerals within the boundaries of a state are vested solely in the State Authority, whereas all minerals outside the mineral jurisdiction of the state, but within the outer limits of the continental shelf or exclusive economic zone of Malaysia, are vested solely in the federal government.

879. Similarly, the power to issue exploration and mining rights on land in the federal territories is within the sole jurisdiction of the federal government, whereas the power to issue exploration and mining rights for all areas within state boundaries, including permanent reserved land, is within the sole jurisdiction of the respective State Authority.

880. In Malaysia, the main agency empowered with matters pertaining to mineral resources is the Mineral and Geoscience Department under the Ministry of Energy and Natural Resources. The main functions of this Department are mineral

915. *The Encyclopedia of Malaysia: Volume I: The Environment* 22–23 (Sham Sani ed., Archipelago Press 1998).
916. *Smart Partnerships: Key to Sustainable Mineral Resources Development* (Long, Ghiathuddin, et al. eds, Malay. Quarries Assn. Inst. Quarrying Malay. 2005).

exploration, mineral economics, mine enforcement, geological mapping, hydrogeology, engineering geology, environmental geology, information management, laboratory-field-consultancy services and research and development activities with special focus on minerals.

881. The federal government, through the then MNRE, also set up the National Mineral Policy 2 in 2009. Its main objectives are to ensure the sustainable development and optimum utilization of mineral resources; to promote environmental stewardship that will ensure the nation's mineral resources are developed in an environmentally sound, responsible and sustainable manner; to enhance the nation's mineral sector competitiveness and advancement in the global arena; to ensure the use of local minerals and promote the further development of mineral-based products; and to encourage the recovery, recycling and reuse of metals and minerals.[917]

882. The National Mineral Policy provides the foundation for the development of an effective, efficient and competitive regulatory environment for the mineral sector. While the policy aims to expand and diversify the mineral sector through optimum exploration, exploitation and utilization of Malaysia's resources, maximum use of research and development and modern technology, emphasis is also given to environmental protection and sustainable development, as well as the management of social impact. The salient features of the policy include security of tenure, favourable fiscal regimes, high-priority land use for mining, a uniform and efficient institutional framework, and transparent guidelines and regulations.

§3. Legal Framework

I. The Mineral Development Act 1994

883. The Mineral Development Act 1994[918] provides for the inspection and regulation of the exploration and mining of minerals and mineral ores. Specifically, this Act applies to the fossicking, panning, prospecting, exploring, mining and processing of minerals and mineral ores and to mines, minerals and mineral ores generally.[919]

884. Under this Act, the term 'mine', when used as a noun, means 'any place, excavation or working wherein, whereon or whereby any operation connected with mining is carried on together with all buildings, premises, erections, water reservoirs, tailing ponds, waste, other dumps and appliances belonging or appertaining

917. The complete National Mineral Policy 2 statement is available at the Department of Mineral and Geoscience Department's official website at http://www.jmg.gov.my/en/38-mengenai-kami/dasar-jabatan/19-dasar-mineral-negara-2, August 2016.

918. Act 525.

919. Section 2 of the Mineral Development Act 1994.

thereto above or below the ground or in or below the sea for the purpose of winning, obtaining or extracting any mineral by any mode or method or for the purpose of dressing, treating or preparing mineral ores'.

885. The term 'mineral' is defined as 'any substance whether in solid, liquid or gaseous form occurring naturally; as a result of mining in or on the earth; or as a result of mining in or under the sea or sea-bed, formed by or subject to a geological process, but excludes water, "rock material" as defined in the National Land Code 1965[920] and "petroleum" as defined in the Petroleum Mining Act 1966'.[921]

886. Part II of the Act is on administration. Under this Part, section 5 provides for functions and duties of the DG, namely:

- to be responsible for the administration and enforcement of this Act;
- to exercise supervision and control on the safety aspects relating to mines and to the fossicking, panning, exploration, mining, possession, movement, storage and processing of minerals and mineral ores in accordance with this Act;
- to obtain information on and keep records of operations pertaining to the fossicking, panning, exploration, mining, possession, movement, storage, processing, purchase and sale of minerals and mineral ores;
- to perform such functions in relation to this Act as the Minister may from time to time determine; and
- to carry on such other activities as may appear to the DG requisite, advantageous or convenient for carrying out the provisions of this Act.

887. Section 13 requires that fossicking, panning, exploration, mining and mineral processing shall be carried out in accordance with good and safe practices and such environmental standards as may be prescribed under this Act, as well as any written law relating to the environment.

888. Requirements on effluent water are provided in section 18. Under this section, any holder of a proprietary mining licence who uses water in connection with mining shall take such measures so as to ensure that the water so used shall, before it leaves the mine or waste retention area in which it has been used, comply with water quality standards and shall be reasonably free of solid matter and from chemicals and other substances deleterious to human, animal or vegetable life.

889. Requirements on erosion are provided in section 19, which requires every person who undertakes fossicking, panning, exploration or mining to take measures as are reasonable to prevent or minimize the erosion of the land which is the subject of the mineral tenement.

920. Act 56.
921. Act 95.

890. Matters pertaining to enforcement, investigation, evidence, offences and penalties are provided in Part V of the Act. The penalty for various offences is provided in section 39. It states that any person who contravenes or fails to comply with the provisions of sections 9, 11, 13–19 or 20 of this Act shall be guilty of an offence. Section 54 provides for a general penalty for offences which have no specified penalty. Under this section, a person may be liable to a fine not exceeding MYR 50,000, to imprisonment for a term not exceeding three years, or both.

II. Geological Survey Act 1974

891. The Geological Survey Act 1974[922] was enacted to regulate and control geological surveys and to establish geological archives. Under this Act, 'geological survey' means 'any systematic investigation of the surface, or content of the earth with or without the aid of any physical or chemical measurement'.

892. The term 'mineral' means 'any natural occurring homogeneous substance with a definite chemical composition and an ordered atomic arrangement'. Whereas 'rock material' is defined as 'any rock, stone, marble, gravel, sand, earth, laterite, loam, clay, soil, mud, turf, peat, coral, shell or guano within or upon any land'.

893. Part II of the Act is on administration. Section 3 provides for the appointment of a Director General of Geological Survey and his deputies, to carry out the purposes of this Act. Part III deals with geological surveys. The powers of a Geological Survey Officer is provided in section 8, namely:

- to enter upon any land within the designated area;
- to cut, remove or otherwise clear such uncultivated vegetation as may be necessary for the proper conduct of such survey;
- to erect or emplace such pegs and marks as may be necessary for the proper conduct of such survey;
- to conduct a superficial geological survey;
- to conduct an artificial geophysical survey;
- to bore, drill, fracture, dig or pit over the land; and
- to obtain and remove any specimen or sample from the land in furtherance of such survey and to remove and dispose of as he deems fit such superficial or cognate material as may be necessary to obtain the specimen or sample.

894. Part IV of the Act relates to general obligations relating to geological surveys and applies to all persons other than Geological Survey Officers and authorized persons.

895. In a situation where any person conducting a geological survey or prospecting finds any fossiliferous material, section 12 requires that he shall immediately notify the DG of such details as may from time to time be prescribed.

922. Act 129.

Similarly, under section 13, any person who bores, drills, digs or otherwise develops a well for searching for or extracting water therefrom shall notify the DG of such details as may from time to time be prescribed.

896. A general penalty is provided in section 18(1) which states that any person who contravenes any provision of this Act or who fails to comply with any lawful direction, notice, condition or restriction imposed thereunder, shall be guilty of an offence and shall on conviction be liable to a fine not exceeding MYR 10,000, and in addition to a fine of MYR 50 a day for every day during which the contravention or failure continues. Under section 18(2), where no other penalty is specifically provided in any regulations made under this Act, any person who contravenes the provisions of such regulations shall be guilty of an offence against this Act and shall, on conviction, be liable to a fine not exceeding MYR 5,000 and, in addition, to a fine of MYR 25 a day for every day during which the contravention continues.

III. Petroleum Mining Act 1966

897. The Petroleum Mining Act 1966[923] was enacted to make provisions on matters pertaining to mining for petroleum. The enactment of this Act repealed the earlier statutes on oil prospecting licences and oil mining leases, namely:

- the Mining Enactments of the States in Peninsular Malaysia;[924]
- the Mining Ordinance of Sabah 1960;[925]
- the Oil Mining Ordinance of Sarawak;[926] and
- any other state law in force in Sabah or Sarawak relating to mining.

These, in fact, continue to remain in force, except in relation to the exploration, prospecting or mining for petroleum in offshore land and the provisions of the said Ordinances and any such law, so far as they relate to the exploration, prospecting or mining for petroleum in offshore land, are deemed to have been repealed.

898. Section 3(1) of the Act provides restrictions on petroleum exploring, prospecting and mining. It prohibits any person from exploring, prospecting or mining for petroleum upon any land except by virtue of an exploration licence or a petroleum agreement. Under section 3(2), any person who acts in contravention of this section may be fined up to MYR 20,000, imprisoned for a term not exceeding two years, or both.

923. Act 95, revised 1972.
924. F.M.S. Cap. 147, J. No. 69, K. No. 67, Kn. 10/1939, Ps. 1/1340, Tr. 51/1356.
925. Order 20 of 1960.
926. Cap. 85.

899. Section 10(1) prohibits commencement, abandonment and plugging of wells. It states that the licensee shall not commence or, after abandoning in a manner provided in the Act, shall not recommence the drilling of any well, without the consent, in writing, of the Petroleum Authority.

900. Prohibition on the cutting of timber is provided in section 13. It states that the licensee shall not cut or take any timber or protected tree except with the consent of the appropriate authority and on payment of the fees and royalties prescribed by law. Under section 13(2), if the licensee cuts down or takes any other productive tree, he shall pay fair and adequate compensation to the owner thereof.

901. Prohibitions on fishing and navigation are provided in section 14. It states that the licensee shall not carry out any operations authorized by this licence in or about the exploration area in such manner as, in the opinion of the Petroleum Authority, may interfere unjustifiably with navigation or fishing in the waters of the exploration area, or with the conservation of the living resources of the sea.

902. Section 7(5) requires that an exploration licence shall be in the form set out in the Second Schedule. Under this schedule, 'exploration area' means the area of offshore/onshore land specified in the schedule, and where part of that area has ceased to be the subject of the licence in accordance with its terms and conditions, the area as thereby reduced.

Part III. Zoning and Land-Use Planning

§1. General Information

903. Considering that a complex system of government applies in Malaysia, land policy and planning systems need to be implemented within a broader framework and under the supervision of the federal government for uniformity.

904. In Malaysia, land policy has been the result of various successive legislative documents which have been created to overcome numerous land-related issues. This is due to the fact that land is a state matter under the Federal Constitution, allowing each state the prerogative of drawing up its own land policy. At the local government level, there exists further land policy which is based on the state land policy.

§2. Planning Coordination

I. The Constitution

905. Matters pertaining to zoning and land-use planning are not specifically provided in the legislative lists of the Federal Constitution. However, under List II, State List, states are empowered to enact laws on matters pertaining to land, agriculture, forestry and local government, outside the Federal territories of Kuala Lumpur, Putrajaya and Labuan. Under List III, Concurrent List, both the federal and the state governments have the power to legislate regarding town and country planning.

906. For the purposes of coordination and uniformity of policy and law on land matters, Article 91 of the Federal Constitution provides for the establishment of a National Land Council, comprising state representatives, with a federal minister as chairman. The main function of this Council is to formulate a national policy for the promotion and control of the utilization of land throughout the country for mining, agriculture, forestry and any other related purpose, in consultation with the federal and state governments.

907. By virtue of Article 91, the federal government is provided with considerable constitutional powers to undertake national development planning. The Federal Constitution mandates that the federal and state governments follow the policy formulated by the Council.

II. Level of Coordination

A. Federal

908. In Malaysia, there are four levels of coordination within the development planning framework. At the highest level is the Parliament, which enacts federal laws, together with the National Action Council established at the federal level as a coordination and evaluation unit with powers to formulate policies.[927]

909. The second level is the National Development Planning Committee, the functions of which are to consult the National Land Council, National Finance Council, and federal and state governments, before it formulates national policy and makes recommendations to the National Action Council. The committee is comprised of various representatives of ministries and autonomous bodies, and it establishes a link between ministries and relevant agencies, such as the Economic Planning Unit, and the Implementation and Coordination Unit, both under the Prime Minister's Department.

910. The third level of the hierarchy consists of federal ministries and various autonomous bodies, which are responsible for preparing and proposing sectoral strategies. The fourth level is the state level, comprising state and local governments and their agencies. At this level, the sectoral policies which have been decided upon are translated into more detailed instruments for implementation. The state governments perform a regulatory function and ensure that the local authorities carry out the programmes.

B. State

911. The implementation of land policy which is decided at the first level, takes place at the fourth level of the hierarchy. The state is responsible for the general land-use policy in all local authorities within the state. Thus, within the framework of the national policy, each state carries out its land-use planning functions through State Planning Committees and Local Planning Authorities.

912. Strategic implementation of the national development plans is represented by a 'regional development plan' and a 'structure planning system' introduced by the Town and Country Planning Act 1976 and implemented by the local government within its locality. The structure plan and local plan system introduced by the Act constitute a planning vehicle which carries out the following functions, namely:

- to translate national social, economic and physical policies and objectives into a physical development strategy for the state or parts of the state; and

927. Jabatan Perancangan Bandar dan Desa Semenanjung Malaysia, *Garis Panduan Laporan Cadangan Pemajuan [Akta Perancangan Bandar dan Desa 1976]* (Jabatan Perancangan Bandar dan Desa Semenanjung Malaysia 1998).

- to provide the framework for the production of more detailed local land-use plans to guide the agencies concerned with implementation.

913. The states of Sabah and Sarawak have their own individual land policy and planning instruments, distinct from the states in Peninsular Malaysia as provided in Article 95D of the Federal Constitution.

§3. Institutional Framework

914. In Malaysia, the main agency dealing with town and country planning is the federal Town and Country Planning Department, under the Ministry of Housing and Local Government.[928] This Department has the power to formulate and administer policies pertaining to town and country planning nationally, while the state Department of Town and Country Planning serves as an advisory body of the state government.[929]

915. General powers of the local authorities in Malaysia are provided by the Act, including matters pertaining to land-use planning such as:

- local planning authority, including the development planning and control and management functions such as building control, land-use planning, development, creation of industrial estates, etc.;
- licensing authority;
- performance of urban planning and management functions;
- traffic management and control (managing urban public transport systems); and
- power to plan and provide public utilities.

916. The process of land-use control through the Town and Country Planning Act 1976 involves the preparation of the structure plan – a policy document which is approved by the state, and a detailed local plan, which is a map-based plan outlining physical details translating the policies in the structure plan. The local planning authority produces both plans, whereby eventually, the whole country has comprehensive structure plans and local plans.[930]

§4. Town and Country Planning Act 1976

917. In 1976, the Town and Country Planning Act 1976[931] was enacted pursuant to clause (1) of Article 74, clause (4) of Article 76 and clause (2) of Article 80 of

928. For details, *see* the official website at http://www.kpkt.gov.my/, January 2014.
929. *See also* Town Planning Department at http://www.townplan.gov.my/ and Local Government Department at http://jkt.kpkt.gov.my/en/main.php, January 2014.
930. *See* Lynette Taye, *Key Features of the Town and Country Planning (Amendment) Act 2001 – An Analysis of the Impact of the Recent Key Amendments to the Town and Country Planning Act 1976*, 4 MLJ lxv (2002).
931. Act 172.

the Federal Constitution. The main purposes of the enactment are to ensure uniformity of law and policy, to make a law for the proper control and regulation of town and country planning, and to overcome the prior deficiencies of land-use planning for Malaysia.[932]

918. By virtue of the enactment of this Act, existing planning laws were repealed, namely:[933]

- Part IX of the Town Boards Enactment of the Federated Malay States;[934]
- Part IX of the Town Boards Enactment of the State of Johore;[935]
- Part VIA of the Municipal Enactment of the State of Kelantan;[936] and
- Part IX of the Town Boards Enactment of the State of Terengganu.[937]

919. The Town and Country Planning Act 1976 concerns the proper control and regulation of town and country planning through the formulation and identification of a 'structure plan' and a 'local plan'. It stipulates that every local authority shall be the local planning authority. This gave the local authorities the primary physical planning responsibility at a local level, via the local Government Act 1976.

920. The structure plans are the general proposals of the local planning authority for development and the use of the land. They are normally prepared by the federal Town and Country Planning Department and put up for the adoption of the various states. The local plan takes the form of a zoning, density or layout plan, of varying detail, indicating exactly what a landowner can or cannot do with his land.

921. Under this Act, the term 'local plan', in relation to an area, means 'the local plan for the area, and any alteration of the plan, for the time being having effect in the area by virtue of section 15(1)'.

922. In relation to any land or building, 'local plan' means 'the local plan, as so defined, for the area in which the land or building is situated'; and 'draft local plan' shall be construed as the context requires.

923. The term 'structure plan', in relation to an area, means the structure plan for the area, and any alteration of the plan, having effect in the area by virtue of section 10(6); and, in relation to any land or building, means the structure plan, as so defined, for the area in which the land or building is situated; and 'draft structure plan' shall be construed as the context requires.

---

932. *See*, Abdul Haseeb Ansari & Ismawi Zen, *Towards A Sustainable Land Use Planning: An Appraisal With Special Reference to Malaysia*, 6 MLJ cvii (2006).
933. Section 59 of the Town and Country Planning Act 1976.
934. Cap. 137.
935. En. No. 118.
936. 20/1938.
937. Terengganu 12/1355.

924. Another relevant term, 'use', in relation to any land, means 'any use of the land other than merely for the keeping or storage of materials and equipment intended to be employed in the construction or erection of a building on the land, or as a site for temporary buildings for the accommodation of workers involved in the construction or erection of the building'.

925. Part II of the Act relates to policy and administration. Section 2A under this part provides for the establishment of a National Physical Planning Council which consists of the following members:

- a Chairman, being the Prime Minister;
- a Deputy Chairman, being the Deputy Prime Minister;
- the Minister;
- the Minister responsible for housing and local government, if he is not also the Minister responsible for town and country planning;
- the Minister of Finance;
- the Minister responsible for land;
- the Menteri Besar or Chief Minister of every State;
- the Minister responsible for the Federal Territory; and
- not more than seven other members to be appointed by the Chairman.

926. The functions of the Council are provided in section 2A(2), which are as follows:

- to promote in the country, within the framework of the national policy, town and country planning as an effective and efficient instrument for the improvement of the physical environment and towards the achievement of sustainable development in the country;
- to advise the Federal Government or the Government of any state on matters relating to the town and country planning required under this Act; and
- to perform any other functions conferred upon the Council under this Act.

927. Section 2B provides for the appointment of a Director General of Town and Country Planning whose functions shall be as follows:

- to conduct, promote and coordinate research in relation to any aspect of town and country planning;
- to publish reports, bulletins, statistics, monographs and other publications relating to town and country planning and its methodology;
- to provide information and education to the public regarding town and country planning;
- to report to and advise the Council upon matters concerning the use of town and country planning in the conservation, use and development of lands in the country and upon any amendments he thinks desirable to any law affecting town and country planning and upon any matters referred to him by the Council; and
- to establish and maintain liaison and cooperation with each of the State Authorities with respect to town and country planning.

928. At the state level, the State Planning Committee is established under section 4(1) and consists of the following members:

- a Chairman, being the Menteri Besar or Chief Minister of the State;
- a Deputy Chairman, being a member of the State Executive Council, to be appointed by the State Authority;
- not more than three members to be appointed by the State Authority from among the members of the State Executive Council, at least one of whom shall be the member responsible for and whose portfolio is related to town and country planning in the state;
- the State Secretary;
- the State Director shall be the Secretary of the Committee;
- the State Director of Lands and Mines;
- the Director of the State Economic Planning Unit or an officer responsible for such affairs in the State;
- the State Director of Public Works;
- the State Legal Adviser;
- the State Financial Officer;
- the State Development Officer or an officer responsible for such affairs in the state;
- the State Director of Environment or an officer responsible for such affairs in the state; and
- not more than four other members to be appointed by the State Authority.

929. The functions of the State Planning Committee are provided in section 4(4), namely:

- to promote in the state, within the framework of the national policy, the conservation, use and development of all lands in the state;
- to regulate, control, plan and coordinate all development activities in the state;
- to advise the State Government, either on its own initiative or in response to a request by the State Government, on matters relating to the conservation, use, and development of land in the state; and
- to undertake, assist in, and encourage the collection, maintenance, and publication of statistics, bulletins, and monographs, and other publications relating to town and country planning and its methodology.

930. Section 5 of the Act provides that every local authority shall be the local planning authority for the area of the local authority. Their functions as provided for in section 6 are as follows:

- to regulate, control, and plan the development and use of all lands and buildings within its area;
- to undertake, assist in, and encourage the collection, maintenance, and publication of statistics, bulletins, and monographs, and other publications relating to town and country planning and its methodology; and

– to perform such other functions as the State Authority or the Committee may from time to time assign to it.

931. Another body established under this Act is the Regional Planning Committee under section 6A(1) which consists of the following members:

– a Chairman, who is appointed by the Prime Minister;
– six persons representing the Federal Government, at least four of whom shall be public officers, appointed by the Minister;
– not more than four persons representing the Government of each of the states within the region, appointed by the State Authority, one of whom shall be the State Director; and
– the President of every local planning authority within the region if such authority is a local authority.

932. Matters pertaining to the national physical plan are provided in section 6A. Under section 6A(1), the Director General of Town and Country Planning is empowered to prepare and submit to the Council for its approval a draft national physical plan which covers Peninsular Malaysia. Section 6A(3) requires that when preparing the draft national physical plan and determining its contents for submission to the Council, the Director General of Town and Country Planning shall take into consideration the current national urbanization policy or other similar policies and shall consult with every State Authority and such other authorities or bodies as the Council may direct.

933. Part III of the Act deals with development plans. Section 7 in this part empowers the State Director to institute a survey of the state, examining the matters that may be expected to affect the development, or the planning of the development, of the state, and shall in any event keep all those matters under review.

934. Section 8 deals with the preparation of draft structure plans. It requires that the draft structure plan for the state shall be a written statement addressing the following matters:

– formulating the policy and general proposals of the State Authority in respect of the development and use of land in that state, including measures for the improvement of the physical living environment, the improvement of communications, the management of traffic, the improvement of socio-economic well-being and the promotion of economic growth, and for facilitating sustainable development;
– stating the relationship of those proposals to general proposals for the development and use of land in the neighbouring areas that may be expected to affect that area; and
– containing such other matters as may be prescribed, or as the Council or Committee may in any particular case specify.

935. Matters pertaining to the preparation of draft local plans are provided in section 12. Section 2(3) stipulates that a draft local plan shall consist of a map and a written statement and shall contain proposals relating to the area of the local plan, addressing:

- development;
- use of land;
- protection and improvement of the physical environment;
- preservation of the natural topography;
- improvement of the landscape;
- preservation and planting of trees;
- making up open spaces;
- preservation and enhancement of the character and appearance of buildings;
- improvement of communications in; and
- management of traffic.

936. Issues pertaining to approval and rejection of draft local plans are stated in section 15. Under section 15(1A), the Committee may, after considering a draft local plan submitted to it, either approve it, in whole or in part and with or without modifications, or reject it. Under section 15(1C), the Committee then submits the approved draft local plan to the State Authority for the assent of the State Authority, and upon the assent being given, the plan shall come into effect.

§5. OTHER LEGISLATION

I. National Land Code 1965

937. In Malaysia, the National Land Code 1965[938] is the main law relating to land matters and contains provisions relevant to zoning and land-use planning.

938. Land is a state matter under the Federal Constitution. Thus, individual land offices established throughout the states have strong control over land development. This control is derived from the powers conferred by the National Land Code 1965 and takes the form of land subdivision, imposition of special conditions, restrictions-in-interest and category of land use on land titles.

939. Express permission of the State Authority is required before leasehold land can be sold or transferred. This is to ensure that land is not transferred to foreigners and non-Malay individuals and companies freely in states where an implied policy exists to ensure that the local population retain ownership of land.

940. Under the National Land Code 1965, categories of land use, and application thereof to lands alienated under this Act are provided in section 52(1). It states

938. Act 56.

that, for this Act, there shall be three categories of land use, to be known respectively as 'agriculture', 'building' and 'industry'.

941. Section 51 further classifies land as follows:

- 'town land', that is to say, land in any area of the state declared in accordance with the provisions of section 11 to be a town or, by virtue of section 442, deemed to be a town duly constituted as such under those provisions;
- 'village land', that is to say, land in any area of the state declared in accordance with the provisions of section 11 to be a village or, by virtue of section 442, deemed to be a village duly constituted as such under those provisions; and
- 'country land', that is to say, all land above the shoreline other than town land and village land.

942. Under section 52(2), the State Authority may specify any area of the state, and prescribe a category of land use in relation thereto for the purposes of this section.

943. All categories of land use under the National Land Code have to be developed within stipulated periods, which are normally endorsed on the titles. For land with the 'building' category, it must be developed within two years of alienation. For industrial land, the period is three years. If a breach of this condition occurs, the land is liable to forfeiture without compensation.

II. Land Acquisition Act 1960

944. Other relevant legislations on matters pertaining to zoning and land-use planning is the Land Acquisition Act 1960[939] which relates to the acquisition of land by the state government, the assessment of compensation to be made on account of such acquisition and other matters incidental thereto.

945. Under this Act, the state government could acquire land for a specific public purpose. Land could also be acquired for mining, residential, commercial or industrial purposes. The framework allows the government to take possession of the land, even if the compensation is being appealed in court. There are also provisions in the Act allowing the state government to Gazette large areas in which the land is to be acquired, thereby 'freezing' all land transactions in the area.

946. In 1991, section 3 of the Act was amended to provide for the compulsory acquisition of land for any purpose deemed beneficial to the economic development of Malaysia, to the public or any class of the public.

947. Specifically under section 3 on the acquisition of land, the State Authority may acquire any land which is needed for the following purposes:

939. Act 486, revised 1992.

- for any public purpose;
- by any person or corporation for any purpose which, in the opinion of the State Authority, is beneficial to the economic development of Malaysia or any part thereof or to the public generally or any class of the public; or
- for mining or for residential agricultural, commercial, industrial or recreational purposes or any combination of such purposes.

948. Under section 3A, the State Economic Planning Unit, or the Committee for the Federal Territory of Kuala Lumpur, as the case may be, shall consider the application, with regard to the following factors:

- public interest;
- the capacity and capability of the applicant to carry out the purpose for which the land is to be acquired;
- the feasibility of the project; and
- the development approval granted to the registered proprietor.

949. Under section 3A(2), where a development approval is granted in respect of any land, and the acquisition is for the purpose of a public utility, the State Economic Planning Unit, or the Committee for the Federal Territory of Kuala Lumpur, as the case may be, shall determine whether it is appropriate in the circumstances for the registered proprietor to participate in the project for which the land is intended to be acquired.

950. For the purposes of this Act, there shall be established a Committee to be known as the '*Jawatankuasa Khas Pengambilan Tanah*'. Section 3C provides that, in the case of a state, the Committee consists of the following members, namely: the State Secretary, as Chairman; the State Director of Lands and Mines, as Secretary; the Director of the State Economic Planning Unit or his representative; the State Director of Town and Country Planning or his representative; and representatives of other related Government departments or agencies as may be determined by the Chairman.

951. In the Federal Territory of Kuala Lumpur, section 3C provides that the Committee consists of the following members, namely: the Director General of the Economic Planning Unit or his representative, as Chairman; the Under Secretary of the Federal Territory Development and Klang Valley Planning Division, Prime Minister's Department; a representative of the Economic Planning Unit, as Secretary; the Land Administrator of the Federal Territory; the Director General of Lands and Mines or his representative; the Commissioner of the City of Kuala Lumpur or his representative; and representatives of other related Government departments or agencies as may be determined by the Chairman.

952. Under section 3E, on receiving the application, the State Authority may approve or reject the application. Under section 4, whenever the State Authority is satisfied that any land in any locality in the state is likely to be needed for any of the purposes referred to in section 3, a notification in Form A shall be published in the Gazette.

§6. Malay Reservations

953. Article 89 of the Federal Constitution deals with Malay reservations. The definition of a 'Malay reservation' is 'land reserved for alienation to Malays or to natives of the State in which it lies' as set out in Article 89(6).

954. Under the same article, 'Malay' includes 'any person who, under the law of the State in which he is resident, is treated as a Malay for the purposes of the reservation of land'.

955. Article 89 in general seeks to ensure that certain land in the state is alienated only to Malays, and that the land thus alienated or any interest in it will continue to remain in the hands of Malays. Only a Malay may own land or possess an interest in a Malay Reservation area. A Malay Holding includes any registered interest of a Malay proprietor or co-proprietor in any alienated land included in a Malay Reservation Area which has been duly declared and gazetted. Once land is gazetted as a Malay reservation, it can only be sold, leased or otherwise disposed to Malay individuals or corporations.

956. Specifically, Article 89(1) provides that any land in a state which immediately before Merdeka Day was a Malay reservation in accordance with the existing law, may continue as a Malay reservation in accordance with that law until otherwise provided by an enactment of the legislature of that state.

957. Under Article 89(2), any land in a state which is not for the time being a Malay reservation in accordance with the existing law and has not been developed or cultivated, may be declared as a Malay reservation in accordance with that law, provided that:

- where any land in a state is declared a Malay reservation, an equal area of land in that state which has not been developed or cultivated shall be made available for general alienation; and
- the total area of land in a state for the time being declared as a Malay reservation shall not at any time exceed the total area of land in that state which has been made available for general alienation.

958. Article 89(3) empowers the government of any state to declare as a Malay reservation the following lands:

- any land acquired by that government by agreement for that purpose; and
- on the application of the proprietor, and with the consent of every person having a right or interest therein, any other land.

Where any land ceases to be a Malay reservation, the state government must, in accordance with the existing law, immediately declare as a Malay reservation, any other land of a similar character and of an area not exceeding the area of that land.

959. Under Article 89(5), the government of any state may, in accordance with law, acquire land for the settlement of Malays or other communities, and establish trusts for that purpose.

Part IV. Liability Questions

Chapter 1. Introduction

960. This part deals with substantive rules on liability for environmental matters. They include environmental civil liability based on the principles of the law of torts or case law, environmental criminal liability, and administrative liability under statute law.

961. The liability issues to be discussed in this part relate to a large extent to other parts of this monograph, especially the specific sectoral legislation concerning pollution control in Part I and environmental conservation in Part II.

962. In Malaysia, provisions on environmental criminal law are mostly included within environmental statutes regulating pollution control and environmental conservation. Similarly, important aspects of administrative law such as licensing requirements and remedies are also included as provisions within statutory laws and were already discussed in other parts of this monograph.

963. Similar to other countries with a federal system of government, environmental liabilities are scattered, mainly because Malaysian environmental law is largely decentralized in nature, with both federal and state governments having jurisdiction over environmental matters.

964. In Malaysia, tort principles are mainly relied upon for environmental civil liability, as public access to environmental justice within statute law in Malaysia is very limited.[940] However, environmental criminal liability is regulated by statutes, and it comes within the jurisdiction of the federal government, as provided by the Federal Constitution. Thus, environmental criminal matters, including criminal procedures, are regulated uniformly by federal laws.

940. *See* Maizatun Mustafa, *Clean Water: Right and Remedies Under Environmental Law in Malaysia*, in *Integrated Water Resources Management in Malaysia: Experiences and Practices* (Ann Anton et al. eds, Malaysian Water Partnership 2004); and Maizatun Mustafa, *Public Access to Environmental Rights and Justice: A Legal Perspective for an Improved Public Service System of the Local Authorities*, in *Service Delivery by Local Authorities: Issues and Challenges* (Worran Kabut et al. eds (compilers), UPENA 2006).

Chapter 2. Civil Liability

§1. Introduction

965. English common law, which is applicable throughout Malaysia, provides a venue for the public to seek a remedy, directly, for injury inflicted upon them by polluters.[941]

966. The authority for the application of the English common law in Malaysia is provided in sections 3 and 5 of the Civil Law Act 1956,[942] which allow the courts to apply common law in certain circumstances. Common law remedies, in the form of tort principles, are available to any person who has suffered injury as a result of environmental pollution. Civil litigation in respect of environmentally related matters can be established based on these principles.

967. However, it is to be noted that in Malaysia, environmental litigation, either deriving from case law or statute, is rather infrequent. Until now, only a small number of environmental cases have been brought to court, especially under statute laws.[943]

968. Among the reasons for this problem are limited access to environmental justice provided in statute law, and the difficulty in establishing the strict requirement of *locus standi* limiting the number of environmental cases being brought to the Malaysian court.

§2. Liability for Negligence

969. In Malaysia, the rule of negligence is widely applicable within tort, although it is rarely used for environmental protection, as the utility of bringing an environmental action under this rule is rather limited.

970. In order to succeed in an action of negligence, the plaintiff must show that there has been some fault on behalf of the defendant. The plaintiff must also prove several other requirements, such as: that the defendant was under a duty to take reasonable care to avoid the damage complained of; that there was a breach of this duty; and that the breach of duty caused the damage. The rule on negligence originates from the judgment of Lord Atkin in the case of *Donoghue v. Stevenson*.[944]

---

941. *See Environmental Protection and the Common Law* (John Lowry & Rod Edmunds eds, Hart 2000). *See also*, Andrew Harding, *Do Public Interest Environmental Law and the Common Law Have a Future Together?*, in *Public Interest Perspectives in Environmental Law* (D. Robinson & J. Dunkley eds, Wiley Chancery 1995); and Abdul Haseeb Ansari, *Environmental Protection Through The Law of Torts: A Critical Appraisal*, 4 MLJ lxxxi (2000).
942. Act 67.
943. *See* Janet Looi, *Environmental Issues: Major Case Law and Environmental Management*, 3 MLJ cclxxxvii (2002).
944. (1932) AC 562.

971. McGowan & Anor. v. Wong Shee Fun & Anor[945] was an environmental Malaysian case applying the principle of negligence. In this case, the first defendant was the owner and developer of the land. The second defendant was the owner and developer of land adjacent to the first defendant's land. The plaintiff alleged that the defendants had indiscriminately stripped off the top soil of their land and so caused and allowed the stream to become silted due to the erosion of the land, thus causing flooding that caused damage to the plaintiff's land.

In addition, the first defendant had constructed, across the river, a culvert which was inadequate to cope with the water that was likely to flow down the stream during or after a heavy rainfall. The court held that both the defendants were negligent for not having taken all reasonable steps to prevent fine earth from being washed down the sides of the slopes into the stream.

972. In the case of *Guan Soon Tin Mining Co. v. Wong Fook Kum,*[946] an appeal was made against the High Court's judgment alleging that the appellants were negligent in causing pollution of a fish pond of the respondent, by discharging tailings thereto from their adjacent mine. From the evidence, the court found that there was no direct or traceable relation of the cause and effect between the appellants' conduct and the respondent's loss. The court also found no evidence to show that the death of fish was due to pollution of water by the appellants' mining operation. In addition, the fact that the respondent himself stocked the pond again after the alleged discharge, was sufficient to negate the appellants' responsibility, and it was held that the appellants were not guilty of negligence.

§3. Strict Liability

I. Introduction

973. In Malaysia, rules relating to strict liability have been established both under common law and statute law.

974. Under common law, the strict liability principle relevant to environmental matters can be found in the rule on *Rylands v. Fletcher*. Under statute law, certain provisions within the EQA 1974 on pollution control apply the strict liability principle.

II. Strict Liability in Tort

975. The rule in *Rylands v. Fletcher*, which was first established in the case of similar name in 1865,[947] provides another tortious action for the victim of environmental pollution.

945. (1966) 1 MLJ 1.
946. (1969) 1 MLJ 99.
947. (1865) H&C 774.

976. Under the general common law rule, the defendant is liable only if he acted intentionally or negligently as a result of which he has caused harm to the plaintiff's interest. Whereas in *Rylands*, the requirement is made stricter, as a defendant may be held liable even though he has not been negligent or at fault. In this case, Blackburn J stated that 'a person who, for his own purposes, brings on to his land and collects and keeps there anything likely to do mischief if it escapes must keep it in at his peril, and, if he does not do so, is prima facie answerable for all the damage which is the natural consequence of its escape'.[948]

977. One of the two elements necessary to establish liability under this rule is non-natural use of land. One of the earliest Malaysian cases to have applied this rule is *Ang Hock Hai v. Tan Sum Lee & Anor*,[949] where the court held that the defendants brought upon the premises in which they were in de facto possession for the purposes of their business, dangerous materials which would not naturally be upon the premises and they were under an obligation to keep those materials under control, so as not to cause mischief to their neighbours. Thus, the rule in *Rylands* applied here.

978. Another example of non-natural use relating to the environment can be found in the case of *Pacific Tin Consolidated Corporation v. Hoon Wee Thim*.[950] In this case, the appellants maintained on their land, ponds of water for dredging purposes. These ponds were separated from one another by intermediate bunds. A breach in the bund between two ponds caused a violent outflow of water causing damage to lands adjacent to the pond. The respondent claimed damages on the ground of the rule in *Rylands*. It was held, on the basis of natural use of land, that such use does not imply that the appellants can carry out their operation in any manner they think fit, however hazardous to their neighbour. In this case, non-natural use of the land refers to 'some special use' which brings about increased danger. The use to which the sand bund was put in the case was a non-natural use, and hence, the rule in *Rylands* applied.

979. Another main element required to establish liability under the rule in *Rylands* is escape. In *Read v. Lyons*,[951] the House of Lords held that it is a necessary element of the rule that there must be an escape of the substance from the land on which it is kept. The issue of escape raised in the case of *Weng Lok Mining Co. Ltd v. Hiap Lee Brickmakers Ltd*[952] was whether, in order to claim compensation, the plaintiff's injury must be caused by the escape of the thing from the defendant's land. The court held that for the rule in *Rylands* to apply there must be proof of escape. In this case, the defendants were found guilty for allowing the escape of water from a reservoir on their land.

948. (1866) L.R. 1 Ex. 265.
949. (1957) 23 MLJ 135.
950. [1967] 2 MLJ 35.
951. (1947) AC 146.
952. (1972) 1 MLJ 156.

980. On appeal,[953] it was found that the respondent failed to prove the escape of water. The appeal was therefore allowed on that basis.

981. On the issue of strict liability, in the case of *Pacific Tin Consolidated Corporation v. Hoon Wee Thim*,[954] the judge ruled in favour of the plaintiff on the basis that natural use of property does not mean that miners had carte blanche to carry on their mining operation in any manner they think fit. This is because the bund was put to uses for which the appellants knew, or ought to have known, that it was unsuitable and hazardous to their neighbours … and that the bund was put to a non-natural use when it was made to hold water in great quantities instead of slimes.[955]

III. Strict Liability under Statute Law

982. One matter to be considered in environmental criminal offences is the need to prove *actus reus* and *mens rea* of the alleged offender.

983. As compared to other criminal statutes, under the EQA 1974, it is easier to prove liability, as what is required is for the prosecutor to show that a person discharged pollution exceeding the acceptable standards without holding a licence.

984. However, the question of proving *mens rea* can also be tricky. The basic principle of criminal wrongdoing requires that the offender be aware of the nature of his act or its consequences, or that he committed the act intentionally. An issue may arise in a situation where a person contravened the acceptable conditions unintentionally, due to the lack of knowledge or negligently.

985. However, under the EQA 1974, it is possible for some of its provisions to be regarded as strict liability provisions where the requirement of intention or knowledge is not necessary in order to prove guilt.

986. For instance, section 25 provides for situations where a person may be held guilty of an environmental offence, despite the lack of knowledge or intention on his part. The principle of water pollution offences under section 25 is formulated in terms of actions and intentions. Subsection (1) of section 25 states that 'a person is guilty of an offence if he emits, discharges or deposits any environmentally hazardous substance, pollutant or wastes into any inland waters in contravention of the acceptable conditions specified in section 21, unless licensed'.

987. The person is deemed to discharge wastes into inland waters, according to section 25(2), if he does any of the following:

953. *Hiap Lee Brickmakers Ltd v. Weng Lok Mining Company Ltd* [1974] 2 MLJ 1.
954. (1967) 2 MLJ 35.
955. (1967) 2 MLJ 35 at 43.

(a) places any wastes in or on any waters or in a place where it may gain access to any waters;
(b) places any waste in a position where it falls, descends, drains, evaporates, is washed, is blown or percolates or is likely to fall, descend, drain, evaporate or be washed, be blown or percolated into any waters, or knowingly or through his negligence, whether directly or indirectly, causes or permits any wastes to be placed in such a position; or
(c) causes the temperature of the receiving waters to be raised or lowered by more than the prescribed limits.

988. Issue pertaining to the possibility of section 25 being a strict liability provision derives from the wording of section 25(2)(b), whereby a person is deemed to emit, discharge or deposit wastes into inland waters 'if he knowingly or through his negligence, whether directly or indirectly, causes or permits any wastes to be placed in such a position'.

989. The term 'knowingly' under section 25(2)(b) indicates a state of mind and action of a person to constitute environmental offences. Until now, there has been no decided case in Malaysia that examined the wording of this section. However, it is safe to argue that the term 'knowingly' generally refers to the state of mind of the person when committing the offence, and it would therefore be the duty on the part of a prosecutor to prove that a person causes or permits the act knowingly. However, if the wording of section 25(2)(b) is read as 'to permit' pollution, the prosecutor would not be required to establish the existence of knowledge, negligence or fault on the part of polluter, and this would constitute strict liability. If the act he committed is of strict liability, then the person is liable for punishment, as he cannot rely on the absence of fault as a defence.

990. Another strict liability provision is in section 31 of the Act on the power to require owners to install, operate or repair equipment, as applied in the case of *Public Prosecutor v. Cocolin Industries Sdn. Bhd.*[956] In this case, a person was charged under section 31(1) of the Act and punished under section 31(3) of the same Act, for his failure to comply with the Directive Notice issued by the Director of Department of Environment Sarawak for not installing and operating any control equipment within a three-month period from the date of notice. In this case, the court held that section 31(1) is a strict liability offence, where the burden of proof is on the respondents to show that they have installed and operated control equipment, or additional control equipment, to reduce water pollution within three months from the date of the said notice.

956. Criminal Appeal No. 42-14-2007-11.

§4. NUISANCE

I. Introduction

991. The main element of nuisance is that of annoyance or inconvenience based on the maxim of *sic utere tuo ut alienum non laedas* which in essence means the use of one's property must not injure another's, and indicates a condition or activity which unduly interferes with the use or enjoyment of land.[957]

992. Nuisance is divided into two. The first, private nuisance, is in general a civil action for damages and the abatement of an interference with the plaintiff's use and enjoyment of land, caused by the defendant's action on his own land.

993. The second, public nuisance, arises when a defendant's conduct causes an interference with some right common to the general public. Usually a public nuisance is redressable through a suit by a public representative, such as a public prosecutor, for abatement, or recovery of the costs incurred responding to conditions resulting from a public nuisance.

II. Private Nuisance

994. The basic principle of a private nuisance is the balance between competing rights of neighbours to use their property as they wish and the protection of interests in land or water. To form a private nuisance, the act must constitute an unreasonable interference with an occupier's beneficial use of his land, or cause actual damage to the property.

995. The question of reasonableness was discussed in *Saunders Clark v. Grosvenor Mansion Company Limited & D'Alles-Sandry*,[958] which states that 'the court must consider whether the defendant is using his property reasonably or not. If he is using it reasonably, there is nothing which at law can be considered a nuisance; but if he is not using it reasonably ... then the plaintiff is entitled to relief'.

996. A claim for private nuisance is intended to govern the way neighbouring occupiers use their respective property and in this regard can be brought only by the owner or occupier of the land. Where nuisance can be established and consequent damage shown, the remedies which are available to the plaintiff are an injunction to restrain the defendant from commencing or continuing the activity which constitutes the nuisance, and an award of damages to compensate the plaintiff for injury which he has suffered in consequence of the nuisance.

997. There have not been many pollution-related cases in Malaysia tried under the rule of private nuisance. It is, however, worth discussing a case of *Chan Jen*

957. *See* Lord Wright in *Sedleigh-Denfield v. O'Callaghan* [1940] AC 880 at 902.
958. (1900) 2 Ch. 373.

Chiat v. Allied Granite Marble Industries Sdn. Bhd.,[959] which concerned the issue of the interference of a person's beneficial use of his land. In this case, the plaintiff owned land where he constructed ponds to breed commercial worms. His source of water for the ponds was channelled from a drainage system which flowed through adjacent land belonging to the defendant. The defendant carried out earthworks on his land, the excess soil of which affected the flow of water and polluted it. Polluted water killed worms in the ponds, and as a result the plaintiff suffered loss. It was held that the defendant's activity was an interference with the plaintiff's lawful use of the land and hence the defendant was liable for nuisance.

998. In another case, *Pacific Engineering Limited v. Haji Ahmad Rice Mill Ltd*,[960] the plaintiff had brought an action for an injunction restraining the defendant from burning rice husks on their land. The court held that the plaintiff had shown ample evidence of injury to property and interference to personal comfort caused by smoke, ash, rice husks and dust and that these constituted an actionable nuisance in law. The court further stated that it was not necessary to constitute a private nuisance to show that the nuisance complained of should be noxious in the sense of being injurious to health. It was sufficient that there is a material interference with the ordinary comfort and convenience of life. In *Renal Link (KL) Sdn. Bhd. v. Dato' Dr Harman Singh*,[961] the appellant was alleged to have emitted noxious and toxic fumes and gases from his premises to the detriment of the respondent's beneficial use of his premises. It was held that the appellant was liable for the loss suffered by the respondent under the tort of private nuisance.

III. Public Nuisance

A. Introduction

999. Unlike private nuisance, a public nuisance is an interference with the public's reasonable comfort and convenience and it is a criminal offence. A public nuisance is thus an unlawful act or omission to discharge a legal duty, which act or omission endangered the lives, safety, health, property or comfort of the public, or by which the public are obstructed in the exercise or enjoyment of any right common to all.

1000. The definition of public nuisance is given by Lord Denning as 'a nuisance which is so widespread in its range or so indiscriminate in its effects that it would not be reasonable to expect one person to take proceedings on his own responsibility to put a stop to it, but that it should be taken on the responsibility of the community at large'.[962]

959. (1994) 3 MLJ 495.
960. (1966) 2 MLJ 142.
961. (1997) 2 MLJ 373.
962. Refer to Lord Denning, *in A.G. v. PYA Quarries Ltd*, [1957] 2 QB 169 at 191; [1957] 1 ALL. E.R. 894 CA at 908.

1001. In cases of public nuisance, which affect a large portion of the community, a civil action for abatement has to be brought by the Attorney General, who represents the community at large and who is under a duty to protect the public interest. This is provided in section 8 of the Government Proceedings Act 1956,[963] which states that in the case of a public nuisance, the Attorney General may institute a suit, although no special damage has been caused, for a declaration and injunction or for such other relief as may be appropriate to the circumstances of the case.

1002. Specifically in Malaysia, public nuisance[964] is considered an interference with the public's reasonable comfort and convenience, including environmental harm. It is a criminal offence; and the relevant provisions can be found in statutes. The method applied to determine public nuisance under these statutes is non-quantitative. The court looks at the reasonableness of actions rather than restricting conduct to specific levels.

B. Local Government Act 1976

1003. There are several local government statutes that contain provisions on public nuisance. One of these is the Local Government Act 1976,[965] which defines 'nuisance' as 'any act, omission or thing occasioning or likely to occasion injury, annoyance, offence, harm, danger or damage to the sense of sight, smell or hearing or which is or is likely to be injurious or dangerous to health or property or which affects the safety or the rights of the inhabitants at large'.

1004. Under this Act, the control of nuisance includes water pollution within the local authority area. Any person who commits nuisance or deposits any filth in or on the banks of a watercourse commits an offence and is liable to a fine up to MYR 2,000, jail up to one year, and to a further fine not exceeding MYR 500 for each day during which the offence is continued after conviction.[966]

1005. Local government's power to abate the nuisance is through the issuance of an abatement notice, as provided in section 80 of the Act. Where a notice has been served on a person and such a person defaults in complying with any of the requirements of the notice within the time specified, he shall be guilty of an offence and shall on conviction be liable to a fine not exceeding MYR 1,000, to a term of imprisonment not exceeding six months, or both, and in addition the Magistrate's

963. Act 359.
964. The definition of public nuisance is given by Lord Denning as 'a nuisance which is so widespread in its range or so indiscriminate in its effects that it would not be reasonable to expect one person to take proceedings on his own responsibility to put a stop to it, but that it should be taken on the responsibility of the community at large'. Refer to Lord Denning, in *A.G. v. PYA Quarries Ltd*, [1957] 2 QB 169 at 191; [1957] 1 ALL. E.R. 894 CA at 908.
965. Act 171.
966. Section 69 of the Local Authority Act 1976.

Court may issue a nuisance order.[967] Any person who fails to comply with the provisions of a nuisance order shall be guilty of an offence and shall on conviction be liable to a fine not exceeding MYR 100 for each day during the period of his default.[968]

1006. One decided case on public nuisance under section 80 is the case of *Majlis Perbandaran Pulau Pinang v. Boey Siew Than & Ors.*[969] The respondents in this case were alleged to have made structural alterations to a building and to have used it as a restaurant without the approval or the licence of the local authority. The appellants, the local authority, brought an action for public nuisance, seeking an injunction to restrain the respondents from illegally operating the eating house. They also applied for an injunction to restrain the respondents from operating the said eating house until trial of the actions. The respondents applied to strike out the actions, and the High Court upheld their application. The local authority appealed. On appeal, the Federal Court examined sections 80 and 13 of the Local Government Act 1976 on the power to take legal action in cases of public nuisance, and held that, for the protection of public interest, the local authority is given an enabling power and duty to take such action. In giving the judgment, the court upheld the appeal from the local authority allowing them to impose the injunction on the basis of the protection of the public interest in their area.[970]

C. The Street Drainage and Building Act 1974

1007. Another provision on public nuisance can be found in the Street, Drainage and Building Act 1974.[971] 'Nuisance' in this Act means 'any act, omission or thing occasioning or likely to occasion injury, annoyance, offence, harm, danger or damage to the sense of sight, smell or hearing, or which is or is likely to be injurious or dangerous to health or property'.[972]

1008. Section 86 of the Act explains what constitutes nuisance, which includes a foul watercourse, or one that is injurious or dangerous to health. When this situation occurs, the State Authority is empowered to serve notice to the person who

---

967. Section 82(5) of the Local Government Act 1976.
968. Section 82(10) of the Local Government Act 1976.
969. [1979] 2 MLJ 127. This was an appeal case from the decision of the High Court, *see Majlis Perbandaran Pulau Pinang v. Boey Siew Than & Ors* [1978] 2 MLJ 156.
970. *See* Maizatun Mustafa, *Public Access to Environmental Rights and Justice: A Legal Perspective for an Improved Public Service System of the Local Authorities*, in *Service Delivery by Local Authorities: Issues and Challenges* (Worran Kabut et al., eds (compilers), UPENA 2006).
971. Act 133. This is another federal law which amended and consolidated the laws relating to street, drainage and building in local authority areas in West Malaysia pursuant to Art. 76(4) of the Constitution.
972. Section 2 of the Street, Drainage and Building Act 1974.

causes the nuisance to require him to abate such nuisance.[973] In the case of default, and upon conviction, such person shall be liable to a fine not exceeding MYR 500 for each offence.[974]

1009. Under section 53 of the same Act, the local government is also empowered to maintain, keep in repair, improve, discontinue, close up or destroy storm water drains, culverts, gutters and watercourses within its locality. However, the discontinuance, closing up or destruction of any of them shall be done so as not to create a nuisance.[975]

1010. One case where an issue pertaining to section 53 was raised is *Muhamad Saleh bin Hashim & Ors v. Percon Corp Sdn. Bhd.*[976] The plaintiffs in this case brought an action against the defendant for negligence as a result of the defendant's project in building a highway. The plaintiffs' houses were built along the riverbanks of Sungai Kelang, and the defendant's activities caused, among other things, siltation and the rise of the river bed, causing the plaintiffs' houses to be flooded. The defendant alleged that the floods were caused by the inadequate drainage system, and requested a third-party notice against the mayor of Kuala Lumpur City Hall and the Ampang Jaya Municipal Council. In this case, the plaintiffs relied on sections 53(1) and 54(1) of the Street Drainage and Building Act 1974 pertaining to the local government's duties to maintain surface or storm water drains, and to properly clear and cleanse them so that they do not cause a nuisance. However, the plaintiffs' action failed, on the basis that the plaintiffs were illegal squatters who had unlawfully built their houses along the riverbanks. Since the damage pleaded arose directly from the illegal acts of the plaintiffs, the issue of compensation did not arise at all. The local government does not owe any duty to illegal squatters to perform any act in order to ensure that the squatters' property and their belongings are not damaged by flood.[977]

D. The Penal Code

1011. Criminal law is another area of law in Malaysia that provides for provisions on public nuisance. Chapter XIV of the Malaysian Penal Code[978] deals with the crime of public nuisance and offences affecting the public health, safety, convenience, decency and morals.

1012. Section 268 of the Penal Code defines the offence of 'public nuisance' as 'a person who does any act or is guilty of an illegal omission which causes any

973. Section 87(1) of the Street, Drainage and Building Act 1974.
974. Section 87(5) of the Street, Drainage and Building Act 1974.
975. Section 53(2) of the Street, Drainage and Building Act 1974.
976. (2003) 6 MLJ 483.
977. *See* Maizatun Mustafa, *Public Access to Environmental Rights and Justice: A Legal Perspective for an Improved Public Service System of the Local Authorities*, in *Service Delivery by Local Authorities: Issues and Challenges* (Worran Kabut et al., eds (compilers), UPENA 2006).
978. 976 F.M.S. Cap. 45, revised 1997, Act 574.

injury, danger or annoyance to the public or to the people in general who dwell or occupy property in the vicinity, or which must necessarily cause injury, obstruction, danger or annoyance to persons who may have occasion to use any public right'.

1013. Public nuisance involving water pollution is provided in section 277 of the Penal Code. It imposes punishment on a person who voluntarily corrupts or fouls the water of any public spring or reservoir, so as to render it less fit for the purpose for which it is ordinarily used. The punishment imposed for this section is imprisonment for a term which may extend to three months, or with a fine which may extend to MYR 1,000, or both.

1014. Public nuisance concerning air pollution is dealt with under section 278. It states that whoever voluntarily vitiates the atmosphere in any place so as to make it noxious to the health of persons, in general, dwelling, carrying on business in the neighbourhood, or passing along a public way, shall be punished with fine which may extend to MYR 1,000.

1015. Section 291 of the Penal Code further states that whoever repeats or continues a public nuisance, having been enjoined by any public servant who has lawful authority to issue such injunction, not to repeat or continue such nuisance, shall be punished with imprisonment for a term which may extend to six months, or with a fine, or with both.

1016. Under section 291 of the Penal Code, a person may also be held guilty of public nuisance if he does any act which causes any common injury, danger, or annoyance to the public, or to the people in general who dwell or occupy property in the vicinity, or which must necessarily cause injury, obstruction, danger, or annoyance to persons who may have occasion to use any public right.

E. Criminal Procedure Code

1017. Provision on public nuisance is also set out under Chapter IX of the Criminal Procedure Code.[979] Section 89 empowers a First Class Magistrate to order that:

- any unlawful obstruction or nuisance should be removed from any way, harbour, lake, river or channel which is or may be lawfully used by the public or from any public place;
- any trade or occupation or the keeping of any goods or merchandise by reason of its being injurious to the health or physical comfort of the community should be suppressed or removed or prohibited;
- the construction of any building or the disposal of any substance likely to occasion conflagration or explosion should be prevented or stopped;

979. Act 593, revised 1999.

- any building or tree is in such a condition that it is likely to fall and thereby cause injury to persons living or carrying on business in the neighbourhood or passing, and that, in consequence, its removal, repair or support is necessary; or
- any tank, well or excavation adjacent to any such way as aforesaid or to any public place should be fenced in such a manner as to prevent danger arising to the public.

1018. Under section 89, the Magistrate may make a conditional order requiring the person causing such nuisance to take certain steps to remove the nuisance.[980] Furthermore, if the Magistrate, while making an order under section 89, considers that immediate measures should be taken to prevent immediate danger or injury of a serious kind to the public, he may issue an injunction to the person against whom the order was made, and may order any person not to repeat or continue a public nuisance.[981] In the case of *Loke Kui Thong v. Public Prosecutor*,[982] an action was brought under section 89 where a person was required by the Magistrate to cease to trade, as this was injurious to the health and physical comfort of the public.

§5. Remedies

1019. The object of damages under tort law is to compensate the plaintiff on the principle of restitution *in integrum*, namely, to put the injured party in the same position as he would have been in if he had not sustained the wrong for which he is being compensated.

1020. In a situation where the property is totally destroyed as a result of the defendant's tort, the normal measure of damages is its value at the time and place of the destruction as decided in *Dodd Properties Ltd v. Canterbury City Council*.[983] If the plaintiff's injury, caused by the defendant, deprived him of some enjoyment of life, he may be compensated for loss of amenities such as decided in the case of *Yang Salbiah & Anor v. Jamil B. Harun*.[984]

1021. Another type of remedy is injunction, which is an order of court restraining the commission or continuance of some wrongful act, or the continuance of some wrongful omission. It is the court's discretion to issue an injunction in any case in which it appears to the court to be just and convenient.

1022. If the plaintiff is an owner of property, as a landlord, he is entitled to an injunction to restrain a tortious act, such as a nuisance caused by the defendant, even though he may not produce evidence of any particular harm.

---

980. The procedural requirement for the removal of public nuisance is elaborated in ss 90–95 of the Criminal Procedure Code.
981. Sections 96 and 97 of the Criminal Procedure Code.
982. (1933) MLJ 20–21.
983. (1980) 1 WLR 433.
984. (1981) 1 MLJ 292.

1023. In Malaysia, the source of law relating to injunctions is provided by the Specific Relief Act 1950.[985] Section 4 of this Act provides for instances where specific relief is given, including by ordering a party to do the very act which he is under an obligation to do; by preventing a party from doing that which he is under an obligation not to do; or by determining and declaring the rights of parties otherwise than by an award of compensation.

1024. Injunction, being an equitable remedy, can be either temporary or perpetual. Section 51(1) of the Act provides that temporary injunctions are such as are to continue until a specified time, or until the further order of the court. They may be granted at any period of a suit, and are regulated by the law relating to civil procedure. Under section 51(2), a perpetual injunction can only be granted by a decree made at a hearing and upon the merits of the suit; the defendant is thereby perpetually enjoined from the assertion of a right, or from the commission of an act, which would be contrary to the rights of the plaintiff.

1025. In imposing an injunction on the defendant, the court may also order him to perform a positive act through a mandatory injunction. In the case of *Morris v. Redland Bricks Ltd*,[986] the defendant excavated on his own land, but caused subsidence on part of the plaintiff's land. The plaintiff obtained damages and a mandatory injunction requiring the defendant to restore support to their land. On appeal, the House of Lords removed the injunction and laid down stricter principles for the grant of a mandatory injunction, namely, in situations where damages will not be an adequate remedy for the plaintiff. Where the defendant had acted reasonably, the sum of money to be incurred will be considered, but where he has acted wantonly, it is immaterial; and that the mandatory injunction must enable the defendant to know exactly what he has to do, so that he could instruct his contractor accordingly. One Malaysian case where the Supreme Court upheld a mandatory injunction is *Tinta Press Sdn. Bhd. v. BIMB*,[987] where the Supreme Court found that, if the injunction had not been granted earlier, the plaintiff would have suffered irreparable damage and greater hardship.

§6. *Locus Standi*

1026. One issue that need to be considered in bringing a civil case to court is that pertaining to *locus standi*.[988] In Malaysia, judicial recourse is available only to persons who can demonstrate sufficient *locus standi* in the subject in dispute. Thus,

985. Act 137, revised 1974.
986. (1970) AC 657.
987. (1987) 2 MLJ 192.
988. *See* Andrew Harding, *Practical Human Rights, NGOs and the Environment in Malaysia*, in *Human Rights Approaches to Environmental Protection* (A.E. Boyle & M.R. Anderson eds, Oxford U. Press 1996).

even though common law allows for judicial remedies in environmental cases, in order to undertake such litigation, a person must go through the procedural hurdle of *locus standi*.[989]

1027. Under the rule of *locus standi*, if all members of the community suffer equally, none may sue because it is an inconvenience common to everyone else.[990] For a private person to initiate a civil suit, he must prove that he has a genuine private interest to protect, over and above that of any other member of the public. Otherwise, he has no right to sue.

1028. The requirement of *locus standi* in Malaysia is very strict, as established in the case of *Government of Malaysia v. Lim Kit Siang, United Engineering (M) Berhad v. Lim Kit Siang*.[991] In this case, Mr Lim relied on his position as a road user, tax payer, Member of Parliament and Leader of the Opposition to justify his standing in challenging the legality of a government contract offered to United Engineers (M) to build a highway. The court held that he could not prove any special distinction between himself and other road users, and he had no intimate links with the company; therefore, he had no standing.[992]

1029. The issue of *locus standi* was also raised in the case of *Ketua Pengarah Jabatan Alam Sekitar & Anor. v. Kajing Tubek & 2 Ors*.[993] This is a case pertaining to the application of the EIA requirement under section 34A of the EQA 1974 on a hydroelectric project located in a remote area of the state of Sarawak known as Bakun. The aggrieved party were the natives of Bakun, who argued for the vindication of their right to inspect the EIA report before it was approved by the Department of Environment. One of the issues raised by them was on the basis of *locus standi* in obtaining a relief of declaration. In this case, the Court of Appeal rejected the appeal and ruled that the natives had no substantive *locus standi* on the following bases.

989. *See* Maizatun Mustafa, *Clean Water: Right and Remedies Under Environmental Law in Malaysia*, in *Integrated Water Resources Management in Malaysia: Experiences and Practices* (Ann Anton et al. eds, Malaysian Water Partnership 2004); and Maizatun Mustafa, *Public Access to Environmental Rights and Justice: A Legal Perspective for an Improved Public Service System of the Local Authorities*, in *Service Delivery by Local Authorities: Issues and Challenges* (Worran Kabut et al. eds (compilers), UPENA 2006).

990. For example, *see* the judgments in *R. v. Lloyd* (1802) 4 Esp. 200 and *Attorney-General v. PYA Quarries* [1957] 2 QB 169.

991. [1988] 2 MLJ 12. *See* Ranjit Singhs & Looi May Mei, *A Comparative Study of Approaches to Public Interest Litigation* (*Government of Malaysia/Uem v. Lim Kit Siang Revisited*), 3 MLJ i (2003).

992. This judgment has been confirmed in other cases such as *Abdul Razak Ahmad v. Kerajaan Negeri Johor* [1994] 2 MLJ 297; *Abdul Razak Ahmad v. Majlis Bandaraya Johor Baru* [1995] 2 AMR 1174; *Lee Freddie v. Majlis Perbandaran Petaling Jaya* [1994] 3 MLJ 640; *Kajing Tubek & Ors. v. Ekran Bhd. & Ors.*[1996] 2 MLJ 388; and *Ketua Pengarah Jabatan Alam Sekitar & Anor. v. Kajing Tubek & 2 Ors.*[1997] 3 AMR 2521.

993. [1997] 3 AMR 2521. *See also*, Gurdial Singh Nijar, *The Bakun Case: A Critique* 3 MLJ ccxxix (1997).

1030. First, on the basis that no private person can bring an action to enforce criminal law based on the fact that section 34A(8) of the Act creates a criminal offence, and thus, it was for the Attorney General, and not the aggrieved party, to decide on matters of prosecution.

1031. Second, that the natives suffered no special injury over and above the common injury suffered by the other native persons. This is because although there is deprivation of life, as this deprivation is being done in accordance with the existing and valid law of Sarawak, the requirements of Article 5(1) of the Constitution are satisfied, which states that there can be no deprivation of life and liberty save according to law.

1032. Third, the action brought by the natives was not representative in character, and the other affected persons were not before the court. As a substantial number of other persons whose rights were equally affected by the project were not before the court, it was held that the declarations ought not to be made, because the harm complained of was not peculiar or special to them.

1033. The final basis was that the trial judge, which was the High Court judge, did not have sufficient regard for public interest. Here, the judge failed in exercising his discretion to take all the relevant circumstances into account, and, crucially, the question of whether public and national interests are better served by the granting or refusal of the declarations sought by the natives, and whether the remedy, if granted, would cause greater harm than if denied. The declarations sought were refused by the Court of Appeal.

Chapter 3. Criminal Liability

§1. Environmental Criminal Law in Malaysia

1034. In Malaysia, the penalty imposed for environmental criminal offences can be found in the respective statutes creating the offence. For these offences, the type of punishment includes the payment of a fine or a jail sentence. However, in more serious cases, the death sentence may be imposed.

1035. With regard to investigation of environmental offences, some statutes such as the EQA 1974 and the Exclusive Economic Zone Act authorize the Director General of the Department of Environment to take up this task. However, criminal prosecution and criminal trial are conducted in accordance with specific criminal procedures at the civil court.

§2. Sources

1036. Discussion in earlier parts of this monograph has shown that in Malaysia criminal sanctions relating to environmental pollution have been incorporated within statutes.

1037. The application of criminal sanctions to punish environmental offences, mainly through public nuisance, are available in penal legislation, such as the Malaysian Penal Code and Criminal Procedure Code, apart from local authority's legislation.

1038. Environment-related legislation also contains criminal provisions within the statutes. A typical example is the EQA 1974. This statute is the most comprehensive legislation on environmental pollution, and it relies on criminal sanction for environmental offences committed therein. This was especially so during the early years of its enactment. In later years, especially in 1996,[994] the Act was extensively amended to provide for stricter punishments for environmental criminal offences. This included increasing the amount of penalty from the maximum of MYR 10,000–MYR 100,000 for pollution offences, and MYR 500,000 for more serious offences such as scheduled wastes pollution and marine pollution.[995]

1039. However, modern environmental legislation does not rely solely on criminal sanction as a form of punishment. Other methods of sanctions are relied upon by these statutes to cater for different types of environmental offences. These sanctions will be discussed in a later part of this monograph.

994. Environmental Quality (Amendment) Act 1996, Act 953.

995. *See* Maizatun Mustafa & Mariani Ariffin, *A Review on Environmental Forensics and Environmental Law in the Malaysian Perspective*, in *From Sources to Solution* (A.Z. Aris et.al., eds, Springer 2014), and Maizatun Mustafa & Nurah Sabahiah Mohammed, *The Development of Environmental Crime and Sanction in Malaysia*, 11(25) Eur. Scientific J. (2015).

§3. CIVIL CLAIMS UNDER CRIMINAL LAW

I. Environmental Quality Act 1974

1040. In general, statutory law in Malaysia does not provide for any provision allowing the victim of environmental harm to bring a case directly to court for claiming compensation for any damage suffered.

1041. Under the EQA 1974 and any other environmental legislation, prosecution remains exclusively with the respective DGs. The public, even those who are directly affected by the conduct of the offender, have no right under the Act to bring a case against the polluter, even though they can still rely on tort law for a civil remedy.

1042. In relation to the EQA 1974, prior to its amendment in 1996, there exists no statutory provision that recognizes the right of an environmental victim to obtain damages due to harm done by the offender. In other words, the court was not given any power by the Act to order such an offender to pay compensation for losses incurred by the said victim, or damage to property, due to an offence caused by the offender.

1043. In 1996, the Act was amended to introduce a new provision relating to the polluter's financial exposure, through the payment of compensation under section 46E.[996] This section provides that, after a person has been convicted for an offence against the Act or its regulations, and the court finds that another person has suffered loss or damage to any property due to the commission of, or the omission resulting in the offence, the court may, in addition to imposing a penalty for the offences, order the offender to pay to the other person the costs and expenses incurred, or compensation for loss or damage suffered by that person.

1044. However, until now, the applicability of section 46E in providing protection to the victim of environmental harm is still unresolved. The wording of this section seems to suggest that it is the court that has the power to require the offender to pay for the damage. Thus, it is presumed that the victim still has no rights under the Act to directly seek compensation for such damages. It is only after the case is brought to court by the Director General of the Department of Environment that the court will decide whether damages to the victim should be awarded, or otherwise. Until now, this section has never been invoked by the Malaysian court; thus, it is not possible to gauge how the court would apply this section, including the method of calculating the amount of compensation awarded to the victim.

996. Environmental Quality (Amendment) Act 1996, Act 953.

II. Exclusive Economic Zone Act 1984

1045. The Exclusive Economic Zone Act 1984 also contained a provision pertaining to the damage caused to any person or property or to the environment in exclusive economic zones or on the continental shelf, as provided in section 40. Unlike section 46E of the EQA 1974, section 40 of the Exclusive Economic Zone Act 1984 recognizes the right of the government and Malaysian nationals to claim for compensation, through specific civil courts, where damage was caused to the victim or his property.

1046. Section 40 states that where, by reason of any act or omission in contravention of this Act or any applicable written law, damage is caused to any person or property in or on, or to any segment or element of the environment or related interests within, the exclusive economic zone or continental shelf, the owner and the master of the vessel, the owner and the occupier of the place on land, the owner and the person in charge of the installation or device, or the owner and the pilot of the aircraft, as the case may be, causing the damage, or the owner and the master of the vessel, the owner and the occupier of the place on land, the owner and the person in charge of the installation or device, or the owner and the pilot of the aircraft from which any oil, mixture containing oil, or pollutant was discharged or escaped resulting in the damage, shall be liable jointly and severally for such damage, unless otherwise provided under this Act or such written law.[997]

1047. Section 40(2) further provides that where the act or omission of a person other than any of the persons in subsection (1) caused such damage, discharge or escape, then such other person shall also be liable, jointly and severally, with the persons mentioned in that subsection for such damage, unless otherwise provided under this Act or such written law.

1048. For liability committed under section 40, such liability extends to the payment of compensation for any damage caused to a person, vessel, gear, facility or structure used in any activity, including fishing and related activities, connected with the exercise of the rights of the government and Malaysian nationals, and of other persons where such rights are exercised with the consent of the government, in the exclusive economic zone or on the continental shelf, and compensation shall also be paid for policing and surveillance activities, and activities for the protection of the environment and shipping necessitated by the damage.[998]

1049. Under section 40(4), any claim for compensation under this section may be brought before any High Court, Sessions Court or Court of a Magistrate of the First Class in Malaysia, as the case may be, according to the value or amount of the claim; and where a claim is so brought, the court concerned shall have full jurisdiction and powers to adjudicate thereon.

---

997. Section 40(1) of the Exclusive Economic Zone Act 1984.
998. Section 40(3) of the Exclusive Economic Zone Act 1984.

§4. Criminal Liability Within Corporate Entities

1050. In Malaysia, general liabilities of corporate entities are regulated by the Companies Act 1965.[999] However, environmental criminal liability of the corporation is available in various environmental statutes.

1051. Under the EQA 1974, three types of people may be prosecuted for the offence committed, namely the 'owner', 'occupier' and 'company director'.

1052. The 'occupier' is defined by the EQA as 'a person in occupation or control of any premises; or in relation to premises where different parts of which are occupied by different persons in occupation or control of each part; or any vehicle, ship or aircraft'.

1053. For any 'premises', an 'owner' is defined by section 2 to mean one of the following, namely:

- the registered proprietor of the premises;
- the lessee of a lease including a sub-lease of the premises;
- the agent or trustee of any of the owners or if the owner above cannot be traced or has died, his legal personal representative; or
- the person for the time being receiving the rent of the premises whether on his own account or as agent or trustee or as receiver.

1054. Under the Act, 'owner' in relation to any 'ship' includes 'the person registered as the owner of the ship, the person owing the ship, the country that owns the ship, or agent or trustee of the owners'. In relation to 'vehicle or aircraft', an 'owner' is defined by the section to mean 'the person registered as the owner of the vehicle or aircraft'.

1055. Another person that may be held liable under the Act is the company director and other company officials or their agents under section 43. In 2007, this section was amended to include the 'chief executive officer', when his company, firm or society commits such offences.[1000]

1056. Section 43 provides that, where an offence against this Act or any regulations made thereunder has been committed by a company, firm, society or other body of persons, any person who at the time of the commission of the offence was a director, chief executive officer, manager, or other similar officer or a partner of the company, firm, society or other body of persons or was purporting to act in such capacity, shall be deemed to be guilty of that offence unless he proves that the offence was committed without his consent or connivance and that he had exercised

999. Act 125, revised 1973.
1000. Am. Act A1315: s. 3.

all such diligence as to prevent the commission of the offence as he ought to have exercised, having regard to the nature of his functions in that capacity and to all the circumstances.

1057. To avoid conviction under this section, it is necessary to prove that the offence was committed without his consent and that he had exercised all diligence as to prevent the commission of the offence.[1001] Where the court is satisfied that the offence had been committed by a servant or agent when acting in the course of his employment, the principal shall also be held liable for such contravention, unless he proves that the offence was committed without his knowledge or consent, or that he had exercised all diligence to prevent the act.

1058. Under this section, in a case where a company has committed a polluting offence, the burden of proof is on the director or persons holding similar office, or the employer, to prove that the offence was committed without his consent or permission. Even if the employer or the director was later found guilty of the offence, a proviso in section 45 states that nothing in this section shall be deemed to exempt such clerk, servant or agent from liability in respect of any penalty provided in the EQA 1974 or its Regulations for any contravention proved to have been committed by him.

§5 Endangerment Crimes

1059. The existence of an administrative strategy within environmental statutes such as the EQA 1974 through the requirement of licences, means that it is possible to punish an offender based on the abstract endangerment of environmental values. This means that criminal provision is not applied directly against the offender, but only as a supplement to an administrative strategy.

1060. As already discussed in earlier parts of the monograph, under the EQA 1974, pollution control through administrative sanction is applied by allowing the DG to control the discharge of pollution from various sources. Here, the control is done through the imposition of specific licences which are based upon certain environmental quality standards.

1061. The licences contain particular effluent standards which prescribe the allowable limits of such effluent emitted into the environment. The requirement of acceptable conditions sets a way to ensure that below that limit, discharges of wastes are legal. In a circumstance where wastes are discharged above the prescribed limit, there is an allowance for contravention by way of licence.

1062. Thus, under the licensing strategy, the criminal law protection is provided in separate provisions on the restriction or prohibition of environmental pollution.

1001. Section 43(2) of the Environmental Quality Act 1974.

These provisions specifically mention that anyone who operates without a licence or violates licence conditions is criminally liable.

1063. One example of such application is section 25 of the EQA 1974, which provides for situations where a person may be held guilty of an offence of polluting the inland waters. Subsection (1) of section 25 states that 'a person is guilty of an offence if he emits, discharges or deposits any environmentally hazardous substance, pollutant or wastes into any inland waters in contravention of the acceptable conditions specified in section 21, unless licensed'.

1064. However, there is a weakness in relying on the combined administrative and criminal strategy. Despite its stringent requirement, the main defence to section 25 is that of the possession of a licence. In this sense, criminal offences under this section do not derive from direct environmental harm, but from the breach of administrative requirements. Thus, prosecution under section 25 is imposed on a person not if he has caused harm to inland water, but mainly if he does not hold a licence to discharge effluent exceeding the permitted limit. The same argument can be applied to other pollution offences under the Act which are based on the licensing requirement.[1002]

§6. The Sanction

I. Introduction

1065. In Malaysia, criminal sanctions for environmental offences under statute law are in the form of fines and jail sentences for serious cases. However, the death penalty may be inflicted in very serious cases. For example, under the Water Industry Services Act 2006, on commission of the offence of contamination of water, a person who is found guilty of contaminating any watercourse with any substance with the intention to cause death and where death is the result of the act, shall be punished with death or imprisonment for a term which may extend to twenty years, and where the punishment is not death, he shall also be liable to whipping.[1003]

1066. While traditional statutes still provide low sanctions on environmental offences, modern environmental legislation, including the EQA 1974, is continuously being amended to revise and upgrade the sanction imposed. As a tool for environmental protection, criminal sanction has been applied by the EQA 1974 to provide a direct control over environmental harm. Relevant criminal provisions are as follows:

– section 18 on the occupation or use of prescribed premises without a licence;

1002. *See* the same argument in Maizatun Mustafa, *Legal Approach towards Water Resources Protection and Pollution Control in Malaysia*, in *Water Environmental Planning* 151–176 (Alias Abdullah et al. eds, Intl. Islamic U. Malay. 2004).
1003. Section 121 of the Water Industry Services Act 2006.

- section 22 on the restrictions on pollution of the atmosphere;
- section 23 on the restrictions on pollution of noise;
- section 24 on the restrictions of soil;
- section 25 on the restrictions on inland waters;
- section 27 on the prohibition of the discharge of oil into Malaysian waters;
- section 29 on the prohibition of discharge of wastes into Malaysian waters;
- section 29A on the prohibition of open burning;
- section 31A on prohibition order;
- section 34A on the requirement of EIA; and
- section 34B on the prohibition against the deposit of scheduled wastes.

1067. For criminal offences committed under section 18, any person who is found guilty may be liable to a fine not exceeding MYR 50,000, to imprisonment for a period not exceeding two years, or both, and to a further fine of MYR 1,000 for every day that the offence is continued after a notice by the DG requiring him to cease the act specified has been served upon him.[1004]

1068. For offences committed under sections 22–25, any person who contravenes these sections are liable to a fine not exceeding MYR 100,000, to imprisonment for a period not exceeding five years, or both, and to a further fine not exceeding MYR 1,000 a day for every day that the offence is continued after a notice by the DG requiring him to cease the act specified therein has been served upon him.[1005]

1069. For offences committed under sections 27, 29 and 29A,[1006] the penalty imposed on those who contravene these sections are a fine exceeding MYR 500,000, imprisonment for a period not exceeding five years, or both. For offences committed under section 31A, the penalty imposed is a fine not exceeding MYR 50,000, imprisonment for a period not exceeding two years, or both.[1007]

1070. In the case of EIA, the penalty provided is a fine not exceeding MYR 100,000, imprisonment for a period not exceeding five years, or both, and a further fine of MYR 1,000 for every day that the offence is continued after a notice by the DG requiring the perpetrator to comply with the act specified therein has been served upon him.[1008] For offences committed under section 34B on scheduled wastes, any person who contravenes this section shall be guilty of an offence and shall on conviction be punished with imprisonment for a term not exceeding five years and shall also be liable to a fine not exceeding MYR 500,000.[1009]

1004. Section 18(2) of the Environmental Quality Act 1974.
1005. Sections 22(3), 23(2), 24(3), and 25(3), respectively.
1006. Sections 27(2), 29(2) and 29A(2), respectively.
1007. Section 31A(3).
1008. Section 34A(8).
1009. Section 34B(4).

1071. One example of a criminal offence prosecuted under the EQA 1974 is *Malaysian Vermicelli Manufacturers (Melaka) Sdn. Bhd. v. Pendakwa Raya.*[1010] In this case, the Malacca Sessions Court convicted and sentenced the appellant to a fine of MYR 75,00, and in default one year's imprisonment, on a charge of discharging effluent into inland waters (Malacca river) contrary to Regulation 8(1)(b) of the Environmental Quality (Sewage and Industrial Effluents) Regulations (the Regulations) without a licence. This is an offence under section 25(1) of the EQA 1974, punishable under section 25(3) of the same Act. The evidence of the chemist established that the effluent discharged from the appellant's factory contained substances having concentrations greater than those specified in the acceptable standards set out in the third schedule to the Regulations. The charge against the appellant alleged that the effluent discharged from the appellant's factory exceeded the concentration limit set by Regulation 8(1)(b), which refers to standard B in the fourth column of the Third Schedule. The evidence of the chemist revealed that except for PH value, the other substances in the samples of effluent discharged from the appellant's factory were in concentrations greater than the parameter limits set by Standard B. The appellant appealed to the High Court. The High Court, after considering the totality of the evidence provided by the prosecutor, agreed that it had been proved beyond reasonable doubt that the factory was in operation and was discharging effluent into the river, that the charge against the appellant was proven beyond reasonable doubt, and dismissed the appeal.

II. Specific Sanctions

A. *Prohibition Order*

1072. Apart from the conventional method of sanctions, modern environmental statutes such as the EQA 1974 introduce specific measures aimed at restoring the environment after environmental harm. One specific sanction introduction under the EQA 1974 is prohibition orders.

1073. Section 31A empowers the Minister to specify the circumstances whereby the DG may issue a prohibition order to the owner or occupier of any industrial plant or process to prevent its continued operation and release of environmentally hazardous substances, pollutants or wastes either absolutely or conditionally, or for such period as he may direct, or until requirements to make remedy as directed by him have been complied with.

1074. This section further authorizes the Minister, in circumstances where he considers that the environment, public health or safety is under or likely to be under serious threat, to direct the DG to do the following:

– to issue an order requiring a person to cease all acts that have resulted in the release of environmentally hazardous substances, pollutants or wastes; and

1010. (2001) MLJU 359.

- to effect and render any machinery, equipment, plant or process of the person inoperable.

1075. The penalty imposed on any person who contravenes the prohibition order is a fine not exceeding MYR 50,000, imprisonment for a period not exceeding two years, or both.

1076. Another prohibition order is provided in section 33 of the Act on the prohibition on licensed persons against accumulative discharge of pollution. Under this section, where several persons are licensed under this Act to emit, discharge or deposit environmentally hazardous substances, pollutants or wastes into the environment and it appears to the DG that each of such persons is complying with the conditions of the licence, but nevertheless, the collective effect of the aggregate of such wastes is likely to cause a worsening of condition in that segment or element of the environment, such as to affect the health, welfare or safety of human beings, or to threaten the existence of any animals, birds, wildlife, fish or other aquatic life, the DG may, by notice served on each of the licensees, require each of them to abate such emission, discharge or deposit in the manner and within the period specified in the notice. Any person who contravenes the notice issued shall be guilty of an offence and shall be liable to a fine not exceeding MYR 50,000, to imprisonment for a period not exceeding five years, or both, and to a further fine not exceeding MYR 1,000 a day for every day that the offence is continued after service on him of the notice.

B. Requirement on the Installation of Equipment

1077. Another sanction provided in the EQA 1974 is under section 31 on the requirement of the occupier to install equipment. Under section 31(1), where any environmentally hazardous substances, pollutants or wastes are being or are likely to be emitted, discharged or deposited from any vehicle, ship, premises or aircraft, the DG may by notice in writing require the owner or occupier of the vehicle, ship or premises, or aircraft, to do the following:

- install and operate any control equipment or additional control equipment;
- repair, alter or replace any equipment or control equipment;
- erect or increase the height of any chimney;
- measure, take a sample of, analyse, record and report any environmentally hazardous substances, pollutants, wastes, effluents or emissions containing pollutants;
- conduct a study on any environmental risk;
- install, maintain and operate a monitoring programme at the expense of the owner or occupier; or
- adopt any measure to reduce, mitigate, disperse, remove, eliminate, destroy or dispose of pollution within such time and in such manner as may be specified in the notice.

1078. Section 30(2) further empowers the DG to direct the owner or occupier of any vehicle, ship, or premises, or aircraft, to emit, discharge or deposit environmentally hazardous substances, pollutants or wastes during such periods of day as he may specify, and may generally direct the manner in which the owner or occupier shall carry out his trade, industry or process or operate any equipment, industrial plant or control equipment therein.

1079. The penalty for the contravention of this provision is stated in section 30(a) which is a fine not exceeding MYR 25,000, imprisonment for a period not exceeding two years, or both, and a further fine not exceeding MYR 1,000 a day for every day that the offence is continued after service on him of the notice.

1080. The provision in section 30 was applied in the case of *Public Prosecutor v. Cocolin Industries Sdn. Bhd.*,[1011] where the respondent was charged under section 31(1) of the EQA 1974, and punished under section 31(3) of the same. In this case, the defendant was charged for failing to comply with the Directive Notice issued by the Director of the Department of Environment Sarawak, under section 31(1) of the Act for not installing and operating any control equipment or additional control equipment to reduce water pollution within the stipulated three-month period from the date of Notice.

C. *Recovery of Costs and Expenses*

1081. Another specific sanction provided under the EQA 1974 is section 47, which provides that where any segment or element of the environment is polluted by any person in contravention of this Act, the DG may take such action as is necessary to remove, disperse, destroy or mitigate the pollution and may recover from that person all costs and expenses incurred in connection therewith.

1082. Section 47(2) further empowers the DG to issue a certificate that it is of the DG's opinion that the person named in the certificate is responsible for such pollution, which shall be prima facie evidence for the purposes of any proceedings under this section. The same section further provides that the sum incurred in carrying out all or any of the works required is a conclusive proof of the sum due and shall not be subject to any appeal or review in any court.

1011. Criminal Appeal No. 42-14-2007-11.

Part V. Juridical Actions of Individuals

Chapter 1. Administrative Remedies

§1. Jurisdiction

I. Appeal Board

1083. What is meant by administrative remedies? These are procedures whereby individuals can ask an administrative authority to revoke, annul or modify an administrative decision. It is possible to have statutes that provide for administrative remedies. There are various environment-related statutes in Malaysia that provide for such administrative remedies.

1084. For example, under the EQA 1974, there are several provisions that allow for administrative appeal. One of these is through the establishment of an Appeal Board, as provided in section 6.

1085. Administrative appeal to the Appeal Board on matters under the EQA 1974 is provided in section 35, namely:

- on a refusal to grant a licence or transfer of a licence;
- on the imposition of any condition, limitation or restriction on his licence;
- on the revocation, suspension or variation of his licence;
- on the amount which he would be required to pay under section 47;
- on any decision of the DG under subsection 34A(3) or (4); and
- on any decision of the DG or any officer under subsection 48A(2) or (5).

1086. One situation under the EQA 1974 where an appeal can be made to the Appeal Board is regarding the imposition of conditions on licences. Under section 3(1), the authority to issue licences is conferred on the DG. If a licensee fails to comply with any terms or condition of the licence, the DG may revoke the licence. However, under clause (2) of sections 11 and 12 of the Act respectively, a licensee is given the right to appeal against the decision of the DG relating to the imposition of conditions. By virtue of these sections, any condition so attached has no force until the time limit for appealing against the condition has expired and, where an appeal against the condition has been duly made, until the hearing of the appeal confirms the decision of the DG imposing the condition.

II. Water Forum

1087. The enactment of the Water Services Industries Act 2006 not only provides for more effective and comprehensive water supply and sewerage services in Malaysia, it also provides for administrative remedies for consumer protection and resolution of disputes, through the Water Forum, under section 69.

1088. The functions of the Forum, as provided in section 70, are as follows:

- to give feedback and make recommendations to the Commission on any matters concerning the interest of consumers of the water supply services and sewerage services;
- to represent the interests of consumers of the water supply services and sewerage services;
- to promote consumers' interests in relation to the tariffs and standards of water supply services and sewerage services;
- to identify and keep under review matters affecting the interests of consumers and ensure that the water supply services and sewerage services companies are aware of, and responsive to, concerns about their services;
- to publicize the existence, functions and work of the Water Forum in protecting the interests of consumers; and
- to carry out any functions as may be determined by the Commission.

1089. Among the administrative remedies provided by the Water Forum are measures relating to consumer protection and the resolution of disputes. For example, for consumer protection, section 68 empowers the Commission, upon the recommendation of the Water Forum, to prepare consumer standards which shall include model procedures, including those for the handling of customer complaints and disputes including a mediation process other than a court, and procedures for the compensation of customers in case of a breach of the consumer standards.

III. Resolution Dispute Committee

1090. Another administrative remedy provided under the Water Services Industry Act 2006 is the setting up of a 'resolution dispute committee' in section 71. This section states that a dispute between two or more licensees or permit holders, or a licensee and a permit holder, regarding any matter under this Act or its subsidiary legislation, shall first be attempted to be resolved by negotiation between the parties to the dispute.

1091. Under section 71(2), if the parties to a dispute fail to reach an agreement, the parties may seek resolution of the dispute by referring the dispute to a committee established by the Commission to hear and resolve disputes. Section 72(1) authorizes the Commission to establish a committee to hear and resolve disputes, although it may only do so under this chapter if it is notified in writing of the dispute.

1092. Under section 73(1), upon receipt of a notification in writing by the parties to the dispute referred to in section 71, the Committee shall, as soon as is practicable, convene to decide the dispute. The Committee shall be bound to convene to decide a dispute if it is satisfied of the following:

- an agreement will not be reached, or will not be reached within a reasonable time;
- the notification of the dispute is not trivial, frivolous or vexatious; and
- the resolution of the dispute would promote the objects of this Act.

IV. Enquiry Commission

1093. Another method of administrative remedy introduced by the Water Industry Services Act 2006 is enquiry by the Commission. Under section 77, the Commission is authorized to hold an enquiry on any matter of a general nature which relates to the administration of this Act or its subsidiary legislation either in response to a written request from a person or on its own initiative.

1094. Under section 78, an enquiry is to be conducted as and when the Commission deems fit; and all inquiries are to be open to the public. Under section 79, if the Commission is directed by the Minister to hold an enquiry, the Commission shall publish the following matters:

- the fact that it is holding the enquiry;
- the period during which the enquiry is to be held;
- the nature of the matter to which the enquiry relates;
- the period, of at least forty-five days, within which, and the form in which, members of the public are invited to make submissions to the Commission about that matter;
- the matters that the Commission would like such submissions to deal with; and
- the address or addresses to which submissions may be sent.

V. Appeal Tribunal

1095. Another form of administrative remedy available under the Water Industry Services Act 2006 is an Appeal Tribunal. The establishment of this tribunal is provided in section 91 for reviewing any of the following matters:

- any directions given by the Commission under this Act or its subsidiary legislation;
- the decision of the Commission not to register any agreement which requires registration under this Act or its subsidiary legislation;
- the decision of any committee established by the Commission to hear and resolve disputes under Chapter 2 of Part V;

- the decision of the Commission to grant or not to grant approvals under section 45;
- the decision of the Commission under section 59; and
- the direction of the Commission under section 64.

1096. Under section 98(1), a person who is aggrieved by a decision or direction of the Commission, or the committee as set out in section 91, may appeal to the Appeal Tribunal by filing a notice of appeal with the Appeal Tribunal. This can be done in writing within thirty days from the date of the decision or direction of the Commission or the committee.

1097. Section 105 provides that a decision of the Appeal Tribunal is final and binding on the parties to the appeal and is not subject to further appeal. A decision given by the Appeal Tribunal may, by leave of the Sessions Court, be enforced in the same manner as a judgment order to the same effect, and where leave is so given, judgment may be entered in terms of the decision.

Chapter 2. Judicial Remedies

§1. Introduction

1098. In Malaysia, judicial remedies for environmental issues can be imposed by the court either in the form of a breach of statutory law, or through tort law. Breaches of statutory law are usually penalized on the basis of criminal law, as compared to tort law, which is a civil matter.

1099. Malaysia has a single hierarchy of courts which enforces both federal and state law, and these courts are entrusted with powers to adjudicate both civil and criminal cases, including those relating to the environment. The jurisdiction pertaining to matters such as civil and criminal procedure and the administration of justice are granted to the federal government by the legislative list of the Federal Constitution.

1100. The hierarchy of the courts, in order of prominence are as follows:[1012]

- Federal Court;
- Court of Appeal;
- High Courts;
- Sessions Courts; and
- Magistrates' Courts.

1101. The three highest courts, namely the Federal Court, Appeal Court and High Courts are superior courts, established under Article 121 of the Federal Constitution and governed by the Courts of Judicature Act 1964.[1013] The three lowest courts are inferior or subordinate courts that derive their jurisdiction from the Subordinate Courts Act 1948.[1014]

1102. Both superior and subordinate courts have jurisdiction to deal with criminal and civil matters and with disputes involving private and public law. Civil matters pertaining to environmental disputes are generally decided by the Sessions Courts and High Courts, whereas criminal matters derived from environmental statutes are usually tried at either the Magistrates' or Sessions Courts. Appeals from Magistrates' Courts and Sessions Courts are heard by the High Courts.

§2. Civil Jurisdiction

1103. The Sessions Courts are established under section 59 of the Subordinate Courts Act 1948. They are courts of general jurisdiction, with authority to try both

1012. *See* Ahmad Ibrahim & Ahilemah Joned, *The Malaysian Legal System* 116–135 (Dewan Bahasa dan Pustaka 1995).
1013. Act 91, revised 1972.
1014. Act 92, revised 1972.

civil and criminal cases. Civil jurisdiction of the Sessions Courts is provided in sections 65–70 of the Act, which includes jurisdiction to try all actions and suits of a civil nature where the amount in dispute or the value of the subject matter does not exceed MYR 250,000, or where there is mutual consent from both parties. Thus, most tort cases are heard by the Sessions Courts, which are civil in nature. In the situation where the defence or counter-claim of the defendant raises matters which exceed the court's jurisdiction, either party may apply for the case to be transferred to and tried in the High Court.

1104. Certain civil remedies are outside the jurisdiction of the Sessions Court even if the amount involved is less than MYR 250,000, as enumerated in section 69 of the Act, including the grant of an injunction, which is within the jurisdiction of the High Courts.

1105. The High Courts are constituted in Article 121 of the Federal Constitution. Subject to the limitations contained in Article 128 of the Federal Constitution, the High Courts have jurisdiction to try all civil proceedings where the cause of action arose, and can try any civil case of any value, although they usually try cases where the amount involved exceeds MYR 250,000. The general civil jurisdiction of the High Court is set out in section 23 of the Courts of Judicature Act 1964.

1106. The power to grant injunctions is provided in section 69 of the Subordinate Courts Act 1948. One decided case that applied this section is *Majlis Perbandaran Pulau Pinang v. Boey Siew Than & ors*,[1015] which is an appeal case from the decision of the High Court.[1016] In this case, the respondents were alleged to have made structural alterations to an eating house without the approval of the local authority. The appellants, the local authority, brought an action for an injunction to restrain the respondents from illegally operating the eating house on grounds of public nuisance. They also applied for an injunction to restrain the respondents from operating the said eating house until trial of the actions. The respondents applied to strike out the actions and the High Court upheld their applications. The local authority appealed and the court allowed the appeal, imposing the injunction, on the basis of the protection of the public interest in their area.

§3. Civil Procedure

1107. In Malaysia, civil actions on environmental claims, usually based on tort principles, are generally tried at the Sessions Court. However, if the amount in dispute or the value of the claim exceeds MYR 250,000, the case is tried at the High

1015. (1979) 2 MLJ 127.
1016. *See Majlis Perbandaran Pulau Pinang v. Boey Siew Than & Ors* [1978] 2 MLJ 156.

Court.[1017] Similarly, Sessions Courts have no jurisdiction in the suit for injunctions,[1018] and such claims must be made at the High Court. The High Court also has jurisdiction to hear civil appeals from subordinate courts. They are governed by the Courts of Judicature Act 1964.

1108. Civil action is normally commenced by a writ of summons to order the defendant to enter an appearance within eight days. The writ must be endorsed with the statement of claim; a concise statement of the nature of claim; or the relief or remedy required. The defendant must enter an appearance within eight days or a judgment in default will be imposed against him. After an appearance has been entered, parties then prepare pleadings.[1019]

1109. Pleadings are written documents which define the issue to be tried and comprise the statement of claim, statement of defence, and reply. Discovery and inspection of documents take place after the close of pleadings. It is possible that settlements outside the court can be achieved at this stage. If a settlement is not achieved, preparations for the trial will take place.

1110. When preparing for trial, one issue to be considered is on whom the burden of proof lies. The general principle is that the person who makes the allegation has to prove his case. Facts are proved through the testimony of witnesses and by documents.

1111. After hearing both parties, the court will give judgment based on the balance of probabilities. The judgment of the court is pronounced in open court, either during the trial or on the hearing of the appeal.

§4. Criminal Jurisdiction

1112. Criminal offences pertaining to environmental matters are provided in statutes, which usually contain a provision on the punishment imposed for the contravention of that law. In such situations, the statutes also provide a provision on the specific court that has jurisdiction to try these environmental criminal offences.

1113. For the purpose of the contravention of provisions under the EQA 1974, section 46 of the Act provides that a Sessions Court in West Malaysia or a Magistrates' Court of the First Class in East Malaysia shall have jurisdiction to try such offences and to award the full punishment.

1114. For environmental criminal offences involving international issues, the national statute would normally lay down the sovereign rights and jurisdiction of

1017. Section 65 of the Courts of Judicature Act 1964.
1018. Section 69 of the Courts of Judicature Act 1964.
1019. *See* Ahmad Ibrahim & Ahilemah Joned, *The Malaysian Legal System* 244–261 (Dewan Bahasa dan Pustaka 1995).

the country over the subject matter. For example, section 4 of the Exclusive Economic Zone Act 1984 provides for Malaysia's sovereign rights in, and jurisdiction over, the exclusive economic zone.

1115. For the purpose of criminal trial for offences committed under the Exclusive Economic Zone Act 1984, section 36(1) provides that, notwithstanding any written law to the contrary, any offence committed under the Act shall be deemed to have been committed in Malaysia for conferring jurisdiction on a court to try that offence, and a Sessions Court or a Magistrates' Court of the First Class shall each have full jurisdiction and powers for all purposes under this Act.

§5. Criminal Procedure

I. Summons and Warrant

1116. For criminal offences committed under the EQA 1974, a person suspected of committing such offences may be brought before the court in any of the three ways:

- summons by a court;
- warrant for his arrest; or
- arrest without warrant for seizable offences.

1117. The most common method of bringing a suspect before the court for offences under the EQA 1974 is through summons. A summons is a document specifying the charges and requiring the person on whom it is served to appear in court to answer the charges.

1118. The procedure pertaining to service of notices for offences under the Act is provided in section 39. Section 39(1) requires that every notice, order, summons or document required or authorized by this Act, or any regulations made thereunder to be served on any person may be served through the following methods:

- by delivering the same to such person or by delivering the same to some adult member or servant of his family;
- by leaving the same at the usual or last known place of abode or business of such person in a cover addressed to such person; or
- by forwarding the same by registered post in a prepaid cover addressed to such person at his usual or last known place of abode or business.

1119. Under section 39(2), a notice, order, summons or document required or authorized by this Act or any regulations made thereunder to be served on the owner or occupier of any premises shall be deemed to be properly addressed if addressed by the description of the 'owner' or 'occupier' of such premises without further name or description.

1120. Section 39(3) further provides that a notice, order, summons or document required or authorized by this Act or any regulations made thereunder to be served on the owner or occupier of any premises may be served by delivering the same or a true copy thereof to some adult person on the premises or, if there is no such person on the premises to whom the same can with reasonable diligence be delivered, by affixing the notice, order, summons or document to some conspicuous part of the premises.

II. Investigation

1121. A criminal prosecution is usually begun by lodging a first information report. For offences under the EQA 1974, investigations are carried out by the Director General of the Department of Environment. Only when the investigations are complete, will the case be sent to the court.

1122. For cases involving marine pollution, the DG is authorized, under section 49, to delegate his investigation power to others. For example, the Environmental Quality (Delegation of Powers on Marine Pollution Control) Order 1994[1020] authorizes the delegation of powers on the investigation of offences under sections 27 and 29 to any police officer commanding a vessel, or appointed police officer, or the Royal Malaysia Police.[1021] The Environmental Quality (Delegation of Powers on Marine Pollution Control) Order 1993[1022] provides authorization to any port officer, any fisheries officer, any officer commanding a vessel of the Royal Malaysian Navy and any officer of customs commanding a vessel of the Customs and Excise Department.

1123. For the purpose of investigation, section 38A(1) of the EQA 1974 authorizes the DG to examine orally any person supposed to be acquainted with the facts and circumstances of the case and shall reduce into writing any statement made by the person so examined. Section 38A(2) further provides that the person referred to in subsection (1) shall be bound to answer all questions relating to the case put to him by the DG or any officer duly authorized in writing by him, provided that the person may refuse to answer any question, the answer to which would have a tendency to expose him to a criminal charge, penalty or forfeiture. It is a requirement under section 38A(3) that a person making a statement under this section shall be legally bound to state the truth, whether or not the statement is made wholly or partly in answer to questions.

1124. Section 38A(5) provides that a statement made by a person under this section shall, whenever possible, be reduced into writing and signed by the person

1020. P.U. (A) 537/94.

1021. Regulation 2 of the Environmental Quality (Delegation of Powers on Marine Pollution Control) Order 1994.

1022. P.U. (A) 276/93. This Order revoked the Environmental Quality (Delegation of Powers) Order 1976, P.U. (A) 51/76.

making it or affixed with his thumb-print, as the case may be, after it has been read to him in the language in which he made it and after he has been given an opportunity to make any corrections he may wish, and where the person examined refuses to sign or affix his thumb-print on the statement, the DG or any officer duly authorized in writing by him shall endorse thereon under his hand the fact of the refusal and the reason for it, if any, as stated by the person examined.

1125. By way of comparison, under the Water Services Industry Act 2006, an 'authorized officer' for the purpose of this Act includes any public officer or officer of the Commission. Section 148 of the Act empowers the authorized officer to investigate the activities of a licensee or other persons material to his compliance with this Act or its subsidiary legislation. The officer carrying out an investigation may exercise all or any of the powers in relation to police investigation, except the power to arrest without warrant.

III. Public Prosecutor

1126. There is a restriction on the power of the DG to institute an environmental case, and normally the order of the public prosecutor is required. This requirement is provided in section 44 of the EQA 1974, whereby no prosecution shall be instituted for an offence under this Act or the regulations made thereunder without the consent in writing of the Public Prosecutor. The Magistrate will then inquire into the matter and will send notice to the other party to appear, and the case will proceed according to the procedure laid down in the Criminal Procedure Code.

1127. A similar requirement of obtaining the order of the public prosecutor is provided for under other legislation. For example, section 38(1) of the Exclusive Economic Zone Act 1984 requires that a prosecution for an offence under the Act shall not be instituted except by or with the consent of the Public Prosecutor, provided that a person who is to be charged with such an offence may be arrested, or a warrant for his arrest may be issued and executed, and any person so arrested may be remanded in custody or released on bail, notwithstanding that the consent of the Public Prosecutor to the institution of a prosecution for the offence has not been obtained, but the case shall not be further prosecuted until that consent has been obtained.

1128. One decided case that can be referred to pertaining to this issue is *Pai San & Ors v. Public Prosecutor.*[1023] The appellants in this case were charged at a Magistrate's Court for fishing in Malaysian waters without an international agreement allowing the same or a valid permit issued under section 19 of the Fisheries Act 1985, thereby committing an offence under section 25(a) of the Act. At the end of the prosecution's case, the appellants were called upon to enter their defences. The appellants raised a question of law on the validity of the prosecution, which was conducted by an officer of the Fisheries Department. The learned magistrate refused

1023. (2002) 4 MLJ 538.

the application, whereupon the appellants filed a notice of motion in the High Court for the orders that the prosecution of a charge under the Fisheries Act 1985 can only be conducted by the Public Prosecutor, and that the prosecution conducted by an officer of the Fisheries Department was void and *ultra vires* the Federal Constitution. The High Court dismissed the appellants' application, and the appellants appealed to the Court of Appeal. The court dismissed the appeal on the basis that, in the instant case, although there was no provision in the Fisheries Act 1985 empowering an officer of the Fisheries Department to conduct the prosecution under the Fisheries Act, the Act should be read together with the Exclusive Economic Zone Act 1984. Section 38 of the Exclusive Economic Zone Act 1984 provides that 'a prosecution for an offence under this Act or any applicable written law shall not be instituted except by or with the consent of the Public Prosecutor … ', and the expression 'or any applicable written law' was defined in section 2 of the Exclusive Economic Zone Act 1984 as any written law provided to be applicable in respect of the exclusive economic zone, continental shelf or both. In relation to fisheries in the exclusive economic zone, the applicable written law was the Fisheries Act. Therefore, the words 'A prosecution for an offence under this Act or any applicable written law' in section 38 of the Exclusive Economic Zone Act 1984 referred, *inter alia*, to a prosecution for offences under the Fisheries Act 1985. Section 38(1) of the Exclusive Economic Zone Act 1984 provides that a prosecution shall not be instituted except by or with the consent of the Public Prosecutor. Here, the powers of the Public Prosecutor are not taken away from him and given to somebody else. His powers remain intact. It is the Public Prosecutor and he alone who may institute or give consent for a prosecution. That is consistent with his powers under Article 145(3) of the Federal Constitution. Therefore, section 38(1) is constitutional and valid and it gives the Public Prosecutor power to give consent to prosecute, and in the instant case he had, in the exercise of that power, given his consent. The officer of the Fisheries Department, armed with that consent, was clearly authorized to conduct the prosecution of the appellants. Therefore, the prosecution by the officer in this case was valid.

IV. Commencement of Proceeding

1129. A criminal prosecution begins after investigations have been completed, and the case has been sent to the court. The court will then inquire into the matter and if there is a case, take cognizance and send a notice to the other party to appear. A criminal case proceeds according to the procedure laid down in the Criminal Procedure Code.

1130. The conduct of a criminal proceeding may either be an examination of complaint, summary trial, or preliminary inquiries into cases triable by the High Court. When an accused is produced or appears before the court, the charge is read and explained to him. During trial, the accused is entitled to cross-examine all the witnesses for the prosecution.

1131. If at the end of the prosecution evidence, the court finds that there is no case against the accused, the court will order an acquittal. However, if there is a sufficient ground to convict him, the accused will be called to take his defence and to produce evidence. At the end of the case, the court may find the accused guilty, when the prosecutor has proved beyond reasonable doubt or otherwise, or not guilty. The accused must be acquitted if there is any reasonable doubt as to his commission of the offence.

V. Proof of Evidence

1132. Criminal proceedings are open to members of the public. Where the accused is brought to court and refuses to plead or does not plead, the court proceeds to hear the evidence presented by the prosecutor. Matters pertaining to evidence for the purpose of the EQA 1974 are provided in section 40 of the Act. Section 40(1) requires that the contents of any document prepared, issued or served under, by virtue of or for the purposes of this Act, shall, until the contrary is proved, be presumed to be correct, and the production of any book purporting to show the licences issued under this Act shall be prima facie proof of the issue, lack of issue or date of expiry of such licences.

1133. Under section 40(3), in any proceeding for offences against this Act, where it is necessary to prove that any person was or was not licensed, or that a licence was suspended, a certificate in writing signed by the DG setting out that such person was or was not licensed, or that the licence of such person was suspended, shall be prima facie evidence of the facts stated therein. And the DG shall not be cross-examined on the contents of such certificate.

1134. During trial, the accused is entitled to cross-examine all the witnesses for the prosecution. If at the end of the prosecution evidence, the court finds that no case against the accused has been made, the court will order an acquittal. However, if the court is of the opinion that there are sufficient grounds to convict the accused, the accused would be called upon to make his defence and to produce evidence.

1135. Under the Water Services Industry Act 2006, section 157 provides that if any person is charged with an offence under this Act, any statement, whether the statement amounts to a confession or not or whether it is oral or in writing, made at any time by that person to or in the hearing of an authorized officer or other person, shall be admissible in evidence at his trial and, if the person charged tenders himself as witness, any such statement may be used in cross-examination and for impeaching his credit.

VI. Imposition of Punishment

1136. At the end of the case, the court may find the accused guilty or not guilty. If the accused is found guilty, the court proceeds to sentence him according to the law. Usually the person is allowed to plead in mitigation before sentence is passed.

1137. Under the EQA 1974, penalties provided include a fine, or imprisonment, or a combination thereof. For more serious offences, the court may even impose the death sentence on the accused person. In Malaysia, the death penalty is the most severe punishment that can be imposed on a person and this penalty can be found under section 121 of the Water Industry Services Act 2006 for the offence of contamination of water. Under section 121(2), a person found guilty of an offence under subsection (1), on conviction, where death is the result of the act, shall be punished with death or imprisonment for a term, which may extend to twenty years, and where the punishment is not death, he shall also be liable to whipping.

1138. Modern environmental legislation in Malaysia tends to reflect the policy of the government in using criminal sanction as a deterrence measure in criminal related offences. The introduction of the death penalty, the longer period of imprisonment, the introduction of whipping and the imposition of higher amounts as penalties for environmental offences, show that severe punishments are intended to result in a reduction of crimes against the environment, regardless of the actual effectiveness of this policy in protecting the environment.

Selected Bibliography

§1. Government Publications

Forest Department Sarawak. *Sarawak Forest Policy 2019*. Sarawak: Forest Department Sarawak, 2020.

Jabatan Alam Sekitar Malaysia. *Environmental Impact Assessment (EIA): Procedure and Requirements in Malaysia*. Kuala Lumpur: Jabatan Alam Sekitar, 1993.

Jabatan Perdana Menteri. Unit Pemodenan Tadbiran dan Perancangan Pengurusan, Malaysia, *First Malaysia Plan 1966–1970*. Kuala Lumpur: Jabatan Percetakan Negara, 1970.

Jabatan Perdana Menteri. Unit Pemodenan Tadbiran dan Perancangan Pengurusan, Malaysia, *Second Malaysia Plan 1971–1975*. Kuala Lumpur: Jabatan Percetakan Negara, 1971.

Jabatan Perdana Menteri. Unit Pemodenan Tadbiran dan Perancangan Pengurusan, Malaysia, *Third Malaysia Plan 1976–1980*. Kuala Lumpur: Jabatan Percetakan Negara, 1976.

Jabatan Perdana Menteri. Unit Pemodenan Tadbiran dan Perancangan Pengurusan, Malaysia, *Fourth Malaysia Plan 1981–1985*. Kuala Lumpur: Jabatan Percetakan Negara, 1981.

Jabatan Perdana Menteri. Unit Pemodenan Tadbiran dan Perancangan Pengurusan, Malaysia, *Fifth Malaysia Plan 1986–1990*. Kuala Lumpur: Jabatan Percetakan Negara, 1986.

Jabatan Perdana Menteri. Unit Pemodenan Tadbiran dan Perancangan Pengurusan, Malaysia, *Sixth Malaysia Plan 1991–1995*. Kuala Lumpur: Jabatan Percetakan Negara, 1991.

Jabatan Perdana Menteri. Unit Pemodenan Tadbiran dan Perancangan Pengurusan, Malaysia, *Seventh Malaysia Plan 1996–2000*. Kuala Lumpur: Jabatan Percetakan Negara, 1996.

Jabatan Perdana Menteri. Unit Pemodenan Tadbiran dan Perancangan Pengurusan, Malaysia, *Eighth Malaysia Plan 2000–2005*. Kuala Lumpur: Jabatan Percetakan Negara, 2000.

Jabatan Perdana Menteri. Unit Pemodenan Tadbiran dan Perancangan Pengurusan, Malaysia, *Ninth Malaysia Plan 2006–2010*. Kuala Lumpur: Jabatan Percetakan Negara, 2006.

Jabatan Perdana Menteri. Unit Pemodenan Tadbiran dan Perancangan Pengurusan, Malaysia, *Tenth Malaysia Plan 2011–2015*. Kuala Lumpur: Jabatan Percetakan Negara, 2011.

Jabatan Perdana Menteri. Unit Pemodenan Tadbiran dan Perancangan Pengurusan, Malaysia, *Eleventh Malaysia Plan 2016–2020.* Kuala Lumpur: Jabatan Percetakan Negara 2016.
Jabatan Perdana Menteri. Unit Pemodenan Tadbiran dan Perancangan Pengurusan, Malaysia, *Twelfth Malaysia Plan 2021–2025.* Kuala Lumpur: Jabatan Percetakan Negara 2021.
Jabatan Perhutanan Perhutanan Semenanjung Malaysia, *National Forestry Policy Peninsular Malaysia 1978 (Revised 1992).* Kuala Lumpur: Jabatan Perhutanan Perhutanan Semenanjung Malaysia, 1992.
Kementerian Sains. Teknologi dan Alam Sekitar, *Dasar Pelbagai Biologi Kebangsaan.* Kuala Lumpur: Kementerian Sains, Teknologi dan Alam Sekitar Malaysia, 1998.
Kementerian Sumber Asli dan Alam Sekitar Malaysia. *Environmental Quality Report 2012.* Kuala Lumpur: Jabatan Alam Sekitar, 2012.
Kementerian Sumber Asli dan Alam Sekitar Malaysia. *Annual Report 2012.* Kuala Lumpur: Jabatan Alam Sekitar, 2012.
Kementerian Tenaga dan Sumber Asli, *Dasar Perhutanan Malaysia.* Putrajaya: Kementerian Tenaga dan Sumber Asli, 2021.
Ministry of Economic Affairs, *Shared Prosperity Vision 2030.* Putrajaya: Ministry of Economic Affairs, 2019.
Ministry of Energy, Science, Technology, Environment and Climate Change. *Malaysia Third National Communication and Second Biennial Update Report to the UNFCCC 2018.* Putrajaya, Ministry 0f Energy, Science, Technology, Environment and Climate Change, 2018.
Ministry of Energy, Water and Communications, Malaysia. *The Water Tablet: Malaysian Water Reforms.* Kuala Lumpur: Ministry of Energy, Water and Communications, Malaysia, 2008.
Ministry of Environment and Water, *National Marine Litter Policy and Action Plan 2021 – 2030.* Putrajaya: Ministry of Environment and Water, 2021.
Ministry of Environment and Water. *Third Biennial Update Report to the UNFCCC 2020.* Putrajaya: Ministry of Environment and Water, 2020.
Ministry of Natural Resources and Environment Malaysia. *Malaysia Biennial Update Report to the UNFCCC 2015.* Putrajaya: Ministry of Natural Resources and Environment Malaysia, 2011.
Ministry of Natural Resources and Environment Malaysia. *Malaysia Second National Communication to the UNFCCC 2011.* Putrajaya: Ministry of Natural Resources and Environment Malaysia, 2011.
Sabah Forestry Department, *Sabah Forest Policy 2018.* Sabah: Sabah Forestry Department, 2018.

§2. Books

Abidin, Zainal & Zubaid Akbar (eds). *Conservation and Faunal Biodiversity in Malaysia.* Bangi: Penerbitan Universiti Kebangsaan Malaysia, 1996.
Ahmad Bagader, Abubakr, et al. *Environmental Protection in Islam.* Switzerland: IUCN World Conservation Union, 1994.
Aiken, Sir Robert, et al. *Development and Environment in Peninsular Malaysia.* Singapore: McGraw-Hill International, 1982.

Aiken, Sir Robert & Colin H. Leigh. *Vanishing Rain Forests: The Ecological Transition in Malaysia*. Oxford: Clarendon Press, 1992.

Harding, Andrew. *Law, Government and the Constitution in Malaysia*. The Hague: Kluwer Law International, 1996.

Hasan, Surtahman Kastin & Abd Ghafar Ismail. *Alam Sekitar: Permasalahan dan Pengawalan*. Kuala Lumpur: Dewan Bahasa dan Pustaka, 1997.

Hassan, Mohd. Nordin, et al. *Kepelbagaian Biologi: Implikasi Kepada Malaysia*. Bangi: Penerbitan Universiti Kebangsaan Malaysia, 1997.

Hassan, Mohd. Nordin, et al. (eds). *National Review on Environmental Quality Management in Malaysia: Towards the Next Two Decades*. Bangi: Institute for Environment and Development, Universiti Kebangsaan Malaysia, 1998.

Ibrahim, Ahmad & Ahilemah Joned. *The Malaysian Legal System*. Kuala Lumpur: Dewan Bahasa dan Pustaka, 1995.

Kathirithamby, Jeyamalar & J. Wells. *Nature and Nation: Forests and Development in Peninsular Malaysia*. Singapore: Singapore University Press, 2005.

Koh, Hock Lye. *Pemodelan Alam Sekitar dan Ekosistem*. Pulau Pinang: Universiti Sains Malaysia, 2004.

Komoo, Ibrahim & H.D. Tjia, *Warisan Ekologi Malaysia: Pembangunan Sumber Untuk Pemuliharaan dan Pelancongan Tabii*. Bangi: Institut Alam Sekitar dan Pembagunan, 2000.

Md. Jahi, Jamaluddin. *Impak Pembangunan Terhadap Alam Sekitar*. Bangi: Penerbitan Universiti Kebangsaan Malaysia, 1996.

Md. Jahi, Jamaluddin. *Striking a Balance Between Environment and Development: Is Malaysia Prepared to Management the Environment to Face Challenges in the Next Millennium?*. Bangi: Universiti Kebangsaan Malaysia, 1999.

Md. Nor, Shukor & Neeta D. Sinnappah-Kang (eds). *Kepelbagaian Biologi & Ekologi Fauna di Malaysia*. Bangi: Universiti Kebangsaan Malaysia, 2003.

Mohd Isa, Zaki (ed.). *Perhutanan dan Alam Sekitar*. Kuala Lumpur: Institut Penyelidikan Perhutanan Malaysia, 1995.

Mottershead, Terri (ed.). *Environmental Law and Enforcement in the Asia Pacific Rim*. Hong Kong: Sweet & Maxwell, 2002.

Othman, Fadil. *Permasalahan Alam Sekitar*. Petaling Jaya: Centre for Environmental Technologies, 1995.

Othman, Sahir, et al. (eds). *Management and Status of Resources in Protected Areas of Peninsular Malaysia*. Kuala Lumpur: Department of Wildlife and National Parks Peninsular Malaysia, 2006.

Persidangan Pertubuhan Bangsa-Bangsa Bersatu Mengenai Alam Sekitar dan Pembagunan. *Agenda 21, Program Tindakan Untuk Pembangunan Mapan: Deklarasi Rio: Kenyataan Mengenai Prinsip Hutan*. Kuala Lumpur: Jabatan Alam Sekitar, 1997.

Phang, Siew Nooi. *Sistem Kerajaan Tempatan di Malaysia*. Kuala Lumpur: Dewan Bahasa dan Pustaka, 1989.

Sani, Sham. *Pembangunan dan Alam Sekitar di Malaysia: Isu dan Pengurusannya*. Kuala Lumpur: Dewan Bahasa dan Pustaka, 1990.

Sani, Sham. *Environmental Quality Act 1974: Then and Now*. Bangi: Institute for Environment and Development, Universiti Kebangsaan Malaysia, 1997.

Sani, Sham. *Environmental Management Issues and Challenges in the Next Millennium in Malaysia*. Bangi: Universiti Kebangsaan Malaysia, 1999.

Siwan, Chamhuri. *Pembangunan Mapan: Strategi 'Menang-Menang' Untuk Pembasmian Kemiskinan dan Pemuliharaan Alam Sekitar*. Bangi: Penerbitan Universiti Kebangsaaan Malaysia, 2004.

§3. Articles

Ansari, Abdul Haseeb. 'Environmental Protection Through the Law of Torts: A Critical Appraisal', *MLJ* 4 (2000): lxxxi.

Ansari, Abdul Haseeb. 'Legal Issues in Forest Management in India and Malaysia: A Critical Appraisal', *MLJ* 2 (2004): xxi.

Ansari, Abdul Haseeb. 'Prevention, Abatement and Control of Pollution of Straits: An Appraisal with Special Reference to the Straits of Malacca', *MLJ* 3 (2005): xxxvii.

Ansari, Abdul Haseeb & Ismawi Zen. 'Towards a Sustainable Land Use Planning: An Appraisal with Special Reference to Malaysia'. *MLJ* 6 (2006): cvii.

Ansari, Abdul Haseeb, Parveen Jamal & Maizatun Mustafa. 'Meaning and Scope of the Precautionary Principle'. In *Land Use Planning and Environmental Sustainability in Malaysia: Policies and Trends,* edited by Hunud Abia Kadouf & Sharifah Zubaidah Al Junid. Kuala Lumpur: International Islamic University Malaysia, 2006.

Ariffin, Mariani & Maizatun Mustafa. 'International Wildlife Trade Regulation and Its Enforcement in Malaysia'. 1 *LNS(A)* (2013): xlvii.

Hamid, Abdul Ghafur. 'Malaysia's Commitments under International Conventions and the Need for a Harmonized Legal Regime Regulating Marine Pollution'. *MLJ* 6 (2007): cxxiv.

Harding, Andrew. 'Do Public Interest Environmental Law and the Common Law Have a Future Together?'. In *Public Interest Perspectives in Environmental Law*, edited by David Robinson & John Dunkley. London: Wiley Chancery, 1995.

Harding, A. 'Practical Human Rights, NGOs and the Environment in Malaysia'. In *Human Rights Approaches to Environmental Protection*, edited by A.E. Boyle & M.R. Anderson. Oxford: Oxford University Press, 1996.

Looi, Janet. 'Environmental Issues: Major Case Law and Environmental Management'. *MLJ* 3 (2002): cclxxxvii.

Mustafa, Maizatun. 'River and Water Pollution: Are Our Laws Adequate?'. *Infoline* (November/December 1997).

Mustafa, Maizatun. 'Legal Approach Towards Water Resources Protection and Pollution Control in Malaysia'. In *Water Environmental Planning*, edited by Alias Abdullah, Norio Okada & Mohd Kamil Yusoff. Kuala Lumpur: International Islamic University Malaysia, 2004.

Mustafa, Maizatun. 'Clean Water: Right and Remedies under Environmental Law in Malaysia'. In *Integrated Water Resources Management in Malaysia: Experiences and Practices*, edited by Ann Anton, et al. Kuala Lumpur: Malaysian Water Partnership, 2004.

Mustafa, Maizatun. 'Public Access to Environmental Rights and Justice: A Legal Perspective for an Improved Public Service System of the Local Authorities'. In

Service Delivery by Local Authorities: Issues and Challenges, edited by Worran Kabut et al. (compilers). Selangor: UPENA, 2006.

Mustafa, Maizatun & Sharifah Zubaidah Aljunid, 'Legal and Institutional Framework for Pollution Prevention in Malaysian Rivers'. *MLJ* July/August (2008).

Mustafa, Maizatun. 'Environmental Quality Act 1974: Development and Reform'. *MLJ* 2 March/April (2009).

Mustafa, Maizatun. 'Water Availability and Policies in Asia'. In *Global Warming and Climate Change, Prospects and Policies in Asia and Europe*, edited by Antonio Marquina. Hampshire: Palgrave Macmillan, 2010.

Mustafa, Maizatun. 'Environmental Quality Act 1974: A Tool Towards the Implementation and Achievement of Malaysia's Environmental Policy'. *IIUM Law Journal* 19, no. 1 (2011).

Mustafa, Maizatun. 'The Role of Environmental Impact Assessment in Addressing Marine Environmental Issues Arising from Oil and Gas Activities: Examples from Malaysia'. In *International Conference on Environment and BioScience IPCBEE vol. 2.* Singapore: IACSIT Press, 2011.

Mustafa, Maizatun & Mariani Ariffin. 'Protection of Marine Biodiversity from Pollution: Legal Strategies in Malaysia'. *International Journal of Bioscience, Biochemistry and Bioinformatics* 1, no. 4 (2011).

Mustafa, Maizatun. 'The Application of Law on Pollution Control Towards Marine Biodiversity Conservation in Malaysia'. In *International Conference on Environment and BioScience IPCBEE vol. 21.* Singapore: IACSIT Press, 2011.

Mustafa, Maizatun, Khairil Azmin Mokhtar & Mohd. Hazmi Rusli. 'Mitigating the Implication of Offshore Oil and Gas Activities on the Marine Environment in Malaysia: Some Measures through Environmental Impact Assessment'. *Australian Journal of Basic and Applied Sciences* 6, no. 11 (2012).

Mustafa, Maizatun, et al. 'Coping with Climate Change through Air Pollution Control: Some Legal Initiatives from Malaysia'. In *Environment, Energy and Biotechnology: International Proceedings of Chemical, Biological and Environmental Engineering, vol. 33.* Singapore: IACSIT Press, 2012.

Nijar, Gurdial Singh. 'The Bakun Case: A Critique'. *MLJ* 3 (1997): ccxxix.

Index

The numbers here refers to paragraph numbers.

Index

www.ingramcontent.com/pod-product-compliance
Lightning Source LLC
LaVergne TN
LVHW011112300926
849160LV00008B/355